FROM
THEOCRACY
TO
RELIGIOUS LIBERTY

FROM THEOCRACY TO RELIGIOUS LIBERTY

Connecticut's Journey from Thomas Jefferson's "Wall of Separation" Letter to a State Constitution, as Told Through the Newspapers of the Time

CHRIS RODDA

Published by the author
Highland Park, NJ

From Theocracy To Religious Liberty: Connecticut's Journey from Thomas Jefferson's "Wall of Separation" Letter to a State Constitution, as Told Through the Newspapers of the Time

ISBN: 9798673356357

*Dedicated to the memory of all the
journalists, satirists, and poets
of the first decades of the 1800s
whose wonderful writings
provided the material
for this book.*

❧ **Contents** ❧

❦ **Introduction** ❧

On January 1, 1802, Thomas Jefferson wrote his now-famous letter to the Danbury, Connecticut Baptists, in which he coined the phrase "separation between church and state."

Jefferson was replying to an address from the Danbury Baptist Association in which the Baptists, after congratulating him on his election to the presidency, told him of the oppression they faced as a dissenting sect under the Congregationalist-Presbyterian theocracy of their state.

It would be another fifteen years before Jefferson, upon hearing of the Republican victory in the 1817 Connecticut election, would write to John Adams:

> I join you therefore in sincere congratulations that this den of the priesthood is at length broken up, and that a protestant popedom is no longer to disgrace the American history and character.[1]

This book, through newspaper articles from the time, tells the story of what happened over that eventful decade and a half to transform Connecticut from a "protestant popedom," as Jefferson put it, into a state with a constitution that guaranteed religious freedom.

It's hard not to draw parallels between the political parties of

1. Thomas Jefferson to John Adams, May 5, 1817. Albert Ellery Bergh, ed., *The Writings of Thomas Jefferson,* vol. 15, (Washington D.C.: Thomas Jefferson Memorial Association, 1907), 109.

the first decades of the 1800s in New England and the political parties of today. The Federalists, like today's Republicans, were the conservatives, the party that believed the rich should rule, feared that more people being able to vote would put them out of power, regarded immigrants with contempt, and hypocritically boasted of having "all the religion." The Federalist clergy, like the right-wing clergy of today, were outspokenly political, preaching that it was a religious duty to vote for Federalists. The Republicans, the party of Jefferson, also called Democrats and Democratic-Republicans, were, like today's Democrats, the liberal party. The Republicans labeled the Federalists aristocrats, monarchists, and religious hypocrites. The Federalists labeled the Republicans disorganizers, infidels, and Jacobins,[2] claiming that they wanted to destroy all religion, and, among the charges that sound very familiar today, wanted to do away with the institution of marriage. In the election of 1800, the Federalist press and clergy warned that if Jefferson was elected president, Bibles would be burned, churches leveled to the ground, and the clergy driven from their pulpits and even killed. The Federalist cry of "religion is in danger" would be kept up throughout Jefferson's administration, although even after years of his being in office none of the dire predictions made before his election had come true.

In the election of 1800, all of the states had gone Republican except the New England states, New Jersey, and Delaware, with Jefferson and Aaron Burr defeating Federalists John Adams and Charles C. Pinckney. In 1804, Jefferson won reelection in a landslide, getting 162 electoral votes to Pinckney's 14. But while the Federalists had been soundly defeated nationally, and even the other New England states had gone for Jefferson, Connecticut, which supplied 9 of Pinckney's 14 electoral votes, remained a Federalist stronghold. That Jefferson won the other New England states in the 1804 presidential election did not mean that Federalism was dead in those states. Far from it. Federalism, and the animosity between the Federalists and the Republicans, remained very strong in the other New England states, particularly in Massachusetts.

---

2. The Federalists, only a quarter of a century after the American Revolution, were pro-British, and rabidly anti-French. To stir up fear of the Republicans, they equated the democratic principles of the Republicans with those of the Jacobins of France, the most radical political group of the French Revolution that instituted France's Reign of Terror.

Nowhere, however, did the Federalists have the absolute stranglehold on the state government that they did in Connecticut.

The established religion of Connecticut was the Saybrook Platform, named for the town of Saybrook where, in 1708, acting on an order from the legislature directing the colony's Congregationalists and Presbyterians to hold a synod to form one church system for the colony, the two denominations were united to become one established order. For this reason, in the articles in this book, the established clergy and church are sometimes called Congregationalist and sometimes Presbyterian, terms that at this time in Connecticut were interchangeable. In both cases, the articles are referring to the Saybrook Platform establishment.

For taxing purposes, it was presumed by the government that everyone in Connecticut belonged to the established church and were taxed to support that church unless they "certificated off," as it was called. This is what the Danbury Baptists were referring to when they wrote in their letter to Jefferson:

> ...what religious privileges we enjoy (as a minor part of the State) we enjoy as favors granted, and not as inalienable rights: and these favors we receive at the expence of such degrading acknowledgements as are inconsistant with the rights of freemen.[3]

This was the certificating off process, as it was explained in one newspaper by someone who on a sample certificate cheekily had John Calvin certificating off the Presbyterian Church:

> MR. BARBER.—It is a lamentable fact that in this State, and in this enlightened age, those persons who, to answer a good conscience have left the Presbyterian (or established) order and attached themselves either to Episcopalian, Baptist or Methodist churches, are called on for taxes by the aforesaid established order, and these taxes are rigidly exacted, although the taxed never attend their meeting nor desire to. Many of the writer's friends are in this predicament,—

3. The Danbury Baptist Association to Thomas Jefferson, after October 7, 1801. Barbara B. Oberg, ed., *The Papers of Thomas Jefferson*, vol. 35, (Princeton, NJ: Princeton University Press, 2008), 407-408.

and from observation I am induced to believe that a large number of our citizens are in the same situation; these circumstances have influenced me to send you the enclosed Certificate, which by being properly filled out, and deposited in the Society Clerk's office, will prevent a repetition of the call for taxes after one year.

A Countryman.

THIS CERTIFIES, That I differ in sentiments from the Worship and Ministry of the ecclesiastical Society in this State, constituted by law within certain local bounds, called the *Presbyterian Society* within the town of *Saybrook,* to which I have before been joined, and I choose to join myself to another denomination of Christians, which have formed themselves into a different Church or Congregation, for the maintenance and support of the public worship of God, known by the name of *Methodists,* ordinarily holding communion in the town of *Saybrook.*

WITNESS MY HAND, IN *Saybrook,* this *25th day of December* 1816.

JOHN CALVIN.[4]

Although Connecticut's official nickname is the "Constitution State," it was actually one of last of the original states to have a constitution. At the time of the American Revolution, all of the states except Rhode Island and Connecticut had adopted state constitutions. Connecticut, however, did not write a constitution, but continued under its 1662 royal charter granted by King Charles II, with the Connecticut General Court declaring in 1776:

That the ancient form of civil government contained in the Charter from Charles the II, King of England, and adopted by the people of this state, shall be and remain the civil constitution of this state, under the sole authority of the people hereof, independent of any king or prince whatever.[5]

As the Danbury Baptists described this lack of a constitution in

4. *Columbian Register,* New Haven, CT, January 4, 1817, 3.
5. James Bradley Thayer, *Cases on Constitutional Law,* vol. 1, (Cambridge: Charles W. Sever, 1895), 433.

their letter to Jefferson:

> ... our constitution of goverment is not specific. Our antient
> charter, together with the Laws made coincident therewith,
> were adopted as the Basis of our goverment, At the time of
> our revolution; and such had been our Laws & usages, &
> such still are; that religion is consider'd as the first object
> of Legislation ...[6]

The Federalists insisted that the 1662 charter of Charles II
was a constitution. The Republicans did not consider it to be a
constitution. They wanted a state constitution that was voted on by
the people.

Religious liberty was, of course, a primary reason that a state
constitution was needed, but there were also other reasons. One
was the state's lack of a separation of powers, particularly between
the legislative and judicial powers. In the government as it existed,
the same twelve-member Council was both the state's senate and
its highest court, the Court of Errors. The governor had no veto
power, leaving no separation of powers between the executive and
legislative branches. The governor also presided over the Court of
Errors, leaving no separation of powers between the executive and
judicial branches. The Council, in effect, held all the power. With
a majority of seven Council members having the sole power to
approve or disapprove any act, seven Federalist lawyers, as the
Republicans put it, ruled the state. Another major issue was suffrage,
which, as things were, was restricted to those who met property
qualifications. The Republicans wanted extend the right of suffrage
to virtually all white males. None of these things would be remedied
without a constitution.

Also at issue were the state's election laws, which were designed
by the Federalists to keep their party in power.

Connecticut's government consisted of a governor, a lieutenant
governor, the twelve-member Council, whose members were called
assistants, and a House of Representatives, which had between 190
and 203 members during the time period covered by this book.

---

6. The Danbury Baptist Association to Thomas Jefferson, after October 7, 1801. Barbara
B. Oberg, ed., *The Papers of Thomas Jefferson*, vol. 35, (Princeton, NJ: Princeton University
Press, 2008), 407-408.

There were two elections each year, one in September and one in April, which took place at Freeman's meetings in each town. New members of the House of Representatives were chosen at both elections, in September for the October legislative session, and in April for the May session. Council assistants, the governor, and the lieutenant governor were all elected for a term of one year. The election of the Council assistants was done in two phases over the two elections. In the September election, each freeman would submit twenty names for nomination. The twenty names with the most nominations across the state were then published as a list of nominees to be voted on in the April election, at which each freeman would select twelve out of the twenty on the list. April's freeman's meetings were also known as proxy days because, although the Council assistants, governor and lieutenant governor were voted on at this meeting, this wasn't the end of the election. The freemen would also vote for a deputy as their proxy to take their town's votes to the general election in Hartford in May, where the final election and tallying of the votes took place.

The opening of the May session of the legislature was marked by the annual General Election Day festival, an event with the pomp and pageantry of a royal coronation, including a procession and a typically very political election sermon delivered by one of the established clergy. The spectacle was described in one newspaper as the "usual exhibition of the symbols and representations of the mystical and practical union of church and state," at which the "relics of our colonial dependence and of royalty have been carefully preserved."[7] The regal procession was followed by a public dinner, with the governor, lieutenant governor, and Council at the first table, the clergy, which could number up to a hundred or more, at the second table, and the representatives at a third table. After the dinner, the counting of the votes took place, followed by an election ball and a more exclusive formal ball.

Connecticut's elections, particularly for the all-powerful Council, were far from fair. By law, the top twenty nominees for Council assistants from the September election had to be published as a list, but the law did not say that the names had to be listed in order of the number of votes received. So, what the ruling Federalists did

---

7. *The Times, Hartford*, CT, May 13, 1817, 3.

was list the nominees in order of who *they* wanted on the Council, making the first twelve names on the list their preferred Federalist brethren, regardless of the number of votes they had gotten. By law, the list of nominees had to be read off at the freeman's meetings in the order in which it was printed, with each nominee being voted on one at a time as their name was read, and each freeman voting for that nominee by handing in a slip of paper with the nominee's name written on it. Anyone who hadn't used up all twelve of their slips of paper by the time the twelve Federalist-preferred nominees on the list were read off would be known to the Federalist-appointed officer presiding over the meeting, the ever-present clergyman, and any of their neighbors who were keeping track, risking, if they lived in a heavily Federalist town, being spurned by their community. To prevent anyone from pretending to vote for any the first twelve nominees by handing in a blank slip of paper and throwing away that vote, it was illegal to hand in a blank slip of paper.

The election of Jefferson spurred Connecticut's Republican party to solidify and become a far more organized force in the spring of 1801, running candidates for governor and lieutenant governor in the April election. Then, in the September election, they published a list of names for Republicans to nominate for the Council. While no Republican received enough votes to make it onto the list of twenty, the move was quickly answered by the Federalists, who, at the October 1801 session of the legislature, passed *An Act in addition to, and alteration of the Statute entitled "An Act for regulating the Election of the Governour, Lieutenant-Governour, Assistants, &c." And in addition to and alteration of the Statute entitled "An Act for regulating the Election of Senators and Representatives for this State in the Congress of the United States."* — better known as the "stand-up law."

The stand-up law was designed to make anyone voting for a Republican so conspicuous that it would deter them from doing so, making it as unlikely as possible that any Republican could get enough votes to make it into the list of twenty Council nominees. The law completely changed the way that Council nominees were nominated at the September freeman's meetings. Prior to the stand-up law, each freeman simply handed in a written list of their twenty choices. Under the stand-up law, each freeman had twenty blank slips of paper, and as one freeman advanced a name, all others who wished to vote for that nominee had to stand up to be counted, or to raise their hand if the meeting place couldn't accommodate the freemen to be seated, dropping one of their slips of paper with each vote to keep count that they had voted for twenty nominees. There was no longer any secrecy whatsoever to the voting. Anyone who advanced the name of a Republican, or stood up to vote for a Republican, marked themselves as a radical who wanted to "revolutionize" the state — an infidel, an atheist, a disorganizer, and all the other epithets for Republicans that filled the Federalist papers and Federalist preachers' sermons.

This was the stand-up law:

> ...That before the freemen are called upon to vote for persons to stand in nomination for assistants or representatives in congress, the presiding officer shall appoint a suitable number of tellers not exceeding four, for the different parts of the house or area where the freemen are assembled, and shall also direct the freemen to provide each for himself a number of slips of paper equal to the number which by law are to stand in nomination, and when provided, he shall if the accommodations will admit thereof, order the freemen to be seated, and on any persons being named by any freeman to stand in nomination, the presiding officer shall call upon all those who would vote for the person so named by any freeman to stand in nomination, the presiding officer shall call upon all those who would vote for the person so named to signify it by rising, or when the accommodations will not admit of the freemen's being seated, shall call upon them to vote by holding up the hand, which being done, the tellers in the quarters assigned them shall count the numbers voting, and shall successively with an audible voice declare the numbers, which numbers, the presiding officer with a like audible voice shall successively repeat and cause to be taken down, and the aggregate to be entered against the name of the person voted for, and the same proceeding shall be repeated as often as any person shall be so named by any freeman; but no freeman shall vote for more in number than are by law to stand in such nomination, and every freeman on voting as aforesaid shall each time drop one of the said

slips of paper that he may not be exposed through mistake to vote for more than the prescribed number.[8]

While this book tells the story of Connecticut's journey from theocracy to religious liberty, it is impossible to tell that story without including other states — primarily the rest of New England, and particularly Massachusetts, where Federalism and political religion ran high. There were also Federalist pockets in other states, just as there are red parts of blue states today, and wherever Federalism was strong, so was the politicized religion that went along with it, but it was New England that stood apart from the rest of the country as the Bible Belt of the day.

In 1774, John Adams described the religious establishment in his state of Massachusetts as "the most mild and equitable establishment of religion."[9] The 1780 constitution of Massachusetts, with Adams as its principal author, guaranteed freedom to all religions, but still retained much of the state's religious establishment, which wouldn't be abolished until 1833.

After two decades of a new Federalist brand of religion that was anything but "mild," but had become an engine of party politics and a weapon to be wielded in the most vicious attacks and seditious rantings by the clergy, Adams changed his tune. When Jefferson wrote to him in 1817 about the Connecticut election, saying that "a protestant popedom is no longer to disgrace the American history and character," Adams, who had once favored a "mild and equitable religious establishment," replied:

> Oh! Lord! Do you think that a Protestant Popedom is annihilated in America? Do you recollect, or have you ever attended to the ecclesiastical Strifes in Maryland, Pensilvania, New York, and every part of New England? What a mercy it is, that these People cannot whip and crop, and pillory and roast, as yet in the U.S.? If they could they would.[10]

---

8. *The Public Statute Laws of the State of Connecticut,* (Hartford, CT: Hudson and Goodwin, 1808), 252.

9. Charles Francis Adams, ed., *The Works of John Adams, Second President of the United States,* vol. 2, (Boston: Charles C. Little and James Brown, 1850), 399.

10. John Adams to Thomas Jefferson, May 18, 1817. J. Jefferson Looney, ed., *The Papers of Thomas Jefferson, Retirement Series,* vol. 11, (Princeton, NJ: Princeton University Press, 2014), 363.

By the time John Adams wrote those words, the Federalist party had come to an end nationally, running its last presidential candidate in 1816, but not before seeing a resurgence during the War of 1812. At no other time was the divide between the New England Federalists and the rest of the country so great, with some Federalists going as far as calling for the New England states and New York to secede from the rest of the nation and negotiate a separate peace with England. Also at no other time did New England's Federalist clergy behave so scandalously as to draw attention both nationally and internationally, preaching sermons that were so pro British that they were often described in the Republican newspapers as treasonous.

At few times in our country's history has religion been used so successfully to politically divide the American people as it was during the time period of this book and as it is today. At both times have "common people" been induced to vote for the party of the rich against their own interests because they were told that it was their "religious duty" to do so. At both times has the party with "all the religion" been the party to shamelessly lie, spread wild conspiracy theories, and demonstrate the most blatant hypocrisy, and yet maintain the unwavering support of the party, and religious, faithful. And the press, of course, took political sides just as it does now — papers like the Federalist *Connecticut Courant* were the *Fox News* of their day, and Republican papers like the *American Mercury* were the *MSNBC*.

This introduction, and the chapter that follows on the year of 1801, particularly Republican leader Pierpont Edwards's description of Connecticut to Thomas Jefferson, written to explain his state to a southerner, will set the stage for the articles in the chapters that follow, beginning with the Danbury Baptists' address to Jefferson and Jefferson's famous New Year's Day 1802 reply.

∽ **1801** ∼

On March 11, 1801, the Republican party of Connecticut held a large festival in Wallingford to celebrate the inauguration of Thomas Jefferson. Dubbed a "General Thanksgiving," an irreverent jab at Connecticut's public thanksgiving and fast days, the celebration, reportedly attended by over a thousand Republicans from across the state,[1] was an all-day-long affair, with an artillery display and music, a banquet and a fireworks display in the evening. The participation of the state's leading Republicans included a reading of the Declaration of Independence by Gideon Granger, the Republican candidate in the upcoming election to fill a vacant seat in the U.S. House of Representatives, a reading of Jefferson's inaugural address by party "boss" Pierpont Edwards, and an oration by Abraham Bishop, an already-popular orator who had turned his talents to promoting the Republican cause in 1800. A sermon was preached by Republican clergyman Rev. Stanley Griswold, who the federalists in his parish tried to drive from his pulpit, not because he preached politics there, but simply for being a Republican.

Abraham Bishop, a figure whose name appears often in the articles presented in this book, was a lawyer, orator, writer, and an alumni of the Federalist-controlled Yale College. In 1800, Bishop was invited to give the Phi Beta Kappa address at that year's Yale commencement, which at that time was held in September. Rather than choosing an academic topic for his oration, as was the usual

1. *American Mercury*, Hartford, CT, March 19, 1801, 3.

1

practice, Bishop planned to deliver an anti-Federalist political address, titled "The Extent and Power of Political Delusions." When he submitted his address to the committee in August, however, his invitation was promptly rescinded. Not a man to be muzzled, Bishop delivered his oration at the White Meeting House in New Haven on the evening before the commencement, drawing a larger audience than the commencement, and quickly had it printed, reaching an even larger audience. Ironically, one of the orations that was delivered at the commencement was on "the consequences of the invention of printing."[2]

In his 1801 oration at the Wallingford festival, Bishop covered all of the grievances of the Republicans — the union of church and state, the Federalists' political clergymen, the state's lack of a constitution, the aristocratic and monarchist views of the Federalists, the inequity of the state's election and suffrage laws, and the desire of some Federalists for the New England states to separate from the rest of the Union. Bishop repeatedly used phrases in this oration that will become very familiar when reading the articles in this book — the "steady habits" of Connecticut that were boasted of by the Federalists; the "friends of order," as the Federalists styled themselves; and "Moses and Aaron," referring to Connecticut's union of church and state.

By December 12, 1800, John Adams knew he had lost the presidential election. Regardless of the fact that Jefferson and Aaron Burr had tied with 73 electoral votes apiece, and it was yet to be determined by the House of Representatives which would be president and which would be vice president, it was certain that one of them, and not Adams, with 65 electoral votes, would be president. Nevertheless, Adams continued making appointments to federal offices, almost all of which were given to Federalists. These "midnight appointments," as Jefferson called any appointments Adams made after December 12 on a list that he drew up, are most well known for the judicial appointments, but also included many other federal offices. One of these was the Collector of the Port of New Haven, Connecticut, a highly desirable and lucrative position to which Adams had appointed Federalist Elizur Goodrich, Sr. after the death of the former collector in February 1801.

2. *Windham Herald*, Windham, CT, September 25, 1800, 3.

Once in office, Jefferson began removing Federalists from office and replacing them with Republicans, an action decried by the Federalists. The Federalists of Connecticut, however, arrogantly believed that Jefferson wouldn't dare dismiss any Federalist officers in their state. They were wrong. Jefferson did, in fact, remove Goodrich from his collector position, an act that outraged Connecticut's Federalists.

What follows is the correspondence between Jefferson and Pierpont Edwards regarding Goodrich's replacement, which also contains an extensive description of virtually all aspects of the state of affairs in Connecticut politics.

Replying to Edwards's prior letters about the replacement of Goodrich, Jefferson wrote on March 29, 1801:

> You will doubtless have long ago learned that the office which was the subject of your two favors to me was filled by mr Adams some days before he went out of office. I have not considered as candid, or even decorous, the crouding of appointments by mr A. after he knew he was making them for his successor & not for himself, even to 9. aclock of the night, at twelve of which he was to go out of office. I do not think I ought to permit that conduct to have any effect as to the offices removeable in their nature. of course this would leave me free to fill mr Goodrich's place by any other person. this is a subject worthy of mature consideration, & therefore Judge Lincoln[3] will ask of yourself, & some few of your fellow laborers, who best know all [the] circumstances which ought to weigh, to consult and advise us on this subject ...[4]

After consulting with other Republican leaders in Connecticut, Edwards replied on May 12, 1801:

> ...There is but one Opinion among the intillegent republicans in Connecticutt, respecting the case of Mr. Goodrich; all agree, that a removal will be right, in itself, and that the

3. Levi Lincoln, Jefferson's Attorney General. A native of Massachusetts, Lincoln was also one of Jefferson's advisors on New England politics.

4. Thomas Jefferson to Pierpont Edwards, March 29, 1801. Barbara B. Oberg, ed., *The Papers of Thomas Jefferson*, vol. 33, (Princeton, NJ: Princeton University Press, 2006), 489.

Measure is necessary, as it regards the general cause in Connecticutt. We have "consulted and Advised on the Subject,
taking a broad view of the general as well as local." The Manner of his appointment has been considered by you in its
proper light, as to that Point therefore I forbear to make any
remarks—"Taking a broad view of it," we are convinced,
that his being continued in office, instead of reconciling his
friends, or any part of the federalists to republicanism, and
to your Administration will Strengthen them in there Opposition—They boldly Assert that you dare not dismiss any
federal Officer in Connecticutt.—And they assign two reasons—"That you know, that if your administration is supported at all in Connecticutt, it must be supported by the
federalists," and "that you have no confidence in any of the
republicans, because you consider them as Men unfriendly
to all regular Goverment"—They have the Affrontery to pro-
mulge these sentiments in every corner of the State, and
with vast industry; and to [evince?] that these sentiments
are just, they refer to your conduct with respect to officers
in Connecticut—; they say, "Mr. Jefferson has displaced no
Officer in Connecticutt; he has in other States; and is it because the Officers in Connecticutt are more republican than
in other states? No, they are the strongest federalists in the
United States; the true cause of his thus conducting is, he
dare not trust a republican in Connecticutt, he knows they
are, what we Assert them to be, disorganizers." Every hour
that the work of displacing is deferred gives strength to this
delusion. I should not have mentioned what I have, were it
not constantly and hourly said by the most influential and
distinguished of the federal party. ...[5]

Before getting to his recommendation for Goodrich's replacement,
Edwards described at length all aspects of the state of affairs in
Connecticut and the level of animosity among the state's Federalists
towards anything Republican, and towards Jefferson in particular:

...Our Southern brethren, I presume, have no Just concep-

---

5. Pierpont Edwards to Thomas Jefferson, May 12, 1801. Barbara B. Oberg, ed., *The Papers of Thomas Jefferson*, vol. 34, (Princeton, NJ: Princeton University Press, 2007), 91.

tion, as to the state of things in Connecticutt; the malignity
of the federalists here is wholly inconceivable to any, but
such as are Eye and ear witnesses to all; we should be as
slow to beleive as they, if we had not had the evidence of
our own senses, as to there conversation and conduct—The
federalists here are a corps most systimatically organized.
The Governor and Council joined to the corporation of
Yale College, which was originally wholly eclesiastical, (and
thirteen out of twenty one are now eclesiastics,) makes all
the arrangements; these are communicated to those general
meetings of our established Clergy, one holden at the general
election in May, one holden in July, called a general association, and one holden at the Commencement in September;
from these general Meetings the plans are communicated to
the County consociations, and there are generally two in each
County; these are composed of all the established Clergy
living within the limits of the respective consociations—
from them it is communicated to all the true federalist of
each Parish—By this means they act with perfect uniformity; they are also, in this way, taught an uniformity of
speech, on all political questions; so that if you hear any
thing said by a federalist of tolarable respectability here, you
may be sure that the same thing is prepared to be said every
where—Since your elevation to the Presidency they have
formed a plan, which looks more like producing some serious mischief than any that has ever yet been adopted by
them: the Clergy are all to inculcate, with ernestness, in
private conversation, and from the Pulpit the necessity of
submitting to Goverment, the danger of speaking evil of
those who administer the Goverment, so long as they administer it well they are to shew the fatal effects of not
Observing this sort of Conduct; by stating, that if good
Men, who are in Office, are calumnited; it will very proba-
blely be the means of bringing into Office bad Men, Deists,
men of no religion, men profligate in their Morals; and to
shew clearly that such will be the effect of calumniating
good Officers, they are to tell the people, to looke at recent
events. several sermons have already been dilivered in
Perfect conformity to this Plan—the federalists here do

not consider themselves conquered; they are putting every faculty to the torture to effect the overthrow of your republican Administration—our leading federalists are all royalists; they think as our Clergy do "Moses & Aaron here walk together"—The throne and the Alter have here entered into an alliance offensive and defensive. If they cannot effect a change in the administration, they are resolved to divide the Union—this measure however, even in their minds, has its difficulties; the Republicans are Numerous even in Connecticutt, in Rhode Island they are decidedly a majority, in Massachusetts about seven fifteenths are republicans, in New Hampshire two fifths, in Vermont half are with us— The plan of dividing the Union therefore affords but a gloomy prospect of success, unless the republican Party can be lessined; this must be effected. To accomplish an event so desirable, has given them much thought, and no small share of trouble; but it is at last determined, so far as Connecticutt is concerned, to adopt the following measures—to disgrace the republican party, as a party, as much as posible; for that purpose to teach, that Mr. Jefferson has no confidence in them. A few are to be taken off, by courting them, bringing them into Office here, but wholly by the force of federal Votes and influences to relax on the Measure which they have heretofore adopted, of turning out every man, who was not a federalist; to reinstate two or three, who have very good connextions, that in the rage of party were turned out; but on all Occasions to teach it for doctrine, that the Democrates in Connecticutt, are a set of Men of no talents, no property, no Morals, and unfriendly to all Goverment. with these facts in full View, we do not hesitate to say, that a temporizing policy will be, here, a ruinous policy. The Collector at Middletown deserves a dismission on more grounds than one—Violent, unstable, priest-ridden, implacable, a ferocious federalist, and a Most indecent enimy to you and your administration,—One of the toasts drunk on the 4th. of July last at Middletown was, "Thomas Jefferson may he receive from his fellow Citizens the rewards of his Merits", he drank it, adding, "a halter." I could fill a quire of paper with speaches of his equally Violent and indecent ...[6]

Returning to the subject of who should replace Goodrich, Edwards advanced the name Samuel Bishop, father of one the Federalists' most reviled Republicans, none other than Abraham Bishop:

> ... As to Mr. Goodrich's Successor we all agree, that Samuel Bishop Esqr. of this town, Mayor of our City Cheife Judge of our County Court, and a Deacon of one of our established churches aught to be the Man. In him will be embraced the respectability, integrity, religion "Steady habits" and firm republicanism. ...[7]

To the Federalists, this wasn't only seen as a reward for Abraham Bishop's exertions during the presidential election of 1800, but in effect giving the appointment to Abraham Bishop himself, since his father, although still very active as the mayor of New Haven and in other positions, was seventy-seven years old, and Abraham would likely succeed him. And succeed him he did. When Samuel Bishop died two years later, Jefferson, who among other things was a fan of Bishop's writings,[8] appointed him as his father's successor.

Connecticut's spring 1801 election marked the first appearance of Republican candidates for governor and lieutenant governor. The candidate for governor was New London mayor Judge Richard Law, a federal district judge nominated by George Washington, who, among many other distinctions, had been one of Connecticut's delegates to the Continental Congress. Running for lieutenant governor was Colonel Ephraim Kirby, a Revolutionary War veteran, lawyer, publisher of the first volume of law reports in the United States, and member of Connecticut's General Assembly. Incumbent Federalist governor Jonathan Trumbull easily won reelection with 11,156 votes to Law's 1,056, as did Federalist lieutenant governor John Treadwell, with 9,066 votes to Kirby's 2,028. The other significant race in the spring of 1801 was that to fill a vacant seat in the U.S. House of Representatives. That race was won by

---

6. Pierpont Edwards to Thomas Jefferson, May 12, 1801. Barbara B. Oberg, ed., *The Papers of Thomas Jefferson*, vol. 34, (Princeton, NJ: Princeton University Press, 2007), 92-93.
7. Ibid., 94.
8. Ibid., vol. 41, 207.

Federalist Calvin Goddard, who received 7,397 votes to 3,256 for Republican Gideon Granger. In the state's House of Representatives Federalists outnumbered Republicans about five to one.

In the fall election, the Republicans issued a list for Council assistants for the first time, which included a few moderate Federalists. Of the Republicans, the highest number of votes went to Gideon Granger at 3,963, which was 1,240 votes below the lowest number received by any candidate who made the list of twenty from which twelve would be elected the following spring. Republican representation in the House remained about the same as it had been in the spring. It was after this fall election that, as explained in the introduction, the Federalists, threatened by the state's rising Republican party, enacted the stand-up law.

∽ 1802 ∾

ADDRESS TO THE PRESIDENT.

The Address of the Danbury Baptist Association,
in the State of Connecticut; assembled
October the 7th, 1801, to THOMAS JEFFERSON, Esq.
President of the United States of America.

SIR,

AMONG the many millions in America and Europe who rejoice in your election to office; we embrace the first opportunity which we have enjoyed, in our collective capacity, since your Inauguration, to express our great satisfaction in your appointment to the chief magistracy in the United States: and tho' our mode of expression may be less courtly and pompous, than what many others clothe their addresses with, we beg you, Sir, to believe that none are more sincere.

Our Sentiments are uniformly on the side of religious liberty—That *religion* is at all times and places a matter between God and individuals—That no man aught to suffer in name, person, or effects on account of his religious opinions—That the legitimate power of civil government extends no further than to punish the man who *works ill to his neighbour:* But, Sir, our constitution of government is not specific. Our ancient charter, together with the laws made coincident therewith, were adopted, as the basis of our government, at the time of our revolution; and such had been our laws and usages, and such still are; that *religion* is considered as the first object of legislation; and therefore what religious privileges we enjoy (as a minor part of the state) we enjoy as favors granted, and not as *inalienable rights:* and these *favors* we receive at the expence of such degrading acknowledgements as are inconsistent with the rights of freemen.—It is not to be wondered at therefore, if those, who seek after *power* and *gain,* under the pretence of *government* and *religion,* should reproach their fellow men—should reproach their chief magistrate, as an enemy of religion, law and good order, because he will not, dares not assume the prerogative of JEHOVAH and make laws to govern the kingdom of Christ.

Sir, we are sensible that the President of the United States, is not the national legislator; and also sensible that the national government cannot destroy the laws of each state; but our hopes are strong that the sentiments of our beloved president which have had such genial effect already, like the radiant beams of the sun, will shine and prevail thro' all these states and all the world till Hierarchy and tyranny be destroyed from the earth. Sir, when we reflect on your past services and see a glow of philanthropy and good will, shining forth in a course of more than *thirty years;* we have reason to believe that America's God has raised you up to fill the chair of state, out of that good will which he bears to the millions which you preside over. May God strengthen you for the arduous task, which Providence and the voice of the people have called you to sustain; and support you in your administration against all the *predetermined* opposition of those, who wish to rise to wealth and importance, on the poverty and subjection of the people. And may the lord pre-serve you safe from every evil, and bring you at last to his Heavenly kingdom, thro' Jesus Christ our glorious Mediator.

Signed in behalf of the Association

> Nehemiah Dodge,
> Ephraim Robbins, } Committee
> Stephen S. Nelson

To Messers. Nehemiah Dodge, Ephraim Robbins and Stephen S. Nelson, a committee of the Danbury Baptist association in the state of Connecticut.

GENTLEMEN,

The affectionate sentiments of esteem and approbation which you are so good as to express towards me, on behalf of the Danbury Baptist association, give me the highest satisfaction; my duties dictate a faithful and zealous pursuit of the interests of my constituents and in proportion as they are persuaded of my fidelity to those duties, the discharge of them becomes more and more pleasing.

Believing with you, that religion is a matter which lies solely between man and his God, that he owes account to none other for his faith or his worship, that the legitimate powers of government reach actions only, and not opinions, I contemplate with sovereign reverence that act of the whole American people which declared that their legislature should "make no law respecting an establishment of religion, or prohibiting the free exercise thereof," thus building a wall of separation between church and state. Adhering to this expression of the supreme will of the nation, in behalf of the rights of conscience, I shall see with sincere satisfaction the progress of those sentiments which tend to restore to man all his natural rights, convinced he has no natural right in opposition to his social duties.

I reciprocate your kind prayers for the protection and blessing of the common father and creator of man, and tender you, for yourselves & your religious association, assurances of my high respect and esteem.

THOMAS JEFFERSON.

January 1, 1802.[1]

⤳

In January 1802, when Jefferson wrote this now-famous letter to the Danbury, Connecticut Baptists, coining the phrase "separation

---

1. *American Mercury*, Hartford, CT, January 28, 1802, 3.

between church and state," the government of Connecticut was firmly under Federalist control, and with the new stand-up law and other inequitable election laws, was designed to stay that way.

In the spring 1802 election, Jonathan Trumbull, governor since 1797, was reelected with 11,368 votes to Republican Ephraim Kirby's 4,525. John Treadwell, also in office since 1797, was re-elected lieutenant governor with 9,085 votes to David Trumbull's 3,913. Only about 55 seats, a little over a quarter of the House of Representatives, went to Republicans. The Council remained entirely Federalist.

While some Republicans boasted of having elected 78 members to the House of Representatives in the fall election, Federalist newspaper the *Litchfield Monitor* rightly questioned that number, given that Republican party leader Ephraim Kirby received only 36 votes for Speaker of the House out of 153 members present. With candidates for the House not formally declaring a party affiliation, an exact count is not possible. For most, it was only possible to guess at their party leanings by how they voted after they were in the House. As the *Monitor* put it, "When the House is collected, it is presumed some question will be stated by them which will shew who their 78 are."[2]

In 1781, Samuel Peters, an Anglican minister from Connecticut published a book titled *General History of Connecticut, from its first settlement under George Fenwick, to its latest period of amity with Great Britain prior to the Revolution,* in which he listed what he purported to be Connecticut's original "blue laws" from the first settlement of New Haven in 1639. These laws, according to Peters's book, included such things as a law forbidding a mother to kiss her child on the Sabbath. Peters's list has been dismissed by historians, as Peters, a loyalist writing in England during the Revolution, was clearly trying to paint Connecticut and the American colonists in as bad a light as possible, and also because there was no written record of these laws, as Peters acknowledged in his book. The first written blue laws, drafted by Governor Theophilus Eaton in 1655,

2. *Litchfield Monitor,* Litchfield, CT, October 27, 1802, 1.

did, however, contain some similarities to Peters's list, such as a law forbidding a husband and wife to kiss on the Sabbath, and a law permitting parents to kill a disobedient child over the age of sixteen. Peters wrote in his book that the term "blue laws" was used by people in the other colonies to refer to Connecticut's laws, a claim that has also been dismissed by many historians, with some accusing Peters of inventing the term himself. This, however, is not true. The term "blue laws" was, in fact, in use in America prior to Peters's book.

A 1775 advertisement for an almanac for the year 1776, described the almanac as "Containing besides the usual Calculations, &c. &c. some curious and entertaining Extracts from the ancient Records of New-Haven, vulgarly call'd the BLUE LAWS."[3]

And an interesting article in a New York paper from 1755 also used the term. In this article, the author recounts a dream in which he is transported twenty years into the future to 1775, to a world in which there had been a revolution in England, a new Protectorate government installed, and the Toleration Act of 1689 repealed:

> I dreamed, that there had been a great Revolution in England; that another *Lord Protector*[4] had usurped the throne; that all Laws and Customs were entirely changed, and every Thing moddled and put upon the same Footing as they were in the Days of OLIVER CROMWELL, whose Laws were revived and re-printed; in Consequence whereof Independency was established, and Bishop's Lands, Tythes, and other ecclesiastical Revenues, were invested in the new Clergy; that the Act of Toleration[5] was repealed, and *Presbytery* and *Independency*, were, by Proclamation, declared to be synonymous Terms; and that we had been under a

3. *Connecticut Journal*, New Haven, CT, November 29, 1775, 2.

4. Oliver Cromwell ruled Britain as Lord Protector, head of the Protectorate government that followed Britain's civil wars. The most plausible theory for the origin of the term "blue laws" traces back to the derisive term of "bluestockings" for the Puritans in Cromwell's short-lived "Barebones Parliament" of 1653, which preceded the Protectorate government of 1653 to 1659.

5. England's Toleration Act, enacted in 1689. In the American colonies, this act gave Quakers and other Protestant dissenters the right to worship. In the New England colonies, dissenters were no longer exiled or subject to corporal punishment, although they continued to be discriminated against in all other ways.

protectoral Government four Years in this Province, and the Governments of New-York and Connecticut were united.

While these visionary Ideas were disturbing my natural Repose, I dreamed, that I heard the Printer's Man, crying the *New-York Gazette,* of whom (as I was ever desirous of knowing the worst of Things,) I purchased one, which made such a strong Impression on my Mind, that I perfectly remember the Contents yet; which are as follows.[6]

One of the items the dreamer saw in his imagined future newspaper of 1775 was:

Hartford, (in Connecticut) May 12. Since the happy Revolution, and the Revival of our old Blue Laws, we have the pleasure to see the Lord's Work go on with Success; all different Persuasions do now again pay our Ministers, which is said to be a great Help to many of our Towns in the back Settlements.[7]

The following item from May 1802 begins with a quote from Samuel Peters's version of Connecticut's blue laws, and while the quote from Peters might or might not be accurate, the description of the control of religion and the clergy over New England is.

"No one shall dance, or play on any instrument of music except the Drum, Trumpet, and Jews-harp."
BLUE LAWS.

THE venerable code from which the foregoing is an extract is the prototype of the "steady habits of Connecticut."

Tho some of its precepts have been repealed and its principles forgotten—yet their influence remains unimpaired in many of our villages *where* the obsequious multitude *tamely* submit to clerical dominion and dare not elect even a Corporal in the militia without the "advice and consent" of their wig-clad oracle—*where* prayer and fasting precede elections—*where* elections *civil, military, and*

6. *The New-York Mercury,* New York, NY, March 3, 1755, 1.
7. Ibid.

ecclesiastical, are headed by sermons; and the "Pulpit Drum Ecclesiastic," loudly beats the federal long roll, "Religion is in danger," and nominates the candidate*—where the grateful magistrate rewards the faithful orator, by *procuring* generous contributions from the deluded flock: and an extensive spread of the means of *delusion*—Magazines, Speeches, &c. stigmatizing the government to *support* order! advocating a dissolution of the union to preserve the Constitution! and warning from their precincts teachers of good manners to *secure Morality and Religion!!*—But in no part of our country is this *goodly work* so conspicuous as in the town of Boston, where an unusual alarm has lately been excited by opening a dancing school, and the appearance of democracy—as may be seen in the following letters, which would have been sooner submitted to your consideration had not my master expected "further trouble" from his honorable correspondents.

A FIDDLER.

To the MASTER and SCHOLARS of the Dancing Assembly in North-Boston.

GENTLEMEN and LADIES,

WE the Subscribers, having received a petition signed by a considerable number of the inhabitants of said society, praying to have said school discontinued—and it appearing to us a matter that demands our immediate attention, have unanimously agreed to address you on the subject, hoping you will be persuaded to give it up without any further trouble.

It is with serious concern that we view the progress of vice in our land—that infidelity stalks abroad with a bold front—that the councils of our nation are divided thereby, which threatens to ruin and destroy all order and government, both civil and religious:—Under such circumstances we cannot think it a proper time for merriment; it is a time to mourn, and not a time to dance, when we are on the brink of ruin: It is like dancing at our own funeral: we think it will also be of pernicious consequence in society; the young people will divide into parties, and their parents will join their children—by which means the whole parish will be in parties; and all this sore evil, without any substantial good to be obtained by any one, but a great mispence of time and money:—We also hope, the parents and guardians of children will take the matter into their most serious consideration, and by their seasonable advice and interference, prevent the bad consequences which are likely to follow such a loose kind of education: we wish not to hurt the feelings of any person; but we think it our duty to give you this friendly admonition, hoping you will turn your attention to that which will conduce more to your present and future happiness.

With the purest friendship we subscribe our names—

> *Samuel Carver,*
> *Oliver King,*   } *Justices of the Peace.*
> *Jared Cone, jun.*

> *Samuel Howard,*
> *Cornelius Roberts.* } *Select-men.*

Boston, March 17th, 1802.

———

To the Civil Authority and Select-men
of the Town of Boston.

GENTLEMEN,

I *BOW* with reverence to the *constituted authorities* of our country, civil and ecclesiastical—But when our venerable clergy proclaim from the pulpit,† that every species of reformers from the Sage of Monticello, to the dancing master of Hebron, are "jacobin philosophers, demoralizing the world"—when our pious Magistrates *officially* denounce "the councils of our nation" and the village *Ball,* as nurseries of vice, and sources of *"infidelity,"* I doubt the infallibility of the one—I deny the jurisdiction of the other.

Be not deceived, nor alarmed my respected friends—the laws of Congress were not given by inspiration, and should a few more of them be repealed, it would not affect an article of our holy religion, nor "destroy all order and government, civil and religious"—and you may rest assured, that there is not a single particle of *Deism* or *Jacobinism* in the sound of a violin, or the graceful movements of a dancing assembly.

Your advice, Gentlemen, I receive with gratitude, and will certainly comply with your wishes "without further trouble," whenever my pupils or their parents *discontinue their favors.*

I "wish not to hurt the feelings of any person, but I think it my duty to give you this friendly admonition," that the morals and manners of the good people of Boston are in no danger from an intercourse with polished society—and cannot be injured by *that* which is every where considered as a genteel and useful accomplishment.

Be pleased, gentlemen, to accept my most respectful and grateful acknowledgements for the unusual mildness of your proceedings against an *odious offender,* which I have reason to hope will be *graciously* continued *until the laws permit you to do otherwise.*

Wishing that your "mourning" may speedily turn to joy—and that you may happily escape from "the brink of ruin."

"With the purest friendship I subscribe my name"—
FREDERICK A. FULLER.

S. *CARVER,* Esq. &c.

Boston, March 22d, 1802.

———

* *In a sermon delivered at the Freeman's meeting in Boston the last year of the reign of terror, the* Rev. E.K. *after pointing out the mode of electing the President, and the importance of the subject, exclaimed with great emphasis* "Look out Freemen, if you send such men to the Assembly as you have in sessions past we shall have democratic electors and that wicked Jefferson, that Deist that Atheist will be President." J.C. Jun. Esq. humbled himself and was re-elected, but poor J.W. Jun. had not a single vote.

† *See an elegant, pious, and learned discourse, lately delivered at E. Haddam, by the Rev. Mr. Lyman, wherein he suggests that dancing masters and fiddlers are of the order of the illuminati—and that "dancing schools are a*

part of the modern system of infidel philosophy" &c. *!!* [8]

The Federalist cry of "religion is in danger," begun during the election of 1800 — that if Jefferson was elected Bibles would be burned, meeting-houses leveled to the ground, ministers removed or even killed — continued well into Jefferson's presidency, despite the fact that even after years in office none of these predicted calamities had occurred.

"RELIGION is in DANGER!"

This cry has been reiterated by the anti-republicans, it has been falsely rung by the tories, till in fact it has lost the power, which it once had, of alarming the people—After the experiment, the people find that Religion is as well attended to and shines with as benign a lustre, under the administration of *Thomas Jefferson,* as of a *Washington,* or *John Adams!*—None of our Churches have been attacked; no Minister of the Meek and Beneficent Redeemer has been disturbed in his Divine functions, nor *his salary;* no sect has been oppressed;—every man enjoys the divine and constitutional right of worshipping THE DEITY "according to the dictates of his own conscience"—in a word, Religion was never more regarded and never *flourished* more in America, than within the last two years — ...

The measures, rather than the *professions,* of men, must determine whether they be wise and GOOD rulers, or whether they be evil and imprudent.—But the Tories must try some other way to destroy the confidence of the American People in the patriotic JEFFERSON, than *smiting their breasts* and crying from the *house-top,* "Religion is in danger! the *democrats* will destroy it."...[9]

8. *American Mercury,* Hartford, CT, May 27, 1802, 2.
9. *Republican Gazette,* Concord, NH, December 16, 1802, 3.

One of the most controversial laws passed during the Adams administration — or the "reign of terror," as the Republicans called it — was the Sedition Act of 1798. Under this law, which was to expire on the last day of Adams's term, it became punishable by fines and imprisonment to:

> ... write, print, utter or publish, or shall cause or procure to be written, printed, uttered or published, or shall knowingly and willingly assist or aid in writing, printing, uttering or publishing any false, scandalous and malicious writing or writings against the government of the United States, or either house of the Congress of the United States, or the President of the United States, with intent to defame the said government, or either house of the said Congress, or the said President, or to bring them, or either of them, into contempt or disrepute; or to excite against them, or either or any of them, the hatred of the good people of the United States ... then such person, being thereof convicted before any court of the United States having jurisdiction thereof, shall be punished by a fine not exceeding two thousand dollars, and by imprisonment not exceeding two years.[10]

Over two dozen individuals were prosecuted under the law, many of them Republican editors, but also Matthew Lyons, a U.S. congressman from Vermont, who was fined and jailed. Lyons had written and published the following opinion of Adams:

> As to the executive, when I shall see the efforts of that power bent on the promotion of the comfort, the happiness, and accommodation of the people, that Executive shall have my zealous and uniform support: But whenever I shall, on the part of the Executive, see every consideration swallowed up in a continual grasp for power, in an unbounded thirst for ridiculous pomp, foolish adulation, and selfish avarice; ... when I shall see the sacred name of Religion employed as a state engine, to make mankind hate and persecute one

---

10. *An Act in Addition to the Act, Entitled "An Act for the Punishment of Certain Crimes Against the United States,"* July 14, 1798.

another, I shall not be their humble advocate.[11]

Lyons's constituents continued to support him, reelecting him to Congress while he was in jail.

While their party was in power, the Federalists supported the prosecutions under the Sedition Act, with Federalist clergy preaching that Republicans should submit to the ruling party, but as soon as Jefferson was in office, it was the same clergy, along with the Federalist press, preaching and publishing all manner of "false, scandalous and malicious writing or writings against the government of the United States" and the president, designed "to bring them ... into contempt or disrepute; or to excite against them ... the hatred of the good people of the United States." The blatant hypocrisy of this was of course pointed out by the Republicans.

LET it be remembered that two years past, to publish a falshood or even to advance an opinion against the then ruling party, which should be called by them untrue, was considered and prosecuted as Sedition. Let it be remembered that victims of persecution were invariably indicted and shamefully punished. Let it be remembered that many of our pious Clergymen, many who would wish to be ranked as first characters, were the men who aided and abetted this persecution; that they disclaimed sedition, and avowed a determination to submit quietly to the majority.—And henceforth let it be treasured up in our minds, that some of the same Clergymen are now the defamers of a government chosen by the voice of the people; and that the papers are filled with their anonymous publications, which have a tendency to alienate the affections of the people from their government. And that it is a fact that they advance the most gross and abusive falshoods; ample proof, and our own senses can testify. ...

Calumny and abuse, although practised by many, does not tend to forward the cause of truth, but operates rather to irritate than to enlighten those to whom it is addressed. The height of my wishes is that the characters of men may

11. *The Bee,* New London, CT, November 14, 1798, 2.

be fairly investigated;—and that the people might then see for themselves. If a Priest profanes his pulpit with politics in lieu of teaching his audience the religion of which he calls himself a teacher, let the people know it and esteem him as he is, the servant of a party, but not a teacher from God. ...[12]

A story that first hit the news in 1802 that would be brought back up incessantly throughout Jefferson's presidency was his invitation to notorious infidel Thomas Paine to return from France to America on a national ship. To the Federalists, who were on the prowl for anything that they could use as evidence to support their hue and cry that the Republicans were plotting to annihilate religion, Jefferson's invitation to Paine was red meat. Word of Jefferson's invitation had come from the London papers in the spring, and in August the *Gazette of the United States,* a Federalist paper in Philadelphia, printed Jefferson's actual letter to Paine, which was reprinted in papers throughout the states.

LETTER TO TOM PAINE.

We are happy to have it in our power at length to lay before our readers the following celebrated and affectionate letter of our president to the most infamous and odious creature of our species. It was at first incredible that a man in Mr. Jefferson's station should even write to such a man as Paine, and the fact was never fully believed till confirmed and vindicated by the National Intelligencer, the President's official paper. What would at that time have been the feelings of the American people had they known the tenor of this letter which is now copied from a London paper. ...

Copy of the letter.

"You expressed a wish in your letter to return to America by a national ship; Mr. DAWSON, who brings over the

12. *The Pittsfield Sun,* Pittsfield, MA, May 3, 1802, 1.

treaty, and who will present you this letter, is charged with orders to the Captain of the Maryland to receive and accommodate you back, if you can be ready to depart at such a short warning. You will, in general, find us returned to sentiments worthy of former times; in these it will be your glory to have steadily laboured, and with as much effect as any man living. That you may live long to continue your useful labours, and reap the reward in the thankfulness of nations, is my sincere prayer.—Accept the assurance of my high esteem and affectionate attachment.

THOMAS JEFFERSON.[13]

Jefferson's phrase "useful labours" in referring to Paine's work became a go-to example for the Federalists of proof that Jefferson's desire was to turn America into a country of infidels.

From the Federalist *Litchfield Monitor:*

The president mentions the infidel Tom Paine's "useful" labors. Now what are they? Pulling down government, attempting to pull down religion—and writing libels against Washington. These useful labors, the President expresses his hope that Paine will continue. He wishes to have Paine here to pursue this laudable business, and offers him a public ship to bring him over. Now, if there is one fair minded democrat in the state, to him I appeal, and ask, whether any jacobin newspaper can complain with any face of reason, of the abuse of Mr. Jefferson? Is not his own conduct the worst imputation that can be thrown upon him? Is not the simple truth the most biting of all satire, the most blackening to his fame of all libels? ...[14]

Even before Jefferson's actual letter hit the papers, and the only news from the London papers was that Jefferson had sent an "affectionate" invitation to Paine, the Federalist papers were working this invitation into their "religion is in danger" pieces, as in this piece from the *Monitor,* commenting on some extracts from the

13. *Gazette of the United States,* Philadelphia, PA, August 10, 1802, 2.
14. *Litchfield Monitor,* Litchfield, CT, September 1, 1802, 3.

Temple of Reason, a deist weekly published by Denis Driscol in Philadelphia:

> These extracts have been made, my Countrymen, with a double view: The writer wishes to have you acquainted with the designs of these genuine republicans, as they call themselves, who are attempting to prostrate the religion of Jesus, and erect upon its ruins the impious dogmas of infidelity. He also wishes to convince you, that the alarm among Federalists, lest our institutions and our religion should fall a sacrifice to the madness and folly of Democracy, is not a pretence, as democrats would persuade you. Altho Democrats may feel perfectly satisfied, when Infidelity, assuming a most formidable attitude, erects her horrid crest against the Heavens; yet to Federalists, it is a source of the most serious apprehension, when they find a Temple erected in one of our largest cities; that periodical papers are publishing for the same purpose; that men who do these things are devoted to the *"Democratic Executive* of the United States," as they stile the President, and that this President has written an affectionate letter to Paine the reviler of Christianity, offering him a passage to this country in a National ship.—Is there no cause of alarm, my countrymen? Shall the delusions of Democracy still prevail? May the God of our Fathers snatch us from impending ruin![15]

Driscol's *Temple of Reason* was a popular target of the Federalist papers, held up as proof that all Republicans were on a crusade to destroy religion. From the *Middlesex Gazette,* another Connecticut Federalist paper:

> The following is extracted from a paper published weekly at *Philadelphia,* patronized by Democrats, (alias Republicans) and professedly devoted to the cause of Atheism. Speaking of the BIBLE, it says, *"would it not be felicity to future generations, were the book, and the blind tenets deduced*

---

15. *Litchfield Monitor,* March 31, 1802, reprinted in the *Republican Farmer,* Danbury, CT, April 6, 1802, 2.

from it, scouted from the earth, and blotted from the memory of man."—Would it have been credited a few years since, that the period was so soon to arrive, when any man should have been suffered publickly to deny the existence of a GOD, and to treat with derision the GOSPEL of his son. Surely we have fallen on evil times, when the open and infamous blasphemer is permitted to publish his blasphemies, and spread his poison, not only without any interference of the civil authorities but even without the pointed and vigorous opposition of every class of honest and sober citizens.

No nation, but the Jewish, ever received such signal favors from the Almighty, as this. No times of the greatest darkness, when all hope from human exertion has failed, we have beheld, through the goodness of Heaven, the clouds which overshadowed us, suddenly to dissipate, and the sun of our prosperity to shine brighter than ever.

But we are provoking the vengeance of Heaven; and if we tolerate within our bosoms a nest of villains without religion, without common decency, without any regard to truth or decorum, we cannot expect to avert it.[16]

Paine wasn't the only infamous infidel returning to America. It was reported in 1802 that Joel Barlow, a Connecticut native who as America's consul at Algiers in 1796 had drafted the much-quoted Treaty of Tripoli, which stated that "the Government of the United States of America is not, in any sense, founded on the Christian religion," was also planning a return.

BIRDS OF A FEATHER.

It has been announced that Joel Barlow "purposes to return to his native country in the course of the next year." Thus is the *Theistical Society* likely soon to be strengthened; Paine, who has already arrived, and Barlow, those mighty champions in the cause of infidelity and democracy. Barlow in a letter to a friend, dated Hamburgh, May 23, 1795, expresses himself thus; "I rejoice at the progress of

16. *Middlesex Gazette*, Middletown, CT, July 5, 1802, 3.

good sense over the damnable imposture or christian mummery. I had no doubt of the effect of Paine's Age of Reason. It must be cavalled at a while, but it must prevail.— Though things as good have been often said, they never were said in so good a way. I am glad to see a translation, and so good a one, of Bolanger's Christianity unveiled. I wish Mr. ——would go on and give us in the next volume, the history of that famous mountebank called St. Paul." ...

... That Barlow, upon his arrival will not be able to change the "steady habits" of Connecticut is certain, and he will be viewed as an object of horror and contempt. Better had both he and Paine, with all deference to Mr. Jefferson be it said, been advised to remain in Europe, where there is so much king craft and priest craft, where their labors are so much needed; for in this country we have so many reformers, that we will probably arrive at the summit of perfection, without their assistance.[17]

While the Connecticut's Federalists liked to boast that the state's "steady habits" could not be changed by the infidels, and that the Republicans' plan to "revolutionize" the state was failing, they at the same time continually warned of Republican plots against religion, that the Republicans wanted to, among other things, do away with the institution of marriage, and what the next article calls "one of the most insidious plots" — the plot to "prostrate the clergy":

OUR Democratic Republicans cannot withhold the expression of their chagrin and disappointment, at not being able to revolutionize the New-England, as they have done the Southern States—they have not, however, spared their exertions in this quarter of the Union, but fortunately have had more *knowledge* and *sagacity* to encounter here than farther South. It is not a set of ignorant Germans—of newly imported united Irish—of proud but uninformed slave holders, whom they have to contend with, but *free men*— an *industrious, intelligent, moral* people, who could distin-

17. *Windham Herald,* Windham, CT, November 25, 1802, 2.

guish between misrepresentation and truth—between the doctrines of anarchy and those of rational liberty.

In order at once to *democratize* and *demoralize* New-England, one of the most insidious plots—one of the most favorite schemes, with the anti-federal party, has been to prostrate the *Clergy.* For this purpose, every effort has been tried, first, to sap religion by the publication and dissemination of all the infamous French publications, or those written by such Franchified creatures as Paine and Barlow, against the Christian religion—and when it was found that a plan of this nature could not succeed in America as it had done in France, the next effort is to be tried against the Ministers of the Gospel. Because like honest men, they adhere to what they consider as right, rather than what is polite—because they continue to be the friends of Washington and Adams, altho' one is in his grave and the other in retirement, they are represented as "tories, as hypocrites, as friends of sedition," &c.—Abraham Bishop, the *virtuous, immaculate* Abraham Bishop, has written a book to prove them to be enemies of religion and government, and therefore, with a certain description of people, the fact is considered as *proved.* The next measure with this class of politicians would be to withdraw from religion and morals, all the protection they derive from the law—to let the people, simple and gentle, break the Sabbath, get drunk, swear, game, blaspheme, as often as they please—marry and *un*-marry when they choose without any *legal* restraint, because, if they were restrained by law, this would be an "union of Church and State"—this would be calling the *civil* authority to repress crimes and offences against *morality,* which are equally offences against the *christian religion.*[18]

Republicans in New England did denounce the clergy — the political clergy who used their pulpits and influence to preach Federalist politics, electioneer for Federalist candidates, viciously malign Republicans, and not only spread the lies, rumors, and anti-Republican propaganda from the Federalist newspapers but wrote

18. *Litchfield Monitor,* Litchfield, CT, December 22, 1802, 1.

a good part of it. New England's Federalist clergy would reach new heights of brazenness and notoriety during the War of 1812, with certain clergymen becoming household names throughout the country, one preaching a sermon that was so pro-British that it was reprinted in Canada as an "unparalleled" example of British patriotism and recommended to Canada's ministers to imitate. Though the Republicans hadn't yet started using the word "treason" to describe the Federalist clergy's sermons as they would a decade later, the union of church and state that existed between the political clergy and Connecticut's Federalist government, or "Moses and Aaron," as Abraham Bishop put it in his 1801 oration, led to to numerous articles like the following:

A FREE people cannot well be too jealous of *sacerdotal interference* in their *political concerns;* for it has been in all ages, and in every country, the source of innumerable evils, and those of the greatest magnitude. Even the loss of religious liberty by the establishment of ecclesiastical tyranny; and the destruction of civil liberty, by an alliance between such establishment, and the civil authority, has seldom failed of being its effects. The attempts of many of our clergy to hold an undue influence over our minds in political matters, and particularly about the period of the last presidential election, was highly alarming. At that time, there issued from several of our pulpits the most dreadful *anathemas* against such as thought it would be beneficial to the country, to place at the head of its affairs a person whose conduct in the most eminent stations, for a series of years, had evinced him to be a steadfast supporter of its interests and rights. But, alas! this man was *accused* of being a *philosopher*—an enemy to religious persecutions; and without doubt he was guilty! He believed, too, that all sects of religion ought to be equal in the eye of the law,—an opinion that was sure to bring upon him the wrath of the clerical bigots; and if ever the man who labored for the happiness of his species, by inculcating the principles of toleration, and equal rights, deserved such execration, JEFFERSON *earned it well.* True it is, had he been the *seducer of a Maria,* and an *advocate for monarchy, aristocracy,* and *priest craft,* he would have been a favorite,—yea, a mighty favorite of those *holy* political meddlers. ...[19]

Similar articles were found in the Republican papers of Massachusetts, a state that would give rise to some of the most infamous political preachers in the years to come.

On the Sabbath preceding the first monday of April, 1802, a Clergyman in one of the towns within the County of *Berkshire,* preached upon the duty of choosing such men as rulers, as had the qualifications described in the Sermon; and mentioned one of the then candidates for the office of Chief Magistrate of the Commonwealth, as a gentleman possessing those qualifications. This, I believe, the Preacher and his hearers will agree is a correct statement of the case; on which the question arises, whether such a mixture of religion and politics, of Church and State, is proper? Could anything be more directly ELECTIONEERING?—If it was proper for him thus to preach in support of his favorite Candidate, would it not be as proper for another minister, who preferred another Candidate, to inculcate upon his congregation the religious duty of voting for him? If it is proper thus solemnly and persuasively to interfere in the election of a Governor, is it not equally proper to interfere, in the same manner, in the elections of Members of Congress, Senators, town Representatives, Militia Officers, Selectmen, &c? If it is proper for the Preacher in his Pulpit, on the Sabbath, thus publicly to electioneer for a Candidate, would it be improper for his hearers, during the intermission, to form themselves into an electioneering Caucus, appoint a Committee to distribute votes and adopt other measures for promoting the election? In short, where will the practice end? ...[20]

Few political thinkers held the high esteem of Federalists more

19. *The Patriot, or Scourge of Aristocracy,* Stonington-Port, CT, January 22, 1802, Vol. 1, No. 27, 209.

20. *The Pittsfield Sun,* Pittsfield, MA, October 11, 1802, 3.

than Edmund Burke, making the passage from Burke's *Reflections on the Revolution in France* quoted in the following article extremely popular among Republicans as the go-to quote to throw in the Federalists' faces.

Edmund Burke has long been the great *Preceptor of the "Old School."* The full-blooded, high-toned, Hamiltonian, *Sulpiciated* Federalists, have long inculcated a reverence for his doctrines, approaching to devotion; and a respect for his name, bordering on adoration. He has been their infallible political *Prophet,* and the clerical advocates of *"Church and State,"* have preached Sermons, expressly designed to shew the fulfilment of his prediction. Jeremiah, Ezekiel, Isaiah and the rest have been neglected, and this second St. Edmund has engrossed the attention of the Federal *Crusading* Divines. To them, therefore, I shall merely propose a text from their favorite Book of Prophecies, and leave it to them, (as it is perfectly within their province) to compose the Sermon.

Your serious and candid attention then, is, requested, Reverend Sirs, to that passage, which you may find recorded in the 7th Page *Newyork* Edition of Burke's *"Reflections on the Revolution in France."*

"Politics and the Pulpit are terms that have little agreement. No sound ought to be heard in the church, but the healing voice of Christian charity. The cause of civil liberty and civil government, gains as little as that of religion by this confusion of duties. Those, who quit their proper character to assume what does not belong to them, are, for the greater part, ignorant both of the character they leave, and of the character they assume. Wholly unacquainted with the world, in which they are so fond of meddling, and inexperienced in all its affairs, on which they decide with so much confidence, THEY HAVE NOTHING OF POLITICS BUT THE PASSIONS THEY EXCITE. Surely, the church is a place, where one day's truce ought to be allowed to the dissensions and animosities of mankind." ...[21]

21. *Salem Register, Salem,* MA, October 14, 1802, 1.

One story widely reported on in late 1801 and early 1802 was that of the "mammoth cheese," as it was called by the Federalists. Weighing in at 1,235 pounds, the cheese was made in the town of Cheshire, Massachusetts, and delivered to Jefferson on New Year's Day 1802 as a large, edible token of the town's esteem.

The cheese was made by the ladies of Rev. John Leland's church. Like the overwhelming majority of Baptists, Leland, a Baptist minister who had lived in Virginia during that state's struggle for religious freedom, was overjoyed by Jefferson's election to the presidency. The Cheshire cheese was personally transported from Massachusetts to Washington by Leland and Darius Brown, beginning its journey in November and arriving at the end of December. Upon the cheese's arrival in Washington, Leland was invited to preach a sermon on religious liberty before Congress and the president.

News of the making of the cheese and its journey to Washington was met with much mocking from the Federalists, countered by articles like this one from the Republican *Pittsfield Sun:*

> One of the principal subjects of *Federal* complaint against President JEFFERSON seems to be the '*Mammoth Cheese,*' (as the *Opposition* writers have generally called it) made by a number of the ladies of Cheshire, to be presented to the President as a mark of respect, and for the encouragement of the staple production of that grazing town. This intended PRESENT, and the appointment of ABRAHAM BISHOP'S Father, Collector of New-Haven in the place of Mr. GOODRICH, have probably drawn forth more federal objections against the New Administration than any other two measures. The Cheshire Cheese has not yet been seriously represented to be in itself a violation of the Constitution: but presenting it to the President is thought to be inconsistent with the monopoly of a *federal* market, and consequently a crime nearly related to that of taking '*their daily bread away from meritorious federal officers;*' and it is an alarming principle of disorganization and modern philosophy, that upon every change of administration subordinate officers and marketers must be deprived of their *Bread and Cheese!* It is shrewdly suspected that ALBERT GALLATIN,

the Genevan instigator of whiskey insurrections,[22] instigated the good women of Cheshire to enter into the Cheese Plot, the particulars of which may be expected in the *Appendix* of Dr. MORSE'S[23] next *Thanksgiving Sermon*.[24]

One thing that there was no shortage of in the newspapers of the period was poetry. There was no subject that couldn't be set to rhyme, and the address to Jefferson from the town of Cheshire upon the presentation of the cheese was a natural for this treatment. Here is the actual address, followed by the versified version from a Federalist paper:

The address of the inhabitants of the town of Cheshire, Berkshire county, Massachusetts; to THOMAS JEFFERSON, president of the United States of America.

The greatest CHEESE in America,
FOR THE
Greatest MAN in America.

SIR,

Notwithstanding we live remote from the seat of national government, and in an extreme part of our own state; yet, we humbly claim the right of judging for ourselves.

Our attachment to the national constitution is strong and indissoluble. We consider it a description of those powers which the public have submitted to their Magistrates, to be exercised for definite purposes, and not a charter of

---

22. Albert Gallatin, Jefferson's Secretary of the Treasury, was a frequent target of the Federalists, not only because he was a Republican, but because being born in Geneva he was a foreigner, although he had become a U.S. citizen in 1785. Gallatin settled in Pennsylvania. He was a U.S. senator from Pennsylvania when the Whiskey Rebellion broke out in 1794, and was also elected to represent his county in the assembly formed by the farmers and small whiskey producers who were protesting the tax on whiskey, a tax that was unfair to the small producers, who paid a higher tax per gallon than the large producers. Gallatin was actually a moderating voice in this assembly, speaking out against an open rebellion against the government, but his involvement, which he himself later called his "only political sin," was never forgotten by the Federalists.

23. Massachusetts clergyman Rev. Jedidiah Morse, known for broadcasting the most ridiculous rumors of Republican plots through his sermons.

24. *The Pittsfield Sun*, Pittsfield, MA, November 16, 1801, 3.

favors, granted by a sovereign to his subjects. Among its beautiful features, the right of free suffrage, to correct all abuses. The prohibition of religious tests, to prevent all hierarchy. The means of amendment, which it contains within itself, to remove defects as fast as they are discovered, appear the most prominent. But for the several years past, our apprehension has been, that the genius of the government was not attended to in sundry cases; and that the administration bordered upon monarchy:—Our joy, of course, must have been great on your election to the first office in the nation;—having had good evidence, from your announced sentiments and uniform conduct that it would be your strife and glory to turn back the government to its virgin purity. The trust is great! The task is arduous! But we console ourselves that the supreme ruler of the Universe, who raises up men to achieve great events, has raised up a JEFFERSON for this critical day, to defend Republicanism and baffle all the arts of Aristocracy.

SIR, we have attempted to prove our love to our President, not in words alone, but in *deed and truth.* With this address, we send you a CHEESE, by the hands of Messrs. *John Leland,* and *Darius Brown,* as a pepper-corn of the esteem which we bear to our chief Magistrate, and as a sacrifice to Republicanism. It is not the last stone in the Bastile, nor is it of any great consequence as an article of worth; but as a free-will offering, we hope it will be received. The Cheese was not made by his Lordship, for his sacred Majesty; nor with a view to gain dignified titles or lucrative offices; but by the personal labor of free-born farmers (without a single slave to assist) for an elective President of a free people; with the only view of casting a mite into the scale of Democracy.

The late triumphant return of republicanism has more animated the Inhabitants of Cheshire, to bear the burthens of government, and treat the characters and persons of those in Authority with all due respect, than the long list of alien—sedition—naval, and provisional army laws, ever did.

SIR, we had some thoughts of impressing some significant inscription on the Cheese; but we have found such inconveniency in stamps on paper,[25] that we chose to send it in a plain Republican form.

May God long preserve your life and health, for a blessing to the United States, and the world at large.

Signed by order of all Cheshire,

> *Daniel Brown,*
> *Hezekiah Mason,*
> *Jona. Richardson,* } Committee.
> *John Waterman,*
> *John Wells, jun*

P.S. The Cheese was made July 20, 1801.—Weight 1235 lbs.[26]

⤳

From the WESTERN STAR.

MR. WILLARD,

I SEND you a versification of the Great Speech, which accompanied the Great Cheese, when it was presented to the Great Chief, who now commands. In elegance of diction, and pith of sentiment, it stands unrivalled in the annals of literature excepting only the solitary instance of Gen. Jackson's Speech.[27]—Yours, X. Y. & Z.

———

The greatest Cheese American!
For Jefferson the greatest Man!

ALTHO' far distant from the seat
Where you preside and Congress meet;
Although by chance it is our fate
To live in corner of *our* State;
We hope we have a right to think,
And now sit down with pen and ink,

25. Reference to *"An act laying duties on stamped vellum, parchment and paper,"* passed by the Adams administration in 1797. This act, commonly referred to at the time as the "Stamp Act," laid a tax on virtually any type of written or printed document.

26. *American Mercury,* Hartford, CT, January 28, 1802, 3.

27. The fiery pro-Republican, anti-Federalist address of Georgia governor James Jackson to his constituents upon leaving the office of governor to depart for Washington to serve as a U.S. senator from his state in 1801. The address was described by one Federalist paper in Massachusetts as "one of the most extraordinary productions even of Democratic Republicanism." (*Western Star,* December 12, 1801).

That we are well to let you know—
"Hoping these lines will find you so."
Our liking to the Constitution
Is strong as steel; past dissolution;
We think it quite a charming creature,
When we behold in every feature
A frown upon that kingly barter
Which deals out favors by a charter.
The right of suffrage too we see,
Like running water, pure and free;
And should her foes e'er dare impeach her,
They'll quickly meet *"correct procedure."*
Religion too, by prohibition,
Is freed from tests of superstition;
Should Feds perchance or break or bend it,
Tools are at hand to patch and mend it;
(And tinkers too who think it fun
To make two holes in patching one)
Yet many years we have been scar'd
For fear a Monarch should be rear'd,
And freedom's genius under trample;
In proof we give you an example:—
Old *Washington* once thought that he,
Or soon or late, a King shall be;
No sooner was this scarecrow gone,
Than up starts *Adams* on his throne.
Think then, dear Chief, how fill'd with joy
Our cup of bliss, without alloy,
When first we heard that you, dear Sir,
Was president, instead of *Burr,*
Your predecessors went astray,
And led the people far away,
In harlot's mazy paths to wander,
Like geese led on by cunning Ganders;
Yours is the task to turn them back
To *virgin purity's* old track;
'Tis yours to strive, yours is the glory,
To put in whig, and turn out tory:
In you we hope to see what's rare,

Good precepts with good conduct square;
Your task is hard; your trust is great;
But we console ourselves that Fate,
Who rules with gods, or one or twenty,
Has in his store such gifts in plenty,
Kindly to spare a JEFFERSON,
T' eclipse the fame of WASHINGTON.
Such prodigy these gods did send us,
From oligarchy to defend us.

    Words are but air, and cannot prove
To you, kind sir, our ardent love;
We therefore send it (hope 'twill please)
By Parson Leland in a CHEESE,
Drawn by a lusty six-horse team,
The *pepper-corn of our esteem.*
Old fashioned folks in ancient times,
(When doing penance for their crimes)
Offr'd up lambs' and bullocks' blood,
A sacrifice to appease *their* God,
But we with faith and plighted vows,
Now offer up the milk of cows.
Think not, dear sir, that 'tis a stone
By *"infuriate man"* from Bastile thrown;
'Twas made of milk, pray sir believe it,
A free will offering, so receive it.
Perhaps you may suspect this thing
Was made by Lords to please their King;
'Twas made by *our own Cheshire ladies,*
And making cheese their only trade is;
By their fair hands the curd was made,
Without the sooty slave to aid;
'Tis not with us as in Virginia,
Where dairy maids all come from Guinea.
Now, from your well assorted dish,
We ask for this, nor loaf, nor fish;
The democratic scale is light,
We therefore just throw in this *mite,*
In hopes, when weigh'd, 'gainst milk and cream,
The Fed'ral scale will kick the beam.

Democracy triumphant reigns,
Gives us great joy, relieves our pains;
The burthens which we could not weather,
Are now as light as hum bird's feather;
Once men in power had our neglect,
But now, *the homage* of respect.
    We would have stamped on this great Cheese,
Some pretty lines your grace to please,
But stamps of all sorts we detest,
And therefore tho't it would be best
To send it from its native press,
In homespun democratic dress.
    May *all our gods* your life preserve,
That you may long our country serve;
Then for your last reward you'll reap
The blessings of eternal sleep.
    By order of all Cheshire town,
    Accept our homage,
        DANIEL BROWN.[28]

A frequent theme of newspaper poetry was the Federalist and Republican papers taking shots at each other. Such was the case in 1802 when the Republican paper *The Bee* moved from New London, Connecticut to Hudson, New York, home of the rabidly Federalist paper *The Balance*. With *The Bee* moving to their town, the publishers of *The Balance* started up a new paper for the sole purpose of satirizing *The Bee*, calling this new paper *The Wasp*. The following poem appeared in the first issue of *The Wasp*.

DEMOCRATIC DING-DONG;
OR A
BELL TO SETTLE THE BEE.

THE Democrats—(I know them well)
Their heads are like a crier's bell—

28. *Newburyport Herald*, Newburyport, MA, March 9, 1802, 1.

A hollow sconce—a noisy thing
Hangs in the middle, pealing—*ding*—
    Ding—dong—a pealing bell,
    A Demo's head will do as well.

A Demo's head is made of brass;
His bawling beats the bray of ass;
His tongue an iron, noisy thing—
Touch it with whiskey—how 'twill *ding*—
    Ding—dong—a pealing bell,
    Whiskey suits the Demos well.

"The Bee" starv'd out and took his flight,
And on our shores he next would light—
The Demo clappers 'gan to ring,
But all was noise, and nought but *ding*—
    Ding—dong—a pealing bell,
    Demo's support a printer well.

Hark! hear the pan's* bewitching sound—
Hark! hear the bee come buzzing round—
See him prepare his pointless sting,
While all the Demo's clappers *ding*—
    Ding—dong—a pealing bell,
    The Bee will sting the fed'rals well.

But, hold! suppose support should fail,
And the poor Bee should shew his tail;
Another tune would Demos sing,
And quite forlorn their bell would *ding.*
    Ding—dong—a solemn knell
    Would sound the dying Bee's farewell.

* *A pan and stick are frequently used for settling a swarm of bees.* [29]

The first return shot at *The Wasp* came not *The Bee,* but from

29. *The Wasp, Hudson,* NY, July 7, 1802, 4.

The Centinel of Freedom, a Republican paper in New Jersey.

> *The following is a parody on a piece which appeared in a paper published at Hudson, in the State of New-York, entitled "The Wasp."*

A tory's head for naught is good,
'Tis senseless as a log of wood;
A thick, impenetrable "thing,"
Nor sense nor reason make it "ding:"
    "Ding dong?" Ah no! 'tis gone,
    A tory's head is like a stone.

A tory's head of horn is made,
By Nature's journey-wench, (a jade!)
There's nought on th' outside or within,
Nor could a "ding" be forc'd by gin.
    "Ding dong?" How sad a tale,
    For rum nor wine can aught avail!

A little *"Wasp,"* with buzzing sound,
Now flits the tories head around,
And though it goads them with its sting,
The hard, dull sconces never "ding."
    "Ding dong?" 'Tis all in vain;
    Their heads are form'd with *leaden brain!*

But hark! methinks I hear a sound,
Advancing o'er th' adjacent ground,
A *"Bee"* comes humming o'er the plain,
And lo the *"Wasp"* in battle slain,
    And now methought a tory's head,
    Would "ding," but no, the brain was lead!

T' inter the *"Wasp"* with honors due,
O *"Balance"* men* belong to you,
But still your heads will never "ding,"
Like log of wood, quite senseless thing:
    "Ding dong?" not e'en a knell,

For *"Wasp"* defunct, or last farewell!

* The conductors of the *Balance,* printed at Hudson, are said to Edit the Wasp.[30]

30. *The Centinel of Freedom,* Newark, NJ, August 3, 1802, 4.

∽ **1803** ∾

On March 9, 1803, the Republicans held another large festival, this time in New Haven. Republican newspaper the *American Mercury* published the agenda for the day, which was to begin before sunrise and go into the night:

> Flag to be displayed at day-break—Cannon on Neck Rock to fire once, 10 minutes before sunrise—then instrumental music on the public square to play till sunrise—then Bells to ring 10 minutes—then a salute of 17 guns—then Drums and Fifes 10 minutes—then three discharges from the Rock—then Bells 15 minutes—then instrumental music.
>
> At 15 minutes before 11, bells to give notice to all Republicans to repair to Mr. Isaacs' to form the procession.
>
> After exercises in the house a salute of 17 guns to be fired before the procession returns.
>
> Dinner to be on the table at 2—the fireworks in the evening to commence at half past six—after which the Ball.[1]

Afterwards, the *Mercury* described the day:

> The morning was saluted by discharges of artillery from the public square and from the neighbouring rocks.

1. *American Mercury*, Hartford, CT, March 3, 1803, 3.

The concourse of people was beyond all expectation, and the procession consisted, at the time of reaching the Meeting-House, of One Thousand One Hundred and Eight persons.

The exercises were opened and closed with very pertinent prayers by the Rev. Mr. Cowles and the Rev. Mr. Austin.—The Republican Proclamation was read by Roswell Judson, Esq.—Mr. Jefferson's inaugural Speech by Ephraim Kirby, Esq.—The principal performance was an Oration by Pierpont Edwards, Esq. which in point of argument and eloquence equalled the expectations of the audience; to have exceeded them was impracticable. The vocal and instrumental music was highly approved.

On the audience leaving the house the return procession was saluted by a discharge of 17 guns. ...

In the evening was a splendid exhibition of fireworks under direction of Mr. William Hull. A full conception of this Festival can rest only with those who witnessed it. ...[2]

The most long-lasting thing to come out of the festival, however, which would be brought up by Republicans for years to come, was the song "Moll Carey," written by the poet laureate of the Federalists, Theodore Dwight, brother of Yale president Timothy Dwight. The Republicans had chosen Psalm 148 from Isaac Watts's *Psalms of David*, frequently read on thanksgiving days, to be read at the festival. Dwight, in a parody of the psalm, published in *The Connecticut Courant* on March 2, had Moll Carey, the madam of a notorious brothel in New York, visiting the festival. The song was immediately denounced by Republicans as blasphemous, obscene, and the height of hypocrisy from the party that boasted of having "all the religion."

SONG,

To be sung at the close of the Republican exercises within the house, at New-Haven, March 9, 1803.

1

YE tribes of Faction join,

2. *American Mercury*, Hartford, CT, March 17, 1803, 3.

Your daughters, and your wives,
MOLL CAREY'S come to dine,
And dance with *Deacon* IVES[3]—
    Ye ragged throng
    Of *Democrats,*
    As thick as rats,
    Come join the song.

2

Old *Deacon* BISHOP[4] stands
With well-befrizzled wig,
File-leader of the Bands,
To open with a jig—
    With *parrot-toe*
    The poor old man,
    Tries all he can
    To *make it go.*

3

Director POWELL[5] leans,
And takes a pinch of snuff,
His words like *little beans,*
His neighbours' pockets stuff—
    Let all who please,
    Their footsteps ply,
    And from him fly—
    Or stay and sneeze.

4

But O ! what human pen
Can ABRAHAM'S[6] self describe?
The *first* of mortal men,
The *last* of treason's tribe—
    With mighty voice,
    The patriot cries—
    "Let earth, and skies,

---

3. Dr. Levi Ives, a festival manager. The festival managers had derisively been referred to as "Deacons" in a February 15 letter in *The Courant* in response to the managers' festival proclamation published in the *Mercury* on January 27.

4. Samuel Bishop, a festival manager and father of Abraham Bishop.

5. William Powell, director of the festival.

6. Abraham Bishop.

And hell, rejoice ! ! ! [7]

5

"Rejoice that man is free
From law, and moral strife,
From truth, and decency,
From shame—and eke his wife—
    Here let me stop—
    My box of glass,
    Will never pass
    With—"THIS SIDE UP."

6

Behold a motley crew,
Comes crowding o'er the green,
Of every shape, and hue,
Complexion, form, and mien—
    With deafening noise,
    Drunkards, and whores,
    And rogues in scores,
    They all *rejoice*—

7

In meek and humble state,
"Old PORPOISE" [8] bends his way,
The Virtues on him wait,
The Graces round him stray—
    While at his side,
    Black, white, and grey,

---

7. The festival proclamation repeatedly used the phrase "We will rejoice" preceding each thing about the Jefferson administration to be rejoiced at the festival.

8. *Porpoises* was a term for those in Connecticut who couldn't vote because they didn't meet the property qualifications. The term originated in an 1802 debate in the Connecticut House of Representatives on a Republican bill to extend suffrage, when Federalist Noah Webster, in attacking the bill, related the following story, which was published in the *Mercury* (December 2): "The introduction of this bill reminds me of a circumstance which took place in Philadelphia while Commodore Truxton and his crew lay there.—The crew were all invited up to Freeman's Meeting, and their votes were handed them, and they voted according to the wishes of a party. Not long afterwards, when they were returning up the Delaware from a cruise, they saw a school of Porpoises making towards Philadelphia. One of them asks the other, where are these Porpoises going; why damn it replies the other, to freeman's meeting to vote for ———." Webster explained his story: "I tell this anecdote barely to shew the sense which all persons have of the impropriety of admitting persons to vote who have no property or families to attach them to the interests of the state." The Republicans afterwards proudly adopted the term *Porpoises,* with Abraham Bishop writing a series of essays for the *Mercury* through the spring of 1803 titled "The PORPOISES of Connecticut."

In wanton play,
"*Seven young ones*" ride.

8

The CANDIDATE*[9] is there,
Cur *David*[10] at his back,
POTTER,[11] and HEYLEGAR[12]
The friends of *white,* and *black*—
    Lo ! as he goes,
    A negro-fume
    Thro' every room,
    Regales each nose.

9

All *energies* at play,
The amusements now begin,
A few without doors stay,
But *fun-alive's* within—
    With fainting voice,
    And closing eye,
    The songsters cry,
    "*We—will—re—joice.*"

10

MOLL CAREY leads the van,
And boldly scours the field,
She takes them *man by man,*
And makes the stoutest yield,
    Great *Potter* pants,
    And *Kirby* crawls,
    And *Wolcott*[13] falls,
    And *Bishop* faints.

11

All pale the *Deacons* stand,

---

9. Ephraim Kirby, Republican candidate for governor.

10. David Parmele, a Republican leader who, although not one of the managers of the festival, had a conspicuous role in it, according to one Federalist account taking the stage several times (*Connecticut Centinel*, March 22).

11. Dr. Jared Potter, a celebrated physician and member of Connecticut's House of Representatives, often assailed in the Federalist papers as one of the Republican ringleaders.

12. John Heylegar, a festival manager.

13. Alexander Wolcott, the Republican party leader in Connecticut's House of Representatives from 1796 to 1801, one of Jefferson's advisors in Connecticut, appointed Collector at Middletown by Jefferson in 1801.

And see their troops expire,
Each begs, with wig in hand,
Permission to retire—
    MOLL opes the door,
    And bids them fly,
    And never try
    Their *courage* more.

12

Thus ev'ry year we'll meet,
And keep Thanksgiving day,
We'll drink, *rejoice,* and eat,
And then *forget to pay*—
    Thus shall our wives,
    And daughters, find
    How very kind,
    Is DEACON IVES.

* *For Governor* [14]

As expected when Jefferson appointed the 77-year-old Samuel Bishop collector of New Haven in 1801, when the elder Bishop died in 1803, Abraham Bishop was appointed to succeed him. The censure of the Federalists was also as expected, with articles like the following appearing in the Federalist papers, painting the appointment of Abraham Bishop as evidence of Jefferson's plot to destroy religion in America:

> We hope the office Mr. Jefferson has now given to Abraham Bishop, will render it unnecessary for him to deliver public lectures against the Christian Religion, to gain a wretched subsistence. O America, how is thy character degraded! Must taverns and rookeries be haunted for subjects of public favor? Is every species of irreligion to be fostered by the smiles of Executive patronage? When such events as these were predicted, a few years since, the anxiety of the virtuous was ridiculed as the ungenerous insinuations of malice, but day unto day *uttereth speech*. Religion, which was once

14. *The Connecticut Courant,* Hartford, CT, March 2, 1803, 3.

considered as the glory of a nation, is now become the mockery of triumphant Revilers.—Religion which exalteth a nation is *now but tolerated;*—the day of persecution is approaching; for among our heads of department we have seen it already justified.

This town has been remarked, and we would hope with some degree of justice, for the sober habits and serious sentiments of a christian people. The time is come when their sincerity is put to the test. The true friends of religion will withdraw their confidence and support from him, who selects its most virulent opposers for his open approbation, or they must renounce their faith in Him, to whom unrighteousness is an abomination.

We address these remarks, not to the thoughtless scoffing infidel; (such we have among us, who will never visit the house of God;) but to those who, notwithstanding the tide of opinion, flowing from our present popular system of politics, retain a reverence for those sacred principles, which, to our ancestors were dearer than their native soil.—A republican government is not *necessarily* the hot-bed of vice, but it becomes so without the utmost vigilance of the firm, the thoughtful and discriminating. The chief magistrate of a nation is sometimes subject to imposture from those who recommend obscure characters, but in the present, as in many other instances that can be no apology. The true reputation of Abraham Bishop has been sounded through America.[15]

During the election of 1800, a key part of the attacks on Jefferson were about his religious beliefs. Absolute proof of his infidelity, said his attackers, could be found in his own writings, specifically his book *Notes on the State of Virginia.* The book's most frequently cited passage, in pamphlets, newspapers, and sermons, both in 1800 and throughout Jefferson's presidency, was:

The legitimate powers of government extend to such acts only as are injurious to others. But it does me no injury for

15. *New-England Repertory,* Newburyport, MA, October 12, 1803, 3.

my neighbour to say there are twenty gods, or no god. It neither picks my pocket nor breaks my leg.[16]

This passage was so frequently quoted that after a while it became unnecessary to quote the whole thing, with just the words "twenty gods" being enough for everyone to know what it referred to. Other passages from the book were also sometimes quoted, and every once in a while someone would find a new one that hadn't been harped on before, as in this typical item on Jefferson's religion from a Massachusetts paper:

Jefferson's Religion.

The President, in his Message, congratulated Congress upon our being *"blessed* with order and *religion at home."* We should be glad to hear what kind of religion Mr. Jefferson refers to, and what sect of religion he belongs to? That he is not a christian we have ten times more evidence than what would be sufficient for hanging a letter stealer at the Old Bailey. Setting aside the invitation of Thomas Paine, there is a passage in his "Notes," which has never been quoted by his enemies, which alone would establish his being an atheist. The words are these:

"The first glance of this scene hurries our senses into the opinion that this world was created in TIME."

From this passage, it is evident, that the writer considered the world as having existed from all eternity. In this case, it is plain that the supreme being did not create the world. If he did not we can have no reason to see why he should govern it, since it can go on without him. The English of all this amounts to a denial of his existence; for an omnipotent being, that he *has nothing to do,* is a contradiction in terms.[17]

Republican papers hit back with articles like the next one, asserting that the Federalists, with their union of politics and religion,

16. Thomas Jefferson, *Notes on the State of Virginia,* (Philadelphia: Mathew Carey, 1794), 231.

17. *The Salem Gazette,* Salem, MA, April 7, 1803, 1.

were doing more to advance infidelity than any deist ever could:

> Neither *Shaftbury* nor *Bolingbroke,* neither *Hume* nor *Gibbon,* neither *Voltaire* nor *Paine,* nor any other of the Deistical writers, have ever offered an argument against Christianity, so difficult to be answered, or so likely to convince, as the conduct of some of the professors and even preachers of it, in representing *Federalism* to be the Religion, which they preach and profess, and charging *Republicanism* with the infidelity which they effect to deplore; while in many of our towns, (in the County of *Berkshire* for instance) a majority of the members of our churches are decided *Republicans.* God, in his providence, may bring good out of this evil practice; but, according to the common course of human affairs, this system of hypocrisy, this federal pharisaism, this impious prostitution of religion to the temporary support of a party, is calculated to impress the rising generation with doubts, if not a disbelief, of a Religion thus blended and corrupted with a system of party passions and politics. Ye conscientious followers of him, *"whose kingdom is not of this world,"* be entreated to think seriously of the lasting consequences of this *federal* fashion. Let christians of all parties unite in keeping Religion and Politics distinct and separate. For whenever they have been connected, such connection has produced corruption and degeneracy. No political party have much cause to boast of their religion, or to say to their opponents, *"stand by yourselves, we are holier than you."* [18]

Most of Connecticut's Republicans, not all being the infidels and atheists that the Federalists claimed them to be, attended church. And many of them attended churches that had Federalist clergymen, often outspokenly political Federalist clergymen. And while the Republicans complained of this political clergy in the press, they did not try to cause trouble for them in their parishes or try to drive them from their pulpits, even in Republican majority towns where they could have. The same could not be said for the way

---

18. *The Pittsfield Sun,* Pittsfield, MA, June 20, 1803, 3.

the Federalists treated Republican clergymen, as this next article explains.

All the religion in the State, is on the side of federalism.
The democrats have no religion.
                                                    Federal Sayings.

Or, FEDERAL RELIGION and REPUBLICAN RELIGION,
            compared and tested by facts.

DOCTOR TRUMBULL of *North-Haven,* might be ousted from his place, or left in the lurch for his support, were the REPUBLICANS of his parish disposed to give him trouble by refusing to vote his salary, or be seceding from his ministration.

The same of Mr. SMITH, of *Stamford,* of Mr. NOYES, of *Wallingford,* of Mr. GAY, of *Suffield,* of Mr. HUNTINGTON, of *Litchfield,* and of several other high-toned federal Clergymen, that might be mentioned, in Connecticut. And in many parishes where republicans are not a majority, yet their numbers are so respectable, that if they were thus inclined, they might give their Clergymen very serious trouble, by maligning their reputation, proffering charges against them, or by seceding from them and uniting with other societies.

Yet where have we heard of *Republicans* undertaking to do any such thing?—With wonderful patience they have set under political declamation, from the pulpit for a long time, and been witnesses to exertions to influence the people in favor of federalism. In many instances have they tamely suffered their ears to be wounded with the vilest abuse, with the grossest attempts of delusion, with the foulest falshoods, and the bitterest calumnies. Yet what federal preacher has been dismissed merely on account of his politics? what one has had much trouble made for him by the secession of his hearers, or by their endeavors to wound his reputation, or by withholding their support, or in any way seeking to render his life uncomfortable?

Look at the reverse of the picture.

No sooner is a Clergyman known to be republican

(though he preaches no politics on a Sunday, or on Fast and Thanksgiving days,) that *Federalists* are immediately up in arms against him.—Plots and schemes are set on foot—his ruin is decreed—he is proclaimed an Infidel—no vice is too low to be falsely ascribed to him;—attempts are eagerly made to oust him from his place, or to silence him, at any rate to render his life uncomfortable.—If, however, he rise superior to these their machinations, then their way is to neglect his ministrations, forsake GOD'S house and worship, and even *change their religion* to accomplish their *pious* views. A *little* thing has been noticed, (which by the way no body cares for) their *magnanimously* refusing to honor REPUBLICAN Clergymen with the usual title of Mr. and of Rev.—Their stile more commonly is, *that fellow, that rascal,* and epithets of similar *politeness.*—This is of a piece with what is said *Doctor Trumbull* declared before an Association of Clergy not long since, *'that sooner than assist in licensing or ordaining a Democrat, he would saw his own arm off'!*—Where is the Republican Clergyman who has not met with the forementioned abuse?

What was the conduct shewn towards Mr. GEMMIL, late of *New-Haven?*—No worthier man ever filled a pulpit in that town. He preached no politics.—But he was a REPUBLICAN. —This was enough.—The pious federalists,—even the *Lawyers,* with a *Councillor* at their head, instantly began an attack, when this was known; they most shamefully abused him whom but lately they almost adored; they meanly attempted to deprive him of his salary, but failed: story upon story, lie upon lie, calumny upon calumny were heaped up against him, till the worthy man felt his life unsupportable there—and he left the State.

Mr. JONES, son of Mr *Isaac Jones* of *New-Haven,* on the expiration of his license to preach, applied to the association for its renewal; but was rejected, because he like his father, was found to be a *Republican.* On that occasion it was that Dr. Trumbull is said to have talked about *sawing his own arm off.*—Mr. JONES, has since been honored with a license in *Georgia* by the unanimous consent of the Clergy there.

Mr. M'KNIGHT, son of the *Rev. Doctor M'Knight* of *New-*

York, as worthy a young candidate as ever preached in Connecticut, was called last fall to be settled at *Greenfield.*—He was suspected of being a *Republican* like his venerable Father, tho' he never meddled with politics in any shape at all.—But bare suspicion was enough:—the warm federalists of the parish abused him—they played off several low tricks upon him—remonstrated against his settlement there, and held themselves ready to *renounce their religion* in case he were ordained, tho' highly approved of by a large majority of the parish. To say nothing of the preliminary *doings* of the REVEREND COUNCIL that was called to ordain him, the young gentleman saw the *spirit* that was possessed, and for his own peace requested a suspension of further proceeding, and left the State.

Mr. GRISWOLD, late of *New-Milford,* has since been employed at Greenfield, and finds the same imbittered foes that Mr. *M'Knight* left, conducting towards him precisely in the same manner,—tho' of the two *worse,* as his *republicanism* is more known than that of his predecessor. Within a few weeks some of them have even *changed their religion* because Mr. G. was invited to continue there a season longer! Before they did this, they were for a long time in the habit of neglecting GOD'S *worship* when a republican preached. To shew how much of *conscience* governed them, it is understood that they declared in open meeting, that *in case the parish would not agree not to hire a republican priest, they would continue to belong to it and would not CHANGE.* On being refused this gratification, they hove in their certificates which they had ready prepared in their pockets! The treatment which Mr. *Griswold* met with from the federal clergy of the county of Litchfield, is notorious, and speaks a volume on the subject in question.

Mr. COWLES of *Grandy,* has experienced treatment from his *federal* parishioners similar to the foregoing. After endeavoring to make him all the trouble in their power, several have *changed their religion* and gone off! And all this without any conceivable reason but that Mr. C. is a republican. ....[19]

---

19. *American Mercury,* Hartford, CT, August 4, 1803, 2.

An argument often heard today by advocates of maintaining separation between church and state is that if churches want to be involved in politics they should have to pay taxes. This argument is not new. It was made by the Republicans in New England long before the days of the I.R.S. and federal tax exemptions for churches, who argued that clergymen had no right to preach politics and use their pulpits for campaigning when they paid no taxes to the state. The Federalists, not surprisingly, argued the opposite, contending, as in this item from a Federalist paper in Massachusetts, that if clergymen owned enough property to qualify to vote, even if their property wasn't taxed, they had the right to preach politics.

... Whether the clergy have the right of suffrage, none, who knows the nature of property, and has read the Constitution, can doubt. Whether they may agitate in the pulpit political questions, admits dispute. To inculcate morality, which con-sists in conformity of actions to natural and revealed laws, is a grand duty of ministers. But, as politics are sound or defective in proportion, as morals are pure or corrupt, the reverse is true; and in proportion, as morals are pure or cor-rupt, politics are sound or defective. Since then politics and morals reciprocally influence, who will deny that it is a *right* of clergymen, and *that they always may;* who will dispute that it is a *duty* of clergymen, and *that they sometimes must* mingle civil with religious concerns? *They are not taxed, say Jacobins,* and therefore they have no interest in gov-ernment. Does immunity extinguish right? Because a man is excused from the duty of taxation, is he deprived of the right of suffrage? Possession of taxable, not taxed, property constitutes the right of suffrage; and the right of suffrage supposes interest in Government.[20]

One whopper of a Federalist rumor making news in 1803 was that Kentucky was in a state of rebellion against the government of the United States, and had mustered thousands of militia who were preparing to march on New Orleans. The rumor was launched on

---

20. *New-England Repertory,* Newburyport, MA, August 17, 1803, 2.

March 4 by two Federalist papers in New York City, the *New-York Evening Post* and the *New-York Commercial Advertiser.*

From the *Evening Post:*

IMPORTANT.

Kentucky in arms.—we have at this moment conversed with a gentleman of intelligence and integrity direct from Washington, from whom we have received the following very interesting intelligence:

That on Saturday last about eleven o'clock, an express arrived at the city of Washington, charged with a Memorial from Kentucky, addressed to Mr. Davis, as their favorite representative.

The Memorialists stated that they had waited with the greatest patience and anxiety for the interference of government in their behalf; that events pressed every day harder and harder upon them, and had almost exhausted their forbearance, but that they were yet willing and desirous of making another appeal to the general government for protection, and that expecting to receive this promptly, they had prepared to hold themselves in readiness to march at a moment's warning; and that for this purpose, they raised by subscription $50,000,* for the purchase of arms and ammunition, and had embodied, organized, and equipped, 15,000 men, who had already been three days in camp. Mr. Davis, it is said, expressed extreme regret, that the messenger had not arrived nine hours sooner, that is, before the Breckenridge resolutions had passed.

* Of this sum the present Governor subscribed 2000 and the last Governor 1500 dollars. [21]

The *Commercial Advertiser* upped the militia number to 20,000:

HIGHLY IMPORTANT.

By a gentleman from Washington, we are informed, that on Saturday last an express had arrived at that city from

21. *New-York Evening Post,* New York, NY, March 4, 1803, 3.

Kentucky, with a Memorial from the inhabitants at large, addressed to Mr. Davis, the purport of which was, that 20,000 men had embodied under arms, and had been encamped five days, for the purpose of descending the Mississippi, to maintain the rights and privileges of the free navigation of that river; that $50,000 had been subscribed by the present and late Governors, and the public in general, for the purchase of arms; that the inhabitants of the western waters wished to act in perfect union with the administration, and that while a negotiation was carrying on abroad to settle the important question of the freedom of the Mississippi, they would on their parts secure their present rights by the means with which the God of Nature had endowed them.[22]

So, why would the Federalist papers start such a rumor? Because the pro-British, anti-French Federalists had long wanted to go to war with France. They wanted a reason for war, and when Spain ceded Louisiana back to the French in 1801, it looked like they might get their wish. Under a 1795 treaty with Spain the United States had been granted the rights to use the Mississippi River and to store goods in New Orleans for shipment on outgoing vessels, called the "right of deposit." Although the treaty only granted these rights for three years, Spain had made no move to revoke them when they expired. With Louisiana under French control, however, the United States would lose these rights, devastating the trade of the western states.

Spain had agreed to cede Louisiana back to France in a secret treaty in 1800, with Napoleon planning to send a large military force to secure "New France," and the cession was formalized in another treaty in 1801. But France was slow to take control of the territory, which is why it was actually Spain, and not France, that decided in July 1802 to revoke the United States' right to deposit, with the order being sent to the Spanish agent at New Orleans. The order was received by the agent on October 14 and published on October 18.

Jefferson and Secretary of State James Madison instructed Charles Pinckney, America's minister to Spain, to get the order reversed, and Pinckney was able to successfully do so, with the order

---

22. *New-York Commercial Advertiser,* New York, NY, March 4, 1803, 3.

to restore the right to deposit being sent from Spain on March 1, 1803, and the port being reopened to Americans on May 17.

The war-hungry Federalists, however, were unaware in March 1803, when the Kentucky rumor was being circulated, that the order to restore America's right to deposit was on its way from Spain. They also assumed that it had been France, not Spain, that had revoked the right, giving them a much hoped for reason for a possible war with France.

Some versions of the rumor, like the one described in the following article from a paper in Maryland, reported to have come from a Federalist clergyman, had Kentucky in rebellion against the United States government, raising the hopes of some Federalists that a civil war with the Republican western states might be on the horizon.

On Sunday last the inhabitants of this town were considerably agitated with a report, that the state of Kentucky was in open rebellion against the general government, and that the inhabitants had embodied, and were marching down to take possession of New-Orleans, contrary to an existing treaty, (which is a law of the land) between the United States and Spain. To the gentleman who first informed us of this rumor, we pronounced it to be a FEDERAL FALSEHOOD. We were told, however, that it must be correct, because the intelligence had been brought from the City of Washington by a *Minister of the Christian Gospel.* ...

We have been particular in stating that this information was propagated by a Minister of the Gospel—we were so informed, and we believe it to be a fact—It is our wish to arraign such atrocious conduct wherever we find it; and we conceive it to be particularly reprehensible in one whose business it is to promote friendship and harmony among his fellow-creatures, and not to propagate fictions to excite to discord. He that preaches the Gospel of Christ, ought to let politics alone. The pulpit and the political cabinet, in a free country, ought to have no connection with each other. The present administration of this country tolerates *all* religious sects; let *all* religious denominations, therefore, *tolerate it*. But in this instance we see a man, professing to be a

Christian teacher, speaking to the people *firebrands and rebellion against their government!* God of Abraham, of Isaac, and of Jacob, who are we to believe if thy Ministers speak falsely!

But who were those who smiled on the occasion?—*They were federalists.* "Did you hear the GOOD news?" cried they.—Heaven and earth! what a question!—We verily believe, that were these fair states plunged into the miseries of a civil war; were Kentucky to rebel, and all the Western Country to follow the example, were all our seaports blockaded, (the certain consequence of war) and the produce of our farmers to rot upon their lands, the leaders of the federalists would exult in the dreadful scene, and glory in the general ruin.

We trust that our fellow-citizens will be cautious how they grant their belief to tales such as we have been describing. There are men in the country who wish to involve it in a war, to promote their own views. Be vigilant, therefore, and circumspect.[23]

Napoleon's plans for a "New France" in North America never materialized, of course. The Haitian Revolution and his troops being ravaged by yellow fever, and the impending war with Great Britain, put the financial strain on France that would lead to the sale of the Louisiana territory to the United States. As the Federalists' Kentucky rumor was spreading in March of 1803, James Monroe was already on his way to France to join Robert Livingston in negotiating the purchase. The Louisiana Purchase, being a peaceful resolution, not to mention doubling the size of the country, was the last thing the Federalists wanted.

With their dire predictions that religion would be destroyed if Jefferson was elected president not coming to pass, but wanting to keep alive the alarm bell of "religion is in danger," the Federalists were always on the lookout for anything at all that could be used as evidence that a Republican plot against religion was afoot. This next story is rather long, but is included here in its entirety to show just how far the Federalists of Connecticut would go when they had the

---

23. *Republican Advocate*, Frederick, MD, March 18, 1803, 2.

slimmest bit of so-called evidence of this nefarious Republican plot — in this case a simple comment made by a Republican in a post office about the clergy.

RELIGION is in danger! This is the rallying cry of federalism; it has seemed to inspire their fainting troops with fresh vigour; it has animated them to perseverance in a hopeless combat against truth and every manly principle. But, many honest but mistaken men, who have long been unworthily abused by sounds, begin to hesitate. Religion is in danger says the Priest. Sir, says the honest parishioner, you have constantly told me the same thing for years past, and I have believed you implicitly, but I am told I am deceived, that the cry that religion is in danger is a mere pretence, to cover and aid certain projects of ambitious men, hostile to the interests and liberties of the people, and these ambitious men are a large potion of the priests, combined with the men in office in this State, and who, it is said, have been raised to office by the influence of those same priests. I am a friend to religion, but am also a friend to truth. I recollect that previous to the election of Mr. Jefferson to the presidency, you told me that religion was at stake, that if Mr. Jefferson should obtain the election a general massacre of the Priests and a destruction of the churches, together with that of our bibles, would be the speedy and terrible consequences. Mr. Jefferson has now been president for two years, and I have been constantly and fearfully looking out to see the work of slaughter and conflagration commence. Hitherto all your predictions have failed of their accomplishment; no movement, that I can perceive, is made against religion, or its professors or teachers. I do indeed hear the priests, at least very many of them, charged with ambition, and hypocrisy. Now, Sir, I tell you with sincerity, I am at a loss what to believe. If you have no unjustifiable motive for sounding alarm, and for exciting discontent and terror in the minds of your parishioners, tell me why it is that none of your predictions are verified? Did you believe what you told us would happen on the election of Mr. Jefferson, or did you not believe it? If you did not yourself believe it, for what purpose have you imposed upon us? And if you believed what you then asserted, and which has in no particular come to pass, if you were then sincere, but mistaken, what proof can you give me that you are not now mistaken, and that, supposing you to be honest, you are not the dupe of your own jealousy, or the art of some man more knowing, but less honest than yourself? These sentiments, or sentiments like these, are spreading very rapidly among the honest men of the federal party, and their leaders are aware of it. They know that the absurd, hackneyed cry of RELIGION IS IN DANGER, has lost much of its effect, that, though there are some men whom they can lead implicitly and blindfold into any measure, however destructive, and into any opinion, however false, and absurd, yet, that, the great body of the men who compose their party, are of a different character, that they act on principle, and though they may be led to adopt wrong measures, and to support hypocritical and wicked men, yet they will not do it in implicit obedience to any man, but they must be deceived by a plausible sem-blance of truth, by something that their minds receive as proof. Proof then must be obtained that democrats harbored designs hostile to religion, and its teachers; the following circumstances will explain what the federalists call proof, and the manner in which it is obtained.

On the 22d of March last, Mr. Thomas Tisdall, of this town, being at the Post-Office, entered into a political con-versation with several gentlemen present. It seems that in the company, standing by, were several young, and very pious federalists, on the look out for proofs of a conspiracy against religion. It seems too, that Mr. Tisdall was pretty frank in his animadversions on the conduct of our political Priests, and their political religion—that is, their hypocriti-cal, and contemptible cant of piety, whilst uttering the most miserable, and false stuff about the piety of federalists, and the impiety and infidelity of republicans.—Whilst on this topic, Mr. Tisdall expressed his astonishment that men who professed to believe that there was any thing sacred in reli-gion, or its ordinances, should dare to make the most revered of those ordinances, to wit the Lord's Supper, a mere engine of faction. That this censure was sincere, there is no reason to doubt; that it was just will be the opinion of the large portion of the religious part of society; but to say that it intimates a spirit hostile to religion itself, is of all absurdities the most absurd. Mr. Tisdall expressly exempted from this censure a great number of venerable and worthy Priests, and this is, we think, going the whole length of charity. To a Stephen Dodge, who was present, and who had uttered sentiments which Mr. Tisdall supported contrary to those taught in the Bible, he said, you are a pretty Bible man, I advise you to go and study the contents of that book which you so noisily profess to hold sacred.

To the Federal gapers after conspiracies against religion, this was a precious feast—Here's a plot, says Dodge! the Priests are all rascals, and I am a pretty Bible man; besides, something, I cannot tell what, about Bread and Wine.—Yes says Stedman Adams, the pupil of Theodore Dwight; yes says William Merell; yes says Jesse Porter, as sure as a gun there is a conspiracy to overturn religion, or else how can Dodge be a Bible man and the Priests rascals. Tisdall says they are ALL rascals, and if he does not we will swear that he does, for it must be twice as much of a conspiracy to call them ALL rascals as it is to call part of them honest men. And I will swear the same thing says Algernon Sidney Griswold, the son of Shubael Griswold, who had been promoted in the militia for his religion, that is, his subserviency to Priests and their upper servants. I am a young man says Algernon, I will recommend myself to favor by suppressing part of the truth in my affidavit. Thus would these HONEST Federalists by a little HONEST swearing to what was not in fact true, have proved this dreadful conspiracy beyond all controversy, had not several republicans been present at the conversation, and maliciously disposed to tell the whole truth. Still however the alarm of a dreadful plot against religion has got abroad; here is proof, damning proof, says the Priests, that the Democrats meditate the destruction of religion, Thomas Tisdall says the Priests are rascals, he says we shall be deprived of the use of the sacraments; and, says a Priest, at the distance of fifteen miles from Hartford, Tisdall has publicly sworn to wash his hands in the blood of the Priests. All this would be sufficiently ridiculous were it not for the consideration that the security of fame, property, and life itself, depends, in society, on the truth of testimony; and we ask any man, of any sect, whether, if men will bear false witness against their neighbour for the paltry purpose of promoting the success of an election, it does not cut asunder the strongest bands of society and leave man an insulated being, without confidence in, or attachment to his fellow men. In this point of view the transaction is a subject of just alarm.

Dodge, Adams, Merrell, Porter, and Griswold, voluntarily came forward and made their affidavits which were as follows:

Hartford County, ss.
Hartford, April 1st, 1803.

STEPHEN DODGE, jun., of said Hartford, of lawful age deposeth and saith, that on or about the 22d day of March last past, the deponent went to the Post-Office in said Hartford, after being there a few minutes, some conversation was introduced by Thomas Tisdall with the deponent, to which he replied calmly—said Tisdall then observed that the deponent was a bible man, and attended Doct. Strong's conference meetings, where said Tisdall remarked, all the deeds of darkness originated, and that all who attended such meetings are hypocrites—said Tisdall then said that they might enjoy themselves, that they might eat their Bread and drink their Wine, and intimated that the time was coming when such privileges would cease—but the deponent cannot be particular as to the expressions made use of, and further saith not.

STEPHEN DODGE, jun.
Sworn before me,
THOMAS Y. SEYMOUR, *Just. Peace.*

Happening at the Post-Office on or about the 22d of March, I heard a conversation held between Mr. Thomas Tisdall and several others, one of whom was Mr. S. Dodge. After many observations of a political nature, the conversation turned upon things pertaining to religion. When Mr.

Tisdall observed, that he believed the Clergy of Connecticut were a vile pack of rascals, or something to that import; whether I make use of the same phraseology is to me uncertain. To which I replied, that it appeared very ungentleman-like to stigmatize any class of men with such general epithets, and requested him to point out some particular ones. To which he said, I shall call no names. Mr. Dodge then having made an observation, Mr. Tisdall replied (at the time patting him on the shoulder) that he perceived him to be one of these Bible men and laughed heartily. After this, as near as my memory serves me, some conversation passed between Maj. Hart and myself; at which time I recollect of hearing something said concerning Dr. Strong's conferences, of eating bread and sipping wine, but as my attention was not wholly directed to their conversation, I cannot tell how these observations were to be applied.

STEDMAN ADAMS.

Mr. Tisdall asked Mr. Adams this question. Whether he did not recollect that he wished not to be misunderstood with regard to the observations he had made with respect to the clergy; and whether he did not say that he considered there were many worthy respectable characters among that class?

Mr. Adams's answer is, that he thinks Mr. Tisdall made an observation to that import towards the close of the conversation.

Sworn before me,
THOMAS Y. SEYMOUR, *Just. Peace.*

WILLIAM MERRELL of Hartford in Hartford County of lawful age, deposeth and saith, that on or about the 22d of March last past, the deponent being at the Post-Office in said Hartford, heard Thomas Tisdall observe, that those people who eat bread and drink wine, would be obliged to quit it in another year; and the deponent further saith, that said Tisdall put his hand on the shoulder of Stephen Dodge jun. who was present, and told him he was a bible man.

WILLIAM MERRELL.

Dated at Hartford, April 1st, 1803.

Sworn before me,

THOMAS Y. SEYMOUR, *Just. Peace.*

JESSE PORTER of Hartford in Hartford County of lawful age, deposeth and saith, that he was at the Post-Office on or about the 22d day of March last past, and heard Thomas Tisdall say to some person present, that he was a bible man, and he looked like one, and that his countenance shewed it—and further saith not.

JESSE PORTER.

Dated at Hartford, April 1st, 1803.

Sworn before me,
THOMAS Y. SEYMOUR, *Just. Peace.*

East Hartford, April 11, 1803.

Then personally appeared ALGERNON S. GRISWOLD of said East-Hartford and made oath that on or about the 22d day of March last, he was at the Post-Office in Hartford, and heard Thomas Tisdall say, that the Clergy were a set of damned rascals, and made more difficulty than any set of men—and further saith not.

Sworn before me,
ELISHA PITKIN, *Just. Peace.*

Mr. Tisdall having been notified of the design of taking affidavits attended with sundry Gentlemen of high respectability, who were present and listened to the conversation. They immediately made the following deposition:

Hartford County, Hartford, April 1st, 1803.

JOSEPH HART, HARRIS OLCOTT, DANIEL OLCOTT, and JOHN DODD, all of Hartford of lawful age, depose and say, that they were present at the Post-Office, on or about the 22d of March last past, that Stephen Dodge, jun., Jesse Porter, William Merrell and Stedman Adams were present, and the deponents have severally attended and heard the depositions or affidavits of the said Dodge, Porter, Merrell and Adams this day sworn before Thomas Y. Seymour, Justice, of the Peace, and that they the deponents heard nothing said by Thomas Tisdall, tending to ridicule religion or its ordinances, as mentioned in the said affidavits, except that said Harris saw said Tisdall put his hand on the shoulder of said Dodge, and tell him he was a pretty bible man, that he had better go home and study and reflect upon it; and the deponents further heard Mr. Tisdall remark, that he wished the gentlemen would not disperse and mutilate his conversation relating to the Clergy, for that he meant to make an exception in favor of many reputable men of that class, whom he knew.

JOSEPH HART,
HARRIS OLCOTT,
DANIEL OLCOTT,
JOHN DODD.

Dated at Hartford, April 1st, 1803.

Sworn before me,
THOMAS Y. SEYMOUR, *Just. Peace.*

———

It was denied by the Federalists, that this deposition in any manner contradicted those of Dodge and others—as it declares only that the deponents heard nothing said by Tisdall ridiculing religion and its ordinances &c. It is however to be remarked that in this deposition they swear that Tisdall expressly requested that his remarks relative to the clergy might not be misrepresented, for that he had excepted from them many worthy men of that class whom he knew. This admonition however was forgotten by Dodge and others when they testified, for they make no mention of the exception of many republican clergymen—Adams does indeed when questioned, confess with apparent reluctance, that the exception was made. But to obviate all objection to the inexplicitness of the deposition of Messrs. Hart, Olcott, &c. the following affidavits were taken:

DANIEL OLCOTT, John Dodd and Harris Olcott, all of Hartford, of lawful age, testify and say, That being at the Post-Office in said Hartford, on or about the 22d day of March last past, when Thomas Tisdall and Stephen Dodge, jun. were in conversation of a political nature; in the course of which said Tisdall said he was surprised that men who sat down at the communion table and there partook of the bread and wine should tell such stories, and conduct in the manner that some of them do; which was all that Tisdall said respecting the communion table or those who partake at it. In speaking of the Clergy he disproved at the conduct of some of them, but made an exception in favor of many respectable men of that class whom he said he knew. We each of us being within a few feet of said Tisdall and Dodge during the whole of said conversation, attended to it and heard the same distinctly.

Dated at Hartford, this 18th day of April, 1803.

> DANIEL OLCOTT,
> JOHN DODD,
> HARRIS OLCOTT.

I agree to the foregoing deposition excepting the conversation respecting the clergy which I did not hear, as I was not present at the whole of the conversation.

> JOSEPH HART.

Hartford County ss.

Hartford, April 18, 1803.

Personally appeared Daniel Olcott, John Dodd, Harris Olcott and Joseph Hart, and made oath to the truth of the above deposition, before me.

> A. KINGSBURY, *Just. Peace.*

Harris Olcott, of Hartford, of lawful age, testify and say, That on or about the 12th of instant April I asked Algernon S. Griswold what his deposition against Thomas Tisdall was? He answered that said Tisdall said all the Clergy were damned rascals. I then asked him if Mr. Tisdall did not make an exception. He answered that Mr. Tisdall after some pause did make exceptions.

> HARRIS OLCOTT.

Hartford County ss.

Hartford, April 18, 1803.

Personally appeared Harris Olcott, and made oath to the

truth of the above deposition, before me,

A. KINGSBURY,

———

With the state of the business at this time the Federalists were as Dodge expresses himself, perfectly satisfied, that the circumstances, by their consent would never have been published. No, Mr. Dodge we believe that you never wished the circumstances published—But if you were perfectly satisfied with the state of the business at that time you are an extraordinary man—what you had sworn to had been flatly contradicted by four men of unimpeachable veracity—and those who had most charity for you believed that you was mistaken.

But the great point was gained, for which, loss of reputation was, on federal calculation, but a small sacrifice; the charges against Mr. Tisdall could be repeated and magnified, and they were supported by the solemn oath of pious, that is federal men. This went into the general mass of federal villainies preparatory to the election, and had its effect. The transaction was thought too barefaced, and too vile to pass without comment, and some remarks in one of our former papers, drew forth in the Courant a mutilated publication of the testimony, accompanied with remarks suitable for that paper. The design of the present publication is to set before our readers, of all facts, a full view of the transaction, that they may be enabled to form their own opinions. For ourselves we are free to say, that in our opinion, taken all together, the black records of federalism cannot produce a transaction more detestable, at least so far as relates to the principles that produced it. We do not say that Dodge and others were guilty of WILFUL PERJURY—no, it MAY BE that they are not, it may be that they really testified of the conversation according to their understanding and recollection of it, and when we say this MAY BE, we go to the utmost stretch of charity, of what is reasonable to believe on this head, we leave our readers to judge. But it is true that Mr. Tisdall did not speak disrespectfully of religion or its ordinances; he did not threaten any man with a privation of those ordinances; he did not say that the Priests were all rascals, but he did say that Dodge was a pretty bible man.

We believe this, because no projects against religion were ever entertained by the republicans. They are men who as sincerely believe the scriptures, who are as strongly attached to the christian religion, and its ordinances as the federalists are; 'tis true their religion is not up for sale, they therefore make less clamour about it. ...[24]

In Connecticut's spring 1803 election, voter turnout for both parties increased dramatically. Governor Trumbull was reelected with 14,375 votes, but Ephraim Kirby had a strong showing with 7,848, more that a third of the vote. Republican representation in the House, however, decreased to about 40. The Council as usual remained entirely Federalist, and John Treadwell was reelected lieutenant governor with 13,147 votes to Republican William Hart's 6,057. The fall election saw a gain in the House for the Republicans, with over 60 of the 203 seats.

24. *American Mercury,* Hartford, CT, Apr 28, 1803, 3.

⌇ 1804 ⌇

The Republican festival for 1804, held on May 11 in Hartford, was promoted as a celebration of the Louisiana Purchase. The issue brought to the forefront, however, was Connecticut's lack of a state constitution, and how this lack of a constitution perpetually kept control of the state in the hands of seven men. As Abraham Bishop explained in his festival oration:

> The charter of Charles 2d. gave to Connecticut power to raise armies, levy war and do many things, wholly inconsistent with our relation to the federal government, but provided well enough, for the day of it, the means by which the people of this, then thinly settled colony, might govern themselves.
>
> At the declaration of independence this charter became of no effect, and it was proper that the people of this free state should, like the people of other free states, have been convened to form a constitution: But the legislature, which was not impowered for that purpose, and which may repeal at pleasure its own laws, USURPED the power of enacting, that the form of government, contained in the charter of king Charles, should be the civil constitution of this state. Thus by the pleasure of his majesty all the legislative, executive and judicial powers of government tumbled into a common mass,* together with the power of raising armies, whenever the stockholders of power should think best.

This precise condition of society, absurd and unsafe as it is in theory, has proved far more so in practice. At the present moment all these powers, TOGETHER WITH A COMPLETE CONTROL OF ELECTIONS, is in the hands of seven lawyers,† who have gained a seat at the council board.— These seven virtually make and repeal laws as they please, appoint all the judges, plead before those judges, and constitute themselves a supreme court of errors to decide in the last resort on the laws of their own making. To crown this absurdity, they have repealed a law which prohibited them to plead before the very court of which they are judges.

In the Congressional debate on the repeal of the new judiciary law our federalists insisted strongly on the great excellence of the federal constitution, because it kept distinct and independent the three great branches of government, but the same federalists are now invincibly opposed to a similar distinction and independence in our own government.

† These seven lawyers are, Mess'rs Daggett, Smith, C. Goodrich, Brace, Allen, Edmond, and E. Goodrich, holding the same undefined powers, which their predecessors have held, and which their successors will hold, till we shall have a constitution. The term, seven men, will be used (as was the term, directory, under the French government) signifying the depository of supreme power. Every obnoxious act in force will be justly considered their act, till they shall repeal it.[1]

Bishop went on to propose:

... that the people shall be convened to form a CONSTITUTION WHICH SHALL SEPARATE THE LEGISLATIVE, EXECUTIVE AND JUDICIAL POWERS,—SHALL DEFINE THE QUALIFICATIONS OF FREEMEN SO THAT LEGISLATORS SHALL NOT TAMPER WITH ELECTION LAWS, AND SHALL DISTRICT THE STATE, SO THAT FREEMEN MAY JUDGE OF THE CANDIDATES FOR THEIR

1. Abraham Bishop, *Oration in Honor of the Election of President Jefferson, and the Peaceable Acquisition of Louisiana, Delivered at the National Festival in Hartford, on the 11th of May, 1804,* (New Haven, CT: Sidney's Press, 1804), 9-10.

SUFFRAGES.[2]

The Republican committee, headed by Pierpont Edwards, did what Bishop proposed, calling for a "Meeting of Delegates." The delegates, from 97 towns, convened on August 29 in New Haven, issuing an address to the people of Connecticut prefaced with the following preamble:

> WHEREAS it is the unanimous opinion of this meeting, that the people of this State are at present without a Constitution of civil government,—Resolved, that it is expedient to take measures preparatory to the formation of a Constitution, and that a committee be appointed to draft an Address to the people of this State on that subject, and make report thereof to this meeting.[3]

The address, which was published in the *Mercury,* and 10,000 copies of which were printed for distribution, began by quoting the passage from the Declaration of Independence on the people's right to alter or abolish their government:

> We hold these truths to be self-evident—that all men are created equal—that they are endowed by their Creator with certain unalienable rights—that among these are life, liberty and the pursuit of Happiness. That to secure these rights governments are instituted among men, deriving their just powers from the consent of the governed: That whenever any form of government becomes destructive of these ends, it is the right of the PEOPLE to alter or to abolish it and to institute new government, laying its foundation on such principles and organizing its powers in such form, as to them shall seem most likely to effect their safety and happiness.

A constitution was necessary, argued the address, to secure the

2. Abraham Bishop, *Oration in Honor of the Election of President Jefferson, and the Peaceable Acquisition of Louisiana, Delivered at the National Festival in Hartford, on the 11th of May, 1804,* (New Haven, CT: Sidney's Press, 1804), 16.

3. *American Mercury,* Hartford, CT, September 6, 1804, 2.

people's rights from being at the mercy of the legislature.

> ... As our situation now is, what one legislature does may be revoked by the next, but what the people do in their collective capacity is done permanently for every man and cannot be revoked in haste or without the consent of the people.—
>
> If a constitution shall declare taxation and representation inseparable, the legislator cannot separate them with his breath.
>
> If a constitution shall declare all men free in the exercise of religion according to conscience, so far as it can be done without violating public order, the legislator cannot bind over one denomination to another.
>
> If a constitution shall give permanence and independence to judges, the legislator cannot make judges annually dependent on his will.
>
> If a constitution shall separate the legislative, executive and judicial powers, the legislator cannot unite them in his own person.[4]

The address ended:

> Whether the State shall have a
> CONSTITUTION,
> be settled finally and forever—ingloriously, (if such must be the effect of invincible prejudice)—but gloriously, we trust, for we are persuaded that on our part we have truth and reason, which must sooner or later impress all ingenious minds beyond the power of opposition.[5]

Whether or not the state of Connecticut should have a constitution became the primary issue of the September election, with the choice of representatives being a referendum of sorts on the constitution question. In the months preceding the election the newspapers were filled with arguments by Federalists insisting that the state did have a constitution, and by Republicans that it did

4. *American Mercury,* Hartford, CT, September 6, 1804, 2.
5. Ibid.

not. It was a Federalist pamphlet, however, widely circulated just before the election that did the most damage to the Republican cause. The persuasive pamphlet, titled *Count the Cost,* was written by Council member David Daggett, under the pseudonym "Jonathan Steadfast."

Daggett began his pamphlet with a lie, claiming to be "an individual who neither holds an office nor seeks one—who can have nothing in view but the maintenance of that order of things which shall most effectually promote public and private happiness."[6] Although not running for reelection, Daggett was still a Council member at the time he wrote the pamphlet and would be until the following spring.

In the pamphlet, Daggett argued, "Our constitution and government are perfectly free, and our laws are mild, equitable and just."[7] He then went on to list the "projects" of the Republicans.

> One of these projects is the repeal of all laws for the support of religious institutions. The language of those who favor this measure is, that religion will take care of itself— that no external aid is necessary—that all legislative interference is impious. Many, and it is believed by far the greater part, of those who make these declarations, intend to throw down all the barriers which christianity has erected against vice. They are obstinately determined to banish from the public mind all affection and veneration for the Clergy, all respect for the institutions of religion, and to reduce Connecticut to that condition which knows no distinction between "him who serveth God and him who serveth him not." They wish to see a Republic without religion; and should they be gratified, the consequence would speedily be, a miserable race of men without virtue, wallowing in vice and ripening for a dreadful destruction. If infinite truth is to be credited, "God will pour out his indignation on the heathen who know him not." ...[8]

---

6. Jonathan Steadfast (David Daggett), *Count the Cost, an Address to the People of Connecticut, on Sundry Political Topics, and Particularly on the Proposition for a New Constitution,* (Hartford, CT: Hudson and Goodwin, 1804), 3.

7. Ibid., 4.

8. Ibid., 5.

... Again, it is insisted by those people who oppose universal suffrage, and the reader is desired to notice the remark with attention, that no community can be safe unless the power of elections resides principally with the great body of the landholders. ...

Landholders have an enduring interest in the welfare of the community. They are lords of their own soil, and of course, to a certain degree, independent—they therefore will resist tyranny—they will equally oppose anarchy because they are aware that in any storm which may arise they must abide its fury. The merchant, with his thousands, can seek a shelter—to the mere bird of passage, who has no "abiding country and who seeks none to come," it is of little moment whether stability or confusion dominate, but to the farmer who is enchained to the State, peace and order is of inestimable value.

What, my fellow citizens, is the attempt now making? What is the language of those who advocate universal suffrage? It is nothing less than an effort to wrest from the farmers of Connecticut that control over the elections which is their only fortress of safety. Let men who wish to protect their invaluable rights ponder on these things, and let them at the same time, remember that no nation in which universal suffrage hath been allowed, hath remained free and happy. ...[9]

A still more mischievous and alarming project is, that of making a new Constitution for Connecticut. This project originates entirely in a spirit of Jacobinism—it is a new theme on which to descant to effect a revolution in Connecticut. The object is, by false assertions, to induce a belief that no Constitution exists and that tyranny prevails. This party always address the passions and never the understanding. ...

Festivals under the pretence of honoring the election of Mr. Jefferson and Mr. Burr, and of extolling the wisdom of the purchase of Louisiana, but with a real design to blazen

9. Jonathan Steadfast (David Daggett), *Count the Cost, an Address to the People of Connecticut, on Sundry Political Topics, and Particularly on the Proposition for a New Constitution,* (Hartford, CT: Hudson and Goodwin, 1804), 8-9.

the fame of those who assume the character of friends of the people that they the more readily destroy the most free and equitable Government in the world, are continually holden, and the discontented, the factious, the ambitious and the corrupt, are collected and flattered with declamations in the various shapes of prayers, sermons and orations. Thus a people enjoying the heighth of prosperity are cajoled into a belief that men without virtue, without the restraints of the gospel, without a particle of real regard for their fellow men, are their best friends, and are anxiously laboring to promote their good. ... Mr. Bishop in his oration on the 11th of May, declared, among other outrageous and wicked falsehoods, that Connecticut had no Constitution. Such a gross absurdity could never have been promulgated till the mind was in some degree prepared, by being accustomed to misrepresentation. ...[10]

Daggett wrapped up by instilling fears that the "revolution" that the Republicans wanted in Connecticut would end like the French Revolution:

In this view of the subject we will briefly ask ... is it proper to make the proposed changes—to adopt these projects? If no benefits will result—if much evil will probably ensue—the course of duty and interest is plain. Aware, however, that it may be said many of the dangers are imaginary, and are founded upon the supposition that we shall act with as little discretion and prudence as the people of other countries, it is important to observe that revolutions are the same, in nature in every nation. Those who speak of a new Constitution, and of thorough reforms, should recollect that the promoters of these schemes in France, constantly amused the people with the idea that a new order of things—new rights—new principles, were to arise. Who does not recollect to have read of the perfectibility of human nature—of the enlightened age of regenerated France? She

10. Jonathan Steadfast (David Daggett), *Count the Cost, an Address to the People of Connecticut, on Sundry Political Topics, and Particularly on the Proposition for a New Constitution,* (Hartford, CT: Hudson and Goodwin, 1804), 10-12.

boldly proclaimed herself the example of the world, and all nations were invited to see her glory, and enjoy her blessed liberty and her glorious equality. But mark the issue—Not twelve years have elapsed before she has returned to an inglorious despotism—She has exchanged her Capets for a foreign usurper, with an incalculable loss, and here her history ends. Such is the constant terminations of such revolutions, and shall we claim to be an exception? How do we judge as to the propriety of any course of life except by observation, experience or history? We see industry and Integrity rewarded with competence or wealth—we see intemperance and sloth followed with disease, loss of reputation and poverty. These are sure grounds on which to predict respecting our neighbors, and by which to regulate our own conduct. On similar principles a wise people regard the conduct of other nations, and are solemnly admonished by their example. Let not the projector persuade us to adopt his theories with proofs of their danger thus glaring before our eyes. Look at the conduct of our revolutionists for four years past, and see if you do not discover the genuine principles of the Jacobins of France—recollect also that they had first a Convention—then an Executive Directory—then a Consul for years—then a Consul for life, and then an usurper with an hereditary descent in his family. At each successive revolution the people were courted—were flattered—were promised transcendent felicity. The people swore eternal hatred to Monarchy, and eternal fidelity to Constitutions, till, heaven, weary of their perjuries, sent them a despot in his wrath.

My fellow citizens human nature is the same here as in France—Then before you give ear to the songs of enchantment Count the Cost—Before you sell your birthright for a mess of pottage Count the Cost. Before you consent to yield up the institutions of your wise and pious ancestors, Count the Cost—Before you admit universal suffrage Count the Cost—Before you submit to the mischievous doctrine of district elections, Count the Cost.—Before you reject from office the men whom your hearts approve, Count the Cost, the great cost of weak and wicked rulers.—Before you consent to be governed by men whose impudence, and vice constitute many of their claims to promotion, Count the Cost. This evil you can prevent by attending with punctuality on our elections. ... Before you neglect an election Count the Cost—If the loss of your vote should prove the loss of an election of a single man, then you will not have Counted the Cost. ...[11]

The Federalist campaign against a constitution was effective. Towns that had voted for Republican representatives in the spring election went Federalist in the fall. The number of Republicans elected to the House in the spring had increased to nearly 80. In the fall, however, Republican representation decreased by about 15 seats.

In the spring 1804 election, Governor Trumbull was reelected with 11,108 votes to new Republican challenger General William Hart's 6,871. John Treadwell was reelected lieutenant governor with 9,592 votes to Asa Spalding's 5,919.

The Council remained entirely Federalist as usual, and in October, in the wake of the downturn for Republicans in the fall election, decided to display its power by removing five Republican justices of the peace from office as retribution for their having attended the New Haven convention in August. One of the five, William Judd, had been the chairman of the meeting. Council member David Daggett, who in his anonymous pamphlet "Count the Cost" had claimed not to hold any office, led the prosecution.

The Council sent a Bill to the House, as reported in the Federalist paper the *Connecticut Centinel:*

We are informed from New-Haven, that on Wednesday last the Governor and Council sent a bill to the House of Representatives stating, That whereas William Judd, Agur Judson, J.H. Tomlinson, Hezekiah Goodrich, and N. Manning, Justices of the Peace, on the 29th of August, at New-Haven, with divers others did assert and publish that we had no constitution; and whereas it was improper that persons who

11. Jonathan Steadfast (David Daggett), *Count the Cost, an Address to the People of Connecticut, on Sundry Political Topics, and Particularly on the Proposition for a New Constitution,* (Hartford, CT: Hudson and Goodwin, 1804), 20-21.

believe the government a usurpation should exercise its powers—Therefore the sheriff was directed to cite those gentlemen to appear on the 25th inst. to shew reason why their commissions should not be revoked. Our informant adds, that this bill excited some sensibility in the house. Samuel Hart, of Berlin, very impudently remarked that argument would be unavailing where there was the disposition and the ability to pass a bill. The question on passing the bill was taken by yeas and nays, and there were 126 for it and 43 against it. The House then passed a resolution desiring the Speaker to reprimand Hart.[12]

Republican paper the *Republican Farmer* reported it a little differently:

On Thursday last, Messrs. Judd, Tomlinson, Goodrich, Judson and Manning, republicans, and Justices of the Peace, were deprived of their offices, by the Legislature of this State, for attending a peaceable, public and lawful meeting on the fifth Wednesday of August last, at New-Haven, and then and there publishing their political opinions!!!! This was the reason given by their accusers; and no other crime was suggested during their trial!

A year or two since a federal Justice, of Fairfield County, was convicted, in that same house, of a CRIME, which has fixed an eternal stigma upon his character—and that Justice still holds his office! This fall another federal Justice of the same county attended a secret caucus (on the evening which his denomination holds to be a part of the Sabbath) to promote his own election; and that same justice, in the house of Assembly, voted for depriving the five Republican Justices of their offices, on the above mentioned grounds! People of Connecticut, think of this, and judge whether it is right![13]

What Samuel Hart, the Republican representative who was

12. *Connecticut Centinel,* Norwich, CT, October 30, 1804, 2.
13. *Republican Farmer,* Danbury, CT, November 7, 1804, 3.

reprimanded by the Speaker of the House had said was the same thing that two Federalists had also said — that any debate on the bill or trial was unnecessary because it was a foregone conclusion how the vote was going to go. Hart, however, being a Republican, was the only member who was reprimanded for making these comments.

William Judd would end up not only losing his office as a result of this Federalist retaliation, but losing his life. Judd, who was in poor health, wanted to defend himself before the Assembly, and in spite of his health traveled to New Haven to do so. The exertion of the trip and preparing his defense rendered him too ill to appear in person, but he was determined to publish a summary of his defense for the public. The further exertion and return trip from New Haven proved to be too much, and he passed away the night he got home.[14]

The four other justices had the support of their communities, with all four being elected to represent their towns in the next Assembly.

Always on the lookout for proof that their dire predictions about a Jefferson presidency were coming true, the Federalists thought they had the goods when it was reported that a church in Lebanon, Connecticut, had been torn down by a riotous mob.

The story was first reported by New York Federalist paper the *New-York Commercial Advertiser*. The paper's editor, Zachariah Lewis, a Connecticut native who had studied for the ministry in Philadelphia and been licensed as a preacher before moving to New York and becoming a newspaper editor, was dubbed the "wandering Priest" or "wandering Parson" by New York Republican paper, the *American Citizen*. The following article is from the *American Citizen*, reporting on the "wandering Parson's" report of the destruction of the meeting house. William Coleman, another New York Federalist editor, mentioned in the articles footnote, was the editor of the *New-York Evening Post*, a paper founded by Federalist party leader Alexander Hamilton in the wake of Jefferson's election.

From the wandering Parson's paper.

"*More "useful labours."*"—By a gentleman *direct** from

14. *Republican Farmer*, Danbury, CT, November 28, 1804, 3.

Hartford we are informed that on Friday of last week, a company of *Republican* democrats (in opposition, we suppose Zac means, to *kingly* democrats?) headed by the famous Demo Tilden, a member elect of the general assembly, assembled and commenced pulling down the Meeting House in *Lebanon* (Conn.) and on Saturday they re-assembled and completed their *useful labors,* by levelling it with the ground! This is a fact and may be relied on, and may, perhaps, justly be considered as a leading trait in the character of the *party."* So far the Snivelling Priest.

We warn all good men against placing the least confidence in the above extract. We know nothing of the truth or falsity of the fact stated, but from the character of the paper from which it is taken the presumption is that it is a wicked *calumny. ...*

Those who reflect on the past *tricks* of the federal party, cannot confide for a moment in the information received *"direct"* from Hartford. According to the delusive stories told by our political adversaries previous to and immediately after the election of Mr. Jefferson, all the bibles, Churches and Meeting Houses in the union were to have been burnt and pulled down before this time! ...

Besides, it is evident that the party, who have lately disgraced themselves by joining a faction, anxiously resort to the old legerdemain of illuminati, and the raw head and bloody bones of every monster that revengeful and weak heads can even imagine. Coleman had the other night an essay of the order of St. Tammany, secret oaths and bloody morsels, and, appealing to the fanaticism of bigots and the fears of the credulous and the timid, declared that St. Tammany was only another name for "Jacobin or illuminati." Tammany Societies, therefore, like the *"self-created"* societies of '94—5, were to be hunted down by malevolence and persecution.—What stuff!

In this spirit of folly, the poor Devil Zac, who uniformly sails in the wane of Coleman, or Solomon Lang, or of some other great man, has published the story of pulling down the meeting house at Lebanon. If Colman publishes a lie to-day, Zac will illustrate it tomorrow by a thumper...

* Whenever Coleman tells a lie, the seat of which is at a distant place, it is always stated as received "by a gentleman direct from—" Kentucky, for example, when the militia were in arms to oppose the Government on the New-Orleans question. The wandering Priest follows the example of this notorious offender.[15]

A meeting house actually had been torn down in Lebanon, Connecticut, and it was done by a mob, but it had nothing to do with politics. It was the culmination of a long-running dispute among the church's members over whether their old meeting house should be repaired or be torn down and replaced, and if a new one were built what the location would be. The group that wanted it torn down began tearing it down, were stopped by the group that wanted to repair it, but returned on another day to finish the job.

The story of the Lebanon meeting house spread far and wide, with Federalist papers reporting it as proof that their predictions of churches being leveled if Jefferson was elected president, and Republican papers reporting it as another Federalist lie, as in the following report in a New Hampshire Republican paper. While the tearing down of the meeting house wasn't the amicable decision that this article makes it out to be, the basic story of its being the result of a church vote is correct.

EXPLOSION OF ANOTHER BUBBLE.

The demolition of the Meeting house in Lebanon, Con. has been a favorite theme of late in the papers of the faction. They have not failed to represent it as a Democratic operation, and plumed themselves much on the countenance it appeared to afford their quondam assertions which have hitherto been so miserably supported by fact, that if Mr. Jefferson should be president, "religion would be destroyed, our Bibles burnt, our Meeting houses rased to the ground, &c. &c." — The truth respecting the pulling down of the Meeting house in Lebanon, as communicated by a respectable gentle-

15. *American Citizen*, New York, NY, May 16, 1804, 2.

man of the town, is briefly this,

"The meeting house at Lebanon was an old tottering building, and the taking of it down and erecting another in its stead, have long occupied the attention of the Parish. The meeting house was taken down *agreeably to a vote of the parish,* in which there were nearly two to one in favour of the measure. A difference of opinion, however, arose as to where the new one should be built. The Parish, though not populous, is of large extent, and the contest was between what are termed the up-town and the down-town people. *Politics* were not mingled with the subject. It was strictly a congregational question. Republicans and federalists united in the vote for taking it down."[16]

With Jefferson running for reelection, the Federalists revived their attacks on his religious beliefs, once again raising their old "religion is in danger" alarm, with this next article claiming that while "disciples of Infidelity and Democracy act under covert at present" they "are paving the way for the introduction of their accursed, atheistical tenets, and a consequent revolution in government." Another popular piece of evidence of Jefferson's irreligion, first used in the 1800 election, is also revived in this one — that Jefferson had said to his friend Philip Mazzei,[17] upon riding past a dilapidated church, that the run-down building was good enough for a god who was born in a manger.

MR. JEFFERSON'S INFIDELITY.

AMONG all the misrepresentations continually disseminated throughout the United States by the adherents of Mr. Jefferson, none is more barefaced and more easily detected by reflecting men, than the attempt to create a belief that he is a Christian.

They perceive the time has not arrived, especially in

---

16. *Political Observatory,* Walpole, NH, Jun 16, 1804, 3.

17. Philip Mazzei, a close friend and neighbor of Jefferson, was a Florentine doctor, merchant, and horticulturist who lived in Virginia from 1773 to 1785 on a tract of land at Monticello given to him by Jefferson and additional land that he purchased. A patriot during the American Revolution, Mazzei later wrote the first history of the war published in French.

New-England, when Infidelity shall be openly encouraged and unblushingly protected; thence arises their solicitude to conceal his *real religious sentiments.*

The disciples of Infidelity and Democracy act under covert at present, and, by corrupting the morals of our fellow citizens, are paving the way for the introduction of their accursed, atheistical tenets, and a consequent revolution in government, as well as morality. Infidelity is the grand engine of revolutionists. Voltaire and his coadjutors have been a greater scourge to France than all her arbitrary monarchs and external enemies. When moral principles become corrupted, when the existence of a God and a future state is disbelieved, when oaths are disregarded, or used only to deceive, then is the time, when every enormity, when every crime of the blackest hue will be committed without compunction and without remorse.—people impressed with these principles, or rather people of no principle, are ever ready to engage in the most desperate enterprises. They make vice a trade, and would sooner plunge their bayonets in the bowels of their country than obey the laws.

They are the scum, the curse of every civilized country, who in a revolution are sure to be cast uppermost. *Modern philosophy,* which is synonymous with Infidelity, teaches us to bear no more affection for our own country, than for the most distant on the globe. Nay, one of its axioms directs us to love an inhabitant of Cassiaria as affectionately as a parent, a brother, a sister, a wife, or a child. When such ideas are once instilled into men's minds, they cannot possess a shadow of Patriotism.—They would as soon fight for Algiers or France, as for America. They would deliberately subvert all the venerable institutions of our ancestors, destroy our government, render robbery, raping, and murder universal, and sacrilegiously light the funeral pile of our country. We should be tossed, woefully tossed on the "tempestuous sea of liberty."

Our democrats know all this; it is the object of their nefarious labors. Hence they assault every thing sacred or venerable. The clergy are sure to receive the first attack.— Destroy them, confusion, outrage, and destruction will follow of course. Already have the friends of "anarchy and wild misrule," and among them an influential public officer, discharged at them a volley of thunder; they are denounced in every section of our country as an unprincipled horde, struggling to wrest from you the rights purchased with your blood.—Mr. Jefferson knows the destruction of the clergy will remove a principal obstacle to the introduction of his principles, which are totally repugnant to all order, morality, and good government. Let no one doubt this; it is an absolute fact, the [illegible word] Parson Griswold's[18] falsehoods to the contrary notwithstanding.—Let any candid man read Mr. Jefferson's Notes on Virginia attentively, and take into consideration his expressions and conduct at different times, and he will, he must pronounce him an Infidel. In one place in his Notes, he observes,—*"Millions of innocent men, women, and children, since the introduction of Christianity have been burnt, tortured, fined, and imprisoned;"* as though the introduction of Christianity had been the sole cause of these enormities, and as though burning, torture, fines, and imprisonment were unknown before that period. But have not as great enormities been committed in Pagan countries, where human sacrifices were offered to appease the wrath of their (perhaps twenty) Gods, and where man roams about in a state of "perfectibility," or even in the "enlightened government of France," our "natural ally" and dear "sister republic," since the introduction of Atheism by a legislative decree, as in any Christian country? Mr. Jefferson and every other person must answer in the affirmative. Again, speaking of Pennsylvania and New-York, he says, "Religion is there well supported; of various kinds, indeed, but all *good enough;* all sufficient to preserve peace and order." Can any Christian consider the preservation of "peace and order," as here used, as the grand design of Christianity? No, he considers it as the foundation of his hopes of eternal happiness, as his only consolation; and the preservation of "peace and order," instead of the primary object, as only a necessary effect of

18. Stanley Griswold, the Republican clergyman who had preached the sermon at the 1801 Republican festival, was at this time the editor of the New Hampshire paper the *Political Observatory,* having left his Connecticut church in 1803.

Christianity.

In another place, he endeavors to prove the impossibility of a general deluge and the falsehood of the account of that occurrence in scripture, and in so doing he denies the authenticity and divinity of revelation.

In another part of his Notes, he observes, "Those who labor in the earth are the chosen people of God, *if ever he had a chosen people.*"—Here he expressed a doubt whether God ever had a chosen people, although we are expressly informed in the scriptures, that he had. An elegant writer remarks, "Please to read it again. Perhaps you do not perceive all the delicate and refined sarcasm contained in it."— Observe that the words are in the present tense, "Those who *labor* (at this time) in the earth *are* (now) the chosen people of God, if ever he had a chosen people." This is found, you will remark, in his Notes on Virginia, written for Virginians and accommodated to their notions and habits of thinking. We all know who they *are,* who in Virginia *labor* in the earth. The sentiment would have been more obvious to the people of the middle and eastern States, though we confess not quite so witty, had Mr. Jefferson said, "If God ever had a chosen people, they are, no doubt, our Virginia negroes." Mr. Jefferson speaks about the twenty Gods or no God picking my pocket or breaking my leg, in his usual air of levity when treating religious subjects, but not in the spirit of a Christian. He further asserts, "Had not the Roman government permitted free inquiry, Christianity could never have been introduced." Here he flatly denies the divine origin of Christianity:—for if it was God's will to introduce it into the world and disseminate its truths among all nations, it could not be prevented. To assert the contrary would deny the omnipotence of God. Mr. Jefferson is not correct in his statement. The Roman Emperors did prohibit free inquiry and persecute the Christians. Our philosophical President ought to blush at his ignorance or intentional misrepresentation.

There are concurrent circumstances, which clearly prove him an infidel. Mr. Jefferson was riding with a friend, a stranger in this country, who was a professed Infidel. As they were passing by a decayed ruinous building, the stranger inquired what it was. Mr. Jefferson told him it was a church. Do you suffer your churches, in this country, said the stranger, to go to decay and ruin in this manner? Why, sir, it looks like an old barn.— "O, replied Mr. Jefferson, *it is good enough for a God who was born in a manger.*" If this is disbelieved, the names of the gentlemen on whose authority it is related are given in a pamphlet entitled "A Voice of Warning," written by Dr. Linn,[19] and published in New-York. His invitation to that notorious Infidel, Thomas Paine, to come to this country in a national ship;—his intimacy with him since his arrival;—his disregard of the Sabbath;—and his blasphemous comparison of the Mammoth-loaf feast with the Lord's Supper,[20] clearly prove him an Infidel. Americans! reflect upon these facts and declare whether such a man ought to preside over a Christian people! "When the wicked rule a nation mourns."[21]

The Republican papers, of course, continued to dismiss the claims of a nefarious plot to destroy religion as ridiculous.

A serious question to every HONEST *man.*

Do you conscientiously believe, that the present admin-istration ever had it in their hearts to *deprive you of the Bible, to burn your Meeting-houses, or to destroy your religion?*— Let the question be answered while your eyes are fixed on that Bible which is yet in your possession, or while you bow in that temple which yet stands, or while your soul exults in those hopes which you freely indulge without any to

19. This article incorrectly names Rev. William Linn as the author of "A Voice of Warning." There were two widely distributed pamphlets attacking Jefferson in the election of 1800 that were written by prominent New York Presbyterian clergymen. The one written by Linn was *Serious Considerations on the Election of a President.* The other, *The Voice of Warning, to Christians, on the Ensuing Election of a President of the United States,* referenced in the article, was written by Rev. John Mason.

20. At a party in the Senate to rally support for a naval war with the Barbary States, at which Jefferson was in attendance, Navy bakers brought in a gigantic loaf of bread they had baked to go with what remained of the mammoth cheese. Also served was a giant roast beef and much alcohol, and the party reportedly turned in to a raucous, drunken affair, at which Jefferson allegedly made a comment comparing it to the Lord's supper.

21. *Dartmouth Gazette,* Hanover, NH, November 2, 1804, 1.

make you afraid.—These you have enjoyed for the space of *three years* of Mr. Jefferson's administration. According to the answer which your conscience shall make in presence of these *existing,* solemn witnesses, so be your opinion of those who declared, that if *Mr. Jefferson should be president of the United States, your bibles would be taken from you— your Meeting-houses burnt—and your religion destroyed.*[22]

Looking for fresh evidence of Jefferson's infidelity for the election year, the Federalist papers jumped all over his being a notorious Sabbath-breaker during his first term as president.

It has been more that once alleged that Mr. Jefferson is an infidel; and his own writings have been appealed to as containing the evidence of the charge. It is an old saying, how-ever, that "actions speak louder than words," The following article from the Boston Repertory, will be an illustration of the maxim:

"Jefferson's Religion." At Washington, the President's ar-rival and departure are always announced to the nation, and are generally remarked by journalists throughout the Union; Is it not as scandalous as it is unprecedented that most or all of these notices must be dated on the Christian Sabbath? Mr. Jefferson stands at the head of the American nation. He is the most conspicuous and it is to be presumed the most influential example. Particularly when acting in his official capacity, he commands the attention of all, & whether com-mendable or reprehensible, his conduct will have greater weight in society, than that of any other individual. But confidently trusting there is yet remaining enough of our steady habits to resist the force of bad example, however, dignified, to the eternal disgrace of this giddy, licentious President, as long as he perseveres in his wanton disrespect to the day of rest from labor, we shall with our brethren, give it due notoriety.

Mr. Jefferson went to Washington to attend the last session of Congress on SUNDAY. Mr. Jefferson set out on his journey

22. *Political Observatory,* Walpole, NH, March 10, 1804, 3.

from Washington, at the close of the session, on SUNDAY. Mr. Jefferson, on the 13th of May last, returned again to Washington, on SUNDAY. Mr. Jefferson is announced in the last National Intelligencer we have received, as having arrived at Washington on the 30th ult. which was on SUNDAY.

This is economy, he wishes to save a day. [23]

"The Immaculate Jefferson."

(So they have called him!)

The Observatory says that "the *illustrious example,* which Mr. Jefferson is setting," "will have effect for time to come!" NOW BE IT REMEMBERED, that this same Observatory has re-published from the National Intelligencer an account of Mr. Jefferson's arrival at Washington on the 30th September, which was the SABBATH day!! Mr. J. also came to Washington on the *Sabbath* to attend the last session of congress—at the rising of congress he set out for Monticello on the *Sabbath,* and he returned to Washington again on the Sabbath, the 13th of May. This is an *"illustrious example,"* set by the first officer in America, and is to "have effect for time to come!" SHAME, *where is thy blush?"*

The democratic editors set up a *hue and cry* against Dr. Park for publishing that Mr. J. went home on Sunday. They called him and most of the federal editors, *"liars,"* *"unprincipled assassins,"* and *"rascals."* Mr. J., they said, "went home to visit a sick daughter:" and that only *confirmed the truth* of what had been published, if their acknowledgment may be allowed any weight. Now we believed that Mr. J. held the Sabbath in utter contempt, and would have gone home on that day, if he had had no sick child to visit. And behold: some days after his daughter had died, Mr. J., as if he meant to mock his apologists, came back to Washington on *Sunday!*

The President's actions speak loud enough to rouse

---

23. *Connecticut Centinel,* Norwich, CT, October 30, 1804, 2.

every man of decency; and although we cannot but think such *examples* abominable in a *Chief Magistrate,* yet we should have thought better of some editors, if they had came forward to approve them, instead calling men "liars" for publishing what these same editors publish for truth in their own papers. But they cannot go back now—their trying to justify the President by publishing reasons for his travelling on the Sabbath was a fair acknowledgment that he would be culpable for doing it when these reasons did not exist; and he has done so since, and stands condemned by his own editors. They must not contradict themselves too often now just before election; but they may, as heretofore, hold up Mr. Jefferson as the purest christian, and a supporter of religion. Yet all sober-minded, rational creatures will pause—and, looking at his practices, first say to themselves, *is it really so?* is *he* a paragon of christian virtue? [24]

The *Eastern Argus,* a Republican paper in Maine, which at the time was still part of Massachusetts, took note of the desperation of the Federalists' religious attacks against Jefferson:

When Joab and Adonijah saw they must die, they fled and caught hold of the *horns of the altar,* as the last remedy to preserve life. Our *Tory Faction* have also lately caught hold of the *horns of the altar.* As this is the *last remedy,* I conclude they expect to die soon! By the horns of the altar, in this place, I mean *Religion.*—The opposition have made a great hurly burly in the country, affirming that Mr. Jefferson is a Deist, that he designs to destroy the Bible, &c. It is not love for the Bible, nor hatred of Deism, but to his *political sentiments,* that induces these Hypocrites to belie one of the most moral, benevolent and patriotic citizens in our country. [25]

The Federalists in Connecticut had for several years unsuccessfully tried to convince the overwhelmingly Republican Baptists and

---

24. *Oracle Post,* Portsmouth, NH, October 30, 1804, 3.
25. *Eastern Argus,* Portland, ME, June 7, 1804, 3.

Methodists of their state that the Republicans didn't really care about their religious freedom, and were only using them for their votes. A Baptist petition to the state's General Assembly, which was circulating for signatures in 1801, was claimed by the Federalists to be a fake, that it wasn't written by Baptists but by the Republican leadership as an electioneering trick. The Federalists also attempted to use their "religion is in danger" canard to convince the Baptists and Methodists that they were being fooled by a party of enemies to religion that no genuine Christian could vote for. The Federalists, so said themselves, were the true friends of their religion.

RELIGION AGAIN IN DANGER!

AN attempt is making in this state, (after the example of Connecticut) upon those who are believed by the intriguers to possess some serious regard for religion, particularly the Baptists and Methodists, to prejudice them against the government, by reviving the hackneyed and worn out theme, that *Religion is in danger.*—And what is the amount of their argument on this subject? why, that religion is in danger, because Mr. Jefferson in his political capacity *lets it alone,* lets it have its own free course, is not inclined to interpose with his power in favor of any sect, but is a friend to free, complete and perfect toleration.—The inference they draw from this, is, that he must be an *infidel,* possessing no regard for religion, and of course (reasoning Calvinistically) must hate it, and will embrace the first opportunity to destroy it! ...

Their deductions from his principles of free and perfect toleration, may pass well enough with their own sect (as they mostly consider themselves of a *standing order,*) but are wretched logic to be addressed to *Methodists* and *Baptists.* What! religion in danger from Mr. Jefferson, because he wishes it to have a free course! religion in hazard of being *destroyed* by him, because in his political capacity he *lets it alone,* does not meddle in its concerns with the artillery of his temporal authority! Who clothed him with that authority for the purpose of intermeddling in the concerns of souls? The world has suffered enough from the perversion of temporal prerogatives and power to spiritual purposes.

The Saviour bled, the apostles were slain, hosts of martyrs perished at the stake and millions have been destroyed in persecutions, from this horrid principle.

If the doctrine were ever to prevail in this country (which God forbid) that the chief Magistrate must interfere in matters of religion and employ the thunder of his power in its concerns, or be calumniated as an *infidel,* what has the Baptist to expect—what has the *Methodist* to expect— what has any *humble denomination* to expect? Could either of these expect to become the *favored* sect, the *established order?* If they should, one thing is certain—those who are now wishing to alarm them, would rebel—nothing but mutiny and insurrection might be expected from their chagrine. No, they must have the *establishment,* or it will be worse than none. And on this head they feel secure enough, for both *Methodists* and *Baptists* are too humble and sincere to have their religion become a fashionable one, a religion of state. Whereas the intriguers are just sincere enough to have *their* religion debauched by temporal power, and converted into state grandeur. ...

Look a moment at Greatbritain—for our Anglo-feder- alists want everything to be here as it is there. The civil power there has not *let religion alone,* but has interposed and established a certain sect by law. To support the overgrown clergy of that sect, a *tythe* is collected of every individual, who improves property, in the realm. Baptists, Methodists, Friends, dissenters of every denomination, are compelled by the thunder of the civil power to pay their *tythe* to the established order.—And what is a *tythe?* why it is a *tenth part* of all their earnings, or of the yearly produce of their farms. Where no compromise is made for money, (which is very frequently the case,) the ecclesiastical collector goes yearly into the possessions of the farmer, and takes the *tenth* hay-cock, the *tenth* sheaf of grain, the *tenth* bundle of flax, the *tenth* bushel of apples, of potatoes, the *tenth* pig, the *tenth* lamb, the *tenth* calf, the *tenth* fowl,—in short, the *tenth* of all and every thing that is produced yearly. This goes to the exclusive support of the established church. Whatever expense the *Baptists,* the *Methodists,* &c. incur

to support their *own* persuasion, it is separate from the forementioned *tythe,* and is a mere *free-will* offering—for the
government cares not whether *they* have ministers or not.
And to discourage them still more, *no dissenter* can hold an
office, civil, military or naval.

This is Old England! and it is perhaps the mildest oppression that ever existed, where the civil power undertook
to interfere in matters of religion. Bloodshed, slaughter and
extermination have most usually attended such interference.

Baptists! consider these things. Methodists! consider of
them. Universalists! Friends! all who have a humble regard
for religion, say, is it not best for the civil power to attend
to the objects for which it was ordained, and not undertake
to regulate the affairs of Christ's kingdom, *which is not of
this world?* And must a man be an *infidel,* because he lets
you all enjoy your lives and your religion in peace? Spurn
the hollow-hearted intriguers, for they wish to make you
tools to procure your own destruction.—But you will not be
deceived. You have hitherto been the friends of liberty—you
will continue its friends.[26]

When a piece appeared in the Republican *Eastern Argus* signed
by "A Humble Methodist Teacher," *Jenks' Portland Gazette,* a Maine
Federalist paper in the same town, responded by casting doubt on
the author's authenticity:

CHRISTIANS READ THIS!!!

*"The truth out at last, of Religion truly in danger from the
leaders of the Democratic faction."*

THE editor of the democratic paper, published in this
town, called the *Argus,* has boldly ventured to proclaim
the sentiments of the adherents to the present anti-christian
administration, in regard to the ministers of the glorious
Gospel of Jesus Christ, by the insertion of a piece in his
paper of the 21st inst. signed *"a humble Methodist Teacher."*
Whether the author is a real Methodist or not, may be a

26. *Political Observatory,* Walpole, NH, October 6, 1804, 1.

question—If he be, it is hoped that that class of men will discountenance the publication, lest it should be thought they are disposed to disaffect the people to those regular establishments, which have the greatest tendency to promote Religion and good order in society. Or that they are combined to promote those democratic principles which if persevered in, will e'er long destroy the peace and happiness, as well as the honor and prosperity of the country.

In that publication, which points to one in the Palladium, on the subject of religion, the writer says of Christians—

"They may now plainly discover the designs of the Political Priests, the mere creatures of State Government, whose whole use is to hush the people into silence and acquiescence to the tyranny and slavery of wicked rulers, with whom wicked Priests have ever been in league to destroy the rights of the people.

"This mere political Priesthood are the agents of Satan to enslave mankind; the most wicked and remorseless Tyrants of the Earth have found it impossible to enslave man by any other means but by uniting with such Priests—with their aid the most sacred rights of man have been easily seized. These men have wickedly instructed their dupes that God required of man passive obedience to the most bloody and savage Tyrants, thus have they profaned Religion, (which is intended to bless mankind, both here & hereafter) to the vile purpose of Slavery and Misery. A union of Church with State is more destructive to the happiness of man than any other conspiracy since the first Apostacy and union of fallen Angels. True Christians have but one opinion of those Priests who wickedly prate about a union of Church and State— they believe them to be only wolves in sheep's clothing; they are mere Hirelings; they have no call to preach the Gospel except what they fancy they derive from a College education."

Here, readers, you discover the cloven foot; by this publication you may judge of the principles of those who are devoted to that infidel who sits at the helm of government, and who are duped by those who profess an attachment to him from motives of self-interest.

This discovery, it is hoped will open the eyes of those

who have not viewed through the medium of reason and sound judgment, the cloud which hangs over our once happy country; & will lead men of greater abilities than the writer of this, to develop the designs of its enemies, and establish a discerning power in the minds of its friends.[27]

Massachusetts Republican paper *The Pittsfield Sun* presented the established clergy of Connecticut and Massachusetts with a bit of a theological conundrum — that as Calvinists they should believe that the administration of Jefferson was preordained, and should therefore not try to turn the people against it:

> But there was false prophets also amongst the people,
> even as there shall be false teachers among you.

THE established Clergy of Massachusetts and Connecticut are, in general, Federalists and Calvinists; they believe that God hath fore-ordained whatsoever comes to pass; that he powerfully governs all his creatures and all their actions; and yet they are continually finding fault with the present administration of the general government. They have told us that the President is a Deist and an Infidel—that the Christian Religion is in danger—that persecution will follow. They have conjured up the frightful idea of blood and carnage, with raw-head and bloody-bones, hobgoblins and frightful spectres, to prejudice weak minds against the present administration. They doubtless would be glad to have the ancient laws against Heretics, made by our pious forefathers, revived and put into execution, to clear the country of Heretics. They account it a fine thing to have Religion established by Law. The union of Church and State would suit them well, if they could be the ruling party—but if they had lived in a popish country, where religion was established by law, they would not like to be forced to help build their churches and maintain their ministers.

Since I was a man in years, in Connecticut, men were fined, imprisoned, and treated as vagrants, for the crime of

---

27. *Jenks' Portland Gazette*, Portland, ME, December 31, 1804, 2.

preaching the gospel, without leave of the parish minister. Men were imprisoned, their estates taken and sold by the collectors, at the beat of the drum. Our pious fore-fathers would have cleared the country of all that they esteemed Heretics, if the King and Parliament had not forbid the execution of their cruel, tyrannical laws, for putting men to death for their faith in Christ. These men, upon their own principles, ought not to find any fault with the present administration, seeing God powerfully governs all his creatures and all their actions. Shall the law magnify itself to him that shaketh it? Is a passive machine to blame for being set in motion?—The devil and wicked men are doing the will of God as perfectly as the angels in heaven do, if God powerfully governs them. ...

If God has fore-ordained that Mr. Jefferson shall be President of the United States, and that he shall obtain the cession of all Louisiana to the United States, without one drop of blood being shed, a most important and valuable acquisition, all done by the unalterable decree of God, how dare these federalists find fault with the fulfilment of God's eternal decrees? If God has decreed that the Infidels shall extirpate and destroy Christianity out of the United States, how durst say what doest thou? Of all the people in the land, the Calvinists ought to be quiet, and never grumble nor find fault, let who will be President, for they are as perfect machines as the planets are, and they cannot do any thing contrary to the decrees of God. ...[28]

The Bee, although having moved from Connecticut to Hudson, NY, in 1802, continued to cover Connecticut and Massachusetts politics, publishing this satirical letter from Massachusetts in November 1804 regarding the choosing of electors for the upcoming presidential election:

Berkshire County, Ms. Nov. 10.

FRIEND HOLT,
    AS one of my neighbors is going into Hudson in a day or

---

28. *The Pittsfield Sun,* Pittsfield, MA, April 23, 1804, 1.

two, you will not be surprised at receiving a line from me. Our election for presidential electors is just over, and I suppose the federal candidates are all chosen. Now what I was thinking of is, who are they to vote for, as our great men at Boston have not told us who they mean to put in. Some, it is true, have whispered that they are going to bring Mr. Adams forward again; but I suspect that was only to obtain more votes for our electors, and that it is determined to make a King if they can instead of a president. I don't much like their keeping every thing behind the curtain, as if they were afraid folks should know what they are about; but still I had to vote for the federal ticket, for you know I had rather have a king or any thing else than Jefferson. Besides, our papers say he's got no religion, and travels on Sundays, and sets bad examples to people. These things I should not mind so much, though, if it was not for the examples, because they are so apt to be followed, even by our own party. And they are followed, you may rely, for every year since he was president our federal Boston folks have held their election-eering meetings on Sunday evenings, and been as wicked in many other things as even Jefferson himself. I suppose you democrats will not believe that the President's conduct has so much influence, but it is a melancholy fact that no longer ago than last Sunday night all our great men met at the hall in Boston to forward the election. They gained their point by it to be sure, but to be candid with you, I don't like to have even a good end accomplished by such bad means; and it is all owing to the example of your wicked president. I understand your electors are to meet in Hudson, and as you will be on the spot do let them see this, and beg of them not to vote for Mr. Jefferson, for I am sure he is so bad a man that if he is in four years more, there will not be six cents worth of religion left, at least in our party, I can answer for it. And do tell them too, who I want to have made president, that is general *Pinckney*,[29] for his character is right the re-verse of Jefferson's, and if he should be chosen religion would flourish again, and we should be prosperous and

29. Charles Cotesworth Pinckney, the 1804 Federalist candidate for president.

happy. It is said Mr. P. is president of the jockey club, and how president Dwight[30] berated him for being a Deist some years ago, and a great many such stories are told about him, but I dont believe them, for our printer says they are all jacobin lies. You may depend gen. Pinckney is one of the best men in the country. I can't say who our party would like for Vice President, but I should think lawyer *Ely,*[31] of Springfield, would be the best, for he is one of the greatest friends to the country that I know of. And you know, too, his famous amendment to the constitution; he deserves the vice presidency for that, if nothing else, for no common man would have thought of such a glorious thing.

But neighbor Frost has called before I expected him, and I must soon close. I can't stop tho' till I repeat my request that your electors may see this, as I shall send it to all the New England electors, and I have no doubt but that, if they will only be unanimous they will put in gen. Pinckney and esq. Ely, President and Vice President, and send your Jefferson and such men home to learn religion and morality. Adieu for the present, you shall hear from me again, when I tell you how my plan works among the yankees.

Your old friend,
A FEDERAL FARMER[32]

Yale College was the nursery in which the next generation of Connecticut Federalists was being trained, and its results were vividly described in this excerpt from an essay in the *American Mercury* on the molding of a young Federalist mind:

Every person the least acquainted with the influence of education in giving a decided bent of sentiment to our youth—in giving them strong prepossessions for, and against men and measures, will testify to the truth of the position.

30. Timothy Dwight, Congregationalist minister and president of Yale College, so powerful in both Federalist politics and the Congregationalist Church that the Republicans dubbed him the "Pope."
31. William Ely, Federalist member of the Massachusetts House of Representatives, elected to the U.S House of Representatives in 1804.
32. *The Bee,* Hudson, NY, November 27, 1804, 2.

As has been hinted, every one knows the many prejudiced principles which are imbibed without knowing or understanding the reason why. A stamp of credulity is given them merely upon the authority of those whom we have been taught to respect and reverence.

So it is with the young man about to bid adieu to his collegiate pursuits—He is armed at all points with a weapon furnished him by his instructor. Indeed so deeply rooted are his prejudices, (altho' imperceptible in himself), that upon mixing with the world, he gives little or no credit to any sentiment or opinion, however supported by truth or reason, which breaks upon his *collegiate creed.* He is ready to support with his reputation and with his life, the orthodoxy of his principles. No democratic innovation (because, forsooth it proceeds from a party *called Democrats)* shall shake in his breast the seeds of federal delusion, planted by his unerring president; and which all his instruction, argument and eloquence tended to inculcate, to inspire, and to support. The young man, with his precious federalism, feels the importance of his literary acquisitions, nor will he yield an inch of ground to any but him who can boast a liberal education. ...

We must not take leave of our young politician. He beholds the Clergy, the *Legislators,* and the Magistracy, the latter of whom are dependent on these same *legislating federalists* for their offices, all speaking in one tone, and all repeating the fallacious and superannuated lesson of modern federalism. The youth in fact sees a virtual union of Church and State, *not under that name,* but under the more imposing one of "the union of friends to order, and good government." His mind is fully ripe for embracing the doctrine in detail, of which he had before professed only the *leading principles.* He is smitten with an ardent love for federal glory, and is worked up to a zeal which would do honor to a better cause. With loud and reiterated acclamations, he proclaims it in the streets, and on the house tops, and with the infuriate madness of a demon, blows the contaminating breath of slander upon those who dare to differ with him in sentiment. With the confidence of a fool and a madman he sings the *State song* of "exclusive religion and virtue," in those whose fatal prejudices he has imbibed! This slender thread on which the "pious cause" is suspended, is now ready to break. At the inconsistent and detestable tale, lately told with so much success, the souls of all honest men begin to revolt and to nauseate. The most hardened knave that ever marched in the federal ranks, will feel ashamed to give it currency in *another year*. Mark this ye modern federalists. ....[33]

The prediction that the Federalist Party would be dead within a year was wishful thinking. The ultimate demise of Federalism in Connecticut was still another thirteen years off.

33. *American Mercury,* Hartford, CT, May 17, 1804, 2.

⇜ **1805** ⇝

The constitution question remained the big issue in Connecticut's spring 1805 election. Jonathan Trumbull was reelected governor once again, with 12,700 votes to William Hart's 7,810. The Republicans saw a slight gain in the House of Representatives, but not as much as they had hoped for in the wake of Jefferson's landslide reelection victory. Of the 195 seats, the Republicans won just over a third with 68. In the fall that number would drop to 61. The Council, as always, remained all Federalist.

There was no Republican festival this spring, but the year's 4th of July events were decidedly partisan, being advertised to one party or the other, and a large Republican celebration of America's Independence held in August rivaled the spring festivals of previous years. Many Federalists, however, whose numbers would grow as the country neared the War of 1812, didn't consider America's Independence a cause for celebration, but were of the opinion that separation from England was a mistake. One such Federalist was Yale president Timothy Dwight. There is no overstating the power of Dwight in both church and state in Connecticut. He was the leader of both the state's church and the state's Federalist party and, as such, was dubbed the "Pope" by Republicans.

> The influence of President Dwight in the political affairs of this State is universally known. He is a clergyman and at the head of our principal seminary of literature. These circumstances naturally place him at the head of what is

called the Connecticut Church, that is, of the clerical part of the Church and State league. This is so perfectly understood that by a general tho' tacit consent the very apposite title of Pope has, long since been conferred on him.

As Mr. Dwight is the chief and leader of our political clergy, and as such, gives direction to their efforts; and as the combined influence of this body of political clergy is sufficient to create or destroy at pleasure, and to which the other part of the league is obligated to bend, this Pope is, in fact, the pivot on which the politics of this State turn; or rather, he is the wire worker who makes the political puppets move as best pleases him.

It may be gratifying to the admirers of this puppet show, of this Church and State league, or, in the slang of the confederacy, this combination of religion and talents, to be informed of the true political character of the great magician who directs it. It is for the purpose of giving this information that I request you to publish the following extract of a letter from a young gentleman of the senior class in Yale College to his friend. The letter bears the date of 19th July 1805. The extract is genuine; it needs no comment as it speaks, on the part of the Pope, precisely the principles that we have constantly, and truly ascribed to the party of which he is chief.—The father of our Pope, it is well known, was in our revolution a Tory, and fled to the banks of the Mississippi to avoid being engaged in the contest against his beloved Britain. His son, the Pope, then pretended, though falsely, as now appears, to approve the exertions of his country to obtain an emancipation from British thralldom. In those exertions, it is true, he took no active part, and his patriotism might have been, and probably was, an expedient to prevent the confiscation of his paternal inheritance. However that may be, of his present Toryism I have in my hands sundry proofs which I intend to communicate to the public.

LUTHER.

EXTRACT.

"The Republicans of this College appointed an Orator and made preparations for the celebration of the 4th of July.—*The Pope,* fearing that his character would be injured by a *Republican* celebration, issued a solemn edict against it. He condemned the celebration of the day *as ruinous in its consequences;* and observed that in the existing state of our country *no substantial reasons could be given for celebrating the day.*

"He observed to my class that he had always thought it an unfortunate affair that the United States separated from Great-Britain, *and that he thought so still.*" [1]

It was customary in New England for ministers to change with each other to preach to different congregations, but some Federalists didn't like this when it meant a Republican minister preaching to a Federalist congregation, even going as far as telling people to stay home when a Republican minister was visiting their church.

The federalists have long professed extraordinary tenderness for the Clergy; and in defending them in the public papers of this state, they have even gone so far to say, in effect, that whoever attacked a Clergyman did thereby shew his enmity to our Saviour and his cause. In the meridian of federal glory, it was also held as sacrilege, in other States, to attack a *(federal)* Clergyman. But the following extract will determine whether it was the spiritual or carnal, the *divine* or *political* character of Clergymen that was revered so much by federalists. It is from an Oration delivered in 1799 by Mr. Livermore, of New-Hampshire.

"Shut out the Jacobins!"

"It is happiness to our country to observe, that the ministers of religion are truly *federal,* and only two solitary instances to the contrary can be found in New-Hampshire!!— How can other ministers change with them, or *admit them into their desks? Or how can their* HEARERS *any longer* TOLERATE *them?—Why do they not have councils upon them, and have them dismissed?"*

The following seems to be a kind of note attached to the proceeding:—

"The public are impatient for these gentlemen's names.

1. *American Mercury,* Hartford, CT, September 12, 1805, 3.

We hope they will be published for the benefit of the community, that *true federalists* may STAY AT HOME *when they change with the neighbouring ministers"!!*

Here is genuine federal religion! This shews how much *Christianity* and the preachers are regarded by *"true federalists,"* when separated from political concerns. No accusation was brought against the moral or professional characters of these two ministers; they were merely charged with being republicans; or, in federal lingo, *Jacobins!* And because they dared to entertain these political opinions (for it is not alleged that they *preached* them) the federal ministers were advised not to admit them in their pulpits—their *hearers* not to tolerate but *dismiss* them—and all *"true federalists"* to *stay at home when they preached!*

Just so it is now in Connecticut—*federal* priests are caressed and revered by the federalists, who deem it sacrilege to doubt the perfect holiness of any one of them; and the *grateful* clergymen in return, exert all their immense influence to bolster up their pious friends, and perpetuate their power—all this passes for piety and christianity—But let a Clergyman once be known as a republican—the scene changes—the tenderness of doves is changed to the ferocity of tygers—it is *then* that Christianity can be wounded through the heart of its preacher—because the preacher is a republican! Few people in this and Litchfield County are ignorant of the savage persecution which pursued Mr. Stanley Griswold; and yet some of the very persons who hurled their vengeful shafts at that excellent man, are now, with pious sensibility, whining about the abuse as they call it, which Republicans pour out against the Clergy![2]

Short History of Connecticut.
NO. III.

A CONNECTICUT man, who had *puffed* himself into a

---

2. *Republican Farmer,* Danbury, CT, June 5, 1805, 3.

vastly solemn opinion of himself and the *honor and dignity* of his messmates, may wonder how we should dare to tell what in his sober senses *he knows to be true;* but we have no qualms on this subject. If a man boasts that he is seven feet in height, and that he can therefore see farther and better than his neighbors, and if we measure him by a true scale and find him to be but five feet in height, we dare to pronounce him a *little puffing* man. If a man boasts of being vastly christian, and we compare him with the bible and find him too short at both ends, and that he has no religion of heart and life, we dare to call him a hypocrite, and we will call him an impostor.

As to the little priests, of whom we speak, they are to be blamed for assuming too much and for minding their leaders rather than their bibles. Really when we consider how little the greatest of men know respecting the mysteries of nature and religion, we feel a mixture of indignation and humility, when we see the most moderate of all intellectual beings affect mighty airs of wisdom and infallibility on a subject, of which they are supremely ignorant. The humble class of priests should have their whole trading stock made up of humility and self abasement: but should profess and know their duty, and in their lives shew a disposition to do it.

This has not been the case in Connecticut for many years. So far from it, from one end to the other of it, nearly every priest was a federal politician of the Adams' school: they loved war and taxes and hated liberty, and some of them preached politics and many prayed politics, and nearly all circulated the infamous blunders and forgeries of the papist Barruel, and the monarchist Robison. If a republican clergyman was found among them, he must either renounce his heresies or be persecuted and slandered till he has obliged to leave his flock: for the whole fraternity hated republicanism, not because it would injure real religion, but because it would oblige them to preach and practise it or relinquish their rank and salaries.

Many of these clerical *pretenders* to a divine mission spent more days in securing federal votes for an election, than they spent hours in gathering souls into the garner of salvation.—They circulated pamphlets, they circulated the Courant even with the blasphemous song of *Moll Cary* in it. When it was probable that Mr. Jefferson would be elected president, Linn's *Serious Considerations* and Mason's Voice of Warning were law and gospel to such clergy, and RELIGION WAS IN GREAT DANGER. This is the never failing howl of imposture, when there is a danger of detection. The common people imagine that the religion said to be in danger is the christian religion, but instead of that it is a religion of this world, the first and great precept of which is, *reverence the priests,* and the second is, *let the priests join themselves unto the rulers and lord it over the people.* This is the only religion, which has ever been in danger in Connecticut. It is the same miserable religion, which has crumbled to pieces in Jersey, Massachusetts and New-Hampshire, and which will always be crushed to powder by an intelligent people, resolved to honor God and assert their rights. ...[3]

Connecticut had the sympathies of Republicans in other states, who often described it as "priest-ridden" and "the holy land." The First Barbary War had been ended with the negotiation of a treaty in June 1805, which freed the American captives in Tripoli in exchange for a ransom, but word of the treaty had not yet reached the United States when the toast quoted in the following pair of articles from the *American Mercury* was given at a 4th of July celebration in Windsor, Vermont.

VOLUNTEER TOAST, *given at Windsor, (Vermont) on the 4th of July.*

"*Our brethren in Tripoli and Connecticut*—May the former be freed from Pirates, and the latter from Priestcraft."

OUR Federalists know very well what is meant by piracy at Tripoli, but they affect to be profoundly ignorant about the meaning of priestcraft in Connecticut. The last Courant undertakes to ask us what we mean by the union of Church

---

3. *Political Observatory,* Walpole, NH, May 11, 1805, 2.

and State, and charges us with having sneeringly compared it to the Copartnership of Moses and Aaron.

This comparison has been uniformly made by federalists at all times and in all places: it is their standing comparison on the subject. Look at Trumbull's history, Parson Ely's election Sermon, and to all other election sermons. It has always been contended by them that as Moses and Aaron were united, so Civilians and Priests ought to be united. By virtue of that ancient union Aaron never sat on a woolsack in the House of Lords, but he and his corps had more influence than the whole bench of Bishops.

The Courant very slyly hints that we cannot see this union, and from this would infer that it does not exist. We can see something like it in the Corporation of Yale College, and at Commencements, and on Election days, and in the Missionary Society, and in the Academy of Arts and Sciences, and in the uniform promotion of Priests sons, and sons-in-law and brothers; but these are nothing compared with the sly tricks of our modern Moses and Aaron in the management of newspapers, pamphlets, and proxies. It is true that after Aaron has prayed in the legislature or the courts, he sits down and hears Moses talk, but Aaron does not vote. At dinner time Aaron sits with Moses, and eats and talks; and now, ye holy federalists, do ye believe that Aaron's readiness to be with Moses proceeds from his great zeal to assist Moses in building up the kingdom of Christ? When our political Aarons and our infidel Moses's are shut up, as they often are, in secret caucus, which think you is the greatest theme of discourse, the art of saving souls or the art of gaining votes?

You federalists may affect total inability to answer such questions; but the facts on the subject are perfectly known to both parties. The union of Church and State here, when spoken of, is universally understood, but as the Courant assumes great solemnity in the denial of this union, we shall say enough about it to make ourselves and our policy understood.

The republicans, as a body, are not opposed to the Clergy; if they were, they would soon rout them from republican towns; but so far from this, they have continued to support several, who for their federal bitterness, activity and imprudence ought to be driven off. That Clergyman, who in the midst of a republican parish, will be constantly venting his spleen against the President and the majority of his country and parish, is a pirate; he has no right to the respect or mercy of the people; he has no religion; if he had any, he would conduct with more decency.

There are some infidels and some immoral men among the republicans but not one so immoral as Alexander Hamilton, not one so openly infidel, as several of our federalists in high office. The common cant in federal papers about federal holiness and republican impiety is all penned by infidels. It is impossible for Christians to deal in such gross misrepresentations and slanders. No Christian is soiling the federal papers with charges of infidelity and atheism on republicans. The men, who do this, never entered the doors of the sanctuary, they are trying to climb up some other way.

The Courant would have it that we wish to introduce natural religion; but our only aim on this subject has been to drive out of public confidence those natural religion divines, who have left the preaching of the gospel in order to help on federal nominations. We have fought to keep the Clergy at their proper work, which is preaching the gospel, visiting families, attending the sick, the dying and the mourners, and offering the consolations of religion to all who need them. THIS IS OUR INFIDELITY; but your federal holiness is dragging Clergymen from their work to serve Moses, and it is in public knowledge how many political prayers and sermons you have drawn from them and how regularly you have harnessed them on proxies day mornings to drag your burdens. It is true that Aaron in his turn harnessed Moses; but the harness of the Clergy sits mighty easy and ornamental upon men in power. In the midst of high office, immerciful sees, splendid dinners and the smiles of Aaron, this federal tackling is very easy on our federal infidels. Such we have called, who drags the Clergy from their work.

We say no more at present, but may a merciful God

defend our brethren from Tripolitan piracy, and us from Connecticut priestcraft.[4]

↩

"Our Brethren in Tripoli and Connecticut—May the former be freed from pirates, and the latter from Priestcraft."
                                    Vermont Toast.

Our leading federalists have wished to persuade the people that a republican, even of large estate, would feel amply compensated for the loss of it by having a state of total anarchy insured to him—that republicans. possessed of the reins of government, would throw them out of their hands and trust them to the mercy of every head strong passion—that republicans, of first education, would destroy all institutions of learning and would hasten society to a state of profound ignorance; and that republicans, having souls, are seeking to destroy all religion, so that mankind may live without restraint and may be prepared for eternal misery.—In short, the common people are told that we have an atheist at the head of government, atheists all about him, atheists of his appointment throughout the union—that we are seeking confusion and ruin in this world, so as to prevent an examination into our principles.

Yet the principles, which we are known to maintain, are those, for which our fathers fought and bled—they are those on which heaven smiled during our revolution—they are the eternal principles of civil and religious liberty, which tyranny and priestcraft have always assaulted. Republicanism is the system of government, guaranteed by our Constitution to all the states.

Then what a boundless set of impostors are those, who are thus misrepresenting our cause and its advocates? No federal member of Congress or of Council, no man in federal Nominations, no clergyman or editor believes a word of these stories; yet they are propagated week after week in

4. *American Mercury*, Hartford, CT, July 25, 1805, 3.

correct English—they are read with great joy by political priests and infidel civilians, and we are called on solemnly to venerate these men as christians!! ...

A late Courant, treating of the union of Church and State, asks us to come forward and say boldly and explicitly to the people *"Destroy the Christian religion, root out this vile system of superstition, break its bands asunder and spurn its restraints,"* but explicit as we wish to be, this is not our language: we say to the people, 'destroy *priestcraft* or it will destroy you: root out a vile system of hypocrisy, which is degrading Christianity, break the bands which bind deceiving priests and infidel lawyers together.'...

When we reflect on the noise about meeting-houses, and bibles, and about twenty gods or no god, and the adopted stories of Callender about black Sal and Walker's wife—and the song of Moll Carey, and the election sermons, and the letter of Tom Turner[5] and all the other cast-off and worn-out impostures of the holy fraternity of Moses and Aaron, we respond to our Vermont friends,

'MAY OUR BRETHREN IN TRIPOLI BE FREED FROM PIRATES, AND WE BE FREED FROM CONNECTICUT PRIESTCRAFT.'[6]

In 1804, the Federalist *Connecticut Courant* hired Ezra Sampson, a former minister who had lost his voice, as its first full-time editorial writer. "Parson Sampson," as he was called in the Republican papers, had previously been the co-editor of *The Balance* in Hudson, New York, leaving that paper after being sued for his libelous articles against New York's attorney general. At the *Courant,* Sampson spread and sometimes invented outrageous lies about the Jefferson administration, one of his most notable concoctions being the 1806 story that Jefferson had sent sixty tons of silver to France as a bribe

---

5. A letter published in the Boston *Repertory* on May 31, 1805, and widely circulated in the Federalist papers, signed by a Thomas Turner who claimed to be from Virginia, accusing Jefferson of running away during the Revolutionary War while governor of Virginia, and saying that he had seen proof that the story published by yellow journalist James Callender in 1802 of Jefferson attempting to seduce Elizabeth Walker, his neighbor's wife, was true. The Mrs. Walker story was, in fact, true, as Jefferson admitted to friends after the publication of Turner's letter, writing, when "young and single I offered love to a handsome lady" (Jefferson to Robert Smith, July 1, 1805).

6. *American Mercury,* Hartford, CT, August 15, 1805, 3.

to Napoleon to stop seizing American ships.

A favorite target of Parson Sampson was the *American Mercury,* and a favorite target of Mercury editor Elisha Babcock was Parson Sampson and the *Courant.* In an August 1805 issue of the *Courant,* the paper that had originally published Theodore Dwight's blasphemous "Moll Carey" in 1803, Sampson wrote:

> A female, by the name of "MOLL CAREY," by her frequent appearance in the American Mercury, seems to be a great favourite with *certain people.* Several of the readers of that paper have a strong inclination to scrape acquaintance with this Belle—at least they would be glad to know whether she be black or white, whether she be a federalist, a democrat, or a *Quid.* If Mr. Babcock will be so good as to publish the song that he talks so much about, perhaps we shall all be satisfied. At any rate, we can partake of the music, whilst our republican friends of the higher order are regaling themselves with *Moll.*[7]

The *Mercury,* which had on a number of occasions invoked "Moll Carey" as one of its go-to examples of the pious Federalists' hypocrisy, responded the following week.

> Parson Sampson, in the Courant of last week, requests us to publish the federal song of Moll Carey; or the bawdy and blasphemous parody of the 148th psalm, which made its appearance in the Sunday paper, in March 1803. Notwithstanding the Parson's assurance of the satisfaction which he and his pious friends would derive from its publication, and the pleasure they would enjoy while *"partaking of the music,"* we will not publish it. Our reasons are,
>
> 1st, Although we are ever ready to lash hypocritical professors, who assume to themselves all the religion in the world, but by every act, set at defiance its principles; yet our paper shall never with our consent, be prostituted to the purpose of ridiculing real religion, and blaspheming the name of God and his holy worship.

7. *The Connecticut Courant,* Hartford, CT, August 28, 1805, 3.

2d, Although the federalists charge us with the design of reducing man to the savage state—of destroying the bonds which unite men in society, and by annulling the marriage contract to render women common; yet we will publish no piece which a woman of chastity cannot read without a blush.

If these reasons are not sufficient to satisfy the editor of the Courant, we can publish for his satisfaction that this infamous song has already through the medium of his paper, had a circulation too extensive, for the modesty and piety of his numerous readers.

That the sons of federalists in Wethersfield directly in front of the house dedicated to the worship of God, blasphemed his holy name by singing this infamous production, while a procession of respectable republicans was passing to Hartford to celebrate the 4th of March; and federal fathers looked on and applauded the obscenity and impiety of their sons.

Would to God that the sons of federalists only, had learned to sing this unparalleled union of obscenity and impiety. Their *daughters* too were taught to chaunt this requiem to their departed modesty; while fathers high in office by federal suffrages, listened with pleasure, while in their daughters the blood which once encrimsoned the cheek of sensibility, indignantly returned to its corrupted fountain.

The Courant which contained this song was carried to the houses of worship and read in the intervals of Divine service to groups collected for the purpose, and highly applauded by federal members of the church.

Federal ministers read with applause this infamous parody, in their families—to their wives and daughters—and laughed and read, and read and laughed, till they ridiculed and laughed modesty and religion out of doors.

We hope we have satisfied Parson Sampson—but we know of no medium but the Courant through which the song itself can pass. Perhaps however at some future day, a body of political priests may be found, who to put 10,000 dollars into the pocket of a favorite brother and poet, and take out of the pockets of the people, may recommend an edition of political federal psalms, among which *the parody* may hold high rank. Should this happen, there is no doubt but readers and singers will be found; for it is not uncharitable to believe, that those who can read and sing this song in their families now without a blush; can hereafter read it from the desk and sing it from the holy temples of religion.[8]

Parson Sampson continued on his "Moll Carey" theme the next week with this little item combining "Moll" with the old Federalist charge that the Republicans wanted to destroy the sanctity of marriage:

A correspondent wishes to know, (and at his request we propose the knotty question,) why the man who has openly and explicitly declared, that the marriage covenant was founded in superstition and supported by priest-craft, and that there ought to be no law against the promiscuous intercourse of the sexes even in open day light—why this man should so grievously take to heart the song of Moll Carey, a ballad that appeared in the Courant several years ago.[9]

Maine Republican paper the *Eastern Argus* had a short and simple response to those who warned that Jefferson was a danger to religion:

Many ignorant people are made to believe that the anti-republicans are friends to Christianity, and that the President of the United States has the power of establishing or destroying any kind of Religion at his discretion. Let such be informed, that neither the President of the United States, nor Congress, has any more power to destroy, alter or modify, either Bibles, Meeting-Houses, or Religion, than Captain Kid has, and not half so much as the Deacon of their own Parish. Mr. Jefferson was chosen for President of the United States, and not for a Preacher of the Gospel. ...[10]

8. *American Mercury,* Hartford, CT, September 5, 1805, 3.
9. *The Connecticut Courant,* Hartford, CT, September 11, 1805, 3.
10. *Eastern Argus,* Portland, ME, June 21, 1805, 2.

The Republicans of Connecticut liked to flaunt Jefferson's land-slide reelection victory of 162 to 14 electoral votes as a constant reminder to the Federalists that their party was dying nationally. When a series of essays titled "162 vs. 14" began to appear in the Litchfield, Connecticut *Witness* in the fall of 1805, The *Courant* hit back with "134 vs. 61," the numbers of Federalist representatives to Republican representatives in Connecticut's Assembly, as a re-minder to the Republicans that the Federalists were still in control in Connecticut. It should also be noted in this article that the Federalists were starting to shift the names of the parties, calling themselves "federal republicans," and the Republicans simply "democrats."

134 vs. 61.

The democratic prints in this State are almost constantly displaying with great pomposity, a view of the democratic majority in the Union; and are using this circumstance as an irrefragable argument to compel submission to their principles.—Now our democrats ought to consider that this argument recoils forcibly upon themselves, and that they are wounding themselves with their own arrows. For if the democratic majority in the union affords an all-powerful reason that the federal republicans should yield their prin-ciples respecting the concerns of the general government, the federal majority here affords also an all-powerful reason that our democrats should quietly yield in all matters per-taining to our state government.—They cannot evade the force of this reasoning. ...[11]

While Connecticut remained steadily under Federalist control, the other New England states waffled somewhat, with the Federalists always trying to regain the firm grip they had previously enjoyed, still relying on their "religion is in danger" alarm in hopes of pulling the Baptists and Methodists away from the Republicans.

... It has been urged as an objectional point in MR. JEFFER-

---

11. *The Connecticut Courant,* Hartford, CT, September 25, 1805, 3.

SON'S character that he is a PHILOSOPHER! If any person unacquainted with the tergiversation and artifices and diabolism of the Anglo-federal faction, was to hear that a magistrate was to be repudiated and condemned, because he was a *Philosopher,* how much would he be amazed? He would naturally comprehend that the Gothic night of barbarity was to darken society once more, and that all the refinements of humanity were to be abolished and overthrown. ...

> *"For modes of faith let graceless zealots fight,*
> *His can't be wrong, whose life is in the right!"*

... An attempt is now making in New-England, (after the example of Connecticut), upon those who are believed by the tories to possess some *serious* regard for religion, particularly the *Baptists* and *Methodists,* to prejudice them against the government, by reviving the hackneyed theme, that *Religion is in danger.*—And what is the amount of their argument on this subject? Why that religion is in danger, because Mr. Jefferson in his political capacity *lets it alone,* lets it have its own free course, is not inclined to interpose with his power, in favor of any sect, but is a friend to free, complete and perfect toleration.—The inference *they* draw from this, is, that he must be an *infidel,* possessing no regard for religion, and of course, (reasoning Calvinistically) must hate it, and will embrace the first opportunity to destroy it! ...[12]

A tradition among the papers at this time, both Federalist and Republican, was the New Year's "Address" from the editors of the papers. These addresses were epic poems, often filling an entire page of the paper, in which the events of the year before were set to verse. A typical format for these poems was a section on world events, then national events, then state events. The following is the section about Connecticut from the Danbury, Connecticut, *Republican Farmer's* address for 1805, on the "wedding" of "Miss Church to Mr. State."

12. *The Witness, Litchfield,* CT, October 2, 1805, 1.

Connecticut! we view again,
Thy truant steps with growing pain!
On *Freedom's* robe a dusky spot!
On fair Columbia's amp, a blot!
An ulcer, whose corrosive nature
Deforms our country's fairest feature;
Where vermin, in rank hordes abound,
And fatten in the fester'd wound!
    What whimsical vagaries here,
Have mark'd the annals of last year;
What new delusions, cloth'd in terror,
Have rose, to aid the schemes of Error!
What consternation did, last May, break
Forth about Lebanon's old fabrick!
Each scare-crow prophet, wond'rous willing
To think his prophecies fulfilling,
With zeal vociferated, "lo,
"The work's begun—*I told you so!!*
"Bibles will follow, soon, 'tis fix'd,
"And then God knows what must come next?
Some wore their horses out, or shoes,
To circulate the dreadful news;
"What *infidels!*" each bigot bawl'd,
Old women fainted; children squawl'd;
While grim *Fanaticism* growl'd,
And for her prey terrific prowl'd;
Till in her talons *Tilden* fell,
The victim pleas'd, and all was well!
So Indians erst, with fiend-like revel,
Led on by powaws, rais'd the devil;
And when they long enough had teaz'd him,
Gave him an infant, and appeas'd him:
    A wedding, too, has been on foot;
The question long ago was put;
ELY* proclaim'd the bans of late—
Demure Miss *Church* to Mr. *State!*
To tie the knot 'tis contemplated,
'Gainst the consent of *some*, 'tis stated,
Who call the bride the whore of Babylon,

And to disgrace her set the rabble on!
Others give reasons strong, however,
To prove the union would be clever:
"They're love," say they "while both were young
"wax'd warm, their courtship has been long;
"For each a native of this region is,
"Sprung from the ancient aborigines;
"As when our Luther first came o'er,
"They found them kissing on the shore.†
"And when of yore our pious dads
"For want of ploughs, us'd hoes and spades,
"Did these not kindly help each other—
"Cemented, as it were, together? ‡
"Does *he* not *now* her children bring
"To feast at *his* board ev'ry spring §
"And by *maintaining* ev'ry one,
"Acknowledge them to be his *own?*
"Does *she* not prostitute, each hour,
"Her beauties, to increase *his* power?
"Does *he* not, in return, supply *her*
"With dainty feasts and rich attire,
"Nor any service asks, but just
"To gratify his rampant lust?
"Then sure 'tis time, in marriage station
"To end this scene of fornication!"
Amen! *Moll Carey* ¶ shall be sung,
By every pious fed'ral tongue;
While each a chorus loud shall hal'oo
With all his might, in words which follow:
Lawyers and priests "have met together,"
And *Church* & *State* "have kiss'd each other!

* See his election Sermon of last Spring, in which he eulogizes the connection of Church and State, as a "blessed Union!"
† "These (Indian) paniese, or ministers of state, were in league with the priests, or powaws. To keep the PEOPLE in awe, the pretended as well as the priests, to have converse with the invisible world." TRUMBULL'S Hist. Connecticut,

page 40.

‡ Extract from 5th article of the original constitution of the government of New-Haven—"That church members ONLY should be free burgesses; and that THEY ONLY should choose magistrates among themselves, to have power of transacting all the public CIVIL affairs of the plantation."

§ Alluding to the attendance of the clergy at Election dinners.

¶ A prophane parody on the 148th Psalm, a conspicuous article in the annals of federal piety! [13]

13. *Republican Farmer*, Danbury, CT, January 2, 1805, 2-3.

∽ 1806 ∼

On March 12, 1806, the *Courant* republished a circular letter from Republican state manager Alexander Wolcott, headed "162—Vs—14," which it had previously printed in November 1805. The letter, to the party's county managers, provided instructions for what we would today call a voter registration drive and "get out the vote" campaign. Each county manager was to appoint town managers, who would then appoint district managers for each section of their town, with each being tasked with collecting the names of all men in their district who were taxed, finding out who were freemen, listing which were Republicans, and finding any Republicans who weren't freemen but might be qualified and assisting them with the process of becoming freemen. At the election, the managers were to take note of any Republican freemen who weren't present, and ensure that those who were present stayed for the entire day and voted in all the elections.

In November 1805, the *Courant* had printed Wolcott's letter without comment; in March 1806 Parson Sampson tried to turn the Republicans' voter drive into a scandalous conspiracy, writing:

> ... To the friends of our excellent State Government, this appeal comes with peculiar force. A set of office-holders and office-seekers, under the National Government, are using every possible exertion to destroy this State. By the blessing of GOD, they have hitherto made but little progress towards their darling object. If we are faithful to ourselves, we have

no reason to expect they will ever succeed. We have here exhibited to our view, the extent and the perfection of a daring conspiracy, to overawe our freemen, and to overturn our Government. ...[1]

A few days later, a letter in another Connecticut Federalist paper, the *Middlesex Gazette,* called the voter drive a "stupendous plot." [2]

The Federalists were very fond of plots. There were Republican plots and French plots and, of course, the Republicans plotting with the French.

There had been the "tub plot," in which French agents with designs to incite a slave rebellion had supposedly sailed from Hamburg with secret documents hidden in tubs with false bottoms.

That was followed by the "tailor plot," in which a tailor in Philadelphia was said to have made immense quantities of French military uniforms in preparation for a French invasion.

There was the "powder plot," also called the "lady plot," in which a Frenchwoman was planning to blow up Congress.

There was the slave rebellion instigated by the French, and in some versions aided by the Baptists and the Methodists.

There was a French fleet in the Chesapeake.

And there was the one about the American merchant ship the Ocean being boarded by French privateers who killed all ninety persons on board. This one was preached and published by Massachusetts Federalist clergyman Jedidiah "Granny" Morse, also known for his Illuminati conspiracy theories.

As outrageous as these stories were, they were believed by countless rank and file Federalists, who became genuinely afraid that a French invasion was coming any day.

The Republicans generally mocked the plot stories and the Federalists who believed them.

A PLOT! a new PLOT!! a black PLOT!!!

The federalists are alarmed, they report that a number of French Agents are busily at work buying all the CHARCOAL

---

1. *The Connecticut Courant,* Hartford, CT, March 12, 1806, 2.
2. *Middlesex Gazette,* Middletown, CT, March 14, 1806, 3.

that comes to Market, for the express purpose of shipping it to the West-Indies and France. They say that the French chemists have lately discovered, that Charcoal is a necessary ingredient in making gun-powder, and is used in roasting frogs.[3]

A principle means of spreading these plot stories in New England, and giving them credibility among the people, was through the Federalist clergymen in their Fast Day sermons, as the *New-Hampshire Gazette* satirically noted:

A generous reward will be given for any newly invented story, that may serve as a theme, on which political Clergymen may rail against the Government and traduce Republican principles. The more improbable the better, as it has been found by experience, that the *Ocean* story, the *negro massacre,* the *tailor plot,* the *tub plot* and many other plots, never plotted, but equally absurd and improbable, by being skillfully interlarded in FAST DAY sermons, have passed as current and been more attended to, than the truths of the Gospel would have been, had the preachers step'd out of their usual path to have noticed them. It was expected that the insurrection story of Kentucky, would have done for the next *Fast Day,* but it was imported so soon, that its falsity was detected, before an opportunity offered for making use of it. Had the New-England Fast Days been a little sooner, that story would have had an excellent effect in the hands of an adroit manager. Any plausible high seasoned fabrication will be gratefully received by every political preacher, who regards the traditions of men, more than the commandments of GOD; especially if it holds up the President as a Deist, and Tom Paine as the *Whore* of *Babylon.*

N.B. Evidence of the truth of any tale will not be required, provided there is no danger of its being proved a lie before next Fast Day.[4]

Getting back to Connecticut in 1806, Alexander Wolcott's *get*

3. *The Gazetteer, Boston,* MA, April 30, 1803, 3.
4. *New-Hampshire Gazette,* Portsmouth, NH, Mar 29, 1803, 3.

out the vote effort was effective, with record numbers of Republicans voting in the spring election. The Federalists, however, also had a high voter turnout. Governor Trumbull was again reelected, with 13,413 votes to William Hart's 9,460, and John Treadwell was reelected lieutenant governor with 11,810 votes to Asa Spalding's 7,918. The Republicans won 72 seats in the House, up from 61. The Council, as always, remained entirely Federalist.

This year's Republican festival, held on August 6, was in heavily Federalist Litchfield, where Selleck Osborne, the editor of Litchfield's Republican paper *The Witness* was in jail for libel against a county magistrate, Julius Deming, having printed that Deming attempted to intimidate a Republican voter at the September 1805 freeman's meeting by crossing the room and telling the Republican, who owed him a debt, that he owed him a vote. Osborne was jailed after refusing to pay a fine, becoming a martyr for freedom of the press. The festival's procession, a thousand strong, made a stop at the jail where Osborne was being held, with the military men saluting him at the window and the others taking off their hats to him.

Shortly after the festival, the Federalist papers claimed that the Republicans had forcibly ejected the town's elderly minister from the meeting house, with someone grabbing the minister by the arm and physically escorting him out of the same meeting house where he had preached for fifty years. The Republicans flatly denied the story.

Just before the September election, an anti-Republican pamphlet titled *The Sixth of August or The Litchfield Festival* was published by Hudson and Goodwin, the publishers of the *Courant*. The pamphlet began:

> It is well known that, for about six years past, a party has been organized in this State, for the avowed purpose of changing the government.—It is equally certain that the government is the most democratic of any government in the Union, except that of the State of Rhode-Island, and that it has afforded ample security to the people, in all their important interests, for more than one hundred and sixty years. The exertions of this party, as all prudent men foretold, have produced much discord. The peace of families— of neighborhoods—of towns, and of the whole community

has been almost turned into war, and hatred and revenge have succeeded to kindness and mercy.

Sober men will not fail to enquire for the real cause of this unhappy change and to ask what are the real objects of the leaders of that party denominated democratic. ...[5]

The pamphlet goes on to name all the festivals held by the Connecticut Republicans, and then make the comparison to another group that had festivals — the revolutionaries in France.

It has been fashionable ever since the organization of the democratic party, for their leaders to appoint public meetings and festivals, which all are invited to attend, and on which great numbers do constantly attend.

Thus in March 1801, a festival in honor of the election of Mr. Jefferson as President and Mr. Burr as Vice-President, was holden at Wallingford—in 1802, a like festival was holden also at Wallingford—in 1803, at New-Haven—in 1804, at Hartford to celebrate the purchase of Louisiana—in 1806, at Litchfield to celebrate the independence of the United States—and in 1804, a great number, denominated the representatives from 97 towns, were convened at New-Haven by order of the (then) State-Manager, to devise means for forming a new constitution for this State.

In the last six years, the leaders of democracy have collected together from all parts of the State, their followers once in each year. What was their object?

At one time, the avowed design is to rejoice at the election of a chief magistrate—then to celebrate the purchase, at the expense of fifteen millions of dollars, of a country whose limits are undefined—then to form plans to erect a new government for the State, and then to celebrate our national independence. These, I say, are their *avowed* designs—their *real* object is to influence the public mind by prayer, orations, sermons, or declamations—all dictated by the same spirit—all fraught with statements, opinions and assertions calculated to destroy the confidence of the people in the

5. *The Sixth of August or The Litchfield Festival: An Address to the People of Connecticut,* (Hartford, CT: Hudson and Goodwin, 1806), 1.

Clergy, in our Legislature and in our Courts, and thus to prepare them for revolution.

These measures of those leaders, have been taught them by the successive leaders in the revolutions which have for twelve years distressed France—which have there rent asunder all the bands of society, and have produced more slaughter, death and ruin than any nation ever witnessed in the same period. There Robespierre, and after him the successive heads of faction, summoned their followers to national festivals, till their houses of feasting were emphatically turned into houses of mourning, and till the people sickened at the repeated imposture of their pretended friends, sought and found a dreadful repose from the horrors of anarchy, in the sullen gloom of despotism. ...[6]

The widely circulated *Sixth of August* pamphlet and marred character of the Litchfield festival caused the Republicans in the fall election to lose 11 of the 72 Assembly seats they had won in the spring, bringing their number back down to 61.

A theme that emerged in the Republican papers in 1806 was questioning what the Federalists' political principles actually were, other than religion and being against anything Republican.

In reviewing the federal newspapers of this state for a few years past I find not one attempt to define or defend federalism. There is a dreadful roar against Mr. Jefferson & illumination, infidelity, atheism, jacobinism &c.—There is a great rout about the wickedness of democrats and the holiness of federalists, but not a word about the principles of federalism. It is so long since federalism has been in power and actual operation under the general government, that we wish to have some definition of it on paper.

We know that under Mr. Adams, federalism consisted of standing army, navy, stamp-act, land tax, alien and sedition acts, new judiciary and *universal employment of friends of the administration,* but what it is or can be in Connecticut no man can tell.

6. *The Sixth of August or The Litchfield Festival: An Address to the People of Connecticut,* (Hartford, CT: Hudson and Goodwin, 1806), 4-5.

If the federalists will for one week leave religion in the care of its divine founder and will inform WHAT THEIR federalism is, we should be much obliged.[7]

In the wake of Jefferson's landslide victory in the 1804 election, it also began to be analyzed why Connecticut was so different from the majority of the country.

FEDERAL IDOLATRY.

"Forsake your gods, your IDOL gods,
And pay the Lord your vows."

If a man chooses to be federal, let him set up some political principles and reason from them, and endeavour to convince the people that federalism is worth embracing; but let him forbear to conceal, under a stolen garb of religion, a system, which he dare not openly avow. Every real federalist is a monarchist; he loves a government, where power and profits are in few hands, and where the body of the people are *made* to believe, and *made* to act according to orders; but many, who act on the federal side, are in heart republicans, and would long since have voted with us, had they not been told that priests and religion were in danger.

This is the cunning, by which federalism has, in this State, survived federalism in other States. Here idolatry took early and deep root. In the first settlement of Connecticut the people were taught to suspend opinions and measures, till the Rev. Davenport, or the reverend Mr. Hooker, or some other reverend should tell what the divine will was in the case.

Fathers taught their sons an *idolatrous* respect even for the political opinions of priests; this respect descended from generation to generation, ready to be seized on, as the most valuable of steady habits, whenever ordinary means of keeping the people in subjection should fail. Accordingly in war time their political priests, having an abundance of *secular* motives, were whigs. After the war they were little heard of,

7. *True Republican*, Norwich, CT, February 5, 1806, 3.

except in their proper callings, till the year 1796, when the contest of parties called them out again. Had they fore-known the present state of our country, they might probably have been republicans, but Mr. Adams was coming into power to rear his stupendous fabrics, among which one would naturally have been an *ecclesiastical establishment, with Woolsacks in the senate chamber for the heads of the Clergy. Political priests* love power as carnally as if they were not priests; they lust after power and are wretched without it; of course they took strong hold of federalism; and all the *idolators* followed in mass.

Idolators are the last men in the world to be reasoned out of their errors; nothing will move them but a persuasion that their idols are tottering to the ground. Let them look to their idols, the *political* priests in this State, and see how feebly they stand in public estimation, how feebly they stand in the affections of their people; *political preachers* have nothing before them but an awful looking for the loss of their worshippers, for the loss of their parishes, and for eternal perdition. If they can cooly anticipate such conse-quences of their desertion from duty, their nerves are fitted for their inevitable fate.[8]

The most infamous Federalist plot stories were a number of years old in 1806, but the Republicans still continued to make use of them.

"This is correct."

The Federal Editors are in the habit of publishing so many *"incorrect"* things, that now, in detailing an ordinary piece of news, they put down at the bottom of their para-graphs, *"This is correct."* These words when placed under a particular article, are in fact a libel upon all the rest of the paper. They hold out this language. The above is "correct;" but all the rest are *lies,* and ought not to be believed unless a man silly enough to be caught in a gull trap. The federalists in '98, told us we were in danger of a French invasion. This

---

8. *The Witness,* Litchfield, CT, June 18, 1806, 3.

"was NOT correct." They arrested in Charleston South-Carolina, an old woman, three mulattos, and a negro wench, said to be concerned in a *conspiracy* against the liberties of this country. It was believed that they had hatched a most "damnable plot," commonly called the "terrible *tub plot.*" But it was *"not* correct." They searched the tub, the old woman, the mulattos and the negro wench, (which was a very "correct" procedure) for dispatches; which they (the feds.) said, were sent by the French Directory, to the American JACOBINS, Jefferson, Gallatin, Madison and others; but they found none. Ah cruel disappointment! The tub had not the dispatches neither had the wench!! Of course "This was NOT correct."

Robert Goodloe Harper, said he had discovered another plot, commonly called the Tailor plot, (for the feds. deal largely in plots) but, this turned out almost as unfortunately for federalism, as the aforesaid "tub plot." The feds. had a poor Tailor in Philadelphia arrested, because, like an honest man, he followed his trade, and *made coats and jackets.* After searching his shop most diligently, they found, wonderful to relate!—a quantity of *coats and jackets.* Robert said, that they should soon find a quantity of *pikes* and other implements of war, intended to arm the wild Irishmen. None however were found. The fact was, that the frightened imagination of Robert, had magnified some dozens of *needles* into as many thousand *pikes of ten feet long,* and his *thimbles* into eighteen inch *mortars.* This was all correct in the day of it; but it has since proved, like the rest of federal stories, very *"in-*correct." The federalists have told us, in case Jefferson was elected, that religion would be destroyed, our liberties overturned, the marriage covenant annihilated and Priests massacred. But they now find, that the democrats are as willing to *read their bibles* and to *get married to fine girls,* as themselves. These however were very *"correct" federal* prophecies in their time; but not *"correct"* enough to be much regarded by democrats.

The story of the massacre of the crew of the ship Ocean, which Dr. Morse made so great a handle of, in his Fast Sermon, was very *"correct"* for a *few weeks.* It could not last long;— for it was *not true*. But what cared the feds. and the Doctor for that?—It had answered the purpose for which it was intended. It proved to be, a most excellent *federal* electioneering *trick*. Federalism was helped by it— a source of great consolation it must be confessed to a *pious* federal parson.

The federalists have so long been in the habit of saying so many *"incorrect"* things, that the people of the United States think it the most *"correct"* course to pay no regard to their falsehoods. ...[9]

Also brought up for years after they happened were the national fast days called for by John Adams as president in 1798 and 1799, which were seen as both political and a dangerous mixing of church and state, and the first of which sparked a protest in Philadelphia that forced Adams to hide in his house. Adams himself would later even credit one of them with his loss to Jefferson in 1800.

Describing his 1798 fast day to Jefferson in 1813, Adams wrote:

... I have no doubt you was fast asleep in philosophical Tranquility, when ten thousand People, and perhaps many more, were parading the Streets of Philadelphia, on the Evening of my Fast Day. When even Governor Mifflin himself, thought it his Duty to order a Patrol of Horse and Foot to preserve the peace. when Markett Street was as full as Men could Stand by one another, and even before my Door; when Some of my Domesticks in Phrenzy, determined to Sacrifice their Lives in my defence; when all were ready to make a desperate Salley among the multitude, and others were with difficulty and danger dragged back by the others; when I myself judged it prudent and necessary to order Chests of Arms from the War Office to be brought through bye Lanes and back Doors: determined to defend my House att the Expence of my Life, and the Lives of the few, very few Domesticks and Friends within it. ...[10]

---

9. *Republican Spy,* Northampton, MA, June 3, 1806, 3.
10. John Adams to Thomas Jefferson, June 30, 1813. Lester J. Cappon, ed., *The Adams-Jefferson Letters: The Complete Correspondence Between Thomas Jefferson and Abigail and John Adams,* (Chapel Hill, NC: The University of North Carolina Press, 1959), 347.

Adams wrote to Benjamin Rush in 1812:

The National Fast recommended by me turned me out of Office. It was connected with, the general assembly of the Presbyterian Church, which I had no concern in. That assembly has allarmed and alienated Quakers, Anabaptists, Mennonists, Moravians, Sweedenborgians, Methodists, Catholicks, protestant Episcopalians, Arians, Socinians, Armenians &c, &c, &c, Atheists and Deists might be added. A general Suspicion prevailed that the Presbyterian Church was ambitious and aimed at an Establishment as a National Church. I was represented as a Presbyterian and at the head of this political and ecclesiastical Project. The secret whispers ran through them [all the Sects] "Let Us have Jefferson, Madison, Burr, any body, whether they be Philosophers, Deists, or even Atheists, rather than a Presbyterian President." This principle is at the bottom of the unpopularity of national Fasts and Thanksgiving. Nothing is more dreaded than the National Government meddling with Religion.[11]

In 1806, an article in the *American Mercury* linked the start of Federalist political preaching to Adams's 1798 fast day:

THE CLERGY.

IT will be recollected that in a sermon at Branford on last Thanksgiving day Mr. Jefferson was called *a debauchee, an infidel and a liar.* In commenting on this abandoned outrage on sound things we have presented as a fact, *'that the leading civilians have taken great pains to draw the whole body of the clergy into their service.'*

We might refer the reader to the days of former centuries, and shew how uniformly the influence of the clergy has been courted by civilians in order to bear down on the common people; but it will be sufficient to begin with Mr. Adams' national fast-day. He had advanced rapidly in his wild experiments of St. Marino balances, in his army and navy, in

---

11. John Adams to Benjamin Rush, June 12, 1812. *Old Family Letters: Copied from the Originals for Alexander Biddle,* (Philadelphia: J.B. Lippincott Company, 1892), 392-393.

his increase of debt and taxes, and in his hole of nobles, and
he had talked rather freely in favor of a limited monarchy;
in fact he was so full of the most stupendous fabric of human
invention, that the people had begun to distrust him. Of
course the next process was to institute a reign of terror and
secure the influence of the clergy.

The appointment of a national fast-day was exactly in
point for the last purpose. It was true that we had occasion
to humble ourselves before God for our offences, which had
brought down the heavy judgement of such an administration. We had occasion to be humble, because our brethren
had fought and bled for blessings, which our American nobles
had determined that the people should never enjoy. Stamp-
act, land-tax, alien and sedition act, army and navy, with a
debt rapidly rising above 70 millions of dollars, and swarms
of excise-men to devour the people's substance, were abun-
dant causes of humiliation; but far other motives led up this
national fast-day: the object was to humble the democrats
and to exalt the administration. Mr. Adams had no more right
to appoint a national fast day, or to recommend one, than his
door-keeper, but by this public act he was to place himself,
like George 3d, at the head of his visible Church, and at his
nod all the priests thro'-out the continent were to read his
proclamation, and to convoke their people for *his* praise.

With great pomp Mr. Adams's fast-day was ushered in, and
it was the darkest day for Christianity, which Connecticut
ever experienced. The proclamation was for a general dispen-
sation for preaching and praying politically, and political sermons we had in abundance; far better calculated to make
infidels than all the writings of Mr. Paine. The worst of the
case was, that on this day many clergymen, who had before
kept aloof from politics, were drawn to pray and preach politics. The railing, which had confined the clergy to the neigh-
bourhood of the altar, was on that day broken down; many of
the clergy were on that day let loose, from the peculiar service
of their master, to prate politics among the people, and to
read in their families the slanders of federal papers against
the present President, to electioneer for the slanderers.

If the life of Mr. Adams could be protracted to the term

of that of Methuselah, and the whole of it devoted to the most sincere and solemn services of religion, he could never repair one half of the breaches, which on that day he made in the walls of Jerusalem. While his followers were shouting his high praises, every sincere christian mourned. Productive as this day was of divisions in towns and societies, yet we have to rejoice that it was too late in the day for this miserable farce to have its desired effect; eleven twelfths of the people of the United States abhor the men and measures, which that day was appointed to idolize.

The political effect of that fast-day in Connecticut was, the removal of one Justice of the peace, (Mr. Law of Cheshire) because his hired man ploughed *unhallowed* ground on said day, and the loss of a thousand friends of the administration. In Connecticut, where it was expected that this political fast-day would run and be glorified more than elsewhere, the administration lost ground: many people of this State were not prepared to have a *political* head of the church, nor a President for life nor eternal debt, nor did they wish to leave the appointment of holy days to the nobles of the cabinet.

But though Mr. Adams lost all, though his measures are repealed and his power is at an end, yet the influence of the clergy, secured at that time, has kept up federalism to this time in Connecticut. *Public opinion is now taking this business in charge.* We no longer hear thanks publicly returned for the removal by death of Thomas Jefferson.* We no longer hear him satirically lashed in prayer before the superior court. We often hear prayers that his life may be preserved, and that he may be enabled to discharge faithfully the duties of his exalted station. We now and then hear of a political sermon, in which his friends and measures are abused, and for once we hear that a reverend preacher has called him in his pulpit a debauchee, and infidel and a liar.

* *This was done in consequence of a federal electioneering rumour.* [12]

12. *American Mercury,* Hartford, CT, January 2, 1806, 2.

At Yale, the pro-British views of President Timothy Dwight, which would become more prevalent in the coming years, continued to be instilled in the minds of young Federalists:

The young men at Yale College are taught to believe,

That the constitution and administration of the government of Great-Britain is THE BEST IN THE WORLD.

That the information and virtue of the American people, and their constitution of government, are *inferior to other nations, particularly to Great-Britain;* and that the government of the United States *cannot stand in its present form.*

That government has a right, and ought to establish a *particular kind of religion in preference to any other;* that such an establishment is *indispensably necessary* to save their country from ruin. ... [13]

The following story from *The Witness* was written by a somewhat confused visitor to Connecticut who had attended a church where a Federalist minister was preaching politics. As the editor's note at the end of the story points out, the visitor, who was admittedly unfamiliar with Connecticut politics, mistakenly thought the minister was preaching against the Federalists. Whether the story was genuinely written by a confused visitor or was a clever satire, it's an entertaining story.

Having resolved, from various motives, the principal of which was the improvement of health, to spend some time in Connecticut, I lately arrived at one of your County Towns, on a Saturday. Next morning the bell rang, as I supposed for meeting. Having been from my youth in the habit of strict attendance on public worship (though strange as it may appear, educated far from Connecticut!) I joined the throng of well dressed people, and sat down in the house with them. A man, whom I supposed to be a gospel preacher, though set off with a smart cambric collar, a gold bosom

---

13. *The Witness,* Litchfield, CT, February 5, 1806, 3.

pin, and something of a beau withal, after introductory forms began a discourse; from the nature of which I was soon led to suspect I was mistaken as to the object of the meeting. It was evidently a political oration, instead of a gospel sermon, as I had expected. But still circumstances were irreconcileable. It was on the sabbath, in the pious state of Connecticut, in a house much resembling the meeting-houses in my state, and attended with prayer, singing, and all the introductory forms of divine worship. Was it possible that in *this* state, the sacred day and these solemn forms were prostituted to the purpose of a party harangue? I could hardly be convinced at first that I was not dreaming. Had it been in France, I might have supposed that as the church bells had been cast into cannon, so the churches themselves had been converted into political lecture-rooms; and the prefatory solemnities use by the *atheistical nation* only in mockery. But I was in Connecticut, awake, in my right senses, and saw and heard this!

Two or three times, he slightly noticed some passages of scripture (doubtless to make his politics go down better with his audience) with one of which he began his oration, in the same manner as *gospel preachers* do sermons. He seemed to be in great heat, and his drift was evidently to lash *some* party now existing in the state; I could not then be certain *which,* not having sufficient knowledge of your local politics; and tho' some of the audience exhibited plain tokens of extreme gratification; yet as I did not know their names nor political feelings, this circumstance did not enlighten me on that point. A file of newspapers, however, which I have since read, has given me a clue to the application, of which I will give you my understanding by way of *innuendo;* as I am told you have had some late opportunities to become acquainted with this mode of elucidation.

The orator quoted the following words from Isaiah— "For the terrible one is brought to nought, and the scorner is consumed, and all that watch for iniquity are cut off;

"That make a man an offender for a word, and lay a snare for him that reproveth in the gate, and turn aside the just for a thing of nought."

He said that *such men* as were here described had existed in most countries from the earliest ages to the *present time.* As the first instance he mentioned Cain (meaning that the federalists on Litchfield Hill were like Cain, in waylaying and assaulting their brethren with *clubs* and fists)—that *this sort of men* delighted in making themselves *terrible;* and that when *they* had the power, they exhibited *"a reign of terror indeed!"* (meaning *federalists,* who when in power, endeavor to keep it by making themselves *terrible,* by sedition laws and standing armies, or by *crowbars,* by *stand up laws,* by *cowskins,* by public *prosecutions,* by pulpit denunciations, by prostituting the weight of official character to sanctify abuse and slander, and by all manner of persecutions to crush opposition; which is surely "a reign of terror indeed")—That such men were scoffers at religion, and blasphemers, (meaning that federalists had mocked at religion by burlesquing in the *Chronicles,* and by publishing a blasphemous and obscene parody on a Psalm of David, called *Moll Cary,* in the *Monitor, Courant,* &c.)—That *such men* were always on the watch for some fault or imprudence in their neighbors, of which they might take advantage, for the gratification of their own malice (meaning the close scrutiny with which the *federalists* peruse republican papers, to find some pretence for prosecution, and the strict watch they and their spies keep over the mouths of their republican neighbors, so that nothing which can be twisted into a foundation for an action of slander may escape their notice)—that such men are prone to slander and abuse, and gorge upon the fairest reputations (meaning that federalists have been in the constant habit of publishing false tales of Mr. Jefferson, about *Black Sal, Mrs. Walker,* &c. also declaring in the federal papers that Mr. Jefferson was a *coward,* a *proverbial liar,* a *miscreant,* &c. and calling republicans of the best characters in this state, *swindlers, adulterers, drunkards, atheists,* &c.)—That this description of people "make men offenders for a word: by distorting the words of others, and publishing some and suppressing other parts of a speech or writing, to the disadvantage of the author (meaning, among other things, the shameful manner in which unprincipled *federalists* have misquoted Mr. Jefferson's Notes on Virginia, and his remark to the Italian priest; in order to stigmatize him with indifference to or hatred of religion)—that the men he was speaking of abused ministers of the gospel (meaning that the federalists had abused Mr. Stanley Griswold, insomuch that he had no alternative but to leave the ministry and the state, or engage, in his own defence, in unchristian strife; and that they had stiled him an apostate, and the Rev. Mr. Cowles an *idiot)*—that such men hated and opposed the magistrates, and men who were vested with authority, because they restrained the gratification of their lusts (meaning that the *federalists* revile and oppose the Chief Magistrate of the Union, because he *does not* bestow all the offices on them)—that the settled enmity of *these men* to religion was evinced by their sneering at *Missionaries* (meaning that the *federalists* had, in the Monitor, given the title of Missionaries to *electioneering agents)*—and that this sort of men further evinced that enmity by ridiculing vital piety (meaning *federal* Ellsworth's tumbling St Paul into the dung, and exalting *self-righteousness* above divine grace and mediation.)

He compared them to the persecutors of Daniel (meaning that the *federalists,* like those persecutors, torture their invention to distress every one who will not bow to their standard of opinion.) He compared them to the Pharisees of old (meaning the *federalists,* like the Pharisees, boast of their superior regard to law and order, display their pretensions to religion at the corner of streets and on house-tops, to be seen of men, and say to all other men, "stand off, we are holier than ye!")

I may not have recollected the precise words of the orator, nor every minute division of the Oration; but I am confident that all worth remembering is here, in substance, correctly stated.

However pleased I may have been with this ingenious satire upon *federalism,* I cannot but regret that a time and place proper for reflections of a less worldly nature, should have been appropriated to this business. It is so much of a piece with the conduct of the Jews, who converted God's

Temple into an Exchange. Of the two cases, the former is least impious; for though the Jews profaned the temple, they respected the sabbath.

                                        SOJOURNER.

[Our correspondent has been led into a gross, though a natural mistake. What he supposes to have been spoken for a political Oration against the federalists, was in fact delivered by a federal clergyman, for a sermon! The application of our friend the sojourner is such as occurred to us at the time; nor should we have been certain that it was not *meant* for a blow at his old *federal* friends, had not some of the leaky young feds given notice that the Democrats were to be lashed in that sermon, *a day or two before it was delivered!*][14]

The following excerpt is from *The Witness's* New Year's poem for 1806. To set the stage, the observer is a sailor who has just returned home, having missed the first five years of Jefferson's presidency because he was in Tripoli and had been taken captive there. The returning sailor is shocked to see that the Federalists' predictions about a Jefferson presidency had not come true.

But mark! a steeple meets his eyes!
He stands petrescent with surprise!
'What! Jefferson still in his seat,
'And churches not demolished yet?
'One place of worship yet secure,
'It must be some illusion sure!
'No—'tis the same; for now I see
'Where oft, in youth's mischievous glee,
I sketch'd rude shapes of beasts and birds,
'Upon its walls—and smutty words—
'Perhaps 'tis sav'd for heathen uses,
'Plays, pantomimes, or worse abuses—
'Perhaps Tom Paine from Reason preaches,
'Or Palmer here his doctrine teaches—
'But—heaven bless us?—who comes here,

14. *The Witness*, Litchfield, CT, April 2, 1806, 3.

'Array'd in sanctimonious geer?
'And can one priest be left alive,
'At close on *eighteen hundred five?*
''Tis he, if I can trust my sight,
'Who cheer'd my youth with heav'nly light!
'What! can those pious men have lied,
'Who said, should Jefferson preside,
'Our priests shall fall, our bibles burn,
'And all religion met with scorn?
'Ah! now I have it—here within
'Must be the *place du Guillotin;*
'And here, his worldly efforts baffled,
'The parson marches to the scaffold.
'And some, remaining faithful still,
'Are come to take their last farewell.
'I'll in, and with attentive eyes
'Learn how a pious martyr dies—
—'No scaffold here? No Guillotine?
'Then what does all this bustle mean?
'Sure no religion cheers the realm,
'Where such an infidel's at helm!
'Perhaps this Rev'rence (who can tell)
'For life, has turn'd an infidel!
'From *Reason* we may hear a text—
'A Bible, too! what wonder next?
'A Bible, in this public place!
'May be they hide it on week days.
'Of all strange things, of which we read,
'This is most wonderful indeed.
'That Bible, priest or church appears,
'When Jefferson has rul'd FIVE YEARS!!
'Alas! I fear 'tis but a dream,
'Of bliss a transitory gleam,
'My freedom, too, may be ideal,
'And stripes and bondage yet prove real!'

    A quondam school-mate next he meets,
Who with an honest welcome greets;
Gives joy—asks news from foreign places,
And so forth, usual in such cases.

"To see me, soon, I hope you'll come—
"I've marry'd, since you went from home."
'Married!—when doctrines of *New School*
'Prevail, and Jacobins bear rule?
'Were not we told by pious men,
'Who surely *could* not lie—that when
'Democracy should reign, unhallow'd,
'No marriage contract would be valid—
'Our tender wives be ravish'd from us,
'By that infernal atheist THOMAS?
'And ev'ry man and ev'ry woman,
'Without distinction herd in common?—
'but ev'ry matter fairly weigh'd,
'I'll come and see you next *decade*.'[15]
"*Decade! Decade!* what means my friend?
We've no such here, you may depend!"
'What! no decades! you surely jest!
'Well! I am puzzled I protest!
'Our churches standing—parsons living—
'Our bibles safe—religion thriving—
'No Guillotines built for beheading—
'And couples, thick as ever wedding—
'And sabbaths ev'ry seventh day'
'Recurring in the *good old* way—
'Though we are govern'd, strange to tell!
'By Jefferson, that infidel!'[16]

15. A reference to the French Revolutionary calendar, in which, to remove all religious influence, seven day weeks were replaced by the month being divided into three decades of ten days each.
16. *The Witness*, Litchfield, CT, January 8, 1806, 4.

$\backsim$ **1807** $\sim$

Voter turnout in Connecticut for the spring election decreased significantly on both sides from the high of the previous year. Trumbull was reelected governor with 11,959 votes to Hart's 7,971, and Treadwell was reelected lieutenant governor with 10,851 votes to Spalding's 7,025. The number of Republicans in the House remained about the same, but would rise to 75 in the fall. The Council, as usual, remained all Federalist.

There was no Republican festival this year, and the Chesapeake crisis put a damper on the summer's Independence Day celebrations.

On June 22, in one of the early events in the lead-up to the War of 1812, the British ship HMS *Leopard* fired on and boarded the American ship USS *Chesapeake* off the coast of Norfolk, Virginia, with a search warrant to search the ship for British deserters. Three Americans were killed in the incident, and eighteen crew members were wounded, one later dying from his injuries. Of the four sailors taken by the British, only one was a British citizen. The others were Americans who had been impressed into service in the Royal Navy.

The impressment of American sailors by the British was one of the primary causes of the War of 1812. At war with France in the Napoleonic Wars since 1803, the British Navy had a shortage of sailors. Their answer was impressment, with "press gangs" removing seamen from American merchant vessels and forcing them into service in the Royal Navy, under the guise of looking for British deserters. While there were British deserters who had enlisted in the American merchant marines, only about one in ten seamen taken by the British were British. The rest were Americans or citizens from other neutral countries. An estimated 6,000 American seamen were impressed by the British before America declared war in 1812. Britain and France both imposed trade restrictions, which also disrupted American trade, and France as well as Britain seized American cargoes, although Britain was the primary offender.

In 1806, in response to the seizure of American seamen and goods, Congress had passed the Non-Importation Act, which prohibited the importation from Britain of a list of items that the United States could produce at home, but this act was never put into effect. With Britain issuing a proclamation to impress even more American seamen, and both Britain and France disrupting neutral trade to prevent trade with the other, the Jefferson administration took more drastic action, passing the Embargo Act in December 1807, prohibiting all foreign trade. The embargo would hurt the United States far more than it hurt Britain and became unpopular with both parties.

⌐

In Connecticut, the question of what, exactly, the Federalists' political principles were remained a subject for Republican writers, as explored in this dialogue between a Republican and an "honest Federalist," printed in the Litchfield *Witness:*

> *The following dialogue between an honest federalist and an inquisitive republican exhibits much of the difference between the parties in Connecticut.*
>
> *Republican.*—Do you believe that the common federalists in the state understand the principles and objects of your leading federalists?
>
> *Federalist.*—They certainly do not understand them—they are not capable of comprehending sound principles of government; they must rely on men of information, and follow them.
>
> *Rep.* Would it not be honest for you to tell your principles plainly to the people?

Fed. We have no principles of which we are ashamed— but it would answer no good purpose to enter into explanations with the common people.

Rep. But do not the *"common people"* support the government—and are they not entitled to the whole truth, and nothing but the truth?

Fed. The common people are entitled to be governed upon sound, rational principles.

Rep. What are those principles?

Fed. You know what I was in principle before and during the revolution. I was a monarchist, and am so still. The government of the world is monarchical—all the respectable states of the world are monarchies. I now call myself a federalist, and believe as they do; and they believe and act as I do—you never heard me call myself a federal republican; for I am in no respect a republican. Republics may last for a little time; but they cannot be durable. Frequent elections are more dangerous than standing armies. Power must be vested in some one. Men of education, wealth, and of influential families, will sooner or later get the power, in every country; and they ought to have it; they were born to govern; others were born to obey. You now understand what I mean by sound, rational principles.

Rep. But are these the principles of 1776?

Fed. Surely they are not. The principles of 1776 were too full of your liberty and equality for my notion.

Rep. Are your "sound principles" those of the constitution of the United States?

Fed. Certainly not. I was an enemy to that constitution, because it guaranteed to every state in the union a republican form of government. I abhor all paper constitutions;[1] they are too easily read; they impose undue shackles upon the ruling powers; they give occasion to clamor against the government. If Connecticut had what is called a constitution of civil government, I would emigrate to Canada. Property

---

1. Britain does not have a written constitution. It has the Magna Carta, a bill of rights, and centuries of laws and conventions, which all together are referred to as the British constitution, not unlike Connecticut's charter and laws enacted under that charter's being considered a constitution by the Federalists.

is never secure, so long as the rich and the learned in society can be called to order by the poor and illiterate.—

Rep. Then you acknowledge that Connecticut has no Constitution?

Fed. No man ever heard me call the old Charter or the Bill of Rights, or *certain usages,* a constitution. When the justices were removed I declared to you and others that they ought to be removed for their perverse political sentiments, and for trying to get power out of the hands of their betters; but I frankly declared that Connecticut had no Constitution.

Rep. You always had the credit of frankness: now tell me plainly, do our Governor and Council and Members of Congress and federal Lawyers think as you do?

Fed. You see me often among those men; we visit together; we make up tickets and vote together; we rejoice together over the successes of England; and we mourn together over her adversities. I am proud to say that we harmonize in all respects; and am more proud because I have been uniform in my political course. I held no office and did no business through the war: these federalists, (whom I consider, between you and I, as a second rate set of monarchists) were pretending to be whigs; and some of them were active and violent against the principles which they now support. I am proud of their repentance—and there is another class of men whose influence in *favor of monarchy* is worth more than all the rest. They are what your party profanely call the *political* clergy. With all my moderation, I would freely have executed some of your party for their attacks upon this excellent class of men—monarchs and thrones are more indebted to them than to armies and nobility.

Rep. Then you contend that clergymen have a right to act as politicians?

Fed. I contend that clergymen are in the world, and that they have wives and children and some property in it; and that they have their feelings as well as other men. The old *Saybrook Platform* ministers are all monarchists; The *platform* itself is a perfect model of monarchy. The common people may find some among the humbler orders of ministry who profess to be republicans; but look to the head of our College, and of our Episcopal Church; do you see anything like republicanism in those *high places?*

Rep. But the clergy pay no taxes, and therefore ought not to be represented.

Fed. That is one of your '76 doctrines, which I do not believe in.

Rep. But the gospel seems to be against clergymen's busying themselves with politics.

Fed. That may or may not be. I am no theologian; but am a thorough, open monarchist; commonly called a federalist. I was always sorry to leave George III—but as that is done, it is my wish to have a king, or a president for life, or something else than a representative democracy.

Rep. I have long been persuaded that the leading federalists of this state were monarchists; but have never before heard it acknowledged by one of the party.

Fed. I have always told the federal leaders to come out boldly and avow their principles. I endeavored to shame some of them out of the meanness of calling themselves *federal republicans.* Federalism, as explained and practised by Mr. Adams, was the young growth of monarchy. If the leaders of his administration had come out boldly and told the people, that a republican government was not worth the trouble of experiment, and that a monarchy was the only legitimate government, they would have been in power at this day. Mr. Adams would have borne the title of his majesty JOHN the first of America; we should have had an alliance offensive and defensive with the mistress of the ocean. In the act of besieging slowly the public mind, the federalists were suspected of some dark work, and buried suddenly in the trenches. Want of courage to storm the public mind was the ruin of the best hopes of the country. Hamilton, Ross, Morris and Dayton would have led us to glory; but those who ought to have followed were panic struck.

Rep. Then you approve Adams's administration?

Fed. He made an excellent beginning—eight years more would have crowned the work.

Rep. If you are right in all this, how comes it to pass that so many states, and so many governors and legislatures are republicans—and how happens it that Mr. Jefferson was re-elected by 162 votes against 14?

Fed. Precisely because in this country 162 parts out of 176 are weak and illiterate, and consequently democratic. The 14 parts represent the men whose right it is to govern. When those who ought to obey set up to rule; and those who ought to rule are forced to obey, every thing will go wrong, and you will have just such men as Jefferson, Madison, Gallatin, &c. at the head of affairs!

Rep. But the people are relieved from some burdens, and the national debt is diminished.

Fed. These are only the tricks of Demagogues! a people relieved from burdens will be clamorous about liberty and equality; and the reduction of a national debt destroys the stability of government. England, that wonder of the world, has a national debt of 5 or 6 hundred millions sterling—annually increasing—and the addition of every hundred million has added to her strength. All the cardinal measures of Mr. Adams tended to this great and much desired object; but those of Mr. Jefferson tend directly to the contrary; and if our national debt should, through the weakness of democracy, be entirely paid off, any president after that time, would be *no more than first citizen of the country, for the time being.*

Rep. Are you perfectly persuaded that the leading federalists in this state will agree with you in these explanations?

Fed. Beyond all question, if they will disclose as honestly as I have endeavored to do. It is not their interest to conceal! they have had an awful example of the danger of concealing their principles: the people here cannot long be deceived by the name of *federal republicans;* they already discern more than their votes tell us of. I do not hesitate to allow, that a great majority of the common people are republicans; we have too many demagogues among us. My policy would have saved federalism forever in Connecticut; and it may yet be saved, if the leading federalists will but universally declare in favor of monarchy; if they will universally declare that Mr. Adams's book [2] written in praise of the British monarchical form of government is their "political bible."

The influence of the clergy is still considerable—the influence of the lawyers is great—the privileged orders in this state are numerous and weighty—the power of bestowing offices has effect—political rumors are very useful—decisions of courts may aid the cause—if Moses and Aaron will be awake and united, MY principles will continue to prevail:—but rest assured that monarchy is the life and soul of Connecticut federalism.—I say this in the pride of my heart, and (the cant of jacobins notwithstanding) to the horror of the Trumbulls, the Treadwells, and Ellsworths, who preside over the destinies of our state. [3]

Another article in *The Witness* predicted that the downfall of Connecticut's Federalists would come, as it had in the rest of the country, when the rank and file Federalists rose up against the party's aristocratic leaders:

GENTLEMEN AND SIMPLEMEN.

The political bible has been sustained in Connecticut, as it was under Mr. Adams' administration, by declaring that all the people, except a few infidels, believe in this bible, and in the distinctions of *gentlemen* and *simplemen*.

It was not true under Mr. Adams, but the people were in no condition to express their real sentiments; they feared alien and sedition acts and the universal denunciations about atheism, jacobinism and illuminatism, but at last they broke every restraint and shewed their contempt of the

---

2. Adams's book *A Defence of the Constitutions of Government of the United States of America*, in which he praised the British constitution, writing: "I only contend that the English constitution is, in theory, the most stupendous fabrick of human invention, both for the adjustment of the balance, and the prevention of its vibrations; and that the Americans ought to be applauded instead of censured, for imitating it, as far as they have." The first part of that sentence, "I only contend that the English constitution is, in theory, the most stupendous fabrick of human invention," was quoted by Republicans as evidence that Adams was a monarchist, ignoring that Adams went on to point out the differences in America's government, such as rulers not being hereditary.

3. *The Witness,* Litchfield, CT, February 25, 1807, 3.

political bible and of every man, who endeavoured to palm it upon the public as political truth.

Take off our restraints in Connecticut, call in your *political* priests, restrain your federal papers within the bounds of decency, dismiss your official tools and partizans, and the people will soon give you their opinion of the political bible and you, *gentlemen,* who are palming it and yourselves upon the *simplemen.*

A Catholic priest will tell you that the common Catholics believe in transubstantiation, yet not one of the common people ever believed a doctrine so palpably absurd and evidently false, but how could a common Catholic hazard a declaration of his disbelief? He had before him a certain loss of reputation and property and a probability of torture from a tribunal of Inquisition.

You may boast that the *simplemen* of Connecticut believe the charter of king Charles to be our civil Constitution; they believe it just as much as they believe the ashes of Charles II to be the living governor Trumbull.

You may boast that the people prefer lawyers to all other classes of men for legislators. They know the consequence if they contradict you.

The people of this state, *(simple* as you lawyers deem them) know that our steady habits have been violated, that laws, considered fundamental, have been repealed; that valuable justices have been removed to make way for *hemlock* justices; that many clergy have been pressed into service to prevent rebellion against an order of things full of novelty and oppression; that pulpits and courts of justice have been repeatedly and publicly called on to be prostituted to the service of the *gentlemen* in their contest for all power of the State. Thousands, who have served on the federal side, abhor the service, but they are not yet prepared for your great slaughter-house ...

The system of exalting one class of men in Connecticut to the exclusion of all others is now completed in Connecticut. The distinction between gentlemen and simplemen is as evident as the distinction between lords and commons in England.

Mr. Webster defines a tory to be an advocate for the union of Church and State. A Church and State government is a *tory* government; ours is such a church and state government, or a Moses and Aaron government, in proof of which read a few modern election sermons, attend a few proxies, examine a few federal newspapers. Federal Moses and federal Aaron walk hand in hand in Connecticut. Aaron prays for the *gentlemen* lawyers and Moses prays for the *political* priests.

The government of Mr. Adams appeared strong in 1798; that of Vienna appeared invincible in 1805; that of Prussia bid defiance to the arms of France in 1806; they are all now chop-fallen, as you, *gentlemen* federal lawyers of Connecticut will be, whenever the *simplemen* shall dare to exercise their votes according to their consciences.[4]

On the same theme, the writer of this letter to the *Political Observatory* expressed their "not rightly understanding" why they had become a Federalist:

Messrs. Printers,
Having been taught, from early childhood, to believe in the consummate greatness of John Adams, and the infallibility of his administration, I was naturally led to cooperate with federalists in opposing the election to office of a political sect styling themselves republicans, but which the leaders of our party told us were *democrats.* Not rightly understanding the signification of the word, I was taught to consider them as allied to demons, or devils, and as holding intercourse with them. Between these kindred spirits I supposed a league to be formed, with the intent to overthrow the civil and religious institutions of our country—and when Mr. Jefferson entered into office, I believed the grand project of such an overthrow would soon be accomplished.

Being thus led, by the continual asseverations of federal *great men,* into these absurd opinions; and these opinions being firmly established by seeing the same assertions

4. *The Witness,* Litchfield, CT, April 8, 1807, 2-3.

confirmed in every newspaper my *instructors* and my *prejudice* allowed me to read, I waited, for a long time, with fearful apprehensions, to see RELIGION driven from her once peaceful abodes, and the GODDESS of LIBERTY supplanted by the destroying arm of ANARCHY. But, blessed stars! ye have been more propitious! Instead of rebellion, ye have nursed us in the chambers of peace; instead of taking from us our civil and religious immunities, you have continued to us a government of laws, and increased our stores of general happiness, under an administration guided by integrity and virtuous principles.

My fears of those anticipated disasters having, by degrees, evaporated, as more happy events continued to prove them merely chimerical; and finding no abatement in federalists to excite alarm, by declaring our present rulers to be demagogues and impostors, although these declarations are made against the conviction of open day; I have been led, Messrs. Printers, to doubt the integrity of these men, and my conviction of their dishonesty gains strength by every day's experience.

Now, Messrs. Printers, as I have plainly stated to you the *rise, progress,* and *decline* of my federal principles, and wishing no longer to adhere to a party who have uniformly practised deception on the credulity of many honest votaries to their cause, I would beg, with due penitence for my political folly, to be enrolled on the list of republican followers, whose course, experience has taught me, is the surest way to political happiness.[5]

Republican papers in other parts of the country often remarked about New England's religious establishments, and what enemies to religious freedom the Federalists were. The following is from the *National Intelligencer* in Washington, D.C., the mouthpiece of the Jefferson administration, or Jefferson's "Royal Gazette," as one Federalist paper called it.

... Our revolution established the great principle, not

---

5. *Political Observatory,* Walpole, NH, July 20, 1807, 2.

merely of religious toleration, but of the entire separation of religious from political institutions.

Have the republicans, in a solitary instance, aimed at invading this great principle? Have they erected inquisitions? Have they devised religious establishments in any form? Have they given a preference to one sect over another? Have they laid taxes for the support of religion, thereby making the maintenance of the latter a thing of coercion and not of choice? Have they required religious tests, thereby excluding those of particular tenets from a participation in the government? None of these invasions of conscience, none of these infractions of the great compact that unites us together are, or can be charged upon them. On the contrary, they have passed many laws to guarantee the enjoyment of equal religious privileges, and the principles they invariably inculcate are those of unlimited freedom of conscience and worship. Need we appeal to what is fresh in the recollection of every enlightened man—to the memorable act of the Virginia legislature penned by the most distinguished republican in the union?[6] Need we appeal to the enlightened principles of a Franklin and a Rittenhouse,[7] the illustrious coadjutors of a Penn? Need we appeal to the constitution of the United States, free from the reproach of a religious test, in the formation of which a Madison so largely participated? These are positive, irrefragable proofs that the most distinguished disciples of republicanism are the firm friends of religious liberty.

Contemplate the opposite side of the picture; and you behold whatever remains in our political institutions, or habits, that partakes of the spirit of bigotry, or ecclesiastical establishment, under the special guardianship of federalism. In New-England, until lately, entirely under the rod of federalism, and part of it still remaining in its fetters, there still exists a religious establishment. We say a religious establishment, for, however accommodating the spirit that upholds such an institution may be to the temper of the times, there cannot exist a doubt that the principle of an establishment

6. Jefferson's Virginia Statute for Religious Freedom.
7. American scientist David Rittenhouse.

is still retained, which may hereafter, as circumstances shall justify it, be exemplified in the rage of intolerance and persecution. There a man is compelled to pay a tax for the support of religious worship. So far the act is coercive—so far the civil power maintains an ecclesiastical establishment. This is undeniable. A man, whose temple is his own conscience, who cannot, among the various existing sects, find one congenial to his own sentiments, is constrained to contribute towards the maintenance of an establishment, to which he is in his conscience opposed. Here then is a palpable violation of conscience, one of the great principles of the revolution. This despotism over the conscience, for it deserves not a milder name, is maintained by federalists. Republicans declaim it, and deem it a reproach. In the republican states such a principle does not exist, and would not be tolerated. It will be observed that these last remarks are not intended to be applied to those states in New-England, in which the republican principle has recently triumphed. Time has not yet elapsed for them to destroy the abuses which have crept into their systems under the auspices of federalism.

Contrast these establishments with the memorable act of the Virginia legislature, penned by Jefferson thirty years ago ...[8]

The Witness's New Year's poem for 1807 covered a range of subjects and events — Federalist lies, the prosecution of Federalist publishers and writers by the newly appointed Republican federal district judge, the prosecution and imprisonment of *The Witness's* own editor, Selleck Osborne (the likely author of the poem), and the 1806 Sixth of August festival in the Federalist stronghold of Litchfield.

Some background information is required to understand all the poem's references.

After years of Republican editors in Connecticut being prosecuted for libel in the Federalist state courts, the Republicans attempted revenge. In February 1806, Jefferson appointed Pierpont Edwards

---

8. *National Intelligencer,* Washington, DC, May 6, 1807, 3.

federal district court judge in Connecticut to replace Federalist Richard Law, who had died in January. Jefferson also appointed a Republican district attorney, Hezekiah Huntington. With Connecticut's federal court in Republican control, Huntington brought charges against six prominent Federalists, including two clergymen, for seditious libel and slander against Jefferson. The six, all indicted in April and May of 1806 by Republican grand juries, were Federalist state court Judge Tapping Reeve, writing in the Litchfield *Monitor* under various pseudonyms including "Phocion," Thomas Collier, the *Monitor's* editor, *Courant* publishers Barzillai Hudson and George Goodwin, and Congregationalist minister Azel Backus and ministry candidate Thaddeus Osgood for statements they had made about Jefferson in their sermons.

It was during this time when the Federalists were being indicted by Republicans that Selleck Osborne, the editor of *The Witness,* was prosecuted and convicted by a Federalist state court for libel against Federalist Julius Deming.

The cases against the six Federalists were plagued with problems, not the least of which was the question of whether or not a federal court even had jurisdiction in common law cases.

The cases were scheduled to be heard in April 1807, but the indictments had defects and the trials could not proceed. Edwards dismissed the case against Tapping Reeve, who was married to his niece, Sally Burr, Aaron Burr's sister, and got so frustrated by the defective indictments that when Huntington got to the last case, that of Thaddeus Osgood, he dismissed that one, two. The cases that would go forward, but which couldn't go forward until Justice Henry Brockholst Livingston,[9] the circuit judge for Connecticut, was brought in to decide the question of whether or not a federal court had jurisdiction in these common law cases, were those of Hudson and Goodwin, Collier, and Azel Backus. These cases, with new indictments, were set to be heard in September 1807.

Jefferson wanted Edwards to dismiss these cases. Why? Because in the case of Azel Backus, one of the stories that Backus was planning to use to justify his statements against Jefferson was actually true, and Jefferson did not want this coming out in a trial.

With all the lies spread by the Federalists about Jefferson, the

9. Justice Henry Brockholst Livingston was an associate justice on the Supreme Court. At this time, Supreme Court justices also served as federal circuit court judges.

Republicans, including Judge Edwards and District Attorney Huntington, didn't believe there was any truth to any story told by the Federalists. But two of the stories were actually true — the story of Jefferson's having children by his slave Sally Hemings and the story of his trying as a young man to seduce Mrs. Walker, the wife of his friend and neighbor John Walker, both of which were exposed in 1802 by yellow journalist James Callender, with the Mrs. Walker story being brought back into the spotlight in 1805 with the publication of Tom Turner's letter.

The case against Backus was for his calling Jefferson "a liar, whoremaster, debaucher, drunkard, gambler." In July 1807, Backus's lawyers summoned witnesses from Virginia, including John Walker and James Madison, to testify that the story of Jefferson and Mrs. Walker was true. Jefferson, for obvious reasons, did not want this to happen, so he interfered, asking his postmaster general, Connecticut native Gideon Granger, to get Edwards and Huntington to drop their prosecution of the Federalists, and writing to Madison telling him to ignore the subpoena and to tell the other witnesses to do likewise, saying that they couldn't be legally compelled to appear in court in Connecticut.

The cases against Backus and Collier were dismissed in April 1808. The only case to go forward was that against Hudson and Goodwin. That case would be decided in 1812 by the Supreme Court, which ruled that a federal court does not have jurisdiction in a common law libel case.

When *The Witness's* New Year's poem for 1807 appeared in January, the outcome of these cases was of course not yet known. All that had happened as of that point were the initial indictments, with the first hearings to be heard in April 1807.

> Here let us trace, in stile concise,
> A hasty sketch of fed'ral lies.
> *Black Sal* was brought upon the carpet,
> A worthy theme for feds to harp at—
> In ev'ry state, thro' ev'ry town
> *Black Sal* was bandy'd up and down—
> And all remember, young and old,
> The won'drous tale, so often told;
> Around with't piously they trudg'd,

And would not in their zeal have grudg'd
T' have kiss'd poor *Sal* from cap to shoe,
Could they have *made* the story *true!*

    Scarce can we hit on half the matter,
Newspaper tales and handbill clatter,
That thick as beggar lice, most solemn,
Demurely crawl on ev'ry column;
Yea, to the pulpit take their course,
And keep fast day with *granny Morse.*

    Tom Turner's tale, of direful sound,
With *witch quill life,* danc'd round and round—
French fleet in Chesapeake appear'd,—
French loans! from ev'ry fed was heard;
Ships sold (though on the fed'ral plan)
By Jefferson, that wicked man!
Dire *prophecies* come on in turn,
Churches and bibles all to burn,
Which scar'd old women (as 'twas meant)
And some old fed'ral men, who went
Forth to the field, in doleful dumps,
And hid their bibles in old stumps.
Post and rail fence (our mem'ry reaches)
Jack-knives, cold meat, and vile red breeches;[10]
Tale followed tale, from friend to neighbor,
Till *"Carter's mountain"*[11] fell in labor;
Then rang the cry, from south to north,
Of what the mountain had *brought forth;*

---

10. Jefferson's informal "democratic" behavior as president was a subject of ridicule by the Federalists. He supposedly received a British ambassador in a pair of old red corduroy breeches, and had the "Mammoth loaf" of bread and cold meat brought to the Capitol when Congress was sitting, pulling a jack-knife out of his pocket to cut off a piece of the bread, again in his red breeches.

11. Jefferson's 1781 escape from the British to Carter's Mountain was later turned into a story of cowardice by the Federalists. In June 1781, during the British invasion of Virginia, Jefferson, whose term as governor had just ended, escaped capture by fleeing to Carter's Mountain. The Virginia legislature had fled from Richmond to Charlottesville in May. In early June, Colonel Banastre Tarleton and a British cavalry force raided Charlottesville, hoping to capture members of the legislature and Jefferson. As the legislature fled Charlottesville, some of its members and Jefferson were at Monticello. Jefferson sent his family to safety, and the legislators left, but Jefferson himself did not leave right away. According to a Virginia military officer, Captain Christopher Hudson, who went to warn Jefferson that a party of British cavalrymen was approaching Monticello, Jefferson only left at his urging.

But soon the truth, all things to tell,
Appear'd—and shew'd that all was well—
And, 'spite of ev'ry wild distortion,
It prov'd a fed'ral weak *abortion*.
    Much stuff skipp'd o'er, of fed'ral glory,
We come now to the *tribute story*—
Pronounce it here, before it dies,
The silliest of all silly lies—
Let's tell the tale, and see how't runs—
"Of silver, sixty precious tons
"Was shipp'd—of winds and waves the chance,
"And sent as tribute unto France!"
    "Ye fools and blind!" did ye believe,
By such a *fetch ye* could deceive?
Or think ye would not be detected?
That federal lies must be respected?
If so, why not say out, at once,
"A SILVER SHIP of sixty tons,
"Was made and rigg'd, with masts so tall,
"Of PRECIOUS, *solid silver all!*
"And o'er the waves was seen to dance,
"A tributary ship to France!" ...

    Now to the COURANT let's away,
Briefly, our compliments to pay,
Whose smutty columns, dark and stygian,
Pretend great things, to aid religion—
Supports it (as we see) from wrongs,
With *holy, pure, Moll Carey songs;*
Gives piety a federal dress
Of slander and self-righteousness;
Labors to shew what blessings spring
From Charles the second—Charles the *King!*
But when she finds (to slur her betters)
Tales of *Black Sal* and *Negro letters,*
To deck her pages and her *chapters,*
She's all in transpot—all in raptures—
For nothing charms and makes her free go
Like fœtid scent of female negro—

Then let her sip and taste, at leisure,
Her fill of rapt'rous negro pleasure—
    While we in haste our course pursue,
To take of Litchfield Hill a view—
Great Litchfield Hill! that sacred place
Of righteous bullies—*crowbar*[12] grace—
Where, with great labor, sweat and toiling,
The federal *pot* is constant boiling,
Watch'd over by those *pious* fellows,
Crowding so fierce to ply the bellows,
That each in turn has 'gainst it knock'd,
And got himself most sadly crock'd—
To check these boilings, flames and flaring,
It seems a *cooler* is preparing,
Which Collier may stand chance to get,
When Fed'ral Circuit Court shall sit—
And PHOCION'S *phrenzy* may produce
A *cooler* fitted for his use—
HUDSON and GOODWIN, too 'tis plain,
A *cooler* also may obtain—
While BACKUS, and his loving brother,
OSGOOD, may chance to get another—
If so, perhaps, these last may be
Cool'd down—and brought to know and see,
'Tis more of *gospel* grace and grandeur,
To preach Christianity than slander.
    And now, to save from sad disaster,
Their fame—and serve their evil master,
The *junto*[13] met, without dispute,

12. The article for which Selleck Osborne was sued for libel by Julius Deming included a recounting of the conversation between Deming and Solomon Simmons, the voter Deming allegedly intimidated, with part of the conversation being about a crowbar that a lodger of Simmons's was supposed to have made for Deming, leading the libel prosecution against Osborne to be nicknamed the "crowbar case."

13. The Essex Junto. The term has been attributed to John Hancock, first referring to a group of merchants and lawyers from or with ties to Essex County, Massachusetts who wanted a strong federal government. The group died out once the Constitution was adopted, but was revived when Adams became president, and were Adams's adversaries in the Federalist party. The junto evolved into a small but powerful splinter group of the Federalist party, including influential Federalists from the other New England states as well as Massachusetts.

And there resolv'd to prosecute,
In ev'ry shape, and form and view,
That fed'ral art could twist and screw,
And by their pow'r presum'd to scare—
So that no *Witness* e'er should dare
T' appear against their full leagu'd might,
And bring their hidden deeds to light,
Arm'd at all points, with gracious mien,
They op'd the prosecuting scene—
Strain'd, at a gnat, their throat and skull,
But swallow'd down a *crowbar,* whole—
   Now see men sit, with solemn face,
And judgment give in their own case,
And PHOCION, lest *his* cause should fall,
Act *Plaintiff, ev'dence, judge* and all.
And now behold the victim sent
To dungeon and imprisonment—
As if they thought, by this bold stile,
Their consciences might sleep awhile;
But, sirs, we judge, from what you prate,
Your *conscious ease* has not been great,
But, by detections, has been more
Like paddy's wig, in 'great uproar.'
The sixth of August shew'd such numbers,
As much disturb'd your conscious slumbers,
And made you foam and inward rave,
To see them civilly behave;
Tho' arts were tried, most mean and tricky,
To make them deign to cuff and kick ye,
In vain—ye could not breed a fray,
To break the order of the day—
But then, as *something must be said,*
Of course, lies must be *wholly made*—
So CHAMPION,[14] by the fed'ral rule,
Was made the mighty *scare-crow* tool,
To tell the tale, how he was u'sd,

14. Rev. Judah Champion, the elderly Federalist minister who claimed to have been forcibly kicked out of the meeting house at the Sixth of August festival.

How greatly injur'd and abus'd!
And give particulars in *surplus,*
Merely to *"answer their good purpose"*—
Poor man!—his *cat's-paws* case, we know,
Claims pity from both friend and foe;
But rev'rend Huntington,[15] pure soul!
For his assistance, through the whole,
May think he ought to lay claim unto
Some badge of honor, from the junto;
Then give him, sirs, to strut and wriggle,
A dashy, fed'ral pewter Eagle...[16]

15. Rev. Daniel Huntington, another Federalist minister who was with Rev. Champion at the Sixth of August festival, known for publicly denouncing any clergymen who joined the Republicans.

16. *The Witness*, Litchfield, CT, January 7, 1807, 4.

∽ 1808 ∾

The big issue of 1808 was the embargo. While the Republican papers defended the measure as necessary, a reflection of its unpopularity with the people of Connecticut was seen in the state's elections, with the number of Republican representatives dropping back to 61 in the spring, and then to a low of 50 in the fall. It would also be the last year that William Hart would run for governor, losing once again to Jonathan Trumbull, 12,146 to 7,566. The Council, as always, remained all Federalist.

1808 was also a presidential election year, and although James Madison easily won the election with 122 electoral votes to Charles C. Pinckney's 47, all of New England except for Vermont went for Pinckney.

Connecticut was the only New England state to consistently have both a Federalist governor and a Federalist majority in the legislature. The other New England states had all gone back and forth between Federalist and Republican governments. Massachusetts, for example, had elected a Republican governor, James Sullivan, in 1807. When Sullivan died in office in December 1808, Lieutenant Governor Levi Lincoln, Thomas Jefferson's former attorney general, served out the rest of his term, but was defeated by Federalist Christopher Gore in 1809. The Massachusetts legislature had become Republican, but shifted back to Federalist control in 1808.

The following article from Massachusetts Federalist paper *The Berkshire Reporter* rejoiced in the Federalists' regaining control of New England:

NEW-ENGLAND.

We have always had a strong confidence that NEW-ENG-
LAND would not long be under the dominion of democracy.
True-blooded Yankees, we have constantly said, were never
made for democrats. By the deceptive arts of interested
and unprincipled men, a small majority of the people in
Massachusetts were induced to abandon, for a very short
time, the good old cause of federalism, and forget the advice,
and oppose the principles, of the immortal WASHINGTON.
But the people of Massachusetts were too enlightened, to be
long deceived. They soon discovered that their *pretended
friends,* the leaders of democracy, were their *real enemies,*
and that their only object was to obtain honorable and prof-
itable offices. Looking round them, they saw those old
grey-headed patriots who fought the battles of our revolution,
turned out of office and noisy and unprincipled demagogues
put in their places. The people had heard these same demagogues loudly clamor against *high wages* and *high salaries,*
but they found that the moment they gained their offices
for themselves, they ceased to exclaim against high wages,
and high salaries, and instead of diminishing them, caused
them, on all occasions, to be encreased. The honest people
of Massachusetts could not bear these insults and abuses;
they turned disgusted from democracy, and again embraced
the cause of Washington, and of federalism.—This state is
now decidedly federal. The majorities in both Houses of
the General Court undeniably prove the fact. And, for the
consolation of all who wish for the prosperity and happiness
of their country, it may be added, that the democracy of
Massachusetts is vanishing like a mist. It will soon exist only
in *name.*

New Hampshire has followed the glorious example of
Massachusetts. The late election of members of Congress in
that State clearly shews that the people are no longer the
dupes of designing and wicked men. All of their Members of
Congress lately chosen are decidedly federal. Happy it is for
that State, that the reign of democracy was short!

The dark and pestiferous cloud of democracy has long

hung over the state of *Rhode-Island,* but that cloud is now dispersed by the light of truth. The people of that State have abandoned their once beloved demagogues, and have joined the standard of Washington and federalism.

Vermont will soon be ranked among the federal States. We have great reason to *hope* that a federal Governor is already chosen in that State. Should the democrats succeed at this time, we are *confident* it will be their last triumph. Their cause is fast declining, their idols are falling.

Connecticut never has been, and never will be, seduced from her political creed; that creed which was given to her by Washington. Democracy has always been insignificant in that State, and is every day growing more contemptible.

This is a highly flattering view of *New-England;* and no one will say it is not a correct one.—True-blooded Yankees cannot long be democrats.[1]

The Republicans had been accusing the Federalists of being pro-British ever since the 1795 Jay Treaty,[2] and in 1808 the New England Federalists started to prove the Republicans right. The article from a Massachusetts Federalist paper, written about in the following two articles from Republican papers, one in Massachusetts and one in Pennsylvania, was written anonymously, but other Federalists, particularly the New England Federalist clergy, were echoing its sentiments completely openly.

"Boston Notions."

It is lamentable that any American head or heart could conceive such *foul* and *rebellious* aspersions and calumnies as are contained in the following paragraph extracted from an essay signed *'Brutus'* in the Boston Gazette. No federalist

---

1. *The Berkshire Reporter,* Pittsfield, MA, September 10, 1808, 3.
2. The 1795 Treaty of Amity Commerce and Navigation, between His Britannic Majesty; and The United States of America, negotiated by Federalist John Jay and popularly known as the Jay Treaty, pitted the Republicans against the Federalists, with Republicans arguing that it gave too many concessions to Britain and weakened America's trade rights. It was this pro-British treaty which led the Republicans to label the Federalists, including George Washington, tories and monarchists. When the Jay Treaty expired in 1805, James Monroe and William Pinckney negotiated a new treaty, but it was rejected by Jefferson because the British would not agree to stop impressing American seamen.

can hold such sentiments, or countenance denunciation so bold and so horrible. *Brutus* is said to be a native tory. Let him stand among his fellow-citizens like the blasted oak in the forest; an object of wonder and regret. Let us hope that the number of such men, even in New-England, is small, & their influence nothing.

Read, fellow-citizens—Read!

"Our rulers have promoted the triumph of a blasphemous bloody tyrant, *(Bonaparte)* and have become *partners* in his crimes, by *sharing in his pillage,* submitting to his insults and yielding to his menaces. The *true* American, may yet feel some *pride,* that the *glorious land of our forefathers (Great Britain)* has heroically resisted his mighty power, and *preserved the liberties of the world through a thousand conflicts.*—While we lament that we have aided the projects of the Corsican, under a pusillanimous infidel *(Jefferson)* who is not a *king,* because he is a *coward;* we may rejoice that our elder brethren *(the British)* have rescued the world from the fangs of a monster, who was wading through blood to universal conquest. Would to heaven that we were suffered to *join our arms* to our prayers in aid of the glorious cause. But, alas! the place of our *hero (Washington)* has been usurped by the *minions of a tyrant,* (the officers of government, under the *tyrant* Jefferson) who acquired power by base arts, and prostitutes it to baser purposes!!!"[3]

New England Toryism.—The language of the New England prints is so manifestly hostile to every thing American, that we are surprised their insolence and vulgarity should be countenanced, much less applauded, by men who profess to revere the virtues of Washington, and the principles of '76. In a late *Boston Gazette,* we find an article under the signature of Brutus, than which one more infamous never appeared in print, it is in praise of *Great Britain,* and eulogizing the Spanish *patriots.* Let every American read it

---

3. *The Statesman,* Newburyport, MA, December 15, 1808, 3.

and blush, that in *Boston,* the very first scene of British outrage, and of American patriotism in 1775—such infamy would be tolerated.—

"Our rulers have promoted the triumph of a blasphemous bloody tyrant, *(Bonaparte)* and have become *partners* in his crimes, by *sharing in his pillage,* submitting to his insults and yielding to his menaces. The *true* American, may yet feel some *pride,* that the *glorious land of our forefathers (Great Britain)* has heroically resisted his mighty power, and *preserved the liberties of the world through a thousand conflicts.*—While we lament that we have aided the projects of the Corsican, under a pusilanimous infidel *(Jefferson)* who is not a *king,* because he is a *coward;* we may rejoice that our elder brethren *(the British)* have rescued the world from the fangs of a monster, who was wading through blood to universal conquest. Would to heaven that we were suffered to *join our arms* to our prayers in aid of the glorious cause. But, alas! the place of our *hero (Washington)* has been usurped by the *minions of a tyrant,* (the officers of government, under the *tyrant* Jefferson) who acquired power by base arts, and prostitutes it to baser purposes!!!"

What must every true American who loves his country, and respects its republican institutions, feel upon a perusal of this basest of slanders? One sentiment alone must be entertained by all—that the writer is a tory, of a *British emissary,* employed to disturb our peace, disgrace our government, and destroy, if possible the reputation of those men, to whom the people have committed the exercise of official authority. Its falsehood and malevolence, however, are so glaring, that it must pass by unregarded, further than as a specimen of black hearted toryism, deserving of punishment; but which the people of the United States are so lenient to treat with silent contempt and abhorrence.

Can anyone believe that the United States have become the partners of France and go shares in the pillage of Bonaparte? That they have tamely submitted to his insults and yielded to his menaces? Besides the inconsistency of the charge, when compared with other tory assertions, the capture, burning, and confiscations of American property under the French decrees prove that these assertions are as false, as they are mean and malicious. But "the glorious land of our forefathers," *(Great Britain)* "has nobly resisted his mighty power and *preserved the liberties of the world* through a thousand conflicts!" Are you there Old True-penny? It is *Great Britain* that is the theme of praise to every tory: And *America,* the subject of their reproach and hatred. Great Britain *has indeed* nobly preserved the liberties of the world—by *violating every treaty* she has yet entered into—by *pillaging* in turn every power in Europe, Asia and America, against which she could bring her forces to bear—and by *murdering* millions of innocent people in the four quarters of the globe, merely to preserve their liberties, and save them from their worst enemies, themselves! This is "preserving the liberties of the world through a thousand conflicts," with a vengeance. Yet this tory *Brutus,* who possesses not a single spark of that patriotism which animated the noble Roman, wishes to heaven, that *we were suffered to join our arms* in aid of this glorious cause. God forbid, that ever the United States should so far forget the cruelties and privations of the struggle for liberty in 1776, as to join her arms with the faithless, treacherous, and cruel government of G. Britain, in any cause—for that cause must be bad, which stands in need of such support.

The praise of *Britain,* and abuse of *Jefferson,* is another evidence of toryism.—what man, who has the smallest regard for the government of the U. States, can listen with complacence to the assertion, that the *president of the United States* is a pusillanimous infidel, who would become a *king,* were he not a *coward?* Shame that such infamous libels should be propagated with impunity—that the man who of all others has rendered the most services to his country, should be so shamefully and wantonly traduced. His reward, however, will be the approbation of the *whigs,* like the morning vapour shall dissolve before the rising sun of republicanism, and leave its propagators a prey to envy and remorse.[4]

4. *The Commonwealth,* Pittsburgh, PA, November 9, 1808, 3.

Federalist clergyman Elijah Parish, a Connecticut native and minister in Byfield, Massachusetts, would become nationally known for his over-the-top pro-British Fast Day sermons during the War of 1812, with one of them being considered such a fine example of British patriotism that it was reprinted in Canada and recommended to ministers there to imitate. In 1808, he was just warming up.

FEDERAL GOSPEL!

Mr. PARISH, the minister of Byfield, delivered a sermon on Fast day, in which he attempts to persuade his hearers, that our temporal and eternal salvation depends on going immediately to war with France;—whom he stiles the Antichrist.

He says that more THAN HALF THE AMERICAN NATION *are in friendship with this Antichrist—that they join him hand in hand, "and a covenant with hell is confirmed;" and that "as devil with devil damn'd firm concord holds, so these maintain a combination of spirits, and bid defiance to conviction!"*

After giving a highly exaggerated description, in the most ranting style, of French aggression; and after *abusing the American people* in terms similar to those above mentioned, he turns, with softening tones, to his beloved nation, with the following words.

"'The mother country,' the blest land of our fathers sepulcres, Great Britain, has *nobly* dared to wage a *just* war with this blasphemous Power. What have been the consequences? Her fields have never been robbed or defiled by the troops of Napoleon; they have never spread desolation along the fair coast of England; they have never profaned her churches, nor dragged her sons into their bloody armies; the navies of England ride triumphant in every sea; they chastise her enemies; they waft to her ports the comforts and luxuries of every clime.—Such is the fruit 'of coming out' from Anti-Christ; *while* WE *and other nations,* LIKE MOLES AND BATS, *crawl at the feet of the Conqueror; like serpents eat the dust of his feet, or are chained to his car to swell the splendor of his triumphs. Our incalculable sacrifices;*

our loss of ships, our tribute, our suspension of commerce, are entirely the fruit of our friendship to Anti-Christ."

It is in fact a raving, antichristian thing, both in *matter* and *manner;* replete with abase against republicans, and the government; as full of toryism as it is of falsehood (which is saying enough.) He recommends the revival of political preaching—and, what is curious enough, he gives a very broad and palpable hint to the *rich,* to encourage no poor people except such as are federalists! Precious Christianity! A fine specimen of federal religion.[5]

Federalist papers unabashedly published pro-British, Fast Day sermon excerpts and prayers, and the Republican papers reprinted them, with the expected commentary.

FEDERAL RELIGION! AGAIN!

In our last paper we gave two specimens of *anglo-federal Preaching;* we now give a specimen of *anglo-federal* PRAYING. If the former was seditious, the latter is impious. View a man, clothed in the assignas of the Gospel of Christ, standing in the sacred desk, in the posture of addressing the Throne of Grace—hear nothing from his lips but phrases intended to excite ridicule, contempt, hatred, malice, strife, revenge, and every base passion of which the human heart is suscep-tible, against the government of his country, to which he is taught, by our Divine Master, to be in subjection—and then say, ye followers of the meek and holy Jesus, can this be a man of God!—Is he not rather a child of Beelzebub?

The authority of the following cannot be disputed by anglo-federalists; it is from the Portland Gazette, a paper high in the esteem of that party. Read it without blushing if you can.

————

Mr. ADAMS[6]—If you think the political part of a "PRAYER," delivered on the late fast occasion, worthy of

5. *The Democrat,* Boston, MA, April 23, 1808, 3.
6. Isaac Adams, publisher of Maine's *Portland Gazette.*

publicity, please inset the same in your useful paper:—

"AMELIORATE the state of our pusillanimous General Government. May we no longer be guided by leading strings; suffering and groping in political darkness.—When we see Liberty's lovely form metamorphosed into the most ugly monster, shall we seriously affect the lullaby tone? We would not presume to lift up our voice against great Diana in Ephesus, as tho' she were politically mad; and much less say "that blindness in part happened to" our Congressional Rulers. But from appearing to be rapidly verging to the awful crisis of American phrensy, we most fervently pray that thou wouldst bless the Grand Sachem of the National Assembly, and every member appertaining to that opaque body. However obstinately bent on suicide, may they be saved from being their own Executioners! After much puerile dashing and Gun-boat mania have been figured off there, to puff away the pitiful effects, the tremendous sweeps of the *amphibious* Jeffersonian embargo; and to gratify their French feelings towards the English: by the adoption of a high and forbidding tone, and of the insufferable hauteur and commanding insolence they have assumed with regard to them; may meat be brought out of the eaters of the present administration, and sweetness out of the ill scented secrets of the Executive. LORD, if thou doth not soon appear, our halcyon days will fly away. The terrible prediction of our illuminated Prophet seem to be fast fulfilling. The abomination of desolation is now marching with gigantic strides, and soon will be let loose upon us, unless instantly awoke from the apparent and fatal stupor in which we slumber! Else why this murderous assault on the freedom of speech? Why all these high-toned Gallic partialities? Why this senseless, continued mockery and suppression of facts, in which the interests of our nation are concerned? Convince them of our insanity, O LORD, who have studiously and insidiously wrapped up all communications from France in total, midnight darkness, and secrecy: and when all this mighty splashing of Presidential Gun boats, in attacking ships of the line, shall have terminated in more than half seas over; may every difficulty be done away, and the dark portentous cloud of Jacobinism which now hangs over our political horizon, soon be dissipated. Out of the mouths of political madcaps, and of humdrum politicians, eventually declare the wonders of thy delivering praise. Disembarrass the maritime trade of our seafaring brethren from the shackles of despotism with which it has been fettered.

"May our Mercantile operations receive no further molestation from our unadvised harum-scarum rulers. May the Embargo, that sanguinary Demon of democracy, and of Napoleon Bonaparte, Emperor of Bedlam, promptly be raised; and every measure adopted by our new fangled Choctaws, hostile to our Commerce, Navigation and Fisheries, fall like Lucifer, never to rise again. May the anti-commercial storm of War, be succeeded by a perpetual calm—and the citizens of the union (as in days of yore) bask in the eternal sunshine of political happiness and prosperity; and let all the people say Amen." [7]

America's British loyalists became the source of inspiration for many a poem.

Composed for the especial use of the British loyalists in the United States of America, who are, in their extreme benevolence, so desirous, not only to relieve "the people from their worst enemies themselves," but in their love and kindness, seem willing to save us from the great expence of a president, a congress, and indeed all the trouble of self-government, by soliciting us again to enter into the paternal embrace of his most gracious majesty, George the third.

I.

Proceed, O dearest friends, still sing
The praises of great George your king,
And be the burden of your song,
"His majesty can do no wrong."

II.

The president and congress too,

---

7. *Essex Register,* Salem, MA, Apr 30, 1808, 2.

The public good will ne'er pursue;
Give them in government their shares,
Then farewell to all British wares.

III.

But if to Britain you return,
You then will have no cause to mourn;
She will with kindness you entreat,
Then why her plans will you defeat?

IV.

She kens all things to regulate,
Your trade and commerce, church & state,
And will you be such silly elves
To take this trouble on yourselves?

V.

But if you obstinate will prove
And disregard her tender love,
And if yourselves ye yet will rule,
We beg you not to play the fool.

VI.

At present look with open eyes,
Take our advice for we are wise,
Are "rich in talents, rich in gold,"
A truth you have been often told.

VII.

Then all agree with one consent
That we may choose your president;
We will elect "a man of nerve,"
Who all your plaudits will deserve.

VIII.

Not a cool, shrewd diplomatist,
But one who will act by dint of fist,
Or sword or gun, or shot or ball,
"This glorious chief will conquer all."

IX.

Sure this, our friends, you can't refuse,
For your own sakes then let us choose
A Pinckney,—but no Madison—
A man who never fir'd a gun.

X.

If this our pray'r you should reject,
Britain will never you respect,
She will on you her thunders pour,
Will harass you from shore to shore:

XI.

For she with her tremendous pow'r
Can crush you in a single hour;
But if you speedily repent
All merciful she will relent.

XII.

Quick sue for pardon—bend the knee,
And you will soon be great and free;
She will this vile embargo raise,
And make you happy all your days.

PILL GARLICK,

Poet Laureat to all true British Loyalists,
here and elsewhere.

N.B. This excellent production is to be said or sung, drunk or sober, at all muster fields, and every place of public meeting, until the present presidential election shall be past, and on every 4th of July ever after, instead of that UNMANNERLY thing, usually called "The Declaration of American Independence." The honorable colonel and puissant hero, Timothy Pickering,[8] esq. "that man of nerve," may sing to his favorite tune, two staves, every evening, to compose his system after the fatigues of the day, and to induce refreshing sleep to fit him for the active scene of the morrow.[9]

Fourth of July celebrations always included many toasts, which were printed in the papers. The following are some of the 1808 "Salem Democratic toasts," as printed in the Federalist paper *The*

8. Massachusetts Federalist Timothy Pickering. Dismissed by Adams as secretary of state for his opposition to Adams's efforts to negotiate with France, and elected a U.S. senator from Massachusetts in 1803. The pro-British Pickering began promoting the idea of a separation of the New England states from the rest of the country in 1804, and during the War of 1812 a separate peace between New England and Britain.

9. *The Monitor,* Washington D.C., October 22, 1808, 2.

Salem Gazette, "with proposed amendments":

... Washington, Franklin, Hancock and Adams:[10] departed patriots: their deeds shall never be erased from the recollection of grateful Americans. ——*Washington, Franklin, Hancock and Adams: departed patriots: their deeds shall never be erased from the recollection of grateful Americans, let Jefferson, Duane*[11] *and Tom Paine do their worst.*

The memory of those who fell in support of our glorious revolution. ——*The memory of those who fell in support of our glorious revolution. By St. Patrick, if there are any of them here present let them step forward and not be ashamed of the land of potatoes.*

The Pickerings and the Burrs of the United States: may the people be aware they have internal enemies. ——*The Jeffersons and the Burrs of the U.S. May the people always remember that these gentlemen in 1800 had equally EVERY "REPUBLICAN" ELECTOR'S VOTE in the country.*

The Clergy: When they interfere with Politics may it be in support of the Government of their Country. ——*The Clergy: When the triumph of "Reason" shall condemn them to the Guillotine, let the following be reprieved for their political services, viz. Parson Beatley, Parson Lelland, Parson Allen, Elias Smith, and Tom Paine.*

May the mantle of Jefferson fall on James Madison, and he wear it without alteration ——*"May Mr. Madison be buttoned up in Mr. Jefferson's red plush breeches whether they fit him or not."*...[12]

The embargo was set to rhyme in a Federalist song for the Fourth of July, and afterwards printed in the Boston *Repertory,* and was answered by the Republican *Pittsfield Sun.*

THE EMBARGO.

A song, composed by Henry Mellen, Esq. of Dover, and

10. Samuel Adams.
11. William Duane, editor of the Philadelphia Republican paper the *Aurora.*
12. *The Salem Gazette,* Salem, MA, July 8, 1808, 3.

sung at the celebration of the Fourth of July.

[Tune — *Come let us prepare*]

DEAR Sirs, it is wrong
To demand a *New Song*;
    I have let all the breath I can spare go;
With the Muse I've conferr'd,
And she won't say a word,
    But keeps laughing about the *Embargo*.

I wish that I could,
Sing in Allegro mood:
    But the times are as stupid as *Largo*,
Could I have my choice,
I would strain up in voice;
    'Till it *snapt* all the *strings* of Embargo.

Our great politicians,
Those dealers in visions,
    On paper, to all lengths they dare go;
But when call'd to decide,
Like a *turtle* they hide,
    In their own pretty *shell,* the *Embargo*.

In the time that we try,
To put out Britain's eye,
    I fear we shall let our own *pair* go;
Yet still we're so wise,
We can see with *French* Eyes,
    And then we shall like the *Embargo*.

A French privateer,
Can have nothing to fear;
    She may *load* and may *here,* or may *there* go,
Their friendship is such,
And we love them so much,
    We let them slip through the *Embargo*.

Our ships all in motion,

Once whiten'd the ocean,
    They sail'd and return'd with a cargo;
Now doom'd to decay,
They have fallen a prey
    To Jefferson, worms, and *Embargo.*

Lest Britain should take
A few men by mistake,
    Who under false colours may dare go;
We're manning their fleet
With our Tars, who retreat
    From poverty, sloth and *Embargo.*

What a *fuss* we have made,
About rights and *free trade,*
    And swore we'd not let our own share go;
Now we can't take for our souls
Bring a Hake from the *shoals,*
    'Tis a breach of the *twentieth Embargo.*

Our farmers so gay,
How they gallop'd away,
    'Twas money that made the old mare go,
But now she won't stir,
For the whip or the spur,
    'Till they take off her *clog,* the *Embargo.*

If you ask for a debt,
The man turns in a *pet,*
    "I pay, sir? I'll not let a hair go;
If your officer comes,
I shall put up my thumbs,
    And clap on his breath an *Embargo.*"

Thus *Tommy* destroys,
A great part of our joys:
    Yet we'll not let the beautiful fair go;
They all will contrive
To keep commerce alive,

There's nothing they hate like *Embargo*.

Since rulers design,
To deprive us of wine,
   'Tis best that we now have a *rare go;*
Then each to his post,
And see who will do most,
   To knock out the *blocks* of *Embargo*.[13]

HENRY MELLEN ESQUIRE'S SMART SONG, "THE EMBARGO,"
Parodied by SIMON PEPPERPOT, THE YOUNGER.

———

Now be at your posts, for the mighty man Sin
Stands watching the door, to let Fed'ralists *in;*
For something must rule them, no doubt a wise thing,
And were it the Devil, they'd call him a King.

———

TUNE—*"Come let us prepare."*

DEAR SIR, you are wrong
To tell lies in a song,
   And let all the filth you can spare go;
For the Muse is quite mad,
To view herself clad,
   In falsehood about the EMBARGO.

Our wise politicians
In spite of divisions,
   To Johnny Bull won't let a hair go;
Tho' his friends wish to reign,
And their hoarse voices strain,
   To curse and blaspheme the Embargo.

13. *The Repertory,* Boston, MA, July 15, 1808, 1.

The tories would twist
'Till they steal all the grist,
    And cajole us as far as they dare go;
While like turtles, the feds
Still poke out their heads,
    And hiss at the prudent Embargo.

When Britain did try
To put out our eye,
    Behold she let one of her pair go;
So let us be wise,
And regard not her lies,
    And t'other we'll shut by Embargo.

The French we believe,
Like the British deceive,
    They both want a smack at the cargo;
But our rulers, who saw
The extent of their maw,
    Have sav'd us the whole by Embargo.

Our ships for a time,
Ride safe in our clime,
    Lest with Denmark, we lose ships and cargo:
They'd better decay,
Than be stol'n away,
    By scoundrels who hate the Embargo.

Old Britain has slain
Our Tars on the main,
    On our Land, the Lord knows, she don't dare go;
For when there she was beat,
She took to her fleet,
    As now when kept off by Embargo.

What a fuss they do make
About lobsters and hake,
    And swear we have let all the share go?
But we've pouts and sow fish,

A good Fed'ral dish,
    For those who oppose the Embargo.

Our farmers so gay,
With pork, beef and hay,
    To Europe will not let a hair go;
'Till she is so fair,
As to grant equal share,
    We'll stick to the prudent Embargo.

Whilst Eden's best stores
Enrich all our shores,
    We'll venture to make the old mare go;
But fed'ralists fret
And demand ev'ry debt,
    And father it all on Embargo.

Thus Tommy destroys
Intriguers chief joys;
    But to ruin will not let the Fair go;
For he will secure
Our damsels, so pure,
    By keeping off rogues with Embargo.

When Fed'ralists dine,
And are tipsey on wine,
    No wonder they call it a RARE go;
They sigh for lost POSTS,
Then knock for their HOSTS,
And take on their twentieth EMBARGO.[14]

14. *The Pittsfield Sun*, Pittsfield, MA, August 27, 1808, 4.

∾ 1809 ∾

In January 1809, Congress passed an act "to enforce and make more effectual" the embargo, which allowed the federal government to call upon the state militias to aid in enforcing the embargo. When Secretary of War Henry Dearborn sent a letter to Governor Trumbull requesting that he deploy the state militia to enforce the embargo, Trumbull flatly refused. Instead, he called a special session of the legislature in February to address the embargo, at which he delivered a speech decrying the embargo and its supplementary enforcement act as unconstitutional and a grievous violation of the state's and the people's rights. The Connecticut legislature resolved to band together with Massachusetts, whose legislature had passed a resolution for their state to join with other like-minded states in opposing the embargo.

To the Republicans, the calling of this special session of the legislature, and particularly the joining together of Connecticut and Massachusetts, was rebellion and a sign of a "northern confederacy" forming.

From the Danbury, Connecticut *Republican Farmer*:

Legislative Convention.

For what is the Legislature of this State convened? This is a question put a thousand times a day, and yet no one seems able to give an answer that can justify their assembling. Federalists, more generally, it is believed, if enquired of, unite in declaring their ignorance of the cause, and their disbelief in the propriety of this proceeding. Many, however, unwilling to censure so important a movement, content themselves with believing that without *due consultation,* and a thorough conviction of the necessity of the measure, the governor would never have issued his notices.

For ourselves we beg leave to enquire, in the words of Mr. *Clinton,*[1] "Is this a link of the same chain? Is this a part of a system of severance? Is this the commencement of the *northern confederacy* which was threatened last summer?" In our own opinion, time only can develop what will be done, and even that may be inadequate to the unfolding the real intention with which this extraordinary measure has been countenanced. Still we must believe the grand object to be a *separation of the States,* this will not be avowed, nor immediately attempted. The way to it is difficult and full of danger, and it may be the business of the session only to devise ways and means gradually to prepare for this change, for reducing them to come under a new system, under a *king* and under the protection of Britain!!! For this purpose we expect to see REBELLION against the government encouraged, to see the laws pronounced unconstitutional, tyrannical and oppressive, to see the infamy of Britain palliated: and the disorganizing and factious doings of the Massachusetts Legislature not only countenanced, but seconded and perhaps even extended in extravagance.

Hartford, probably, has been fixed upon for the assembling of the Legislature, as being more nearly connected with Boston than New-Haven is, and as affording therefore a more easy intercourse with that grand encourager of Insurrection.

It is even said that certain noted characters have already taken a journey to Boston to receive orders how things shall be conducted in this State—In this way are the honour and respectability of Connecticut to be prostituted to the furtherance of the crazy schemes of an infuriated faction in the capital of Massachusetts.

---

1. New York Republican politician DeWitt Clinton. At this time, Clinton, a former U.S. senator and future New York governor, was the mayor of New York City.

Citizens of Connecticut, was it for this that your Representatives were elected in September? What can by any possibility justify the convention of the Legislature? What have
they to do with the government of the nation? What can
they do, as it respects the general government without a
manifest and unwarranted interference with concerns that
do not belong to them? What can all this end in but in taxing
you thousands and thousands of dollars for paying the travelling expenses and for the dinners of a set of men who have
done——what?[2]

When the embargo was repealed in March and replaced by the
Non-Intercourse Act, which prohibited trade only with Britain,
France, and their dependencies, the Federalists claimed that the
Jefferson administration had ended the embargo out of fear of Mas-
sachusetts and Connecticut, with the *Courant* saying:

Our weak and wicked administration were so frightened
by the Legislatures of Connecticut and Massachusetts, that
they have relinquished the embargo and substituted non-
intercourse. Do these poltroons suppose that the people will
not discover their folly and cowardice?[3]

Large Republican meetings with attendances in the hundreds
were held in numerous towns across the state in March at which
resolutions were passed stating the Republican position on the
resolutions of the state legislature's special session and pledging
support to the Madison administration.

The Republican resolutions pointed out that the banding together of the legislatures of Massachusetts and Connecticut violated
Article 1, Section 10 of the Constitution, which states that "No state
shall, without the consent of Congress ... enter into any agreement
or compact with another state."

From the Windham resolutions:

Resolved, That we view with deep regret, the late resolves
of this State, for that, by the constitution of the U.S. "no

2. *Republican Farmer,* Danbury, CT, March 08, 1809, 3.
3. *The Connecticut Courant,* Hartford, CT, March 15, 1809, 3.

state shall without the consent of Congress enter into any agreement or compact with another state," &c.: Therefore any attempt to form a combination of the Legislatures of several States for the avowed purpose of controlling the general government,—we deem it directly against the constitution of the U.S. which was made and solemnly adopted in convention by the people.[4]

A number of the meetings resolved that the actions of Trumbull and the legislature were a step towards civil war:

From the Berlin resolutions:

> *Resolved,* 6th. That we look upon the refusal of Gov. Trumbull to obey the lawful commands of his superior officer, and the approbatory resolves of our legislature, as an enormous stride towards treason and civil war—and we would therefore earnestly recommend to every friend of his country to view, with scrutinizing glances, every transaction of these enemies of our Constitution.[5]

As serious and dire as the situation was, it did not stop one Republican writer from satirizing it.

FEDERAL CAUCUS.

HUSHAI[6] in the Chair.

BURLEIGH[7] Secretary.

Secretary. We are upon great preparatory work, Mr. Chairman, and ought to move cautiously. The people know nothing as yet about our intentions. I have sounded them in my town, and talked about the embargo, and the negro states; the people can be trained by degrees. It is my opinion that nothing should be said publicly about *dividing the union* till after harvest. We understand each other. The British officers in the Canadas understand us. The naval

---

4. *Windham Herald,* Windham, CT, March 16, 1809, 3.
5. *American Mercury,* Hartford, CT, March 23, 1809, 2.
6. In the Bible, Hushai was a spy for David, called "the king's friend."
7. Lord Burleigh, advisor to Queen Elizabeth I.

commanders on the station have their secret instructions. Mr. Rose[8] and Mr. Canning,[9] and even the British king on his throne knows what we are about. THE FURTHEST LINE WESTWARD, WHICH CAN BE OBTAINED. Let this be our countersign, and let every man be prudent. Want of prudence prevented the blowing up of the parliament-house. I move, sir, that every member be sworn to secrecy.

2d Speaker. I move, sir, that the secretary be expelled.

3d Speaker. I move, sir, that the member *last up* be expelled.

2d Speaker. Sir, I beg leave to explain. I am, sir, in favor of a *dismemberment of the union,* and of all sorts of *violent* measures as much as any man, but "the least said soonest mended." These things ought to be understood among ourselves, not spoken about. The proceedings of democratic caucuses were divulged by our *chairman, not as they were in fact,* but as the writer wished them to be. Now, sir, our proceedings may be misrepresented. I am for great prudence and circumspection, but at the same time will go as far as any gentleman towards actual dismemberment of the union.

4th Speaker. We ought not to expel any member; but we ought to augment our numbers by inviting the doubtful, (if any there be,) on the other side, to join us. If we declare independence of the union we shall lose many of our best men, and must supply their places by *Refugees.* The very name will be useful to us.

5th Speaker. I understand, sir, that Pennsylvania is raising 30,000 men to aid the enforcing of the laws of the union. I move that three companies be raised in this state to march against Pennsylvania.

6th Speaker. I move, sir, that in addition, there be raised one full company of drummers, and fifers, to be composed of our first men in this kind of warfare, NOISE is of the first importance.

7th Speaker. I do not like the business of military force; but should prefer that the governor of this state should *write*

8. George Henry Rose, British envoy to the United States after the Chesapeake affair.
9. George Canning, British foreign secretary.

a sharp letter to Snyder,[10] and tell him that one Connecticut man is able to drive 20 Pennsylvanians, and that we are about *interposing a shield between the rights and liberties of this people, and the* ASSUMED *power of the general government.*

8th Speaker. I move, sir, that our governor put in a *nota bene* to the governor of New-York, one Tompkins, to suffer our troops to pass through that state or to oppose them at his peril.

9th Speaker. I think, sir, that the interposing shield should be made without delay, and that all the iron and BRASS in the state be appropriated to that purpose.

10th Speaker. I move, sir, to appropriate all the SMITHS in the state to the work of the *interposing shield.*

Chairman. Gentlemen, I approve your order: but many motions are made and none seconded!

11th Speaker. I second all the motions.

Chairman. You, who are in favor of the several motions, say Aye—*Passed unanimously and a committee of two from a county appointed to carry them into effect.*

Cloudy Speech from the Chair.

Gentlemen, to-morrow at 9 be in your places. Resolutions of suitable import will be brought forward according to the decisions of this evening. You have little to do but to *vote.* The laws, about which we complain, *are not in fact unconstitutional,* but it is necessary to hold this up. The sore spot is in fact, that we have no power and are likely to have none under the general government; but our sore spots are not to be shewn to the common people. I wish that the governor had not called this extraordinary assembly, because by our stories about *sixty tons of precious silver* and French Influence we were doing well enough—but we must support the governor and must pass some resolutions and talk strong; but, gentlemen, the burying has gone by, Madison is to be president for 4 years.—We have had great benefits by the carrying trade; this carrying trade has brought on the present state of things; the government adopted its present

---

10. Simon Snyder, governor of Pennsylvania.

course at the solicitation of our merchants; but these things are not to go abroad. *The furthest line westward, which can be obtained,* may be a good countersign, but from my observation the people will not bear a separation from the union.

I would go all lengths with you, my friends, but *half a loaf is better than no bread.* We have the state government now and may lose it if imprudent—I wish you success and hope that you will vote boldly, but if real danger comes, all the precedents in the books treat, that he, *who fights and runs away, may live to fight another day.* I shall be among these troops and they will be the most necessary, because all, who fight the general government and do not run away, will be assuredly sacrifices.—*And so this meeting is adjourned.*[11]

The next several elections would go very badly for Connecticut's Republicans. In the spring, Governor Trumbull was reelected by a wider than usual margin, getting 14,650 votes to Asa Spalding's 8,159. Treadwell was reelected lieutenant governor with 12,795 votes to Elijah Boardman's 6,834. The number of Republican representatives dropped to 45. The Council, as always, remained all Federalist. The Republicans fared little better in the fall, with their number of representatives increasing only slightly to 49, and the highest Republican on the Council assistants list getting only a little over half as many votes as the year before.

The outrageously pro-British sermons of Elijah Parish were rivaled by those of his fellow Massachusetts clergyman David Osgood, whose election and fast day sermons, like those of Parish, would become nationally known as the country moved into the War of 1812.

REMARKS ON THE ELECTION SERMON
OF DR. OSGOOD.

Having accidentally heard a passage from a pamphlet, displaying the terrible consequences of intestine division

11. *American Mercury*, Hartford, CT, March 9, 1809, 3.

and party opposition among a people, and so very applicable to the present state of our own country, I naturally supposed it to be the production of some one who foresaw the state to which sedition was likely to reduce us—But my surprise at learning that it was from the late election sermon, could be equalled only by my curiosity to read this truly wonderful discourse. After having examined it, had the author not been known, I should have concluded either that he was acting the hypocrite, and under the appearance of friendship, attacking his party with the most cutting satire, or that his blind zeal had led him far beyond the reach of common sense. ...[12]

〰

DR. OSGOOD's ELECTION SERMON.

When we perused the two Fast-day sermons of Dr. Spring,[13] we were in hopes *"we ne'er should look upon its like again."* It is presumed the indiscretion of Dr. O. will not disappoint these hopes, by a publication of the jacobinic harrangue, falsely called a sermon, which disgraced the pulpit and disgusted even the federal auditors of the *"Reverend Demagogue,"* on Wednesday last. To name christianity with such malignant raving and dark insinuations, might be considered an undue mixture of *sacred with profane.* The blushes of every one in the house, except the brazen trumpet itself, through which the evil genius of our country blew this blast of seditious fury, declared it insufferably degrading to the character of the scholar and the gentleman. There is, however, one point in which the Doctor is entitled to praise. His discourse, (long and bitter as it was) was the result of much labor. It was entirely committed to memory, and rolled over his tongue with that fervid eloquence, which is usually considered as the evidence of sincerity, and well calculated to enforce better maxims. The undertaker must surely have labored successfully in folly's cause, when he

12. *Boston Patriot,* Boston, MA, July 29, 1809, 1.
13. Massachusetts Federalist clergyman Samuel Spring.

shames his employers, wounds every better feeling of his friends, and gratifies to the utmost the malignity of his enemies. No one will dispute the Doctor's title to this merit. To the grey-headed disciple in the school of that faction, the articles of whose creed are, *"devotion to England, abhorrence of France, and contempt for America,"* to this honored missionary of Juntoism, the "king of the happy isles," may now say, in his favorite strain of sarcastic irony, and with a friendly reciprocity of biting chagrin, *"enter thou into the joy of thy lord."* [14]

The Federalists were regaining strength not only in their stronghold of Connecticut, where they now held an even larger majority in the legislature, but across New England in states that had been turning Republican. Not only did every New England state except Vermont vote against Madison in the 1808 presidential election, but Massachusetts and New Hampshire, which had had Republican governors, went for Federalists in 1809, although by a very small margin in Massachusetts. The Republicans lost their majority in New Hampshire's legislature. Both houses of the Massachusetts legislature had a Federalist majority. The only New England state to both elect a Republican governor in 1809 and control the legislature was Vermont.

In spite of the Federalist resurgence in New Hampshire, the state did have some new converts to Republicanism, like the writer of the following letter to the *New-Hampshire Gazette:*

The True Convert.

My Federal Friends,

I have been in various circles, through different States, and have kept the best Federal company. I have followed the head, and not the tail, of Federalism, more than eleven years. I have leant my assistance, heartily and sincerely, in deluding many thousand innocent people to vote, directly against themselves and against justice, to the great prejudice of a free government.

14. *Boston Patriot*, Boston, MA, June 3, 1809, 3.

There is not one in a thousand, of those who think themselves popular with the federal club, that knows any thing of their real plan: by exerting themselves to make dupes they are assisting to destroy their dear bought liberties.

I have been puzzled for two years past as to the fitness of my conduct: the scandalous proceedings of the federal party, in abusing Mr. Jefferson, the present administration and the Embargo; with the scandalous profanity of the fourth of July in various States, have, thank God, opened my eyes.

There are *six real tories* in Newhampshire, who have been such from the year 1775; *twenty one* in Massachusetts; *five* in Connecticut; and *three* in Vermont. These men have been the principal movers, in the mischievous design, to overthrow the government of the United States and establish MONARCHY ON ITS RUINS. They have combined with them three classes of men, who are aiding directly or indirectly to promote their nefarious designs. 1. Lawyers, with their technical jargon and useless ceremonies, calculated to bewilder and deceive our honest and plain dealing Farmers. They form a class, whose pursuits and habits are distinct from the rest of society, and are growing rapidly to a complete aristocracy. 2. The regular Clergy, with their pride, avarice and thirst for power; aiming to destroy the right of conscience; to connect the Church and the State; and introduce an established Religion. Should the plot succeed, the Clergy will live upon the fat of the land; and *"God's chosen people"* will be compelled to pay tithes (a tenth part of all the produce of their toil) to support a set of men who preach one thing and practice another; and whose doctrines a very large portion of them never will or can approve. 3. The importers of English merchandize, who by their connection with Great Britain, and large credit, are enabled to circulate foreign luxuries through the country, and by means of their *understrappers* who are placed in almost every town, to disseminate the contaminating and poisonous influence of England; which in its pernicious and destructive operation produces political blindness and insanity. When I reflect on my past conduct: when I behold the deluded victims of my former perfidy, strutting in *chains of foreign fabrick,* and ornamented with all the *gew-gaw trappings* of slavery. When I perceive those *flimsy politicians* by means of their flimsy merchandize, acquiring an influence over the minds of free born Americans, and in many instances compelling them in an unconstitutional manner to vote contrary to their inclination. When I contemplate the bigotry, intolerance and persecution which will pervade this "happy land" if the established Clergy succeed in their plot for forming an union of church and state. When I consider what will be the wretched situation of this now FREE PEOPLE, if overwhelmed with the Aristocracy of the bench and bar—When I behold the inhabitants of these fertile plains *"where Peace and plenty dwell"* advancing to the brink of a precipice, infatuated and blinded, by the dark manœuvres of the enemies of their liberties; and within a step of the gulph of arbitrary power. I cannot repress my indignant feelings;—I cannot allay the *"compunctious visitings of conscience;"* I am impelled to exclaim—*"Turn ye blind from your faithless guides! Awake, arouse, arise ye* SLEEPING SAMSONS" of New-Hampshire, ere the Delilahs of Federalism have shorn your locks! [15]

In the remaining New England state of Rhode Island, the Federalists made a strong push in the spring, and although the state's Republican governor was reelected, the Federalists gained the largest majority they had had in the legislature in a decade, winning 47 of the House's 72 seats, up from a majority of only 8. This gain, however, would be erased in the fall, when the Federalists fell back down to having a majority of only 4.

The Federalists' spring electioneering effort was set to rhyme by one Rhode Islander:

ELECTIONEERING INSTRUCTIONS and ADDRESS from His Most Serene Majesty the Grand Leader of the Opposition in Rhode-Island, to his would-be "princes, potentates and powers," and their understrappers—written in *rhyme* to better assist the memory.

15. *New-Hampshire Gazette,* Portsmouth, NH, February 28, 1809, 2.

"Hath not the Potter power over the clay to make one
vessel unto honor and another unto dishonor?"

TO all who wish for place and pensions,
With talents of but small dimensions,
And who of principle have made,
Like cunning merchants, the best trade:
Ye whose whole merit is your wealth,
And love your country less than pelf;
Who look with scorn upon the poor,
And *equal rights* cannot endure,
And wish for such a state of things,
As subjects, nobles, princes, kings,
Hoping that yourselves may be,
Some of the sprigs of royalty:
Ye who delight in revolution,
And think to gain 'midst much confusion:
Ye who prefer (from office driv'n)
"Reigning in hell, to serve in heav'n;"
And would, to mount a despot's throne,
Make orphans sigh, and widows moan,
Your country's fields would die in blood,
With ruins mark where towns have stood;
Ye who of liberty are tir'd,
Whose bosoms are no longer fir'd
With kindred spirit, when the song
Tells of our deeds when we were young.
And freedom's lyre symphonious rings,
And chorus sounds her hundred strings;
Who wish to be "sav'd from yourselves."
By wise and honest federal elves,
And rather follow in the train,
Of kings and nobles, than maintain
The freedom which you now enjoy,
But which you'd barter for a toy,
For sight of pomp and the parade
Of royal balls and masquerade,
Of Coronation shows and feasts,
Of royal slaves and Royal beasts;

Ye who would sever now the union,
No longer wish to hold communion,
With those who will not bend the knee
To the *New-England sovereignty,*
Or who refuse submission unto
Our house of lords—the Essex junto;
Ye who would unite Church and State,
The only way to make us great,
Or in which Government is able,
To stand 'gainst faction, strong and stable,
As two legs are preferred to one,
Whether we wish to stand or run:
In fine, to all, whatever station,
Who feel rebellious 'gainst the nation,
I, at your head by merit plac'd,
With necessary virtue, grac'd,
Send this epistle to you—greeting,
Hoping we soon in merry meeting,
A new success shall celebrate,
When we shall conquer in the State;
Which there's no doubt but we shall do,
If each of you shall *mind your cue,*
And in your harness shall draw true.
To this intent you'll therefore mind,
What here for our good, I've enjoin'd.

  Th' EMBARGO, you all know, was what
Gave us the pow'r which we have got,
This, you know also, is repeal'd,
But this we all must keep conceal'd,
By saying that its substitute
Is the same, and something *worse,* to boot.
Ye who are rich must use your pow'r,
And on the *stubborn debtor* low'r;
For what's the use of all your wealth,
If you can only vote yourself,
And if your influence is confin'd,
To bounds which our laws have assign'd?
These to you give a voice no more,
Than he who has not half your store.

With *threats* and *promises* assail,
And strange if both will not prevail,
For those who will not *sell* their souls,
May yet be kept back from the polls.
You also know there is a way,
To make freeholders for a day,
And, though the law upon this frowns,
The *rich* may safely burst its bounds.
Those you employ no doubt you'll bring
Submissive to the federal ring,
Nor let the *"equal rights of man"*
Prevent your using, all you can,
The pow'r which wealth unto you gave,
To tyrannize and to enslave.
Thus we shall make the people tools,
As *knaves* do always make of *fools*,
And while they fancy that they reign,
More sure our purpose we shall gain.
Fools think that *names* do alter *things*,
But we shall have the pow'r of kings.
A few electioneering lies,
Of due malignity and size,
Such as *"two millions—specie sent—"*
A token of our good intent,
Must be prepar'd to scatter round,
When they're best fitted to confound.
You must not hold your purse strings tight,
The press must groan, and pens must write,
Handbills and pamphlets must be spread,
For thus the people we have led,
Inflam'd those passions that control,
And drive calm reason from the soul.
How did they credulous receive,
And all our red-hot lies believe!
How that Napoleon's *"unseen* hand"
Was seen to rule it o'er our land!
That Madison has basely said
Our money to him *"must"* be paid!
And that "two millions" of our gold

Had been already to him told!
That, although, injur'd much and long,
Great-Britain had done us *"no wrong,"*
But *"Southern States"* wish'd to annoy
Our Commerce, and our trade destroy!
That this produc'd th' Embargo laws,
And yet, *Napoleon* was the cause!
    It is not strange that we despise,
Those who will swallow such strange lies,
And, if they are such downright fools,
We serve them right to make them tools;
This therefore should the conscience ease
Of those whom such lies do not please.
Besides, will not the *end* excuse,
What means soever we may use?
Should these elections vict'ry bring,
To us, and all of *Pickering,*
We'll teach the jacobins to dance,
And all who 'gainst us dare advance.
With Britain join'd as we think meet,
We'll bring them, humble, to our feet;
And, thus supported, bid defiance,
And scorn their forces, or alliance.
New-England then like *old* shall be,
The *(new-world) tyrants* of the sea,
And "Southern States" of us shall crave
For leave to plough the briny wave,
And to our coffers tribute pay.
When, and as much as we may say.
    The glories such, with us invite,
To bribe, electioneer, and fight.[16]

16. *The Columbian Phenix,* Providence, RI, April 8, 1809, 1.

∽ 1810 ∽

1810 was a slightly better year for Connecticut's Republicans, at least for representatives. The number of Republican representatives rose to 57 in the spring, and increased in the fall to 64, but the highest Republican on the Council assistants list sank even lower than in 1809. This would be the last year that the Republicans would put out an assistants list until 1815.

Upon the death of Governor Trumbull in August 1809, John Treadwell had become acting governor. In 1810 there was a three-way race for governor between Treadwell, Republican Asa Spalding, and moderate Federalist Roger Griswold. With none of the three getting a majority of the vote, the election fell to the legislature, which named Treadwell governor. Griswold became lieutenant governor.

In May, in another attempt to get Britain and France to stop seizing American cargoes and seamen and avoid war, the Madison administration replaced the Non-Intercourse Act with Macon's Bill Number 2, the second of two bills introduced by North Carolina Republican representative Nathaniel Macon. This new law lifted the embargo with Britain and France for three months, with the stipulation that if either stopped seizing American cargoes and seamen, the United States would embargo the other unless the other also stopped.

The Reverends Osgood and Parish, with their fiery pro-British political sermons, were becoming household names not only in New England but throughout the country, lauded by Federalists and condemned by Republicans.

IMPIETY AND DISAFFECTION.

The N. England clergymen have long been remarkable for "preaching in politics:" but it will astonish the pious reader, to find a reverend divine so lost to all sense of dignity and propriety, to say nothing of religion, as the author of the following blasphemous and tory effusion, which has been miscalled a prayer.—The man who could so deliberately insult from the pulpit, the Great Object of Adoration, should have been hurled from it headlong.

FROM THE ESSEX REGISTER.—

TEXT.

"We thank thee, O Father, Lord of heaven and earth, that thou hast poured contempt upon the wrath of man, upon the open hostility of France, and the secret grudge and malice of the American government, so over ruling the French decrees and American embargo, devised on purpose for the ruin of Britain, as to render them subservient to the increase of her revenue, and the extension of her commerce."
Mr. Osgood's Fast Sermon.

COMMENT.

Is there a real American, one who is a true friend to his country, who does not blush at the thought, that the temples reared on the soil which our worthy ancestors fled from the hand of tyranny to cultivate, should be thus disgraced. ...

A question is asked in the discourse, from which the above text is taken.—"To whom can the farmer, the mechanic, or the tradesman apply for information, with so much confidence as to his minister?" Let us reply, if opposition to our government be recommended, men had better rely on their own judgment, than follow the dictates of "skulls that cannot teach, and will not learn." [1]

---

1. *The Pittsfield Sun*, Pittsfield, MA, October 17, 1810, 2.

Making news in 1810 was Parish's election sermon, delivered before the Massachusetts legislature on its opening day in May.

Doctor Parish's election sermon, lately delivered before the executive and legislature of Massachusetts.

The drift of this sermon appears to be to demonstrate the existence of national partiality exercised in favor of France, by the majority of our country, and by the government of their choice, and also to prove, what is now no longer disavowed even by the clergy of New-England, that to maintain the party they advocate, an intermingling of religious with political institutions is essential—or in short "that Church and State" must be united before we shall have (the only good one) a federal administration.—Possessed of these opinions, they therefore preach less gospel than politics in their election sermons. This practice we deprecate: we hold that the pulpit is not to be devoted to the promulgation of any but Gospel Doctrines, far less to be polluted with factious political declamation. We hold that the "man who ministers and serves the altar," who professes to inculcate the gospel of HIM "whose kingdom is not of this world" has in the pulpit no *state-duties* to perform.

It is not, however, to be inferred here, that we are less desirous than many others, that our "rulers should be men fearing God and hating covetousness," but we believe men who are silent on religious opinion, no sticklers of squabblers for tenets, who take no part in controversies between Guelphs and Gibbelines, Catholics and Protestants, Calvinists and Methodists, may be qualified to govern and hold places in our administrations, entertain as high a sense of the rights, and as sacred a regard for the welfare of the people, as any other men.—A Jefferson, in politics may be as useful as a Cardinal Woolsey, a Paine, as good as a Jesuit. To establish the system of connection above alluded to, it seems essential to convince the people of the existence of this "national partiality," among the prevailing party in our country, and among those who administer its government in favor of France; because it is asserted that France is an infidel nation; and therefore they who do not hate France are anti-religionists, and heretics. The language, furthermore, is, GOOD OLD ENGLAND, the object of our affection (and to love our mother is a duty) is religious, has what we want, a national church, never burnt our cottages, murdered none of our citizens, nor introduced the scalping-knife among our defenceless frontier inhabitants.

To fasten the opinion, in community, of partiality to France—France must first be rendered *odious,* and mother Britain presented in an *amiable posture.* Hence France is represented as a nest of infidels, her emperor as a *loathsome monster!* and of England "the magnanimity and high sense of Justice of her king," are urged. In order to interweave these subjects, and so to palsy or destroy the people's confidence in their government, that confidence which is its vital support, the Cuckoo-notes "partiality to France—French influence—the hand of Napoleon" &c. are echoed from Halifax to Florida; from Atlantic to the Lakes! ...

Mr Parish "out-herods Herod," in the extracts which follow, and presents incontestible voucher for the truth of our remarks.

EXTRACTS.

... Yet some are heard to say and some few who wear the livery of Christ's ambassadors say, *they* would as willingly elevate an infidel, as a Christian to the highest office on the nation.—While the world in *this instance* is charitable to their veracity, it blushes for their indecency.—Are they not traitors to their Lord and master? Are they not, like the false prophets of Israel, abandoned of Heaven to be the destroyers of their deluded country? Does not Jesus Christ say to them, "Get thee behind me, Satan!"—The woes, which they and their accomplices have already produced, cannot be numbered; the damage and losses, which they have bro't on the country, cannot be calculated: the vices and corruptions, which they have occasioned are infinite; many years of good government would not restore public opinion and morals to their former standard of purity. Unhappy men! are your people so wickedly in love with goodness and good men that they need the charm of your influence to kindle their admiration for the enemies of their Saviour?

An administration is the minister of God for good, by appointing good men to the subordinate offices of the community. These are scattered over the land; these mingle in every company, and carry the light of virtue, or the miseries of the spiritual plague and death to every cottage. I only add that as the alliance of individuals generally give a complexion to their characters and circumstances, so it is with nations. Such is the social nature of man, that he generally assumes the moral complexion of his familiar associates. That government deserves public confidence, and is the minister of God for good, which forms no alliance with a people of opposite religion glorifying in their infamy and crimes. Time was, when an alliance with a nation, which disdains all moral obligations, which blasphemes God and his Son, would have been rejected as improper and dangerous. As a good physician removes his patient from a deadly atmosphere; so a good government forms its alliances where pure religion, sound principles, and christian morals have taken up their abode. The allies of Napoleon are compelled to adopt his interests, to bend to his yoke, and wear his chains. They imbibe his ferocity and atheism. His philosophists instruct them; his officers discipline them; his secret agents as swarms of locusts from the banks of the Nile, now darken the nations of the world. The atheists of France, and the puritans of New-England; was ever an alliance so monstrous! Our temples shudder at the proposal; the spirits of our fathers bend from their thrones of bliss, and enter their solemn protest against such a horrible union.[2]

⌐

"CHURCH & STATE."

Extracts from the PIOUS *Parson's Election Anathema.*

Parson PARISH appears to be greatly disconcerted, because

---

2. *Republican Messenger,* Sherburne, NY, August 7, 1810, 2.

he and his brethren cannot have the government of the country, and consequent power of "unfurling the American standard against France." While the *ministers of religion* are excluded from political broils and contentions, how will it be possible for us, or *them,* ever to prosper! It is a melancholy truth, that too many of our clergy, in these degenerate days, prefer the service of mammon, to that of their beneficent Lord & Master. But we are informed from indubitable authority, that "such men have their reward."

In his election philippic, Parson P. inquires, "If God, when he has *remarkably* prospered his work, has not united magistrates with the *ministers of religion?* Does not history, sacred and profane, (continues the pious parson) bear testimony to this *interesting fact?* We dare go back to the remotest antiquity; we dare rest the merits of the question on experience of ages. Melchisedeck and the Patriarchs were both *Kings* and *Priests of God.* Israel was delivered from Egypt by Moses and Aaron.—When the people were to be reformed, David, and Solomon, and Josiah, were raised to the throne of Palestine." Page 9.

Again, page 10—"In the reign of Jehosaphat the work proceeded more powerfully; he not only banished idolatry, but united himself and the officers of government more intimately with the ministers of religion."

Page 14—"Clothed in the mantle of sensibility, all eye, all heart, man implores protection from the ministers of God, the *political guardians of his country.*"...

Page 19—"If the administration will do a new thing, speak to France the language of an *independent nation,* [that is, declare war against her] we shall hope they are preparing to mount the ladder, *which angels ascend.* The world will applaud the deed of honor."

"*Where* is the voice of general gladness, where is the face of enchanting prosperity, lately so conspicuous? *Why* are our ports solitary and sad? *Why* have the masts been huddled together like groves scorched by the fires of the wilderness? *Where* are our cheerful mariners: *Who,* where is he who has done this mighty mischief? Has famine, has pestilence stalked through our towns? Every child can answer. *The heralds of the General Government have passed through our towns;* like the messengers of Job, each had a tale more affecting than his fellow. They have passed along; before them was the garden of Eden, a virtuous people, obedient to the laws. Behind them is the desert of Sodom, violations of law, perjury and distress. Terrific architects of ruin, can they exult in these tremendous power of annihilation?"

After reading this extract, one would be led to conclude, that the plains of united America exhibited a continued scene of famine and pestilence, of devastation and ruin. That they would rival in misery the fields of Germany, & the vineyards of Spain. But where are these mighty monuments of *distress, annihilation* and *ruin?* In what part of our peaceful country are they discoverable? "The spring has returned with its flowers," the zephyrs of summer now float around us, and the luxuriant verdure of our fields presents to the eye of the husbandman, the promise of a goodly harvest. No despot rears among us his iron sceptre, no tyrannic mandate casts our friends into prison without trial; nor has the blast of war scorched the face of our peaceful country. Yet man, ungrateful man instead of raising the voice with songs of gratulation and praise, impiously inquires, *Why are we solitary and sad!?* This ingrate enquiry, too, is not made by a simple layman, but by a *minister of the Gospel, a professed vicegerent* of Heaven! Who ought to teach us to sing hosannas of thanksgiving and praise for the numberless mercies we receive, instead of wickedly murmuring and repining at our enviable lot.

The Parson goes on to address Mr. GORE,[3] (who was present) in the following strain of adulation and bombast:

"We fondly anticipate the hour, Sir, when the immense resources of our political science, when your undaunted fidelity to your country, when the splendor of your talents, will irradiate a popular branch of our government, and like the flash of heaven display the machinations of our foes. Nor can this possibly be any degradation of rank. The diamond is the same, whether it sparkle in the crown of royalty, or

3. Massachusetts governor Christopher Gore, defeated in the 1810 election by Republican Elbridge Gerry.

slumber on the cross of the pilgrim. The sun is the same shining in meridian splendor, or descending in full orbed majesty, beyond the western hills "to enlighten the lower parts of the earth." Your indefatigable labors of office, your known anxieties for the public good, are pledges that wherever your lot in society shall fall, every effort will be made for the salvation of your country. This shall console us in our fears, while we most devoutly wish you every blessing from the God of heaven." ...

Here, and in the extracts given in our last, Parson PARISH, fully unveils himself. He wishes for a combination of Church and State, founded upon monarchical principles, and for a General of Mr. GORE's renowned *military talents, to "unfurl the American banner against the standard of France."* This is the point, to which the converging clamors and false insinuation dispersed through every part of the parson's libel, all tend. This is the *consummation* which he, and all the *British faction,* so devoutly wish! ...[4]

In the just-held 1810 election, the government of Massachusetts had dramatically shifted Republican. The state's new governor, Elbridge Gerry, was a Republican, the House of Representatives had a large Republican majority, and 19 of 40 in the Senate were Republicans. Parish had been selected by the outgoing Federalist legislature to deliver the customary election sermon on the new legislature's opening day. The response to Parish's sermon by the newly elected Republican legislature was anything but customary.

... It is customary in Massachusetts, on organizing the legislature, to have a sermon preached, in which it is the peculiar province of the Governor, Lieut. Governor, Councillors, and the other branches of government to attend. It seems that the late federal legislature, which took so much pains to whitewash the character of Mr. Copenhagen Jackson,[5] and

---

4. *American Watchman,* Wilmington, DE, June 27, 1810, 3.
5. British diplomat Francis James Jackson. In 1807, Jackson was sent to Denmark to demand that it turn over its entire fleet to the British for use in its war against Napoleon. When Denmark hesitated, British ships bombarded Copenhagen, reducing the city to rubble and killing countless people. He became the new British minister to the United States in 1809, and was dubbed "Copenhagen Jackson" by the Republicans.

to blacken that of the American executive, selected a Dr. PARISH to deliver a sermon before the present administration of Massachusetts. In performing this service he has gone great lengths in reflections on the national administration, as well as on a majority of those recently chosen to bear rule in Massachusetts.—This denunciation of Dr. Parish, the republican members of the Assembly very properly resented; and refused him the customary compliment, viz. to thank him for his discourse, and request a copy for the press. We give the report of the committee to whom the subject was referred, in their own words; and to which is subjoined the decision of the house, expressive of their marked disapproval of the performance.

"That the discourse alluded to, is, in the opinion of the committee, so replete with unjust accusations against the Government of the United States, and those who administer the same; and contains sentiments so disrespectful of those whom the People of this Commonwealth have entrusted the government thereof, couched in language most exceptionable, that it would be highly derogatory to the dignity of this House, to request a copy of such a discourse, much more to return thanks.

This report was warmly debated, and at a late hour in the afternoon was accepted.

   Yeas 293, Nays 163, Maj. 130" !! [6]

Connecticut's Federalists, like their Federalist brethren in Massachusetts, applauded the sermons of Osgood and Parish, with the *Courant* denouncing the Republican legislature of Massachusetts for their resolution not to thank Parish for his election sermon or to request a copy for printing:

For upwards of an hundred years, it has been the practice of the Legislature of Massachusetts, like that of this State, to pass a vote of thanks to the clergyman, who preaches the election sermon, and to request a copy for the press. This year, there being a majority of democrats in the

6. *The Centinel Of Freedom*, Newark, NJ, June 19, 1810, 3.

legislature, this long established custom has been dispensed with, and the Rev. Dr. Parish has not even received the thanks of that body, for his very able discourse delivered before them, on the late election. This sermon, however, has been published by private subscription, and the public are now in possession of this valuable production. In a preceding column will be found several extracts from the sermon in question, which are well worth perusing.[7]

The "several extracts" from Parish's "valuable production" filled nearly an entire page of the *Courant* — five columns of small type from top to bottom of the page — for the perusal of Connecticut's Federalists.

An emerging Federalist theme, which would become even more prevalent as the country entered the War of 1812, was that England was a protector of religion and, therefore, to oppose England was to oppose religion.

THE printer of the Hampshire Gazette published in his paper of the 21st February, a piece pretended to be written by a "Christian Politician," but written in fact by a vile impostor. This piece was extracted from the Palladium. After a long eulogium upon the British, the writer asks, with an air of triumph, "Are not those who oppose such a nation as England, at the hazard of every thing just, pure, lovely, and of good report, enemies in fact of the church?"

If such sentiments as are propagated by this writer, are tolerated, we may bid adieu to our liberties. If such sentiments become prevalent, we shall be prepared to become the most despicable slaves on earth: the slaves of a foreign power. According to this writer, we are not to oppose England, because England is fighting the battles of the church. If England should see fit to burn our towns, to plunder our property, and murder our citizens in cool blood, we are not to oppose her, for she is the champion of true religion! ...

The object of the "Christian Politician" appears to be to involve America in the mud wars of Great-Britain with all

7. *The Connecticut Courant,* Hartford, CT, June 27, 1810, 3.

the world. With this view he affects to have a great regard for religion, which he pretends to believe is in danger. He says,

"Had we not forsaken the God of our fathers, and chosen to have been governed by a French philosopher, by an infidel, as hostile to religion as Voltaire, and whose morals were on a line with those of Mirabeau and Condorcet, England and America would have been at peace, IF NOT ENGLAND IN DEFENDING UNDER THE CROSS, CIVIL AND RELIGIOUS LIBERTY. But the election of Mr. Jefferson was rebellion against heaven.

Americans, are ye ready for an alliance with England? Are ye prepared to fight for the inquisition; or for the established church of Great-Britain? [8]

The following are a pair of satires from Republican papers, the first mocking how a Federalist might imagine a Republican celebration, and the second on the resolutions of a "Grand Federal Meeting."

DEMOCRATIC CELEBRATION AT HUBBARDSTON.

THE anniversary of our Independence was celebrated at Hubbardston on the 4th inst. in such a manner as to afford much *good entertainment* both to mind and body. I am very sorry I was not there to give you a more circumstantial account. I should certainly have attended had it not been for the following melancholy occurrence. I incautiously, for a rarity, went to church last Sunday and our parson, as ill luck would have it, preached against young people's going into bad company, from Prov. XXIV, 1 and 2. *Be not thou envious against evil men, neither desire to be with them; for their heart studieth destruction, and their lips speak of mischief.* The old man's text and Sermon together (for who can tell which was the most pointed) so alarmed me that, in truth, I could not muster courage enough to join the throng. My neighbor *Frizzle,* however, who is always punctual and attentive, saddled his old white mare by sunrise,

---

8. *Anti-Monarchist and Republican Watchman,* Northampton, MA, March 7, 1810, 3.

borrowed a dollar of me to purchase a ticket, and off he rode. He returned late in the evening, but so overcharged with the good entertainment, that he was not able to give me any account to the transactions of the day until next morning. In relating to me the occurrences, I found he was somewhat diverted with the peculiarities, although he thought them rather unfavorable to the cause of democracy. For he made bold to tell me, that contrary to all precedent, they had no prayers upon so solemn occasion. He observed how thankful he was that no federalists were present, for they would certainly have said that the democrats had no religion. On enquiring how this happened, he told me that the Clergy had been so blamed for meddling with politics, that no one ventured to make his appearance. The democrats, however, were determined to have prayers, and therefore, diligently sought for some deacon or justice of trials to officiate as chaplain. But to their great mortification, there was not a man amongst them all who had ever prayed upon any occasion, and they all swore that they would not begin then. Finding themselves frustrated in this attempt, they next agreed that, for decency's sake, some persons present should pass for clergymen on that day, and accompany the orator to the pulpit, read something pretty curious and solemn, and be in readiness to support the orator if he fainted, to prompt him if he halted, and to seize him by the heels and drag him back if, in his great animation, violent gestures, or heart-rending pathos, he should over-leap the pulpit and be in danger of falling headlong upon the dear people. Accordingly Esq. *Whitebush* and Col. *Browntush* were unanimously chosen to put on the sheep's clothing. We now thought all was in a good way, and saw these Reverend clergy walk majestically into the pulpit, each with a big bible under his arm. But here, as if the devil must always "vex his saints" our clergy made a *bull*. For having selected nothing to read, and being little acquainted with bibles, Esq. Whitebush, poor man, unfortunately hit upon the 59th chapter of Isaiah. I liked his manner of reading much, but the old prophet I found was as strong a federalist as any in New England, *Osgood* and *Parish* not excepted. I cannot remember all he read, but I well recollect the following and presume you will find it so in your bible. He represents us the people as saying, *Judgment is far from us, neither doth justice overtake us; we wait for light but behold obscurity; for brightness but we walk in darkness. We grope for the wall like the blind, and we grope as if we had no eyes; we stumble at noon-day as in the night; we are in desolate places as dead men. We roar all like bears, and mourn sore like doves: we look for judgment, but there is none; for salvation, but it is far off from us. For our transgressions are multiplied and our sins testify against us.* Gracious heavens! Was an audience ever so pinched to the heart before? Was a man ever so unfortunate as our Esq? We were all blind and dead men sure enough! The Esq. paused—for he could read no further; he sat down—for he was unable to stand. The "people" were silent—for they could not speak. Their tongue cleaved to the roof of their mouth and their hair stood on end.

After a long and solemn pause, as if the wheels of nature were broken, Col. *Browntush,* arose and opened his great book. Never did a man look down upon an audience so awfully impressed. Never did a people look to a public reader or speaker with so much earnestness and with such full confidence that he would soon console, compose and cherish their desponding souls. The Col. then, I say, opened his great book and read a part of the 7th chap. of Jeremiah as follows, *Thus saith the Lord of hosts—Amend your ways and your doings. For behold, ye trust in lying words, that cannot profit. Will ye steal, murder, and commit adultery, and swear falsely, and burn incense unto Baal, and walk after other gods whom ye know not, and come and stand before me in this house which is called by my name, and say, We are delivered to do all these abominations? Is this house, which is called by my name, become a den of robbers? Behold, even I have seen it saith the Lord.* It would be impossible to give you any idea of the effect which this had upon the assembly. Neighbor *Frizzle* wept as he repeated the words of the prophet. He told me how the whole multitude were thrown into spasms, and convulsions. The females screamed and fainted; old men and young groaned from the bottom of their breasts; the veteran soldier and uniformed officer stood pale, and their trembling knees smote one against the other. Death and dismay were to be seen on every countenance. An awful silence ensued, as if the last dread summons was next to be read, and they cut off in the very act of political chicanery and hypocrisy.

Soon as the people had recovered from the deep emotions excited by reading the prophets, the Orator of the day, who was no less a character than the celebrated Orlando Furioso, &c. &c. &c. arose—advanced—ascended—bowed—recovered—looked—winked—stared—strutted—scraped—opened his mouth—extended his arm—clenched his fist—and last of all, SPOKE!—From this time to the end of his Song every ear was opened like a tunnel and the words fell from his mouth just like oats and peas from a miller's hopper. "He spoke his oration, as tho' he wished he could act a tragedy." Sometimes his voice was as soft and gentle as the kitten's mew. Again the dreadful storm gathered on his brow, which made the isle of England shake, and anglo-feds were struck with his panics at such a hideous phiz. He disgorged from his stomach and entrails such black and fetid gore as would have gagged a Cyclop to have seen it—such boiling burning lava that many thought he was a little Volcano. But as Orlando will probably print all his grand orations for the benefit of distant climes and future ages, I give you no further account of the one now under consideration. When it appears in print I may probably bestow upon it a few remarks, and likewise upon the select and precious toasts, especially the one drank to "Osgood and the prophets."

CAPTAIN SHANDY.[9]

The following resolutions have been some time in our files. They are published, at this late hour, to gratify several of our readers, and particularly as they contain the pith of all the federal resolutions past during the election which has

9. *Thomas's Massachusetts Spy, or Worcester Gazette,* Worcester, MA, July 11, 1810, 1.

terminated so gloriously for the prosperity, honor and dignity of the state of New-York.

SUBLIME RESOLUTIONS,

Passed at the Grand Federal Meeting.

CHRONONHOTONTHOLOGOS,[10] *Ch'n.*

Secretary General Bombardinian mounted upon the gorgeous cupola of the cloud-capt capital, with the brazen lungs, the thousand mouths, and thousand babbling tongues of same, read and pronounced with a loud voice, the following most sublime and potent *resolutions,* which had been moved in superior style by a most honorable renowned patrician federalist, of no plebeian genealogy:

I. *Resolved,* unanimously, most firmly, unquestionably, decisively, irrevocably and eternally, That his *magnanimous* majesty, the king of Great-Britain, never can do wrong; and the mean, blind and stupid, democratic government of the United States, never can do right.

II. *Resolved,* That these are *not free* and *independent* states, as audaciously declared in 1776; and that the declaration of independence, is an impudent libel upon the character of the British king, "whose magnanimous sense of justice" renders him every way fit to be the ruler of a free and enlightened people. Not independent, because it is undeniably true, that they *depend* on his majesty's *Navy* to save and protect this poor, distracted, prostrate, ruined, disheartened, nerveless, dull, lazy, unenlightened, servile, base, cowardly, mean, starved, scorched, cursed democratic country, from the voracious jaws of Napoleon, and from the blasting effects of French influence forever.

III. *Resolved,* That his magnanimous majesty may, of hereditary and divine right, burn our goods, tax them with transit duties, license our trade, or interdict it wholly by proclamation: That his pettiest naval officer may stop and

10. A 1734 English satirical play by Henry Carey on George II and Queen Caroline in which King Chrononhotonthologos and Queen Fadladinida of Queerummania are invaded by a race of strange people called the Antipodeans.

search our vessels, impress and pronounce upon the citizenship of an American, our laws of naturalization, the laws of nature and nations to the contrary notwithstanding; and that he may stamp under foot the American flag, whip and insult our officers, gibbet and shoot our seamen near our shores, or elsewhere upon the king's high seas, and deserves therefore to be promoted to posts of command and distinction—and that his majesty's minister, in any place and in any manner, may directly or indirectly charge the government of the United States and President, with corruption, duplicity and falsehood; and that for so intrepid an assertion of his sovereign master's royal prerogative, he deserves well of Federalism, and shall be entitled to an honorary ticket of admission into our grand fetes and commemorative balls—and that at his entrance the music shall strike in the highest strains, "God save the king!"

IV. *Resolved,* That it is perfectly consistent that his "magnanimous" majesty, as "defender of the faith," undertakes with his right hand a holy crusade to support the sword, the catholic religion in Spain, whilst with his left hand, the same religion in Ireland is rewarded with misery, abolition of hereditary right and paternal authority, taxation, deprivation, degradation, conflagration, dungeons, bayonets, gibbets and exile: That the invaders of Mysore are fit aids and glorious auxiliaries for the pious invaders of Mexico; and that the constitution prohibiting all other but the catholic religion, is perfectly orthodoxical, and for the establishment of which it is pious and glorious for British *protestants* to suffer martyrdom—and the relics of those who fell shall be canonized: That England is the only country of religion, the merited persecution of our obstinate puritanical forefathers, and the proofs of all the British, moral, theological, biographical and historical writers to the contrary, (for the present) not in any wise withstanding—that religion has been ably, piously and effectually supported in Spain as well as in England, by the powerful and convincing aids of the sword, the dungeon and the wreck, the ordeal, the stake and the gibbet.

V. *Resolved,* That Napoleon is not our king—but that he is an usurper—and that Frenchmen are atheists, murderers, maneaters and devils, who have neither reason, feeling nor souls. That Frenchmen, as a nation, or any other people, have no right, discretion or power to choose and establish for themselves a form of government; but that England, and other monarchies of Europe had a right and cause to interfere, and by incessant wars and intrigues, to persecute and harass them till they sought refuge in tyranny and Bonaparte.

VI. And whereas *Tom Jefferson,* in the declaration of independence, did falsely, wickedly and maliciously traduce and libel the good name, fame and reputation of his *magnanimous* majesty, the King of Great-Britain, *France* and *Ireland; Elector of Hanover, Duke of Brunswick, Defender of the faith,* &c. and by his speeches, counsels and writing, aided and abetted the *rebel* Washington and others, his rebel countrymen, to enforce said declaration with their swords: And whereas said Jefferson, long afterwards, when elevated by the suffrages of said rebels to high stations, still moved by the same malicious and rebellious spirit, did advise and procure the appropriation of millions of dollars of fortifications, repairs of vessels and building of new ones, for the protection of our harbors, seaports and trade, to the evident prejudice and annoyance of his majesty's fleets, and to his interests and rights founded upon the sacred and inviolable doctrine of *expediency;* and by proclamations and laws, excluded from our ports *armed* vessels of his majesty, *merely* because his officers in the exercise of their duty, had done nothing more that magnanimously fire at a public vessel of the U. States, carrying the Vice President from the seat of government—blockaded our harbors, impressed, whipped, hung, shot and gibbetted a few American rebels, within cannon shot of our rebellious land; and to oppose these doings, the said Jefferson raised detachments of hundreds of thousands of democratic, ragged, rebel militia, who, for the most part, impudently and outrageously volunteered in this dishonorable service—and whereas the said Jefferson, by the amicable purchase of Louisiana, opened the Mississippi to the western states and territories, and excluded the possibility of danger from a growing nation of Frenchmen and enemies on our rear; making oceans the barriers between us and the old world—and did impoliticly persuade whole nations of savages to abandon the tomahawk and the chace, for the plough and the loom; and has promoted the laying up of stores, magazines, of arms, ordnances, ammunition, and the importation of saltpetre and copper. Therefore—

Resolved, That said Jefferson is a blind, weak and wicked calumniator and traitor.

And whereas the said Jefferson did, in his notes upon Virginia, maintain that the christian religion was evident and strong enough to support itself without the aid of reason: that it needed not the aid of law or the sword; that laws founded upon principles of universal justice afforded equal protection to the persons and properties of all sects and denominations of religion whatsoever, pagan, christian or mahometan, and that in well regulated governments my person and property are secure, whether my neighbor be a polytheist or monitheist, and that in a question of civil right or wrong it is no enquiry for the court or jury what are the religious tenets of the accuser or accused; and because the said Jefferson by such heretical arguments paved the way for the subsequent article of the federal constitution which most heretically secures to all men the liberty of conscience, and destroys the merciful system of the inquisition: and whereas the said Jefferson did subsequently satyrise the Catholic *Mazzei,* for the show and pageantry of the papal Cathedral and place of worship; and did thereafter most iniquitously pollute a public vessel, by permitting Tom Paine, to sail therein from France to America, pursuant to the request of said Paine; as an act of humanity to one whom Congress employed, paid and thanked for his political services.—And notwithstanding his payment of more than any individual in America for the support of the gospel (pursuant to the assertion of a "Christian Politician" in Boston, republished in the Albany Gazette) it is resolved that said Jefferson is a heretic, a deist, and an atheist—and *that the election of Jefferson was rebellion against heaven!!!*—and further, that if our glorious and pious aims are crowned with success, we will use our best endeavors to revive the inquisition, and the process "de heretico comburendo" (the burning of heretics) that we may take spiritual revenge upon the said heretic for asserting that religion could be supported by reason and good sense only, and that the partialities and prejudices of a thousand sects should not bias or swerve the administration of civil justice.

And whereas, said Jefferson is elected by the national institute of France (the most useful and enlightened literary institution in the world, if it were not composed of Frenchmen,) an honorary member thereof, has been awarded the premium upon suggesting the best improvement of the plough-share.—And whereas, while secretary of state, he vanquished the French minister Genet, by hard arguments only, without the auxiliary of hard names, and by the same means held at respectful distance the impetuous Bonaparte, without the aid of bayonets and epithets.—And whereas, said Jefferson actually reads French, speaks French, and has resided in France.—Therefore, resolved, that Jefferson is a French philosopher.

And whereas said Jefferson did, by writing, attempt to prove, that nature was not a European partizan, and most foolishly to prove that the animals of America are as large and as numerous, the plumage of the birds as fair, the men as strong, feeling and courageous as Europeans—to prove that Washington was a hero, Franklin a philosopher, Rittenhouse an astronomer and artist, Logan an orator—in attempting to prove that these were not degeneracies of nature,

Resolved, therefore, That Jefferson is a fool—and that the administration of Jefferson has brought upon our *"beloved country"* miseries which no tongue can tell, nor eye behold!

VII. *Resolved,* That if any person, upon any occasion, speak respectfully of the American government, of Jefferson, Madison, or any republican measures; who shall not on all occasions curse France and French principles, philosophy or Bonaparte, or who shall on any occasion, speak, write, or suggest any thing directly of indirectly impeaching the integrity, infallibility, honor and uprightness of the King ... be deemed unworthy of any place of honor, trust or confidence.

VIII. *Resolved,* That the only qualification necessary for

a candidate for office is, partiality to Britain, hatred to France, philosophy and democracy, and contempt or indifference for America. ...

CHRONONHOTONTHOLOGOS, Chairman.
BOMBARDINIAN,[11] Secretary.[12]

In the Massachusetts *Independent Whig,* the aristocratic and monarchical aspirations of the New England Federalists were set to rhyme:

EFFUSION
of a Staunch federalist.

Mankind at large, I've often heard,
    Were all created free;
Yet of all things, this has appear'd
    The most absurd to me.

For when th' Almighty made mankind,
    The royal part he blest,
And said to them—"you are design'd
    To manage all the rest."

Yea, if we look all nature thro';
    The earth, the sea, or air,
I think that we can clearly view,
    The same distinctions there.

The Lion ranges o'er the field,
    With aspect so severe,
The lesser beasts are forc'd to yield,
    When he approaches near.

Thus the large fishes of the sea,
    A smaller kind devour;

11. General Bombardinian, a character in *Chrononhotonthologos.*
12. *The Albany Register,* Albany, NY, May 4, 1810, 3.

So hens before a hawk will flee,
    And try t' escape the power.

This solemn truth, of so much weight,
    Let no one dare disclaim;
Since 'tis a fact that Church and State,
    Have always held the same.

They both have said, that some were born
    A lov'd and royal race;
That others must be held in scorn,
    As objects of disgrace.

Since kings and priests this doctrine hold,
    And set so greatly by it,
O, how presumptuous, vain and bold,
    Is he who dare deny it!

If heav'n has e'er shewn to man,
Proofs, more concise and strong,
Then let that person come, who can,
    And prove me in the wrong.

Methinks no one can read such facts,
    Without conviction smites,
He might as well think Afric blacks,
    As good as English whites.

How false that doctrine then, must be,
    (A doctrine which I scorn,)
That men of high and low degree,
    Are on a level born.

I'm an American by birth,
    Yet by the heav'nly powers,
So bad a government on earth,
    Does not exist, as ours.

I lik'd the Embargo, tho' 'twas bad,

Because I had a notion,
The people soon would grow so mad,
      They'd rise up in commotion.

This measure really did, in short,
      Give such dissatisfaction,
That all the Greys, of Newburyport,
      Were cock'd and prim'd for action.

Had then the *Northern States* combin'd,
      And made a separation;
Before this day they might have join'd
      The good old British nation.

But ah! since then, we have lost ground;
      The cause is this, I find,
Our friends are not all firm and sound,
      Too many lag behind.

I ne'er was pleas'd, I must need say,
      With Jackson, Rose and Canning;
A thousand bunglers such as they,
      Were never worth a hanging.

We want more men of nerve and force,
      To keep the *rabble* under;
Whose powerful, energetic voice,
      Should strike *their* ears like thunder.

Had we a powerful government,
      To vindicate our cause;
The people, quickly, should be bent,
      To good and wholesome laws.

Then with a few more on our side,
      Like *Osgood, Spring* and *Morse;*
Our doctrines, men should not deride,
      They should go down by force.

If milder measures would not do,
　　In our attempts to turn them;
Then *Cobb's* advice, we would pursue,
　　That is, we'd "hang or burn them." * 13

The *Press* we quickly would restrain,
　　That *engine* of sedition;
And like our worthy friends in Spain,
　　Set up an Inquisition.

We'd let the common people know,
　　This truth, that's worth repeating:
That they were made to *plow and hoe,*
　　And to be drove to meeting. †

It would my happiness complete,
　　To see this glorious day—
Then fervently let me intreat
　　Our faithful friends to pray,

That ev'ry plague which heav'n can send,
　　May on our foes be hurl'd;
Til democratic power shall end,
　　And monarchs rule the world.

ONE OF THE WELL BORN.

* See the Rev. Mr. Merrill's letter on this subject.
† This chaste and elegant sentiment, is thus beautifully
expressed by an honorable gentleman of Connecticut. 14

13. David Cobb, Federalist lieutenant governor of Massachusetts in 1809 and 1810, was accused by Rev. Daniel Merrill of saying that "the civil authority have a right to make laws to bind men to worship all in one way, and if not, then burn." The remark was said to have been made at a gathering at the home of a Rev. William Mason, and published in the Maine Republican paper the *Eastern Argus.* Even a defender of Cobb, recounting the conversation in the Massachusetts paper the *Merrimack Intelligencer,* said that Cobb had in fact said, "burn them, or punish them in any way pointed out by the laws relative to opposition and rebellion against the State," when asked by Merrill what should happen to those who refuse obey an order of the government "to have the Citizens assemble at stated times, at such and such places, where public worship is had, or any where else." (*Merrimack Intelligencer,* March 31, 1810).

14. *Independent Whig,* Newburyport, MA, December 26, 1810, 1.

∽ 1811 ∾

1811 was a pivotal year in Connecticut politics and in the Republicans' hopes for religious freedom. It was the year that the Episcopalians, which represented almost ten percent of the state's vote, voted with the Republicans for the first time. While the Episcopalians were considered by the Congregationalist Federalists to be a more respectable sect than the other dissenters, and had always largely voted Federalist, they were still dissenters and as such would never be treated completely equally. An Episcopalian could not hope to get into the state's highest offices, and despite repeated requests the legislature had refused to incorporate an Episcopalian college. What caused the Episcopalians to break ranks with the Federalists and vote with the Republicans, at least for this year, was that the Republicans' candidate for lieutenant governor, Elijah Boardman, was an Episcopalian. The Republicans didn't run their own candidate for governor this year, but instead backed Treadwell's Federalist challenger Roger Griswold, a moderate, who, most importantly, wasn't the least bit religious. In the months preceding the election, articles like the following, explaining the party's decision to support Griswold, appeared in the Republican papers.

TO THE REPUBLICANS OF CONNECTICUT.

It is no discredit to the bravery of a man, to make terms with his adversary, when further resistance has become manifestly unavailing. Our contest with the federalists of this State, has been long and arduous. Though our adversaries have been protected by all the muniments, and armed by all the enginery, that could be devised by men hackneyed in all the arts of an unprincipled union of church and state—yet our exertions have been of that steady and persevering character, which could only have proceeded from a perfect confidence in the justice of our cause.

The season has again arrived, when it has become a part of the duty of every freeman of Connecticut, to consider of characters proper to fill the executive offices of our state government, for the year ensuing. At such a time, we naturally take into view the present incumbents, and the present enquiry is, can their places be better filled? On this enquiry no republican will hesitate for an answer, for all agree that the office of governor of this state is filled by a man who never has been (and probably never will be) chosen to that office by a majority of the suffrages of the freemen, whose political principles are believed to be hostile to the constitution of the United States—hostile to the federal union, and to the republican institutions of our country. The next inquiry is, is there any probability that by any effort that the republicans would ordinarily make, the office of governor could be better filled than at present? To this we answer, there is not only a probability but a moral certainty that this can be accomplished by the efforts of republicans. Mr. Spalding has declined being considered as a candidate for that office. The vote of last spring fully evinced that the will of the majority did not designate John Treadwell, for governor. The number of his friends has not since increased. On the contrary, many who last year were willing that he should serve for a time, by way of experiment, are now fully satisfied, that the experiment has been sufficiently tried. If then, the votes of those who are unwilling that governor Treadwell should be continued in office, could be united for any one candidate, there is a moral certainty that this candidate would be elected.—The questions then occur, is there such a candidate, and who is he? We have no hesitation in saying that *Roger Griswold*, Esq. is the only man, who probably, would unite those votes. In offering this gentleman to the consideration of our republican brethren, as their candidate for governor, we are fully aware, that he has been, and still is ranked among the federalists. But we feel an interest in promoting the dignity and reputation of this state. How is this to be accomplished? If Mr. Griswold is a federalist, he is a different federalist from Gov. Treadwell. He will not descend to acts of meanness to gratify a party. He will not render our state contemptible abroad, by an affected display of pedantry, nor despicable, by a criminal ignorance on national subjects. He will not hazard the peace and reputation of the state, by encouraging or countenancing a rebellious opposition to the laws of the union, nor by recommending the enacting of laws that shall enable one denomination of religion, to tyrannize over the others. He will not disgrace himself and friends by any narrow system of politics, nor by an overacted intolerant zeal in party religion. ...[1]

Griswold won by a comfortable margin, with 10,148 votes to Treadwell's 8,727.

Boardman easily beat Federalist John Cotton Smith in the lieutenant governor's race, with 5,966 votes to Smith's 1,789, but did not become lieutenant governor. The problem was that Griswold, although running for governor, had also received 7,404 votes for lieutenant governor, meaning that no candidate had a majority of the vote. The choice, therefore, went to the legislature, which in defiance of the will of the voters, named Smith, with less than a third the number of votes of Boardman, lieutenant governor.

Shortly after the election, an article in the *Mercury* laid out the unlikely sequence of events that would have to occur for the standing order Federalists to regain their stranglehold on the state:

THE OLD CHINA BOWL, AGAIN.

We have heard of divisions in Pennsylvania and New-York, but who could ever thought that there could ever be a division among the federalists in Connecticut, holy men, who care for politics, only for the good of religion, and the

1. *American Mercury,* Hartford, CT, March 28, 1811, 3.

advancement of themselves and their children.

Yet such things are, and the venerable governor Treadwell, who has been twice exposed to the suffrages of the people, is, after all his pious prayers and labors, to be sent home in his old age, to sell his land for a support, and all this, because the democrats chose Mr. Griswold over his head; because Mr. Griswold will not decline to serve, and because the democrats will not ever suffer Mr. Treadwell to be lieut. governor. He is a large fragment of the old china bowl, but there is no such thing as restoring him to his place.

The federal party is divided, and there is but one way of uniting them again. That must be by choosing John C. Smith, Esq. to be the lieut. Governor, and he must agree to abide by that office and outlive Mr. Griswold, and then to succeed him, and Mr. Griswold must agree to die in good season, and the democrats must agree to be neutral, and the men of established religion, must agree that though Mr. G. differs from them in some cardinal points, they will regard him as holy *ex officio,* so long as he shall remain in office, and Mr. G. must agree to issue annually a fresh edition of Mr. Treadwell's proclamations for fasts and thanksgivings, and federalism must go on smoothly again; but alas, a damp snow in the night and a frosty morning may be expected, and when you are proudly shewing how the pieces have been put together, the old china bowl will slip and be smashed beyond redemption.[2]

As it turned out, the unlikely scenario of the legislature naming Smith lieutenant governor, Griswold's dying in office, and Smith's succeeding him is exactly what happened. Griswold, despite losing Republican support because of his opposition to war with England, was reelected in 1812, but died in October 1812. Smith became acting governor, was elected in 1813, and was reelected every year through 1816.

But the importance of the election of 1811, although a short-lived semi-victory, was far from insignificant. At least for this election, the Republicans had won over the Episcopalians, without whom the

2. *American Mercury,* Hartford, CT, May 2, 1811, 3.

eventual victory over the Federalists in 1817 would not be possible.

The influence of the Episcopalians in the election was noted by the *Republican Farmer:*

> A letter from Hartford, to the Editors of the Mercantile Advertiser, states that "In 103 towns Roger Griswold has a majority of 830 votes, and will in all probability, be elected Governor." If this statement is correct, it shews that the influence of the Episcopalians is more than a "drop of the bucket, or dust of the balance." [3]

But despite the Episcopalians' voting with the Republicans for governor and lieutenant governor, Republican representation in the House did not see a bump.

The non-religious moderate Griswold was of course intensely disliked by Connecticut's Federalist party leaders, including Yale president Timothy Dwight, the "Pope."

When a correspondent to the Federalist *Connecticut Mirror* calling himself "Veritas," writing about an article in the New York Republican paper *The Columbian,* accused a correspondent to that paper of lying about what Dwight had said about the "infidel" governor Griswold in his sermon at the college's 1811 commencement, the correspondent to *The Columbian* responded by, among other things, calling "Veritas" a "little stupid dunce."

This was "Veritas's" article from the *Mirror,* which quoted in its entirety the article from *The Columbian:*

From a Correspondent.

NEW-HAVEN, Sept 18.

MR. EDITOR,

Please to publish in your paper, the following article from the New-York Columbian, of September 14, with the remarks subjoined:—

"CONNECTICUT POLITICS.

"From a Correspondent.

"*Electioneering in Season.*—It seems that the Treadwell

---

3. *Republican Farmer,* Bridgeport, CT, April 17, 1811, 3.

party of Connecticut, or rather the special-session men, as they are more properly called, are commencing hostilities anew against their present governor Griswold. Dr. Dwight, in his late sermon to the young men who were about to leave the university at Commencement, told them that if the first settlers of Connecticut could rise from their graves, they would blush for the corruption of the age, when they should observe with what reluctance the taxes are paid for the support of Clergymen and schoolmasters; and when they should furthermore find, that their descendants had deserted the old track of steady habits, and appointed an infidel for their chief office of the state; or to use his own language, to see how infidelity has of late "insinuated itself into the chair of majesty." Many of the audience showed evident astonishment at this bare-faced declaration, but it was repeated with a double emphasis, which could not be misunderstood. The other part of the discourse was employed in showing, that religion and politics are so inseparably connected, that the person who preaches the one, acts as a traitor, unless he interlards his observations with dashes of the other. We may of course expect, that the little State of Connecticut will present another scene of "clashing chaos" at the next spring election. The attacks on Governor Griswold have heretofore been carried on by a parcel of contemptible little puppets; while the wires and secret springs which set them in motion have been touched behind the curtain by an unseen hand. But it now seems, that the chief manager of this solemn farce has appeared in person, and even from the sacred desk dares to deal out the anathemas of ecclesiastical wrath. What will be the result of this management is yet to be learned.

"Every nerve will doubtless be strained to bring forward deacon Treadwell again; he has already been dubbed doctor of laws, and styled the venerable father of steady habits by Dr. Dwight; but a majority of the voters of Connecticut say, that this aforesaid deacon, not withstanding his title of L.L.D. is better calculated to sip tea-slops with old maids, and retail the common scandal of a country village, than to accept any office within the gift of the state. In vain may

Connecticut boast of her "enviable situation;" in vain talk
of her long list of worthy governors—her schoolmasters, and
her parsons, if the officers of the state are to be scowled into
contempt by a pontifical glance; if every republican is to be
branded as an infidel; if the tenure of Connecticut liberty is
to be snapped asunder by the mere venom of ecclesiastical
censure, and if all this is federalism too, then away with your
hypocritical cant about happy Connecticut. From such
happiness, "good Lord deliver us."

The above publication was without doubt written in this
City—with what motive the reader will readily perceive. I
have very rarely seen even a *Columbian* publication so
replete with falsehood. The sermon of Dr. Dwight to the
Graduates, was heard by hundreds as well as by myself, and
I appeal to the recollection of every person of *veracity* who
was present, when I assert that there was not a single allusion
to the politics or to the officers of the State of Connecticut,
or of the general Government. The writer of the above article undertakes to support his statement by a quotation, *to
see how infidelity has of late "insinuated itself into the
chair of majesty"*—this is equally false with the rest, no
such expression was used by the preacher.

VERITAS.[4]

Five days later, *The Columbian* acknowledged the *Mirror* article:

President Dwight. It is due to that gentleman to state,
that the circumstance of his having made certain allusions
to governor Griswold, in preaching against infidels, a short
time since, as mentioned in a communication published in
this paper, is denied in a Connecticut print, and waits for
explanation from our correspondent. We give facts as we
receive them, but wish to receive nothing but facts.[5]

Four days after that, *The Columbian* printed its correspondent's
response. Other than correcting a typo, the correspondent stood

4. *Connecticut Mirror,* Hartford, CT, September 23, 1811, 3.
5. *The Columbian,* New York, NY, September 28, 1811, 2.

by his original story:

President Dwight's Sermon—again.

The following explanation from our first correspondent, whose absence prevented his making it before, is received today. It accords with our first impressions on the subject. The inference from the words used, however, being a matter of opinion only.

"*Error corrected.* The publication made some few days ago, in the Columbian, touching on Dr. Dwight's farewell address to his students, it seems, has galled the feelings of the brotherhood most wonderfully. A typographical error occurred in the piece, which provoked a little stupid dunce, who flourishes with a few lines, in the Connecticut Mirror, to accuse us of misquoting. The error alluded to is, that for the word *magistracy,* the word *majesty* was printed. The sentence should have read thus: infidelity has "insinuated itself into the chair of magistracy"; or rather, to give the whole sentence, that it had "insinuated itself into the legislative hall, and into the chair of magistracy." Now, we will repeat again, that this allusion must have had reference to governor Griswold, or it means nothing. It could not have been intended for Mr. Jefferson, because he is not now in office; and there is no other person, in the "chair of magistracy," who has been anathematized by priests, except governor Griswold.

We should now ask "*Mr. Veritas*" if he can smooth down his face again, and swear point blank, that there was no allusion to the politics of the country, in the sermon alluded to." [6]

Nothing more was heard from "Veritas."

With the Massachusetts legislature still in Republican hands, Reverend Parish was not invited to give this year's election sermon. He did, however, deliver a Fast Day sermon, which even some Federalists denounced. Connecticut's *Republican Farmer,* reprinting an item from a Federalist paper in Virginia, noted the difference

---

6. *The Columbian,* New York, NY, October 2, 1811, 2.

between New England's Federalists and Federalists in the south, or what remained of them:

Federalism reproveth itself.

The following notice of Parish's Fast Sermon, by the editor of the Virginia Patriot, is a mark of the difference between the federalism of the Essex Junto and the southern federalists; and shows, also, what an abominable production the sermon must be, when it is severely condemned by a writer of the same political faith.

Columbian

"A Sermon was preached at Byfield, Massachusetts, on a public occasion which has been printed, and which we have noticed in a paper of that state, and which has occasioned some controversy. We regret seeing such a production ranged on the side of federalism. It manifests too much of a religious and political bigot; rage without force, and zeal without discretion; and it is as free from Christian candor and meekness as if the preacher had never seen a bible. As a clergyman said on another occasion, it is fighting the battles of heaven with artillery drawn from hell. We would advise the Rev. Doctor Parish to confine his labors to geographical compilations [7] and pour out hereafter only *religious* damnation on his parishioners at home, who may be fond of it. We regret saying so much against a federal clergyman, but the production is really outrageous." [8]

7. In 1807, Parish had published a schoolbook, *A Compendious System of Universal Geography.*
8. *Republican Farmer,* Bridgeport, CT, June 12, 1811, 3.

~ 1812 ~

To say that Connecticut was strongly opposed to the War of 1812 would be an understatement. Governor Griswold not only opposed the war, but refused to comply with the federal government's call for the state to supply its quota of militia.

Griswold initially agreed to comply with the War Department's orders, in accordance with an act passed by Congress on April 10, 1812, authorizing the president to call upon the governors to organize and arm their quota of a total of one hundred thousand militia. When Madison directed Secretary of War William Eustis to issue an order to the state governors to detach militia units in preparation for the impending war, Griswold agreed to detach his state's requisite 3,000 men. And on June 12, six days before the United States would declare war on Britain, when Eustis wrote to Griswold ordering the militia that had been detached into the service of the United States, Griswold again responded that he would comply with the order, immediately writing to General Ebenezer Huntington, commander of Connecticut's militia, to prepare to execute the order.

On June 18, the United States declared war.

On June 22, Major General Henry Dearborn, commander of the northeast part of the country, sent a communication to Griswold ordering him to detach four of Connecticut's militia companies to Fort Trumbull, near New London, and one company to New Haven, fully expecting, based on Griswold's previous responses, that he would comply. But Griswold didn't immediately respond. Instead, on June 25, he convened the state's Council, which assembled on June 29.

Griswold's hesitation may in part have been caused by receiving a letter from the newly-elected governor of Massachusetts, Federalist Caleb Strong, who had received a similar order from Dearborn for militia. Strong told Griswold that the Massachusetts Council was divided on whether or not Dearborn's order was constitutional. The question was whether or not there was a danger of an imminent invasion. According to the Constitution, there are only three reasons that the federal government can call forth the militia — "to execute the laws of the Union, suppress Insurrections and repel Invasions." Although war had been declared, the declaration would not yet have reached England, so those who opposed Dearborn's order argued that invasion was not imminent. Griswold had also likely conferred with Federalist leaders in Connecticut who raised the same constitutional question.

The Council declared Dearborn's order unconstitutional, not only for the reason of invasion not being imminent, but because the state's militia would be placed under the command of regular Army officers, violating the Constitution's provision reserving to the states the appointment of their militia's officers.

On July 2, Connecticut's lieutenant governor, John Cotton Smith, acting in place of the ailing Griswold, who only had months left to live, communicated to Dearborn Connecticut's refusal to comply with the requisition for militia. Massachusetts and Rhode Island, which had also elected Federalist governors, refused as well to supply their quotas of militia.

Dearborn's response that, with war having been declared and British ships off the coast of America, the danger of invasion was indeed imminent, was in vain.

Massachusetts governor Caleb Strong left no doubt about his pro-British sentiments when he issued a fast day proclamation that began:

> WHEREAS it has pleased the Almighty Ruler of the world in his Righteous Providence to permit us to be engaged in a war against the nation from which we are descended, and which for many generations has been the bulwark of the religion we profess: —And whereas by this awful and

alarming change in our circumstances, the People of this commonwealth are in a peculiar manner exposed to personal suffering, and a loss of a great proportion of their substance: It becomes us, in imitation of our fathers, in times of perplexity and danger, with deep repentance to humble ourselves before Him for our sins, and the ungrateful returns we have made to Him for His mercies:—To ascribe righteousness to our Maker, when He threatens us with the most severe of all temporal calamities, and to beseech Him to avert the tokens of His anger, and remember for us His former loving kindness and tender mercy. …[1]

Strong's statement that England was "the bulwark of the religion we profess" would go viral and not be forgotten for years to come, throughout the War of 1812 and beyond.

THE FAST PROCLAMATION.

We cannot forbear again inviting the attention of our readers to this subject. We cannot forbear enquiring, whether there exists a single individual, possessed of American feelings, who can read *this Proclamation,* and his heart not sicken with disgust, and his blood boil with indignation?

Monstrous spectacle! The Chief Magistrate of Massachusetts, at a time when his country is once more *driven* by insult and outrage to defend its dearbought Independence, panegyrising THE ENEMY as "THE BULWARK OF OUR RELIGION"! Great Britain the BULWARK of the Christian Religion! That nation whose government has spread *murder, desolation* and *rapine* over the fairest portions of the globe; which sends its emissaries into every clime, armed with the daggers of assassination or the gold of corruption; that nation whose almost total destitution of practical religion is known to the whole world, is eulogized by the Governour of Massachusetts as *"the Bulwark of the religion we profess!"* We will not again attempt to delineate the foul and hideous features of this Proclamation issued as a SOLEMN APPEAL TO

1. *Connecticut Herald,* New Haven, CT, July 7, 1812, 2.

ALMIGHTY GOD! It would draw forth censures perhaps too strong to be applied to the officer who has proclaimed it. It has already been noticed by the publick prints of the neighbouring States in terms of the utmost abhorrence. We request our readers to lay it up in their minds. It will furnish fit subjects for reflection previous to *April next. ...*[2]

⌒

HYMN FOR THE MASSACHUSETTS FAST.
BY W. RAY, ESQ.

———

Conven'd on this appointed day,
    We thank the Lord of glory;
That *STRONG* we meet to fast and play,
    The hypocrite and tory.

Give us, Almighty pow'r, to know,
    On Britons our dependance;
To them submission Lord we owe,
    For we are—their descendants.

Of that Religion, mild and good,
    Which we *profess*—not *practice;*
The British have the bulwark stood
    For ages—this a fact is.

And shall we, their ungrateful sons,
    In flesh and faith begotten,
Point at their breasts our loaded guns!
    Better be dead and rotten.

What though they have impress'd our tars,
    And robb'd us on the ocean;
Should we involve ourselves in wars?
    A very pretty notion!

2. *National Aegis,* Worcester, MA, July 22, 1812, 3.

What though the savage, Britain hires,
    To butcher us and plunder;
Her terms are *peace*—all she requires
    Of us is—*to knock under.*

Humble, O Lord, our nation's pride
    Before the power of Britain;
May we, to them so near allied,
    Such noble terms submit on.

Freedom is nothing but a jest,
    A bubble—a delusion;
Our government was much the best,
    Before the Revolution.

Best the religion of our sires,
    When they, to please their Maker,
Consum'd for love of God, in fires,
    The Heretic and Quaker.

Strong is our faith—*Strong* is our hope,
    That this deluded nation,
Will yet her rights yield tamely up
    To British subjugation.

Let not our privateers men go,
    To kill our English brothers;
And save from Beelzebub and co.
    The *Boston folks—no others.*

Be Massachusetts, Lord, thy care,
    And grant us faith and riches;
May we as zealous be in pray'r,
    As when we hung the witches.[3]

Reverend Parish's Fast Day sermon, titled "A Protest Against the War," did not disappoint the pro-British Federalists, and didn't

---

3. *Democratic Republican,* Walpole, NH, August 17, 1812, 4.

fail to get national attention, particularly after it was published in the fall. An article titled "Clerical and Political Insanity," first published in Philadelphia's *Whig Chronicle,* was reprinted in the Republican papers in all the states, including *Mercury* in Connecticut and Boston's *Independent Chronicle* in Parish's own state. This was the article, as reprinted in Wilmington, Delaware's *American Watchman.*

> We give the following as a specimen of that black and vindictive spirit of faction bordering upon downright treason, that impious and base political and religious frenzy, which impel the federal clergy of New-England to trample upon all decency and truth; to insult the majesty of Heaven itself, in the persecuting and blasphemous sentiments they utter from the pulpit towards all who differ from them and all who oppose the "queen of Isles," the "chosen and faithful lamb" of *their* political gods, the "proud bulwark" of *their* political religion, the idol of their incessant worship and adoration.
>
> *Clerical and Political Insanity.*—The Rev. Dr. Parish, of Massachusetts, has published a political sermon, which he delivered last July, and which is filled with falsehood, profligate falsehood, from beginning to end; with traitorous and impious sentiments, at which every good and noble feeling of the human heart shudders with astonishment and horror. This federal Clergyman whose blasphemous principles cannot fail to draw upon his head the vengeance of insulted Heaven, and the curses of every honest man in Christendom: this sacrilegious preacher, whose feet pollute and whose lips prophane the Holy Temple of religion; this impious madman in speaking of the war and of Great Britain exclaims that *"her banners will wave victorious,* WHILE THE BLOOD OF HER ENEMIES WILL FLOW TO THE HORSES' BRIDLES *and the flesh of their vassal kings furnish a* SUPPER for all the Vultures of Heaven!" And is this the benevolent language of federal religion? Is this that language, which in the New England pulpits, and on the floor of Congress, tell us of the impiety of war, teaches us "to love our enemies," and deprecates the effusion of human blood? Yes! this is New England federal

religion; a religion that "swells the song of praise" to England's bloody deeds, that rejoices to behold "the blood of her enemies flowing to the horses bridles" and see the Vultures of Heaven *supping* on their mangled, lacerated, lifeless bodies! This is that religion which thirsts for the blood of all who dare resist the monstrous despotism of Britain, and which weeps at the prospect of the triumph and glory of America! The heart sickens at the horrid sentiments uttered by this clerical madman.

The Rev. Preacher pronounces the contest with England to be "a nefarious warfare," a "war with the lamb," with "the chosen faithful" of the Almighty; he solemnly declares that it is *"nothing more nor less than a license given by a* VIRGINIA VASSAL OF THE FRENCH EMPEROR *to the people of England authorising them in legal form to destroy the property of* NEW ENGLAND;" and adjures his disciples to "FORBID *this war to proceed in New-England,"* and to "proclaim an HONORABLE neutrality!" He calls the brave militia, who have taken up arms to defend their country, to vindicate a cause than which none more just ever called forth the courage of man; he calls these patriotic heroes by the degrading appellation of "drafted conscripts." He says, "our country is now preserved like the prophet in the den of Babylon; THE ROYAL LYONS DISDAIN *to devour the innocent victim."* He asserts that "it is this moment owing to the *forbearance,* the CLEMENCY, the MAGNANIMITY of the ENGLISH, that our cities are not burning from Maine to Georgia;" "that a million of people are not wandering over the ashes of their dwellings, without a home, without employment, without bread." He basely traduces our government by saying that "it can crush its SUBJECTS, but *cannot afford them security.* He compares the President to Nero, who set fire to Rome, merely to enjoy the spectacle of misery, and "played his harp and sung the woes of falling Troy, amid the roar of flames, the crash of falling temples and palaces, the cries of mothers calling for their children, and the shrieks of thousands expiring in the fire!"

Callous to truth indeed, dead to patriotism, to reason, morality and religion, must have been that congregation, who could patiently listen to a man uttering the language and sentiments we have feebly described from the sacred pulpit. But let the reverend madman peaceably pursue his career of folly, treason, political and religious frenzy. His sermons and his writings will open the eyes of many an honest federalist who will quit ranks filed and headed by such impious zealots and treacherous citizens and cleave to the standard of their country.[4]

With the country now at war, the word "treason" started being used to describe the pro-British sermons of the New England clergy, as it was in the title of this reprinting in a Vermont paper of an article about one of Reverend Osgood's 1812 sermons:

MORE CLERICAL TREASON!

We recommend the following articles, the first from the *National Intelligencer,* the other from the *Utica Gazette,* to the reflection of our readers. Never did more abominations pollute the pulpit, than at the present day. Certain our Preachers are bringing to an end their influence, with an eagerness, which a perverted understanding could alone account for. If the people cease to respect them;—we may exclaim, like *Cæsar,* when he mused on the field of *Pharsalia—"They would have it so!"*

PULPIT POLITICIANS.

We copy today an article from the Utica Gazette, exposing the shameful purposes, to which the Pulpit is in some parts of our country disgraced. It is the essence of our government that church and state should be kept distinct; it is the constant effort of some, equally bigotted in their politics as in their religion, to amalgamate them. The pulpit is prostituted to the worst purposes of faction and that which should be the fountain of instruction, is polluted with the diffusion of the most unholy passions. ...

———

4. *American Watchman,* Wilmington, DE, December 9, 1812, 1.

MR. WALKER—If a paper containing the sermon, from which the following extract is taken, has not reached you, and your types do not blush at being made the instrument of recording such infamous sentiments, please give the same a place in your paper, that your readers may learn what doctrine their brethren in New-England hear from the pulpit, and on the Lord's day. The sermon appears in the Providence Gazette of July 25, delivered on the next Lord's day after tidings of the war were received, by David Osgood, D.D. pastor of the church in Medford, Mass.

II. Chronicles, 12, 13

"O children of Israel, fight ye not against the Lord God of your fathers, for ye shall not prosper."

After dwelling some time on the horrors of war, he says—

"Look at this picture, ye self called true Republicans, contemplate its variegated features, then go and advance the war proclaimed, extol to the skies the wisdom and patriotism of its authors, again fill your gazettes with increased floods of abuse on the few surviving friends of the Godlike Washington, on Strong, Pickering, &c.—hasten a new edition of those farragoes of excitement to war and of malignant calumnies against its opposers, contained in the speeches and proclamations of your admired Gerry."

After proceeding to shew the injustice and want of cause for the present war—our affinity to Great Britain, he says—

"If at the command of weak or wicked rulers, they (the people) undertake an unjust war, each man who volunteers his services in such a cause, or loans money for its support or by his conversations, his writing or any other mode of influence, encourages its prosecution, that man is an accomplice in the wickedness, loads his conscience with the blackest crimes, brings the guilt of blood upon his soul, and in the sight of God and his law is a murderer!!

"For myself, from the moment my ears received the tidings, my mind has been in constant agony, not so much at the loss of our temporal prosperity, etc. as at the *guilt* its *outrage* against heaven, against all *truth, honesty,* justice, &c.

"To you my brethren, and to all my fellow-citizens, I say in the language of my text, "fight ye not against the Lord God of your fathers, for ye shall not prosper." *No recent injury has been done us!!* It is therefore the more wonderful and can be accounted for on no other principle but the imperceptible influence which the author of all evil, the spirit that worketh in the children of disobedience, has been permitted to exert in the hearts of *dark-minded,* cool, deliberately *wicked* rulers."

"Were not the authors of this war, in character nearly akin to the *deists and atheists* of France, were they not men of hardened hearts, seared consciences, reprobate minds and *desperate in wickedness,* it seems utterly inconceivable that they should have made the declaration.—Their pretensions in my judgment are either glaring, unblushing falsehoods, or for things so trifling and unimportant that it may be queried, whether they would not be wickedly obtained at the hazard of a single life."

"Conscious of their guilt and danger, but destitute as fallen angels that they have at length become desperate and in a fit of desperation have proclaimed war."

"If at the present period no symptoms of *civil war* appear, there certainly will soon unless the courage of the war party should fail them. The opposition comprises all the best men in the nation, men of the greatest talents, courage, and wealth, and whose *Washingtonian* principles will compel them to die, rather than stain their hands in the blood of an unjust war. Prudence leads them at present to cloak their opposition under constitutional forms!"

Many more and equally inflammatory and seditious sentences might be copied, but are here not enough? If the bandages around the eyes of some federalists do not leap from their fastenings, on hearing such horrid sentiments proclaimed—if the gnawing worm of conscience does not sting their leaders who fixed them there, then vain is our hope to sustain the constitution and present form of government, and vain the hope in heaven's justice, who in that discourse cannot see the climax ascend from party rancor, to deadly hatred of the soil that bears a freeman, to warm affection for the foe—who is so blind as not to see the rebellious strain swell till treason enters. Why did not the reverend father in the language of Pope Gregory the 7th, when he excommunicated Henry the 4th of Germany say "in the name of almighty God I release all christians from their allegiance" to such a government; and administer the oath of allegiance to George the Third? Perhaps he had not yet received the "ring and crosier" from him. The last sentence quoted from the sermon, openly avows the object of the "Washingtonian" (or rather Illuminati) society,[5] "prudence leads them at present to cloak their opposition under constitutional forms." And are these "men of the greatest talents in New-England who would embrue their hands in the blood of their fellow citizens, before they would take up arms against Great Britain? They cannot see "the iron enter the soul" of six thousand American seamen in servitude to this dear nation; neither can they feel their stripes when chained to the main-mast by "the defenders of faith."

Yours, &c.   YEOMAN.[6]

As incendiary and un-American as the sermons of Reverends Parish and Osgood were, the prize for 1812 went to a sermon from another Massachusetts minister, John S.J. Gardiner, who flat out called for a separation of New England from the rest of the country. Gardiner's infamous sermon, delivered on the national fast day called for by a joint resolution of Congress and proclaimed by James Madison, was particularly offensive to Americans in the southern states, who Gardiner described as being "possessed of all the evil qualities of which human nature is capable." This was the response from one southern man:

On the late Fast Day, recommended by the President, a Federal Parson of the Episcopal Church in Boston, embraced the occasion to vent his rage and venom against the constituted authorities of our country, and to urge a division or

5. Federalist political clubs, formally called Washington Benevolent Societies, started in 1808 in New York, with branches forming throughout the northeast, and lasting until 1816, whose main purpose was electioneering.

6. *North Star*, Danville, VT, Oct 31, 1812, 5.

separation of the States. It appears by the Boston papers, that he so far exceeded the *Osgoods, Springs, Morses. Parishes,* and others of that tribe who cloak their hypocrisy and enmity to the government under the garb of sanctity, that he has drawn all eyes upon him. Indeed, in a Boston paper a large reward is offered to any person who will furnish a copy of what is so improperly called a Sermon. But it is said that the wretched declaimer, finding that he has too plainly laid bare his vindictive soul, has cunningly suppressed it, being in dread that he would be apprehended by the District Attorney for treason, or high crimes. The name of this wolf in sheep's clothing is *J.S.J. Gardiner,* and one of his hearers has published a few passages of the slanderous production, in which he has fallen foul of the people of the Southern States, and where he has drawn a character of them which no one but his God, *the father of lies,* could have furnished him with. But read it.

"He told his hearers that he was acquainted with the Southern people; that he had lived among them, and knew them to be possessed of all the evil qualities of which human nature is capable; in short, that they were every thing but Christians; and the sooner we came out from among them the better! I will not undertake to give his precise words; but I will not misrepresent his sentiments. What, said he, have you to lose by a separation? You have nothing to *lose,* but every thing to *gain.* You have nothing to lose but THOMAS JEFFERSON, JAMES MADISON, ALBERT GALLATIN, and FELIX GRUNDY! [7] By a separation you *gain the friendship* of G. Britain, which is worth more than the friendship of all the world besides. Use all your exertions, therefore, for an immediate separation; and then your situation will be infinitely better, though you should be fighting the whole world besides, than to have a treaty with all the rest of the world, and fighting Great Britain alone," &c. &c.

Well done, J.S.J. Gardiner! What, no honest men, no Christians in our country? Have the preachings of the Clergy

---

7. A member of the U.S. House of Representatives from Tennessee, Felix Grundy was one of the most outspoken congressmen in favor of going to war with England, becoming nationally known and reviled by the Federalists.

here for the last thirty of forty years, your own included, been of no avail? Are the Clergy themselves, and those going to be Clergymen, impostors? Has the Bible Society been established in vain? Are all the Societies which claim the name of Christian among us "any this else but Christians"? Can all this be true, or may we not rather think that this same J.S.J. Gardiner is a base defamer, covered with a black coat, but not of so deep a dye as his putrid heart? If this monster is a specimen of Federal Clergymen, how fortunate is he who has no communication with them! I would "sooner say unto corruption, thou art my brother," than to hold converse with them. But I trust he is far, very far, from being a fair sample; and that there are many good men amongst them, though the unworthy practice some of them have suffered themselves to fall into of employing their pulpit as a place from whence to deal out invectives and revile the government, gives no great latitude for charity— and a considerable portion of them, who continue to dabble in politics, will have to change their conduct, or they will draw down upon themselves the execrations of their hearers, as has justly been the case with J.S.J. Gardiner.

This same J.S.J. Gardiner is conjectured to be a little fellow who came to this city some 20 years ago, seeking a livelihood, unburthened with any of the mammon of this world, and by some means obtained a residence at Beaufort, in this state, as a Schoolmaster or Preacher, and remained there for some years. Should this conjecture be true, some account of his labors, *other than Apostolic,* will shortly be collected and laid before the public, as it has now become the duty of those he has so egregiously and so wantonly attacked, to show this pretended *Federal Saint* to the world in his true and genuine colors. The Federal gentlemen in Beaufort, no doubt, must feel themselves highly gratified on reading the *exalted* character this imp of darkness has covered them with, and they will now learn that they have nursed a serpent in their bosoms.

A SOUTHERN MAN.[8]

8. *City Gazette,* Charleston, SC, September 17, 1812, 2.

Gardiner's open call for a separation of the states was a subject of wonder even in New England, where the people were used to outrageous statements from the clergy. One supposed Federalist, apparently having heard that Gardiner made such a statement, wrote to the editors of the Republican *Boston Patriot* asking whether or not it was true. Another supposed Federalist answered that yes, Gardiner had indeed made such a statement. The question and answer were reprinted in other New England Republican papers, including Connecticut's *Mercury* and *Republican Farmer.*

A SERIOUS QUESTION.

Messrs. Munroe & French,

I wish to be informed through the medium of your paper, whether parson GARDINER, rector of Trinity church, in this town, did or did not, in his sermon of yesterday, strongly advocate a SEPARATION OF THE UNION? and whether he did not *enjoin it on his hearers as a Duty?* and whether he did not say that the consequence of such a separation would be the making *Old* England and *New* England a great and happy nation?

A FEDERALIST.

Boston, August 21, 1812.

––––––

Messrs. Munroe & French,

A Federalist in your last number asks if the Rev. *J.S.J. Gardiner,* in his sermon on the last fast day, did advocate a separation of the Union, &c.

I answer, that *he did advocate a separation of the States,* with all the warmth and vehemence which he is capable of! He told his hearers he was acquainted with the Southern people; that he had lived among them, and knew them to be possessed of all the evil qualities of which human nature is capable; in short, that they were every thing but christians; and the sooner we come out from among them the better! I will not undertake to give his precise words, but I will not misrepresent his sentiments. What, he said, have you to lose by separation? You have nothing to *lose,* but every thing to *gain*—You have nothing to lose but Thomas Jefferson, James Madison, Albert Gallatin, and Felix Grundy! By a *separation you gain the friendship of Great Britain,* which is worth more than the friendship of all the world besides. Use all your exertions, therefore, for an immediate separation; form a treaty of alliance with Great Britain; and then your situation will be infinitely better, though you should be fighting the whole world besides, than to have a treaty with all the rest of the world, and fighting Great Britain alone, &c.

This was the language of the rector of Trinity Church; at least, it is a specimen of the whole discourse.

This discourse was given to the printer for publication, but has been suppressed. For the honor of the nation it ought never to appear, but for the good of the public it ought to be published to the world.

AN OTHER FEDERALIST.[9]

The Federalist party was all but dead in the majority of the country. Outside of New England the only state to remain Federalist was the small state of Delaware. Although articles like the following considered the extreme effusions of the Federalists, and particularly the Federalist clergy, as the "last dying spasms" of the party, its ultimate demise was still over four years off, and a bit longer than that in Connecticut. With New Hampshire electing a Federalist governor in 1813, all of the New England states with the exception of Vermont would be under Federalist control for the duration of the war.

The last hope of Federalism.

That the present writhings and groanings of federalists are the last dying spasms of that corrupt faction, it needs no ghost to divine. The hideous cry set up against the government—the many and unwearied labors of their leading men in dispersing lying pamphlets, and seditious sermons—the tremblings and awful denunciations of members of the clergy—are evidence strong as proof from holy writ, that

9. *Republican Farmer,* Bridgeport, CT, September 16, 1812, 2.

Great-Britain is in fact the "last hope" of falling Federalism—
that the interests of one are so identified with the interests
of the other, that the latter must fall whenever the people
are made to see and detest the deformities, the mass of corruption and wickedness which subsist in the former.

But why is it that a proportion of the Clergy at this time
disgorge the saliva of political animosity? Why is it that *they*
cry up Great-Britain as the only "bulwark of the religion we
profess"—why is it, that *they* take so deep an interest in
palliating and justifying the wounds inflicted on American
honor and American interests by the gross injustice of
Great-Britain—while they abuse and vilify every thing
American, and hate the government which protects them
"with the spirit of murderers"?—It was just so in our revolution—A proportion of the Clergy, then as now, were the
advocates for submission to Great-Britain—for her right to
control us in all cases whatever. But the privileges of their
order did not then protect them; they were buried into their
merited obscurity and contempt by the honest indignation
of a people who knew how to value their liberties; and we
trust in God the same fate will follow the men who have the
same prepossessions for Britain, the same desire to prostrate
American Independence, the same desire to perpetuate
aristocracy and demolish every thing republican in 1812,
that those miscreants had in 1775. ....[10]

Connecticut's 1812 elections were dismal for the Republicans.
They no longer supported Griswold, who despite serious health
problems was running for a second term, because he opposed going
to war with Britain. Instead they ran their former lieutenant governor candidate Elijah Boardman for governor. With the primary issue
of the spring election being the impending war, the alliance of the
previous year of the Republicans, the Episcopalians, and moderate
"non-clerical" Federalists, which had gotten the non-religious
Griswold elected, was gone. The Episcopalians were opposed to
going to war, and Boardman, although an Episcopalian, supported
war. With the Episcopalian vote and a reunited Federalist vote,

10. *New-Hampshire Patriot*, Concord, NH, September 1, 1812, 3.

Griswold was reelected in a landslide, getting 11,725 votes to Boardman's 1,487. The alliance between the Republicans, Episcopalians, and moderate Federalists would be revived after the war, when the focus returned to the issue of religious freedom, but for now it was all about the war. Republican representation in the House dropped to an all-time low of 36, where it would remain in the fall election.

1812 was also a presidential election year. The Federalists did not formally endorse a candidate. Instead they supported DeWitt Clinton, a Republican who opposed the war. Although Clinton won all of the New England states except Vermont, as well as New Jersey, Delaware, his home state of New York, and part of Maryland, Madison won reelection by a comfortable margin of 128 to 89 electoral votes.

∽ **1813** ∽

Like Massachusetts with its Parish, Osgood, and Gardiner, Connecticut had its own pro-British clergymen, as described in this article from the *American Mercury* about the state's annual fast day:

> *The Annual Fast* is now over, and our political clergy have disgorged all the venom and filth they have accumulated during the winter. This day is used by many of the clergy of this state, for the same purpose that the *Saturnalia,* or periodical feasts of Saturn were formerly used by the Roman slaves, viz: to defame and blackguard their masters. In this vocation some of our clergy exhibit such ingenuity; they even out-distance the tory editors in Boston, and the Mirror. Last Friday, a clergyman of one of our neighboring towns, after having dealt out the usual doses of *infidelity* and *French Influence* to our national rulers, and having liberally bestowed the usual epithets of *unjust, unholy, unblest,* &c. upon the war, observed that the blockade of *the southern ports by a British fleet and the massacres of the people at the westward by the Indians, were just judgments of Providence upon the southern and western states, for engaging in war with the land of our fathers, and the Bulwark of religion; & that the permission given to the northern states, to trade with the British west-Indies, was a blessing of Providence upon the northern people, resisting*

the prosecution of the war; thus making Providence the instigator of treason, and the author of the grossest outrages of the British government, and of the barbarities of its savage allies. With a political clergyman, the transition from treason to blasphemy is easy and natural.[1]

A few days before the annual fast, John Cotton Smith, who had been acting governor since the death of Roger Griswold in October 1812, was elected governor, with 11,893 votes to Elijah Boardman's 7,201, far from the landslide by which Griswold had beat Boardman in the year before. In the House the Federalists had a majority of 133 in the spring, with the Republicans only picking up a few more seats in the fall.

The ceremonies of May's election day festival, at which the votes cast in April were formally counted, were described by the *Mercury:*

> The Election ceremonies were performed with the greatest propriety—and nothing occurred to mar the pleasures of the day but being insulted with the tune "God save great George our King" by the Band belonging to his Excellency's foot guards.—We are informed that Mr. Lee's Election Sermon was very disgusting to most who heard it, and will not be published (at the public expence) unless altered—Many who heard it think it would be very proper to have it published as delivered, as an appendix to Messrs. Parish's and Osgood's celebrated Fast-day Sermons.[2]

While the Republicans celebrated America's victories against the British, there were Federalists who did the opposite.

> *Federalism without hypocrisy.*—The federalists of Newburyport, (Mass.) tolled the bell, on the receipt of the news of Perry's victory over the British squadron on Lake Erie. Not content with this, they broke the windows of the Phenix building, which was illuminated in honor of the victory.

---

1. *American Mercury,* Hartford, CT, April 28, 1813, 3.
2. Ibid., May 19, 1813, 3.

In Danbury, in this state, a federal captain of the artillery refused the use of the cannon to fire in honor of the same victory. The Republicans, however, took the cannon, and discharged it seventeen times; and drank a number of patriotic toasts, worthy of Americans. It is also a fact, that this same captain, *applied to a Justice of the Peace for a writ,* to prosecute those vile republicans for daring to insult his Majesty by rejoicing in the destruction of his fleet! This is federalism in its true character, without *hypocrisy*—which have rarely separated.[3]

⌒

"We have met the enemy, and they are ours"

The splendid and unparalleled victory, of the gallant Perry, and his brave tars, on the 10th Sept. over a British fleet on lake Erie, superior in guns and in men, was celebrated by the friends of their country, in this city, on Monday the 27th ult. by firing of cannon, and other demonstrations of patriotic feeling.

The contrast exhibited by the cheerful hilarity which beamed from the countenances of the real friends of their country, and the forlorn and dejected looks of those who were "too moral and too pious to rejoice at its victories," was highly interesting. The only expression of exultation which were heard from their polluted lips, were; "Com. Perry is a Federalist—the British fleet is yet safe on Ontario." If Com. Perry is a federalist, God give us a million such federalists. To the pretended federalists of New England who declare they will not lift a finger to support the war, how great is the reproach arising from the conduct of this young and intrepid "Hero of the Lake."—this "Nelson of America," who calls them in a voice of thunder; America expects every man to do his duty.[4]

3. *Columbian Register,* New Haven, CT, October 19, 1813, 3.
4. *American Mercury,* Hartford, CT, October 5, 1813, 3.

"Another victory gained by a FEDERALIST!" the federal papers exultingly exclaim, on the unprecedented achievement of commodore Perry. If it be so, so much the better. It is a pity a few thousand more federalists were not "gaining victories" for their country, instead of disheartening and ridiculing our armies, and rejoicing at the victories of our enemy. (The Salem Gazette, as rank a tory or British paper, as any in the pay of the British government, calls the men killed in battle, in Canada *"murdered."*) How much more honorable to federalists like com. Perry), and what a cutting reproach to his new born eulogists, to be fighting for his country, while they are fighting against it! We are told, however, that Mr. Perry's father was a decided republican, and himself of the same principles.[5]

New England's papers often reprinted and cited articles from other states showing how New England was viewed by the rest of the country, with Republican editors being in agreement with their southern brethren and Federalist editors being outraged by them. The following item from a Baltimore paper about the blind obedience of New Englanders to their states' governments was reprinted in the *Mercury:*

From the BALTIMORE SUN.

Nations in general are made more for feeling than for thinking. The greatest part of them never had an idea of analysing the nature of the power by which they are governed. They obey without reflection, and because they have the habit of obeying. The origin and the object of the first national associations being unknown to them, or at least willfully forgot by them, all resistance to government however absurd appears to them a crime. To this cause is owing the disaffection at this time in the New England states, where the priests, from their pulpits, are continually preaching "passive obedience and non-resistance" and which at this period of warfare and trial is no less than treason to the

5. *Columbian Register,* New Haven, CT, October 5, 1813, 1.

general government of the United States, and favoring thereby the cause of the enemy. It is altogether in those states where the principles of legislation are confounded with those of religion, that this blindness is to be met with. ...[6]

Another Baltimore paper set the editor of Boston's Federalist *New-England Palladium* straight about why the "Southern Editors" were angry with New England:

"The Southern Editors are very angry because the ports of New-England are not declared in a state of blockade as well as those of the south. What do they wish to have done? Do they want the people of the northern states to petition the Prince Regent to include their harbors in his blockades? Or do their southern brethren contemplate petitioning for them?"

Boston Palladium.

The above article was published in a late pious New England federal paper. As the opposition in that quarter lay claim to all the religion and all the talents in the country, one would naturally have imagined that in exposing their infidel republican adversaries of the south, they would not deem it proper or necessary to transcend the boundaries of truth. The "southern Editors" are not "angry because the ports of New-England are not declared in a state of blockade." They are angry, and with ample cause, at the violation of their plighted fidelity to the union, the unjustifiable neutrality in the war, and the negative co-operation with the enemy, by which the federalists of New-England have ignominiously purchased an exemption from the inconveniencies and evils of the war. Were the people of that section to suffer less than those of other parts of the union from natural and necessary causes; had they not deserved the partiality of the bitter enemy of their country by treachery to it, the middle and southern people would never have censured them. Unlike the northern federalists, they possess too much magnanimity to repine at the good fortune of their

6. *American Mercury,* Hartford, CT, January 13, 1813, 1.

brethren in any section of the union. They are intelligent enough to know that no measure, in so extensive a country as this, can fall equally heavy or equally light on all its parts. They are patriotic and wise enough to submit to any partial and temporary evils for the sake of the countless advantages which all derive from a firm union and a general government. They are too generous and too brave ever to skulk from the dangers of war, behind the miserable pretence of aversion to it. At the commencement of the revolutionary struggle, the southern people did not coldly and meanly stop to enquire where the mother country commenced her career of insufferable oppression. They did not doubt; they did not hesitate; they did not disgracefully refuse to aid in the common cause, because the unlawful scene of taxation and tyranny was first laid at Boston. ...[7]

An incident the previous year that caused much embarrassment for James Madison and his Secretary of State James Monroe was their purchase for $50,000 of the Henry letters, and the presentation of these letters to Congress. In January 1812, a very convincing impostor from France, calling himself Count Edward de Crillon, armed with an elaborate backstory about his life, relatives, and estate in France, arrived in Washington and quickly gained the confidence of the French minister, Monroe, and Madison. Crillon claimed to have letters obtained from John Henry, a spy for Canadian governor Sir James Craig, revealing secret intrigues involving the British and New England Federalists who wanted a separation of New England from the United States, and offered to sell these letters to the United States for $125,000. The French minister talked him down to $50,000, which Monroe agreed to pay. While it was true that John Henry was a spy for Sir James Craig and had been in Boston, Crillon was a fraud and the letters he sold revealed no more information about the Federalists' desire for a separation of the states than could be found in the New England newspapers and sermons of the Federalist clergy. Although Madison and Monroe's being duped by the impostor Crillon was an embarrassment for the Republicans, they adopted a new term for Federalists who wanted to dissolve

7. *American & Commercial Daily Advertiser,* Baltimore, MD, May 19, 1813, 2.

the union — "Henryism."

HENRYISM,

Is again showing its baleful head in our Tory papers, encouraged by the Vermonters having chosen a *Federal* Governor, by a majority of ONE vote! [8] There would have been a handsome Republican majority, had it not been that some thousands of that party were gone to fight the battles of their country; and those who had not marched were prohibited voting.—What fools men must be to rely on the Federalism of a State so circumstanced.

The British party may talk and may write their feelings, and their wishes about the dissolution of the Union, and forming a separate treaty with the enemy; but so soon as any one dare *raise a finger in execution of their designs,* and we should not wonder if half Massachusetts should petition Congress to pass an *exile,* or *transportation act,* to clear our country of the Deputies of *John Henry.* A stern band of intrepid Republicans stand ready to guard our country against open enemies, or secret traitors. The Republicans of Boston are not to be scared by Fort Bulwark, even should it be manned by the picked soldiers of the *Washington Benevolents.* The British party may talk treason till they are hoarse, but should they act it, exile or death will be their portion. [9]

Massachusetts governor Caleb Strong's statement that England was "the bulwark of the religion we profess," was invoked in countless articles throughout the country in 1813.

THE BRITISH BULWARK.

The Bulwark of our Religion (as Dea. Strong terms the

8. In Vermont's election, incumbent Republican governor Jonas Galusha and lieutenant governor Paul Brigham had both gotten more votes than their Federalist challengers, Martin Chittenden and William Chamberlain. In this very close election there was a scattering of several hundred votes for other candidates, resulting in no candidate in either race having a majority, so the choice went to the legislature, which voted for the Federalists, who were reportedly chosen by a majority of just one vote.

9. *American Mercury,* Hartford, CT, November 9, 1813, 3.

English) was early exemplified during our revolutionary war. Whenever they entered a town they first began to attack our meeting houses (at that time pre-eminently styled "YANKEE SCHISM SHOPS.") Old South, Old North, West Boston meeting-house, and Dr. Boyles', bore the marks of their depredations on our first coming to town. The New-England clergy were held in the highest contempt, as a set of whining, hypocritical, canting fellows, below the notice of the *Episcopalian gentry.* So abhorrent did they view every thing relating to Presbyterian worship, that a stigma was attached to every person who officiated in their churches. A *Presbyterian Deacon* was always an object of ridicule—and even the choristers were spoken of with the utmost burlesque. Mr. Samuel Adams was a singer at the New South. Among other terms of ridicule, they used to call him *"Sammy the psalm singer."* Suppose the Bulwark should gain an ascendency, how many *federal psalm singers* would become objects of similar ridicule?—*Psalm singing federalists* would become as contemptible as they endeavored to render Mr. Adams. *Psalm singing federalists* are now a rare species to defend the British Bulwark;—choristers will be obliged to hang their harps on the willows.[10]

"*Bulwark of the Religion we profess.*"
C. STRONG.

Never can this emphatical expression, which gives the clue to a long series of strange and interwoven partialities, escape from our memories; or cease to be a proper subject of comment, so long as it furnishes the pretence of attachment to a public enemy. The Governor of Massachusetts must have a very peculiar species of religion, if the British government is the bulwark of it; and as he professes this to be the fact, the principles of the ostensible moral agents in that government, must furnish the *articles of his creed.*

10. *Independent Chronicle,* Boston, MA, October 21, 1813, 2.

First and foremost, at the very apex of the *"bulwark"* stands His Majesty George III. For evils which his reign has brought on the world, the horrors his tyranny spread over this country, the chains his avaricious myrmidons imposed on the hapless chiefs of plundered Asia, the deep and indescribable horrors with which his bigotry and his subserviency to miscreant ministers, have borne down insulted and oppressed Ireland; for these crimes and the distresses they caused, the temporal punishment of gloomy distraction might seem sufficient, and prevent additional reproach; *but it does not make him a part of the "Bulwark of Religion."*

His Royal Highness the *Prince Regent!*—and her Royal Highness the *Princess of Wales.* Will the pious Mr. STRONG designate the mode, in which they aid in supporting that religion, "which is first, pure, then *peaceable, gentle and easy to be entreated, full of mercy and good fruits?"* We have just been perusing a letter from her Royal Highness to her husband. We have no opinion to give on the subject, whether *Her Royal Highness is no better than she should be*—or *His Royal Highness a calumniating tyrant.* Yet here is the dilemma. And thus must the *"bulwark of religion"* be settled, before we shall be able to know which to look to, to support it. In this right pious government and *"bulwark"* it seems the Prince has chosen to separate the *heir apparent* from her mother, and the alleged reason of this separation, is the loose and unfaithful conduct of this consort. She asks an investigation of her conduct. She alleges, that witnesses against her have been "procured by subordination" and that the *suborned witnesses* are PERJURED! Again we repeat it, all we have to say on this subject, is, that we see a great breach in the *"bulwark of our religion;"* for either the woman is depraved, or the man unjust and slanderous.

Shall we look to the sacred desk for any essential parts of the *"bulwark!"* The station of religious teachers is a matter of barter and purchase. Corrupt sycophancy elevates some debased flatterers to high promotion in the Church; while those who are too poor to hire an agent to manage their spiritual concerns with their Heavenly Master, hurry over a prescribed service themselves, like a schoolboy over a tedious task. The dignitaries have enough of extortion in the name of tithes to attend to; and the ten pound-a-year curates look out for the safety of souls, according to prescribed forms, and measure their pious care by the amount of their wages. The settlers of the state, over which STRONG presides fled from the tyranny of these High-Church props of the *"bulwark,"* and it would puzzle an Œdipus to discover why or how, these same oppressors have become necessary to the support of that faith, against which we have the assurance, that *"the gates of hell shall not prevail!"* ...

The assertion of Mr. STRONG may have been grounded on the noted foreign missionary societies. A truly pious man would have avoided an instance, so rank with hypocrisy. These societies for some pretendedly pious purposes, are mere political engines; and the Lord CASTLEREAGH[11] would laugh most heartily at the suggestion, that piety had a share in the patronage they receive from the government. With England religion is merely a political engine. Of what profession it is, scarcely thought of, so it pays a tribute in cash or in services or pretences. The Catholics are to be protected in Spain and Portugal, and persecuted in Ireland—the Dissenters disqualified in England, and patronized in Scotland—and even a permission is sold, for the obscene and bloody orgies of *Juggernaut* in India. Now, we aver, if Great Britain be the "bulwark of STRONG'S religion," she is also the *bulwark of Juggernaut's* disgusting idolatry. She is equally the *bulwark of "Popish superstition,"* against which the clergy of New-England used so fervently to pray; the Great Spirit of her Indian allied butchers; and the polluted shrine of the descendant of Moloch. ...[12]

With Governor Strong's "bulwark" statement getting so much attention from the Republican press, the Federalist *Columbian Centinel* in Boston made an attempt to explain the statement away, publishing a piece from a "venerable correspondent" who expounded on what Strong *really* meant. It was suspected by Republicans that

11. British Foreign Secretary Robert Stewart, Viscount Castlereagh.
12. *Baltimore Patriot,* Baltimore, MD, April 28, 1813, 3.

the *Centinel's* "venerable correspondent" was actually Strong himself.

From the *Columbian Centinel:*

"ENGLAND THE BULWARK OF OUR RELIGION."

IN a late speech of Governor STRONG to the Protestant Legislature of Massachusetts, he intimated that the United States had declared War against a nation (meaning England) *"which had been for ages the Bulwark of the Religion we profess."* And ever since, the writings of democracy, who have not capacity to comprehend the nature and extent of the remark, have made it the cap-and-bells of all their election-eering jingle; and the tag-word of their boyish paragraphs and essays. It was the duty of Governor STRONG to point the immorality of the War; and he would have neglected that duty, had he omitted to have noticed this characteristic of it. We therefor do not think any apology for the TRUISM is necessary, though we readily admit the following remarks of a venerable correspondent on the subject.

———

THOUGH the United States make no profession of reli-gion, in their national capacity, so that it cannot be properly said the nation is Protestant or Papal, Pagan or Mahometan, Jewish or Christian; yet the largest proportions of the in-habitants, having originally emigrated from Christian nations, at present the prevailing religion is Christian. And the more numerous sects are such as have sprung up among Protes-tants, since the reformation in the year 1517. In this way Governor STRONG considers the inhabitants of the United States, as professing the Protestant religion.

It is well known, that ever since the reign of Queen ELIZABETH, England has been decidedly Protestant, and directly opposed in her establishment to all the essential errors of Popery. Many endeavours were made to reinstate the papists, especially by JAMES IId. But through the kindness of GOD, the Prince of Orange was led to invade England, for the security of the Protestant established Church. He was received by the people with great joy, and JAMES abdicated the throne, which was immediately filled by King WILLIAM and MARY, viz.—the Prince and Princess of Orange.—This caused a close alliance with the States of Holland; and all the Protestant States, on the continent of Europe, looked up to England as the Great Bulwark of the Protestant Religion. While France, Spain and Portugal were in alliance with Rome, and endeavouring to destroy the Protestant religion, England was the *Bulwark* which they aimed at; if they could have made a Breach there they supposed the others would have been an easy conquest. It is presumed that was the sense, in which Governor STRONG meant that England has been for ages the Bulwark of our Religion. It must however be acknowledged, that *England* is not at present very particular about her alliances in that matter.—While she is at war with Denmark, Saxony, Bavaria, &c. &c. she is allied to Spain, Portugal, Russia, &c. so that France may be now considered nearly as favorable to the Protestants as the English, while it must be lamented that the nations appear at present to be leaving Religion out of their calculations; such has been the progress of Deism and Atheism. Still all this does not alter what England has been; *"She has been for ages the Bulwark of the Protestant Religion,"* for no nation entered more lively into the Protestant interest than she did.

Her Protestant establishment has been her glory, and what remains of sound principles in the nation, are still to be found among such as are attached to the standards of the Church, among whom may be reckoned the most respectable of the Dissenters, commonly called *Whitefieldites;* these have long lamented the general disregard which now prevails in the nation.

The Governor did not mean that England had defended any particular sect of Protestants, whether Lutherans, Reformed Churchmen, Presbyterians, Independents, &c. but he meant the Protestants as opposed to Papists when he said England *"had been for ages the Bulwark of our Religion."*[13]

13. *Columbian Centinel,* Boston, MA, September 11, 1813, 1.

The response to the *Centinel* and its "venerable correspondent" from New York Republican paper *The National Advocate:*

> *"England, the bulwark of our faith,*
> *As Caleb Strong devoutly saith."*

The Boston Centinel, for a week or two past, has been labouring to rescue Governor STRONG from the contempt incurred by his famous speech to the legislature of Massachusetts. Who may have been a writer or writers of these articles, we neither know nor care. From prima facie evidence we might conclude the first to be Governor STRONG himself, as no other person could so precisely know what Governor STRONG "meant," or what "he did not mean," when he declared that England *"had been for ages the bulwark of the religion we profess."* It seems, according to this "venerable correspondent," he did not mean "that England was at present," or had been very lately such a bulwark, much more than France—but he meant, nevertheless, and notwithstanding, "that she had been for ages the bulwark of the religion we profess." "Ages"—meaning "since the days of Queen Elizabeth"—that is to say, between one and two hundred years, or about the time she held this country in a state of colonial dependency, by the same rule that *once a Governor* means, *always a Governor.* By this kind of logic, he might as well have deplored a war "with the nation which had for ages" claimed and exercised the rights of sovereignty over us; and more especially with her red allies, who unquestionably "had been for ages" the proprietors of the soil, upon which he and his progenitors have *squatted*—and this, we conclude, would also have comported with his political creed.

If Governor STRONG can avail himself of such quibbling, we can only say of him as was said of another New-England deacon, *He is rather twistical or so!*

The long-winded writer, who keeps up this strain, is evidently of the Church of England, and a tory of the stamp of 75, *Non desensoribus istis tempus eget*—but such alone would be found advocating the sentiments contained in

Governor STRONG'S speech. In the dilemma to which this writer finds himself reduced, he is obliged to give up the Deacon to save the Governor—by melting his religion into that of the "established church of England." But since king WILLIAM and "one" BURNET, a Calvinist and an Episcopalian, did find it pleasant to *commune* together—whilst the former was ousting his father-in-law from the throne, and the latter looking after a Bishopric—it may be thought allowable in Mr. STRONG to make some sacrifice to the love of office. ...

We, who have no means of *guessing* what Governor STRONG'S meant, or what he did not mean, but by the plain import of his words, should guess, that by the word "religion"—he must either have meant the *Christian* religion, in its broad and liberal sense,—which we take to be the construction most creditable to an *American* statesman; or, speaking as a sectarian, he must have meant the religion, which he, and a vast majority of his constituents, "profess"— which we take to be most in character for Governor STRONG.

Now, we assert, that in neither of these senses is his position tenable. England has not been the bulwark of either the one or the other. ...

As it appears from the writer's confession, "that there has been in England for the last fifty years a great falling off in zeal for her own establishment"—"that her allies are chiefly Papists, whilst those in France are Protestants;" and as we know she is the bulwark of the Inquisition in Spain, of the temple of Juggernaut in India, and of the *Prophet* in our wilderness—it is difficult to say of what religion, at present, she is preeminently the bulwark. We are inclined to think, that both now and always, she has, like her humble admirers in New England, made religion subservient to the views of her avarice or ambition.

But the distortion of historical truth and other parts of Governor STRONG'S speech is not the most disgusting feature of it. It is the want of patriotism, of manly feeling, of loyalty to the government of his country, and the Jesuitical cant, under which he has attempted to cloak this disloyalty—it is the poverty of spirit, the sheep-like disposition, which could descend to plead the cause of the enemy,

"And lick the hand just raised to shed his blood:—

It is this which has *pickled* him with with Timothy Pickering, and Josiah Quincy,[14] and those other tergiversators, whose names are destined to stain the annals of their country.[15]

14. Josiah Quincy III, as a Federalist U.S. representative from Massachusetts, had suggested impeaching Thomas Jefferson in 1809, and was a member of the Essex Junto, but unlike Timothy Pickering he was not a pro-British secessionist. At the time, however, Quincy's and Pickering's names were often mentioned in the same breath.

15. *The National Advocate,* New York, NY, October 2, 1813, 2.

⤺ **1814** ⤻

Parson Parish had outdone himself with his Fast Day sermon of 1813, so much so that it was reprinted in Canada as an "Unparalleled Political Sermon," so full of patriotism — for Britain — that it was recommended to "all his Majesty's subjects," "every lover of his King and country." The news of the Canadian reprinting broke in the fall of 1813, but it was in 1814 the preface to this *enemy* edition was obtained and printed in the Republican papers.

From HALIFAX!

LISTEN TO THE ENEMY.
"Unparalleled" Political Sermon!!

A gentleman recently from the neighboring British provinces, where he has been detained in prison as a hostage, has politely favored us with the *"Acadian Recorder,"* of Sept. 4, 1813, printed at *Halifax,* by *Anthony M. Holland,* containing a notice of the publication at that place of one of PARISH's incendiary philippics. It is in the following words:

"In the Press, and will be published on Wednesday next, to be had at this Office, at the several Book-stores, of *Mr. M'Dougal,* and *Thomas D. Cowdell,—An unparalleled Political Sermon* delivered at Byefield, State of Massachusetts, on the Annual Fast, April 1813, by *Elijah Parish,* D.D.—[Price one shilling.]"

He has also loaned us the *"Sermon"* itself, (if such a tissue of treasonable ranting can bear that appellation.) It is printed by *Anthony M. Holland,* the same man who publishes the paper.—The following are his introductory remarks:

"Preface.—*Read, mark, and LEARN!* from an unparalleled Sermon, by *Elijah Parish,* D.D. of Byefield, Massachusetts, (United States.)—The Publisher is well aware, that the above Political Discourse is worthy of the study and imitation of every Minister, and claims the most pious regard of all his Majesty's subjects.—Every lover of his King and country, should certainly possess and disseminate its sacred principles. It includes all the constituent parts which form the accomplished and patriotic Orator, shewing to his own countrymen, (our enemies) with all possible truth and brevity, the *cause* and *consequences* of the present unnatural war with Great-Britain. If energy of expression—if perspicuity of style—if elegance of composition ever regaled the eye, ear, and the heart of a British subject, then this Sermon claims *the suffrage of every soul that loves the best of Constitutions*—namely, *that of OLD ENGLAND!* In short, it appears to be the most strenuous and grateful ebullition of a Patriotic, Evangelical and Martyr-like Spirit!"

Thus we find, that the unholy and factious ravings of our own *priests of confusion* are copied by the enemy with the greatest inveteracy! Verily, *"the laborer is worthy of his hire!"* If they betray such extravagant joy at this sermon, if they call upon *their* ministers to *imitate* it, if they view it as tending to prop up the *Constitution of Old England,* (MONARCHY AND ALL) *at the expense of the* FREE and GLORI-OUS CONSTITUTION OF THE UNITED STATES, how must this joy be heightened when they hear the last "unparalleled Political Sermon," from the same outrageous source, and the late immoderate rejoicing of our federal clergy at the triumph of the arms of Britain?[1]

By the time the Canadian edition of his 1813 Fast Day sermon was making news in June, Parish had already delivered his 1814

---

1. *Boston Patriot,* Boston, MA, June 18, 1814, 2.

Fast Day sermon, which also made news throughout the country. In this one, Parish issued an overt call for a separation of the states, comparing a separation of the New England states to the Israelites "separating" from Egypt.

Heresy against Washington, by a High Priest of Faction.

We have seen a sermon preached at Byfield, in Massachusetts, on the 7th inst being the day *professedly* set apart by Gov. STRONG for *religious and devotional exercises,* by the notorious parson PARISH. If any thing were wanting to complete the cup of this man's iniquity, the sermon before us will be found more than sufficient. "That *evil* exists in the world, (says he) requires no proof." This assertion was not necessary, as every one who reads his *atrocious performance* will be fully convinced of that. While *clerical partizans* are thus permitted to prostitute the sacred desk to the basest purposes of faction, and to fulminate their anathemas in the presence of sober citizen; while with unrighteous zeal they defend the cause of the enemy, array themselves against WASHINGTON, preach up a *dissolution of the Union,* and endeavor to bring upon their country the horrors of *civil war,* no other proof of the existence of *deep depravity and evil* is requisite....

... It will be seen by the extract below, that this *clerical declaimer* has attempted, by perverting the holy scriptures, to draw a parallel between the Egyptians and Israelites of old, and the Republicans and Federalists of the present day. But he has totally failed; the effort is so labored, the sophistry so lame, that he has only exposed his *cloven foot,* without effecting his purpose.

PARISH'S FACTIOUS ANATHEMA.

"Had not the barbarous despotism of Egypt extorted fears of blood and sighs of desperation, from the posterity of Jacob, they might possibly, till this day, have been the slaves of her servile princes, the vassals of her imported Mamelukes. The sons of Israel were passionately attached to their union with this Ancient Dominion.—Their separation from the Ancient

Dominion, who had oppressed them, was *the great, the grand result,* of their political miseries. In this event were involved *blessings,* too great to be deserted, *blessings* too numerous to be named. By this, they were freed from their former bondage.—They bid farewell to the brick-kilns and ditches of Egypt. Israel's sons no longer sailed on the great sea, nor on the Red Sea; but were *deafened by the eternal rattle of dismal manufactures.*—These measures of government were as fatal to the prosperity of Israel, as were the ten plagues to Egypt. Israel had submitted to the unlimited control of Pharaoh, a proud infidel, a despiser of religion, a profane scoffer at divine things; *but when Israel separated,* JEHOVAH became their legislator and king. They had been vexed and scourged by petty tyrants, tools of government; now they were under the pious guidance of Moses and Aaron. It was necessary that they should sigh under the rod of oppression, to wake them from their political lethargy, *to dispel their PREJUDICES in favor of the union,* under which their fathers had enjoyed repose and prosperity, to provoke them to seek a better government; to inflame them to noble darings, in bursting the bonds of oppression; in *dissolving their connexion with the merciless slave-holders of the country.*

"Another immense advantage to Israel from *dissolving their union* with Egypt was an escape from the fatal contagion of infidel examples.

"Finally, THEY DISSOLVED THE UNION—they marched —the sea opened—Jordan stopped his current—Canaan received their triumphant banners—the trees of the field clapped their hands—the hills broke forth into songs of joy—they feasted ob the fruit of their own labors. *Such success awaits a resolute and* PIOUS *people.*

"They became weary of yielding the fruit of their labors to pamper their splendid tyrants. They left their political woes: THEY SEPARATED.—*Where is our Moses? Where is the rod of his miracles? Where is Aaron?*

"To conclude the subject, we discover the malignant nature of American democracy. Democracy is the author of all the Egyptian misery and mischief endured in the land.

A new language must be invented, before we attempt to express the baseness of their [*the republicans*] conduct, or *describe the rottenness of their hearts.* Divines had described a dreadful depravity among the sons of Adam; but divines had not described, nor conceived, *such* a depravity.

"What dismal reflections must have torn the bosom of Pharaoh, surveying the miseries which he had occasioned. "I have ruined my kingdom, I have destroyed myself." What must be the reflections of our exalted President, in the silence of retirement?"...[2]

The sermon was even advertised as a call for separation of the states — "deduced from scripture authority," of course.

☞ Dr. PARISH's Fast Sermon,

THIS Day Published, and for sale at the
Newburyport Bookstore—

A DISCOURSE, delivered at *Byfield,* on the Annual
Fast, April 7, 1814—
by ELIJAH PARISH, D.D.

TEXT.—"But he said, ye are idle, ye are idle; therefore ye say, let us go and do sacrifice to the Lord. Go therefore now and work; for there shall no straw be given you, yet shall ye deliver the tale of bricks."—*Exodus,* v. 17, 18.

☞ As the subject discussed in this Discourse is the expediency of a SEPARATION, deduced from scripture authority, it will be read with much interest.[3]

This sermon must indeed have been "read with much interest," given that by the first week of May, less than a month after it first went on sale, a second edition was published.

Starting in the summer of 1814, a campaign begun by the Presbyterians to stop Sunday mail delivery spread across the

2. *Boston Patriot,* Boston, MA, April 27, 1814, 2.
3. *Newburyport Herald,* Newburyport, MA, April 15, 1814, 3.

country, with countless petitions signed by thousands pouring into Congress. While the campaign was unsuccessful, with the post-master general reporting in early 1815 that the Sunday mail would continue, Connecticut, as far as it could, took its own action to protest this disturbance of the Sabbath, enacting a law prohibiting mail stages from carrying passengers on Sundays. This new law from the "holy land" of Connecticut was mocked by Republican papers in other states. The *New-York Herald,* reprinting an announcement of this new law from the *Boston Gazette,* added a paragraph of commentary that was reprinted in many other Republican papers, giving a good reason why the law was counterproductive to preserving the peace on the Sabbath:

> *From the Boston Gazette of November 7.*
>
> A letter from Hartford, (Con.) received by the Enterprize Stage, dated Friday evening, says, "The Legislature of this State, has this day passed a Law to take place on Saturday next, stating that the Mail Stage, or any other Stage, passing through this State on the Sabbath, shall not take any passengers; and that the owners of any Stage who shall take passengers contrary to that law, are to pay a fine of 20 dollars for each one so carried by them."
>
> SUNDAY—Our religious brethren in Connecticut, have made it highly penal to travel, in a Stage Coach, on Sunday. We regard the observation of the Sabbath and its duties as sincerely as they do; but at this time, when every hour is pregnant with important events, it is not the most auspicious moment for promulgating laws against the only means of communicating early information, interesting to millions. Beside, it should be recollected, in Connecticut, if they permit mail coaches to pass, and it is not denied: that the MORE they are LOADED, the LESS they RATTLE.[4]

The "infidel" Thomas Jefferson, now in his sixth year of retirement, was in the news again. Among the losses when the British

---

4. *New-York Herald,* New York, NY, Nov 12, 1814, 4.

burned Washington, D.C. in August 1814 was Congress's library. To replace the destroyed library, Jefferson offered to sell Congress his own extensive personal library, which was more than double the size of the 3,000 volume library that had been lost. While the majority in Congress were all for purchasing Jefferson's valuable collection, objections were raised by some of the pious Federalists. Jefferson's library, after all, would no doubt contain numerous works by deists and atheists.

MR. JEFFERSON'S LIBRARY.

The objections made by federal members of Congress, to the purchase of Mr. Jefferson's Library, are certainly not only extraordinary and illiberal, but they reflect the greatest discredit upon the national character of this country. What can be a greater stigma upon the members of our National Legislature than to assert, that books of a philosophical description are improper for their perusal? Were Mr. Oakley, Mr. Reid and Mr. Grosvenor, the literary censors of the U. States, the works of Newton, Locke, Simpson, Stewart, and all others of equal merit, would doubtless be committed to the flames, and their places supplied perhaps by the Tales of Wonder, the Tales of Horror, and the Arabian Nights' Entertainment. Another great objection is, that Mr. Jefferson's Library contains the Works of Voltaire.—What a pitiful observation! Will it be said that the works of an author which hold the first rank on the shelves of all the Libraries of Europe, and which may be found in the Libraries of Oxford and Cambridge, and in those of the four Scotch Universities, for the express purpose to be perused by students, should be prohibited and forbidden a place in the Library of Congress? Will the force of federal prejudice and superstition be so powerful as to effect this? If Messrs. Oakley, Reid and Grosvenor, prevail in their motion, it will be a matter not very astonishing to see an attempt next made for an established form of worship throughout the U. States. I know this has been a favorite project for some time past, not only with the federalists, but with the adherents of John Randolph. Every step has been taken, and every means adopted in the several states for this purpose. Several extraordinary facts not generally known, which will prove the truth of this assertion, I shall take an opportunity to before long of making public.[5]

In spite of its numerous "books of a philosophical description," Congress bought Jefferson's library in 1815, which would be the start of today's Library of Congress.

⌐

In Connecticut politics, it was another dismal year for the Republicans. As long as "Mr. Madison's War," as the Federalists called it, continued, the focus would be off the state issues that would eventually lead to a Republican victory. Voter turnout was down for both parties in the spring. Governor John Cotton Smith was reelected in a landslide, with 9,415 votes to Elijah Boardman's 2,619. Lieutenant Governor Chauncey Goodrich was reelected with 7,734 votes to Republican Isaac Spencer's 2,794. The number of Republican representatives remained very low, with only 36 being elected in the September election.

⌐

In October came the first news of what would become the biggest story of 1814 by far — the Hartford Convention. This convention, an assembly of Federalist delegates from the New England states, was to be convened in Hartford, Connecticut in December.

A writer using the name "Chatham" had urged in a September piece in the *Courant* titled "The Crisis" that Connecticut lead the way in a united action of the New England States, suggesting that a commission be appointed, but it was Massachusetts that would get the ball rolling, with that state's House of Representatives passing the following resolution on October 16:

Resolved, That persons be appointed as Delegates from

5. *Daily National Intelligencer,* Washington, D.C., October 25, 1814, 3.

the Legislature, to meet and confer with other Delegates from the states of New-England, or any of them, upon the subject of their public grievances and concerns, and upon the best means of preserving our resources, and of defence against the enemy, and to devise and suggest for adoption by those respective states, such measures as they may deem expedient; and also to take measures, if they shall think proper, for procuring a convention of delegates from all the United States, in order to revise the constitution thereof, and more effectually to secure the support and attachment of all the people, by placing all upon the basis of fair representation.[6]

The Massachusetts House and Senate met together on October 18 and appointed twelve delegates to attend the convention.

Massachusetts, which had chosen Hartford as the site of this proposed convention, communicated its resolution and other documents to the other New England states, and the Connecticut legislature, which was then holding its regular October session, passed the following resolution to join Massachusetts and send seven delegates:

Resolved, That seven persons be appointed Delegates from this State, to meet the delegates of the Commonwealth of Massachusetts, and of any of the other New-England States, at Hartford, on the 15th day of December next, and confer with them on the subjects proposed by a resolution of said Commonwealth, communicated to this legislature, and upon any other subjects which may come before them, for the purpose of devising and recommending such measures for the safety and welfare of these States, as may consist with our obligation as members of the national Union.[7]

On November 5, the Rhode Island legislature passed a similar resolution to send four delegates.

---

6. *Republican Farmer,* Bridgeport, CT, October 26, 1814, 3.
7. *The Connecticut Courant,* Hartford, CT, November 8, 1814, 3.

The legislatures of Vermont and New Hampshire did not send any delegates. There were, however, two New Hampshire counties and one in Vermont which held their own meetings, each electing a delegate to represent their county. These three delegates were admitted to the Convention although not officially sent by their states.

In the nearly two months from the first announcement of the convention until it began, the newspapers were filled with speculation about what would take place there, with words like "treason," "insurrection," and "rebellion" frequently seen in the Republican papers.

In the following article from November, the Republican *Boston Patriot* reprints and comments on what one writer in the Federalist *Boston Gazette* said the convention *could* do.

THE CONVENTION.

WARNING TO STOCKHOLDERS.

The views of the *Junto* begin to be developed. The object of the Hartford Convention is proclaimed as follows in the Boston Gazette, and no doubt it is written by the authority of one of the Boston Members of the Convention.

"This Convention can, if they should think proper, take for their example, and the basis of their proceedings, the result of the Convention of 1787, of which the ever revered Washington was President, and form a *new frame of government,* to be submitted to the legislatures of the several States, for their approbation and adoption, and as was the case at that time, this new Constitution can go into operation as soon as two, three, four, five, or any other number of States that may be named, shall have adopted it. The Convention can so form the frame of government to exclude all persons from voting at elections, except *Free, Native Citizens of the Country:* And also so as to give any other States, besides those uniting in the first instance, which they may be willing to admit into the compact, the liberty of joining them whenever they may be so disposed: And they can exclude the *newly created Western States* from this privilege.

"The same frame of government may be so formed, that the public debt, which *originated prior to the present war,* now due to the citizens of the States so associated, shall be assumed, and the payment of the interest provided for, and this may be done for citizens of each State as they shall come into the compact.

"And lastly, though not least important—This frame of government may provide that there shall be no alternative made, or States admitted into the compact, except those named in that instrument, without the consent of *all* the other States.

"Having had the presumption to give these opinions with regard to what might be done, the reader will pardon me if I hazard another, viz.—That should something similar to what is above stated, be the result of the deliberations of this Convention, we shall very soon see all the States, with which New-England *ought* to wish any political connexion, again united in an improved, efficient and equitable government—leaving Madison, Monroe, and his coadjutors, as the first jacobin congress left the judges of the U.S. circuit court; without any jurisdiction. That men of talents and political integrity would again be seen in the councils of the nation.— That the blessings of peace would immediately be restored; and, in fine, that under such a re-organized and re-united government, we should once more be a respected and happy people."

If the above purposes of the Convention be correctly stated, and we have no reason to doubt it, it is full time for the National government to look into the affair. If two or five States meet together and *abrogate the Constitution,* it is treason against the Union. If they should promulgate a new Constitution, dissolving the Union of the States, it will be an overt act of treason. If they refuse to pay their proportion of the debts due by the National Government since the war, it will be a manifest robbery on the national creditors. *Stock-Holders look to this,* and see how far you have encouraged such men.—Men of honor and integrity, whether *federal* or *republican,* will view this proposed stab at the vitals of the national credit in its proper light. They will consider the proposers and authors of it as the tools of the British Ministry, who are hired to sow disunion, and to dishonor the nation. "Men of talents and political integrity, they say, would again be seen in the councils of the nation." If such purposes as are proclaimed are the objects of these men, we shall find none to approbate them but traitors, and men hired by the enemy to aid them in the destruction of the liberties of our country; and we trust in God they will find nerve and spirit enough in the National Government to put down the conspirators. If our rulers view this proposed Convention with contempt, and unworthy of notice, it is well; but if they have every reason to suppose that it will lead to *civil war,* and a dissolution of the Union, we say they are in duty bound, (yes, it is their incumbent duty) to proclaim them traitors to their country, and to take the necessary steps to have them arrested on the first overt act of treason being committed. The people who are ready to aid them; they have but to proclaim them traitors, and their power is gone in a moment.[8]

Another Boston Republican paper, the *Independent Chronicle,* speculated that the convention could "light the torch of civil war":

Hartford Assembly.

The mischief which may arise from the wanton measures which may be adopted by a body of men meeting at Hartford (in the character of representatives from their respective States) may not be realized, till it is too late to remedy the evils which may take place. A few indiscreet men may do a great deal of mischief, which may take thousands of the most considerate to rectify. Have the new-fangled Delegates fully contemplated their *responsibility?* Can they answer to the citizens in general, what a bare majority of the Legislature have authorized them to do? Not a town in the

8. *Boston Patriot,* Boston, MA, November 5, 1814, 2.

Commonwealth has recommended such a measure by *instructions to their Representatives*—Even Boston has been silent on the subject—and yet a certain body of men have the temerity to assemble in another State, and to begin a work, which may eventually lead to a dissolution of the government, and introduce as bloody a contest as was exhibited in France. And pray, who are the men thus authorized to light the torch of civil war in a neighboring State? Are they these, who are qualified either to *fight,* or *pay* those who do? Admit the "dogs of war" are let out among the citizens—that funds are to be raised to pay the armies—Will Mr. C. *Doctor* O. and their associates, assemble in the field of carnage, or have they funds to lend Massachusetts in case of emergencies? ...

It must be presuming in this State to send a body of men to a sister State, to propose a meeting on business of such a disorganizing nature. It is a high affront on Connecticut to oblige them to become the rendezvous of such an assemblage.—By what authority does Massachusetts direct a Committee to meet at Hartford, to take into consideration a subject of such an alarming tendency? It is an insult to their sovereignty to be thus designated without leave or license, as the place of meeting. Modesty might at least have dictated to Massachusetts not to force themselves into Connecticut, to do a mischief of such magnitude, in this "moral and religious State." If the business was necessary, the meeting of delegates should have been proposed within Massachusetts, (say Worcester) and not intrude themselves within the territory of another State. What a pretty figure would Doctor O. make under the arrest of the Sheriff of Hartford; for no body of men have a right to go into another State to hold assemblies, which have a tendency to bring on overt acts of treason. We may expect some humorous tricks to be put upon them; for when mischief is supposed to be brewing, there are always some wags to promote the sport. The merry lads of Hartford may be as frolicksome as the *Merry Wives of Windsor.* ...[9]

---

9. *Independent Chronicle,* Boston, MA, December 12, 1814, 2.

All of the Federalist papers reprinted the same report of the convention's December 15 opening day, first printed in Hartford's *Connecticut Mirror,* the paper edited by convention secretary Theodore Dwight.

NEW-ENGLAND CONVENTION.

On Thursday last, the Delegates from the New-England States, appointed to meet in Convention at Hartford, assembled for that purpose in the Council Chamber of the State-House in this city, at 10 o'clock in the forenoon. On being called to order, they proceeded to organize themselves by unanimously choosing the Hon. GEORGE CABOT, a member from the state of Massachusetts, their president, and THEODORE DWIGHT, Esq. of Hartford, Secretary.

The Convention was opened with a solemn, and impressive prayer by the Rev. Dr. Strong of Hartford. A Committee was then appointed to examine the credentials of the members returned to serve in Convention; who reported that they found the following persons to have been selected by the Legislatures of the following States, viz.

From *Massachusetts*—Messrs. George Cabot, William Prescott, Harrison Gray Otis, Timothy Bigelow, Stephen Longfellow, Daniel Waldo, George Bliss, Nathan Dane, Hodijah Baylies, Samuel Summer Wilde, Joseph Lyman and Joshua Thomas.

From *Rhode-Island*—Messrs. Daniel Lyman, Samuel Ward, Benjamin Hazard, and Edward Manton.

From *Connecticut*—Messrs. Chauncey Goodrich, James Hillhouse, John Treadwell, Zephaniah Swift, Nathaniel Smith, Calvin Goddard, and Roger Minott Sherman.

And, that, from the State of *New-Hampshire,* in the counties of Cheshire and Grafton, Messrs. Benjamin West and Mills Olcott, had been elected in county conventions in their respective counties, and were entitled to seats in the convention.

The Rev. gentlemen who officiate as Chaplains to the General Assembly of this State, residing in Hartford, and the Rev. Dr. Perkins, of West-Hartford, are invited to officiate daily, as Chaplains to the Convention during their session.

All the members of the Convention are present, and assiduously engaged in the important and interesting duties, for the consideration of which they were appointed.[10]

One of the convention's delegates was missing in the above report. William Hall, Jr. of Vermont, sent by his county of Windham, didn't arrive until December 28.

The *Mercury,* also published in Hartford, reported on the day a bit differently:

HENRYAD, OR SNUFF-BOTTLE CONVENTION.

No crazy headed project since the chivalric period when the immortal Knight of La Mancha, and his renowned Squire Sancho Panza, excited alternate paroxysms of laughter and terror, can be compared to the project of crazy Jack[11] and Henry O![12] The oracle of Boston Federalism, the celebrated John Henry, in the spirit of political inspiration, declared, that "should the Congress possess spirit and independence enough to place the popularity in jeopardy by so strong a measure [as to declare war] the legislature of Massachusetts will give the tone to the neighboring states, will invite a Congress of Delegates from the federal states, and create a separate government." The prophecy once made, it must be fulfilled. Jack and Harry took it into their heads; whether into that part where the brain should be, or in the cavities, where in ordinary heads the water is deposited, is not certainly known. Indeed it is doubtful whether either of the parts alluded to was precisely the place, since it has long been proverbial that *"Boston folks are full of notions;"* and it has, as we are told, been demonstrated by anatomists, that an ample vacuity is left in Boston skulls, as a receptacle for schemes and caprices, that would greatly disturb the regular

10. *Connecticut Mirror,* Hartford, CT, December 19, 1814, 3.

11. John Lowell, known as the "Boston Rebel" and "Crazy Jack," was a strong proponent of a separation of the New England states who didn't think the Hartford Convention would go far enough.

12. Harrison Gray Otis, one of the organizers of the Hartford Convention and one of its delegates from Massachusetts.

functions of the brain, in men of common sense. However this may be, the prophecy was made, and Harry and Jack, unusually affected with the Boston malady, conceived that they were the instruments in the hands of Providence, or in the hands of the Prince Regent, to bring about the fulfillment of the much wished for event. Under this impulse they determined to get up a Convention. A Convention chattered the prattling Harry—a Convention by G-d swore crazy Jack—and the Boston heads all full of notions cried out, a Convention—a Convention!

This great event, predicted by Harry, is now fulfilled. "Massachusetts has given the tone to the neighboring states," and the Congress is assembled. Twelve great luminaries from Massachusetts now honour our city with their presence. Four constellations from the *"great Pillar"* Rhode-Island, and seven of our own Lawyers and Councillors, and Judges, and Lt. Governors and Governors, are duly and *constitutionally* assembled. Two northern lights, who are said to represent about one fifth of two counties in New-Hampshire, are come also. And to complete the group, one plane, shot by its centrifugal force (probably by the aid of a late earthquake in Boston) has been ejected from the Green Mountains, but having acquired too great a momentum, has unfortunately shot by and lost its orbit.

It is truly unfortunate for great men, that their greatness is exhibited best at a given distance only. It may be called a Telescopic distance. Further removed, they swim like motes before the eye; approaching too near, they swell like bubbles, and burst in empty air. These men have surely lost their true distance.—Soon after the appointment of the members of the Convention, we heard much about the great and illustrious men, who were to represent the three great pillars of the union, and the Convention was announced to be a very great and *"dignified body."* The 15th of Dec. was a day of great and fearful anticipation. Our doors and windows were crowded with spectators, anxious to view the wonders of the age as they arrived. Our citizens were standing at the corners of the streets and bridges, gaping and staring for Convention men, like a countryman when for the first time he enters such a great and celebrated town as Boston, or London!

A coach, a coach, cries one; a sleigh says another—it has wheels says a third—and bells cries a fourth; then by heaven says a fifth it must be a Tin Cart in style! At length the wonderful machine ceases to move; and a coach it was, a Boston coach, the horses loaded with bells, and the coach with members of the great and dignified body. Who comes forth! "Not a spirit, nor an angel: nor an old man from the wilderness, clothed with a mantle and bending o'er his staff, with silvered beard; but the pretty flippant ——— ———!" Are these the wise men from the East, whose names have been echoed from one end of the continent to the other! The same. Heads filled with sounds and notions!

The Council Chamber was opened. A prayer was made at the opening of the Convention. Under the portrait of the immortal Washington assembled, this "dignified body" called on Heaven for aid. The pious christians who had in the city been duped into a day of humiliation, fasting and prayer, for the success of their measures, had the doors of the Council Chamber closed against them. They were not admitted to high and dignified communion with Heaven, but returned with heartfelt humiliation, to close the day at their conference houses, or in humble family devotion at home. The very men through whose influence and for whose success fasting and praying had become the order of the day thro' New-England, refused to admit their fellow christians to join with them in prayer, for wisdom to direct them in a course best adapted to the public good, or their *"own safety."* [13]

The Massachusetts district of Maine was heard from in the *Boston Patriot,* which reprinted an item from that part of the state:

The Hartford "Assemblage."

The five-and-twenty men who constitute the assemblage at Hartford, met at that place on Thursday last. Mr. *George*

---

13. *American Mercury,* Hartford, CT, December 20, 1814, 3.

Cabot, of Boston, was nominated as principal, and Mr. *Theodore Dwight* second. As it is usually thought indispensable on such occasions to make a great show of *religion,* (the better to deceive the people) *four clergymen* were immediately conscripted into the service, who are to pray alternately.

Since the above, nothing has been heard from them.

A writer in the *American Advocate,* published in *Hallowell,* (Maine) speaking of the above assemblage, calls upon the hardy citizens of that important District in the following nervous and patriotic manner:

"Fellow-Citizens of Maine!

"How long will you be a province of rebellious Massachusetts? Do you doubt the intentions of the Hartford Convention? Read the federal papers which are the organ of their sentiments and it is no longer doubtful. The Constitution is to be abrogated, the standard of rebellion reared, and a separate peace made with the public enemy. Shall the District of Maine be involved in the guilt, and participate in the degradation of Massachusetts? Forbid it Heaven! Arouse then ye hardy sons of Maine. Your children demand of you their birthright; your own characters imperiously demand that your liberties be secured; that you be no longer subject to Massachusetts than she is subject to the Constitution. Your duty to the Constitution and Government are paramount. Action is necessary to encounter action. Be timid and slothful and all is lost—be bold and persevering and you may avert the worst of all calamities, a civil war.—Your cause will be the cause of your country, of liberty and justice; and God will approve it.—*Call a Convention of at least one citizen from every town in Maine to meet at some central place, who may assume the powers of Government as soon as Massachusetts shall throw off her allegiance to the UNION."*

A letter from Washington of the 10th inst. to the Editors of the *Baltimore American,* says:—"As the time for the meeting of the Hartford Convention approaches, the minority in Congress increase in virulence and misrepresentation of the measures of government, and in attempts to excite the eastern people to rebellion. As to the continued threats about resisting the laws, the majority say, let them resist. If resistance were to take place, the thing had as well be settled at once. Col. JOHNSON, of Kentucky, (who commanded the mounted men at the defeat and capture of Proctor's army) hoped, that if a civil war were brought about, it would only consume the traitors who were urging on the northern people to resistance by their advice and virulent conduct against government, and regretted that he had but one life to lay down in quelling and punishing the risings of rebellion.— This created a terrible ferment among the champions of rebellion." [14]

The *Mercury* had a few comments on Theodore Dwight's *Mirror's* report of the chaplains who would officiate at the convention:

> The Rev. gentlemen who officiate as Chaplains to the General Assembly of this State, residing in Hartford, and the Rev. Dr. Perkins, of West-Hartford, are invited to officiate daily, in turn, as Chaplains to the Convention during their session.
>
> *Mirror.*

> One of these gentlemen has declared to a U.S. officer in this city, that he prays with the Convention, but dislikes it as much as any of you military gentlemen. Another greatly to his credit, and much to the satisfaction of nine tenths of his Parish, has declared that he has not been near the Convention, and will not go, and desires that his people should so understand it.—A third it is reported, how truly we know not, that he knows of no form of prayer for treason and rebellion. The fourth is an aged Gentleman, residing about four miles from the place of the Convention; his health is infirm and was it otherwise we presume would not knowingly offer up his prayers for the success of any faction against the government of his country. [15]

14. *Boston Patriot*, Boston, MA, December 21, 1814, 2.
15. The "aged Gentleman," Rev. Nathan Perkins, did officiate on four of the days of the convention.

How will this great and dignified body proceed? The whole christian church in New England were on their knees to get it under way, and prayers must be had during its life, and will be more necessary at its burial, if it is to rise again.

Their Secretary we presume with some trifling addition to his compensation, might read a celebrated and pious paraphrase of the 148th Psalm,[16] and perhaps the church service. The first he would no doubt be able to repeat verbatim; but in the last he should be cautioned not to stumble on an unfortunate, but very appropriate clause of the service; "from treason, privy conspiracy and rebellion, good Lord deliver us." [17]

After two weeks of the convention's being in session, curiosity about what was going on behind its closed doors was building, not only in New England but throughout the country, as reported by the Republican *National Aegis* in Worcester, Massachusetts, reprinting an article from Philadelphia's *Aurora:*

THE CONVENTION.

The publick, we believe, do not feel any distressing anxiety about the proceedings of the Convention of "choice spirits" at Hartford, for providentially, their weakness is proportioned to their malice, and though they will plot mischief, there is no great danger that they will be able to execute it. But we presume our readers have a spice of curiosity like ourselves, and we are sorry we are not able to gratify them. We have no means of prying into the secrets of this iniquitous conclave, who shut themselves from sight that their machinations may not be detected and defeated. If any one should be impertinent enough to ask—"you secret, black, and midnight conspirators, what is't you do?" they probably would answer him—"a deed without a name."

We this day publish from the *Aurora,* an interesting article on this subject; which demonstrates how completely

---

16. Theodore Dwight's infamous 1803 "Moll Carey" parody of the 148th psalm.
17. *American Mercury,* Hartford, CT, December 20, 1814, 3.

the assertions and predictions of the famous spy *John Henry* are verified. It can hardly fail to convince the mind of every honest man that the present wicked and daring attempt at rebellion is the denouement of a conspiracy, formed, years ago, between domestick traitors and foreign emissaries; and that the measures now in operation are intended to lead the way to a connexion with Great Britain, and are known to be sanctioned by that government. So complete is the chain of circumstantial evidence, that no case unsupported by positive proof can be clearer.

"It is a common enquiry, what will this *Grand Convention* do? Republicans do not think them of consequence enough to be alarmed; but they are all a little curious to learn how they will *get out of this scrape?* For our own part, we are satisfied that the business will end rather farcically than tragically. There will be much smoke and no fire. Guilt is almost always cowardly—and we do not believe the conventionists will adopt any bold measures upon *their own* responsibility. They may talk and threaten in a high strain, because they know that words alone will not constitute an overt act of treason. They will try to kindle the passions of the people to a flame. They will denounce the National Rulers as tyrants. They will declare the constitution violated and the northern states released from their obligations to the Union. They will intimate that a speedy remedy must be found for our *sufferings*. But we are much mistaken, if they are not careful to avoid committing themselves by pointing out any definite course to be pursued. They will instigate the blow, but leave it to be struck by others whom they think more insignificant and irresponsible.

"After all there is no calculating upon the actions of men who act without principle. Let us wait till the *mountain brings forth*. We shall do well to be guarded against a *volcanic* eruption; but if, as is most likely, nothing but a ridiculous mouse is born, we shall have a fair chance to divert ourselves at the expense of men who are depraved enough to intend treason, but not brave enough to perpetrate it." [18]

18. *National Aegis*, Worcester, MA, December 28, 1814, 2.

Although the convention would last into January 1815, Boston's *Yankee* satirically predicted its outcome at the end of December:

PROCLAMATION.

By the Hartford Convention.

WHEREAS his Majesty's dutiful and loyal subjects, having met in solemn Convention at the royal city of Hartford, to take into consideration the necessity of severing the New-England states from the Union, and to form an alliance offensive and defensive with our sovereign Lord the King of the British Isles:

And whereas divers weighty matters and things have arisen that place the *objects* and *purposes* of this Convention in an uncertain and precarious state, which will for present *frustrate those desirable objects:*

NOW BE IT KNOWN to all his Majesty's loyal subjects in the said New-England states, that this convention will be adjourned to the first day of April next, commonly called *Fool's Day,* so that the objects and the great and important purposes of this convention may be better matured, and the public mind prepared for the separation from the confederacy of the Union.

And whereas it hath been represented to this Convention that the citizens of the state of Massachusetts do own TWELVE MILLIONS OF DOLLARS *in the national funds*—We therefore warn all persons so concerned in the said funds, to dispose of their stock on or before the said first day of April—and we further order that the state authorities of Massachusetts do forthwith dispose of such portion of the national funds as they now own; it having been represented to us that the authorities of the Union will in case of a separation of the New-England States, refuse to pay the principle or interest on the said *Twelve Millions* of dollars.

And whereas it hath been further represented to us that the people of the district of Maine are now organizing themselves for a separation from old Massachusetts, so soon as this convention takes measures to dissolve the Union of the States; which will leave Massachusetts little more than 6250 square miles standing: This Convention therefore, in consideration of this alarming procedure, are induced to *pause,* and deem it necessary to postpone all further proceedings until the people of the District of Maine are reconciled to the separation of the states.

And whereas it also appears to this convention, that there being *no funds* in the State treasury at the disposal of the authorities of Massachusetts, to pay troops to enforce a separation of the New-England states from the Union, we deem it absolutely necessary to delay our proceedings until we have funds remitted from England, and more troops landed in Maine, to enable this convention to proceed with promptitude and energy in the great work of revolution.

> Given under our hands and seals, in the
> Royal Council Chamber at Hartford,
> in the sixty second year of his
> Majesty's Reign.

> *God save the King.*
> GEORGE C——, Pres't.
> THEODORE D——, Sec'y.[19]

Unbeknownst to the Hartford Convention delegates, or anyone else in the United States, the peace negotiations in Ghent, Belgium between the United States and Britain, which had been going on since August, had been successful, with the American and British representatives signing the Treaty of Ghent on December 24.

19. *The Yankee,* Boston, MA, December 30, 1814, 3.

✍ **1815** ✍

The Hartford Convention ended on January 4, 1815, releasing its report on the same day. The convention did not call for a separation of the New England states or any other overt act of treason. It did, however, call for a second convention to meet in Boston in June if the federal government did not meet the demand in one of its resolutions, which was to negotiate an arrangement whereby the New England states would retain a portion of the taxes assessed upon them by the federal government to fund their own state military forces, each to defend its own state as well as any other New England state whose governor requested help from another New England state. As the Republican papers put it, the convention "postponed" its rebellion.

The convention also called for seven amendments to the U.S. Constitution, including that a president be limited to one term, that no two consecutive presidents come from the same state, that no foreign-born citizen be eligible for any federal office, that to reduce the representation of the southern states no slaves be counted as part of the population, and, with the Federalists' hatred of the western states, that it be made more difficult for new states to enter the union by requiring a two-thirds vote of both houses of Congress.

New Haven, Connecticut's *Columbian Register* printed the convention's resolutions, noting that a second convention was planned "after a few months breathing time," as the *Register* put it:

THE N. ENGLAND CONVENTION, have for the present

raised the siege—they evacuated their strong hold at Hartford, on Wednesday last; but it seems from their resolutions, that after a few months breathing time, they calculate to take a new stand against the administration, at Boston, near Bunker's Hill. The grand Convention, previous to their rising, had prepared and have now sent forth to the world a Report of their Proceedings. From the Report it appears, that the New-England States must not put themselves in hostile array against the Southern, at present. Not having room or time to copy much from their proceedings this week, we will present only the subjoined Resolutions of the Convention:—

THEREFORE RESOLVED—

THAT it be and hereby is recommended to the Legislatures of the several states represented in this Convention, to adopt all such measures as may be necessary effectually to protect the citizens of said states from the operation and effects of all acts which have been or may be passed by the Congress of the United States, which shall contain provisions, subjecting the militia or other citizens to forcible drafts, conscriptions, or impressments, not authorised by the Constitution of the U. States.

Resolved, That it be and hereby is recommended to the said Legislatures, to authorize an immediate and earnest application to be made to the Government of the United States, requesting their consent to some arrangement, whereby the said states may, separately or in concert, be empowered to assume upon themselves the defence of their territory against the enemy; and a reasonable portion of the taxes, collected within said states, may be paid into the respective treasuries thereof and appropriated to the payment of the balance due said states, and to the future defence of the same. The amount so paid into the said treasuries to be credited, and the disbursements, made as aforesaid to be charged to the U. States.

Resolved, That it be and hereby recommended to the Legislatures of the aforesaid states, to pass laws (where it has not already been done) authorizing the Governors or Commanders in chief of their militia to make detachments from the same or to form voluntary corps, as shall be most convenient and conformable to their Constitutions, and to cause the same to be well armed, equipped and disciplined, and held in readiness for service; and upon the request of the Governor of either of the other states to employ the whole of such detachment or corps as well as the regular forces of the state, or such part thereof as may be required and can be spared consistently with the safety of the state, in assisting the state, making such request, to repel any invasion thereof which shall be made or attempted by the public enemy.

Resolved, That the following amendments of the Constitution of the United States be recommended to the states represented as aforesaid, to be proposed by them for adoption by the state Legislatures and in such cases as may be deemed expedient, by a Convention chosen by the people of each state.

And it is further recommended, that the said states shall persevere in their efforts to obtain such amendments until the same shall be effected.

First. Representatives and direct taxes shall be apportioned among the several states which may be included within this union, according to their respective numbers of free persons, including those bound to serve for a term of years and excluding Indians not taxed, and all other persons.

Second. No new state shall be admitted into the union by Congress in virtue of the power granted by the Constitution, without two thirds concurrence of both Houses.

Third. Congress shall not have the power to lay any embargo on the ships or vessels of the citizens of the United States, in ports or harbors thereof, for more than sixty days.

Fourth. Congress shall not have the power, without the concurrence of two thirds of both Houses, to interdict the commercial intercourse between the U. States and any foreign nation of the dependencies thereof.

Fifth. Congress shall not make or declare war, or authorize acts of hostility against any foreign nation without the concurrence of two thirds of both Houses, except such acts of hostility be in defence of the territories of the United

States when actually invaded.

Sixth. No person who shall hereafter be naturalized, shall be eligible as a member of the Senate or House of Representatives of the United States, nor capable of holding any civil office under the authority of the United States.

Seventh. The same person shall not be elected President of the United States a second time; nor shall the President be elected from the same state two terms in succession.

Resolved, That if the application of these states to the government of the United States, recommended in a foregoing resolution, should be unsuccessful, and peace should not be concluded, and the defence of these states should be neglected, as it has been since the commencement of the war, it will in the opinion of this Convention be expedient for the Legislatures of the several states to appoint Delegates to another Convention to meet at Boston, in the state of Massachusetts, on the third Thursday of June next, with such powers and instructions as the exigency of a crisis so momentous may require.

Resolved. That the Hon. George Cabot, the Hon. Chauncey Goodrich, and the Hon. Daniel Lyman, or any two of them be authorised to call another meeting of this Convention to be holden in Boston, at any time before new Delegates shall be chosen, as recommended in the above resolution, if in their judgment the situation of the Country shall urgently require it.

HARTFORD, Jan. 4th, 1815

[Signed by all the members of the Convention.]

Those who are anxious to know the whole amount of the Convention Report, have only to call to mind the different New-England Legislative Reports for some time past, this being merely a repetition of those complaints, &c.[1]

The Republican papers, in articles like the following from the Worcester, Massachusetts *National Aegis,* mocked the convention and its very undramatic outcome.

---

1. *Columbian Register,* New Haven, CT, January 10, 1815, 3.

The Convention Dissolved & Rebellion Postponed!

The friends of government have been anticipating much diversion from the *farcical* ending of this intended *tragedy;* and they are not disappointed. It is impossible to conceive a more ridiculous spectacle than is now afforded by the *Boston Faction.* (For we consider the rest of the federal brawlers in N. England, with few exceptions, as the dupes and instruments of a cabal in Boston.) Year after year they have blustered and threatened and sworn that the "crisis of their *sufferings* was at hand," that the government had better beware, for one step more would drive them to open resistance, that they had *talked* long enough and now they were going to *act!* And then, thro' that convenient organ of faction, a party legislature, they would fulminate a quantity of red-hot Resolutions, which would make a stranger suppose that there was but one mind & one voice in N. England, that a revolution would immediately ensue, and that the warriors of Massachusetts already had their bows bent for the battle. Deceitful appearances! We know pretty well, that these bullies will never fight but upon paper. In vain have the desperadoes *Quincy, Lowell, &c.* endeavoured to inflame their passions and push them blinded with rage, to the mark.—They have never been able and never will be able to shew their courage to the sticking place.

The *Convention at Hartford* was their boldest attempt. They have never gone so far before; they were never before so favoured by time and circumstances; and since they have so miserably failed at the last moment, when the decisive blow was to be struck if ever, it requires no gift of prophecy to foretell, that they will not soon make another open attack upon the Union, though they will be constantly labouring, in secret, to undermine the edifice.

If the *"Report"* or *Manifesto* of the Convention was of any conscionable length, we would publish it for the amusement of our readers. It principally consists of a *tirade* against the administration, full of false statements and unsound arguments. It attempts an apology to the nation for doing so much and to their own party for not doing more. It makes assertions, which, if true, would justify a separation of the States, and then concludes, with affected moderation, that the union ought not to be abandoned but in the last extremity, and that the present is not the time for an enterprize so dangerous in its nature and doubtful in its consequences! The *Resolutions* with which it winds up we have published. They contain all the *substance,* if there is any, of the *last will and testament of the departed Convention.*

The Amendments of the Constitution which the Conventionists recommend, they well know cannot be obtained. Not more than five states will accede to them. All this therefore is nothing but *talk,* to save appearances. The proposed arrangement of the State Legislatures with the General Government in all probability will never be effected—and what is the alternative? What is the *remedy* adopted, after three weeks' deliberation, for the "intolerable grievances of N. England?" Nothing more nor less than that *a new Convention shall be called in June!* This is the rod held *in terrorem* over the head of our National Rulers! Can Republicans be blamed for laughing?—How will the Boston hot-heads scold and rave at this fresh and most cruel disappointment of their sanguine expectations!

It is easy to foresee what the State Legislature will do at their approaching session. Every method which cunning can devise to obstruct the measures of the General Government will be resorted to. Laws will be passed to encourage and protect the evasion if not the infraction of the United States' laws. Every endeavour will be used to keep alive local prejudices, in hopes that they may hereafter burst into a flame. But as to any acts of open resistance, they will very prudently postpone them as the Convention has done.[2]

Convention secretary Theodore Dwight's *Connecticut Mirror,* of course, had a very different opinion of the convention's report, asserting that nothing would be read with such deep interest since

2. *National Aegis,* Worcester, MA, January 11, 1815, 2.

the United States Constitution:

> On Thursday last, the New-England Convention adjourned. Their Report, with some documents and statements, printed by their order, was made public on the same day.— This important State paper, is given to the nation at large, and will serve to shew the baseness and malignity of the many thousand falsehoods and slanders which have been so liberally heaped upon that enlightened and dignified body, by the adherents of the administration, and the supporters of their destructive measures. Rarely has it happened in this country, that so able and distinguished an assembly of statesmen has been collected.—Their Report is signed by all the members of the Convention, and we have no doubt will be read with deeper interest through the nation, than has been the fact with any other State paper, since the publication of the Constitution of the United States.[3]

Boston's *Yankee,* with all its usual satire, published a bill for the convention:

Mr. JOHN BULL,[4]

Dr. to the Hartford Convention,

First Session, begun 15th Dec. 1814.

To the pay of 25 loyal subjects, assembled in convention at Hartford, from Dec. 15, to Jan. 15, 1815, at 20 dls. per day for each member,	15,000
To travel to Hartford and back to their homes, for 25 members, at 60 dols. each,	1,500

3. *Connecticut Mirror,* Hartford, CT, January 9, 1815, 3.
4. A fictional character personifying England, similar to America's "Uncle Sam."

To the clergy for praying in convention,	1,000
To Theodore D———, Sec'ry to do.	1,000
To Judge O———, for a prepared speech,	1,000
To Crazy Jack, for writing the Crisis,	1,000
To Ben Bobadil[5] for printing do.	1,000
To the Daily Advertiser for publishing,	1,000
To the Boston Gazette for do.	1,000
To the Spectator for do.	1,000
To the Connecticut Courant & Mirror	2,500
To 25 sets Henry's Letters, at 100 dls.	2,500
To 25 Snuff Bottles for use of members,	125
To cash paid for a handsome new British crown, cut at Hartford, and set in diamonds,	10,000
To parson G. for praying in private for the glory and DIGNITY of John Bull's Convention,	2,000
To parsons P. and O. for the like services,	4,000
To 8 dozen Witches,	500
To 1 large Cauldron for do.	50
To 5 doz. Brooms for do.	36
To 3 doz. Blue Lights.[6]	75
To 25 sets of Connecticut Blue Laws,	50
	46,336

Given under our hands at the Royal City
of Hartford, this 6th day of Jan. 1815.

G.C. Pres't,
of the Hartford Convention.

T.D. *Sec'y.*

Approved,
A. A. Consul for the N.E. States[7]

---

5. Benjamin Russell, editor of the Federalist Boston paper the *Columbian Centinel*, dubbed Ben Bobadil after the character Captain Bobadil, a cowardly braggart in the 1598 British play *Every Man in His Humour*, for publishing a piece titled "The Crisis" while the Hartford Convention was sitting, blusteringly calling for New England's independence.

6. In 1813, after hauling a captured British ship back to America, Commodore Stephen Decatur, trying to make a nighttime run past British blockaders, was alerted to blue lights burning at New London, Connecticut, a Federalist stronghold, and was convinced that these lights were lit by pro-British Federalists to signal the British ships and reveal his location. This led the Republicans to call pro-British Federalists "blue light" Federalists.

7. *The Yankee,* Boston, MA, January 6, 1815, 3.

In the same issue, *The Yankee* published the final canto of an epic poem in three cantos about the convention. Canto number one opens in Boston with the planning of the convention, and includes a speech by Harrison Gray "Harry" Otis, a description of a Boston clergyman, and the clergyman's speech. In canto number two, we're at the convention. The "little Rebel," John Lowell, also called Crazy Jack, speaks, and Satan appears. In canto number three, copied here in its entirety, the convention has ended, and we're back in Boston, where an angry Satan speaks to the Massachusetts delegates.

The Hartford Convention,
A POEM ... CANTO III.

————

ARGUMENT.
Satan's speech—he is angry—Mr. O—'s attempt to appease him—Satan's indignant reply—The little Rebel in a rage—attempts to strike his infernal majesty, and is transformed into a monkey.

"FROM realms of darkness and despair,
I am commission'd to repair
To Boston, my most fav'rite seat,
And there my friends in council meet;
To solve their doubts and urge them on,
And see their work is fairly done.
Your scheme has been, from year to year,
An object of my greatest care,
And all my subjects have been busy,
To make it safe, secure and easy.
I thought, with proper circumspection,
To leave it to your own direction,
T' appoint the leaders from your faction,
Of those most fit for plan or action,
And leave you, in a thing so simple,
With my instruction and example;
I thought you'd men resolv'd to lead you,
That no disaster might impede you,
And that your hopes and inclination,
Were ripe for acts of desperation:

My *Orator* was smooth and flippant,
My *Doctor* bold and independent,
My *smuggler* rich and influential,
My *British Lawyer* consequential,
My *little Rebel* a *lampooner*,
Devoid of honesty or honor,
My *Speaker* plodding and intriguing,
With Britain and my subjects leaguing;
And *George*,[8] the chief of delegation,
Up to the notch in every station.
That bolstr'd lawyer, who the first is,
Of dunces, on the bench of justice,
Who of the cunning is possessor
He borrow'd of his predecessor,
Would (if he could) pervert the laws,
To sanctify rebellion's cause.
With these, and others, their abettors,
You soon would rise and break your fetters,
And raise a tempest of sedition,
To sink the nation to *perdition.*
I'm jealous, I have been deceiv'd,
I find you're not to be believ'd;
That bickerings and disorders rise,
And feuds and animosities;
Some fear the danger, some the trouble,
Some scout the scheme, as all a bubble;
While others doubt my disposition,
And make me object of suspicion:
Ye 'xpect to dictate and control,
In spite of me you'd rule the whole.
I've listen'd to your scoundrel prating,
And overheard your vile debating
And, in each selfish, boasting story,
Ye fail to render me the glory,
But claim each plot, of my erecting,
As of your own originating.
Your feuds and fears, and jealousy,

8. Convention president George Cabot.

Ambition, pride, hypocrisy,
Your lack of trust and confidence
In my dear bought experience,
Prove you ungrateful and uncivil
Enough to overmatch the devil.

    Ye vile abusers of my pow'r,
Ye unfledg'd devils of an hour,
Would you resist my majesty,
And supercede my deviltry?
Now be it known, I'll crush your schemes,
Dispel your little, foolish dreams,
And blast your visionary glory,
By the black whirlwind of my fury!

    Come, speak, ye asses! what's your plan?
Who's the *chief traitor!* where's the man!
Where's your device, your stratagem,
Your cunning, craft, and all your scheme?
Your systematic revolution,
Your prompt and daring *execution?*
If you're such masters at revolt,
'Tis time *my* safety I consult:
Lest, unawares, ye come upon me
Excite rebellion, and dethrone me."

    All seem'd affrighted, and regretted
To find his majesty so *fretted;*
And look'd to *Harry* to appease him,
And, by his eloquence to please him.

    "Great sire," quoth Harry, "'t *must not be,*
That friends, like us, should disagree;
Our cause is one, we *mean* the same,
The disagreement is in *name;*
We all avow the same intent,
To crush the present government;
To build another in its stead,
With *me* and my friends at its head;
Now all in which we have directed
Is how the thing can be effected.
Likewise in *this* we all agree,
To *pray* in aid your majesty;

To thank, with grateful heart and tongue,
For help which from your bounty sprung,
And homage and devotion tender,
For all the service you will render;
We 'dore thy wisdom and thy might!
We all are humbled in thy sight!
But, pardon me for what I speak,
'Tis *possible* thou may'st *mistake;*
In thy first effort at revolt,
There was some error, or some *fault,*
And all thy wit and desperation
Cannot retrieve thy degradation.
Should this rebellion prove as fatal,
'Twould end in our destruction total.
The same incens'd ALMIGHTY FOE
Would fix our dreadful overthrow,
And doom our mighty combination
To everlasting condemnation.
    Yet, sire, to yield to thy direction,
We do not feel the least objection;
But, as th' affair is difficult,
We claim the right just to consult;
Though we submit to thy direction,
There's wisdom in much *consultation."*
    Satan to whom no sweet delusion
Appear'd as logical conclusion,
With much chagrin and indignation,
Thus interrupted his narration:
"What consultation? and with whom?
On a fine errand I am come!
To bring a plot, so well digested,
To be by *novices protested!*
I know your dark and deep design;
You'd steal the honor, which is mine;
'Tis the invention of a tory,
To rob the devil of his glory.
Do you your puny strife compare
With my immortal, fatal war?
Or can your petty feuds be blended

With battles wherein GODS contended?
Will you refuse my pow'r to own,
Because I *once* was overthrown,
And build your hopes and destiny
On scraps which you have filch'd from me?
When plots were ripe for execution,
Have they not ended in confusion,
And left your party in the *suds,*
In animosities and feuds?
Have I not treated you politely,
And managed your affairs adroitly?
In British treaty, sign'd by JAY,
Did I not, there, provide a way
To get my friends, *the tories,* home,
The democrats to overcome?
Have I not sent you British agents,
Of dupes and pimps and spies and pageants,
To retail politics, and laws,
And *English Goods,* to aid her cause?
Did I not send John Henry here,
A separation to prepare?
And had you done as I directed,
Would the plot e'er have been detected?
Did I not give most sage direction,
In your last Governor's election?
Contrive to get you many voters,
By pledging the insolvent debtors;
Pretending that you would relive 'em,
To gain their *votes,* and then deceive 'em.
When the *militia* were demanded,
That your own coast might be defended,
Was it not by my inspiration,
That S—g[9] deny'd the requisition?
When G—l H—l[10] betray'd his trust,
And basely yielded up his post,
Did I not there direct the TREASON,

9. Massachusetts governor Caleb Strong.
10. General William Hull, who surrendered Fort Detroit to the British in 1812 without firing a shot, was court martialed in 1814, convicted of cowardice and neglect of duty.

And *urge it on in proper season,*
To give the spirit and direction
To your *Clintonian election?*
Whene'er mishap befell the nation,
Did I not prompt their exultation?
Or when your country proved successful,
To weep and wail in strains distressful?
To swear the war was, from the first,
Most inexpedient and unjust;
To argue, plead, exclaim and write,
That British *pow'r* is British *right;*
That these complaints were mere pretences,
Ungrateful, wicked, vile offences;
That Britain's generous endurance,
Her great long *suff'ring* and forbearance,
Her mercy, gentleness and candor,
Disinterestedness so tender,
We subjects which you all might dwell on,
As eggs on which to hatch *rebellion;*
To say she needed your assistance,
As she was struggling for existence,
And hail her as "the world's last hope,"
As freedom's sole remaining prop?
Did I not undertake the task,
To screen you with *religion's* mask,
And Doctor O—d deputize,
To sanctify your cause with lies,
Turn *plagiarist,* ransack and ramble,
To patch up his notorious *Bramble,*
And rob a Scotch itinerant
To fill his brains with what they want?
To suit your purpose and your case,
I've sent you 'postles weak and base,
Of Clergymen, whose *souls* and *sconces*
Were fill'd with deviltry and nonsence;
P—sh, vile, insolent and frantic
And C—nn—g,[11] pompous and pedantic.

11. William Ellery Channing, the liberal Unitarian theologian and opponent of Calvinism, was politically a Federalist who opposed the War of 1812.

Had privateering come in fashion
'Twould made you rich and help'd the nation,
But while it thus was beneficial,
It to the *cause* was prejudicial.
Did I not an expedient try,
Your thirst of gain to gratify,
And lend you my advice and aid,
To *substitute the smuggling trade,*
Whereby you might obtain great wealth,
And suck the nation's blood by *stealth?*
And are not, nearly, all your tribe
Of *printers* bought by British bribes?
And have they not escap'd detection,
By my advice and circumspection?
I am the principal reviewer
Of that most putrid *Georgetown sewer;*
And chief director and adviser
Of your infernal *Advertiser:*
My majesty directs the quill,
Of my great fav'rite, *Bobadil;*
Attends him, when he takes a trip,
To *aid on board of British ship.*
These minions, with their satellites,
Each raggamuffin, who indicts
A tory print, or fed'ral journal,
Is prompted by my aid infernal.
With these, my wisest, best transactions,
Bequests, devices, benefactions,
Ye trifle, sport, and make derision,
And interpose your inquisition.

There's not a blockhead of your faction
Who's fit for stratagem or action;
Your little Rebel is a *fool,*
And ev'ry sottish priest's a *tool,*
Your party is a band of ruffians,
A dastard herd of raggamuffins;
The vilest imp in my dominions
Would scorn the friendship of such minions."

JACK now no longer could restrain

The fire that burnt within his brain;
He swell'd, and froth'd, and gnash'd his teeth,
While sad *perfumes* came from beneath;
He clench'd his fist, and smote his breast,
And thus his devilship address'd:
    "Monster of hell! Infernal elf!
Come here to *deify* thyself!
We Boston folks, I'll let you know,
Can egotize as well as you;
Take back your boasting; eat your words;
Or else, by the infernal Gods,
I'll stamp your majesty beneath my feet,
And end *your* part of this debate:
If you're so mighty great and wise,
It's matter of profound surprize,
That you've been lab'ring year by year,
And nothing yet have brought to bear;
Where is your wisdom, where your merit,
Your energy, and spunk, and spirit?
Your coward skulking is the reason,
That we're defeated in the treason;
With all your subtilty divine,
Your influence, now, is less than mine;
Have you prevented privateering?
Pray what is *your* electioneering?
Have you Great Britain's rights maintain'd,
Where are the vict'ries she has gain'd?
The privateers meet vast successes;
The democratic strength increases;
The British claims are *down* complete,
And British vict'ry is *defeat!*
As to the *clergy* whom you mention,
Why, really, I have no intention
To take them from you, if I could,
As they've done much more harm than good.
My PRINTERS—damn ye, don't ye name 'em;
They're *mine,* and *shall be,* if you claim 'em!
Good devil, don't be quite so fast,
You're sure to have them all at last"—

"You too, you rebel!" Satan cry'd—
"G—d d—n you! little Jack reply'd,
And seiz'd a cudgel, with great speed,
And aim'd a blow at Satan's head.
Satan, by some infernal charm,
Stopp'd short the little urchin's arm,
And, with damnation in his look,
Fasten'd on him this stern rebuke:
"Thou little, puny, grov'ling pimp!
Thou treach'rous, base, infernal imp!
Thou groundling! sick'ning, putrid reptile!
By devils damn'd, as mean and servile!
Infernal torments rack thy breast!
Goblins and ghosts distract thy rest!
Goaded, distracted, brutaliz'd,
By devils, men, and beasts despis'd!
I'll try thee in another shape,
And let thy soul disgrace an *ape!*"
Thus Satan—and this wretch so spunky,
Transform'd, at once, into a MONKEY!! [12]

In late January, in accordance with the convention's resolution, Harrison Gray Otis, Thomas Perkins, and William Sullivan of Massachusetts, and Calvin Goddard and Nathan Terry of Connecticut, were appointed by their respective legislatures as commissioners to go to Washington and negotiate with James Madison to appropriate funds for the New England states' military forces. By the time the commissioners arrived in Washington, however, word that the peace negotiations in Ghent had been successful had reached America. On February 16, the Senate unanimously ratified the treaty, and the war was officially over.

Although the Hartford Convention had not called for the overt acts of treason that some had anticipated, it left a stain on the Federalist party that could not be recovered from. The party's days were numbered, even in New England, although its ultimate demise in Connecticut wouldn't be immediate.

With the war over, attention began to drift back to Connecticut's

12. *The Yankee*, Boston, MA, January 6, 1815, 2.

state issues. With the spring election coming up, Bridgeport, Connecticut's *Republican Farmer* made an appeal to the state's Episcopalians, reminding them of all the ways they were treated unequally by the standing order:

TO THE EPISCOPALIANS OF THE
STATE OF CONNECTICUT.

Permit me to address to your consideration at this time, a few observations relative to your situation, as a distinct Religious Society in this State. The rage of politics, the political state of the country, & the different views which you have entertained of subjects of this nature, have, it is apprehended, divided your minds, and drawn off your attention from the state of your own society as a distinct body of christians, and also as members of this state; subject to its laws, and of course justly entitled to an equal proportion of its privileges and immunities. Now the question is, do you enjoy an equal proportion of the privileges and patronage of the government of this state? Every person, I trust, of any discernment and reflection, will without a moment's hesitancy, answer this question in the negative. On the contrary, it appears evident to me, and I believe to many others, that an uniform object of the government of this State, has been and still is, to encourage, patronize and support, one religious denomination only, and leave the others *to take care of themselves:* Nay, to discountenance, and bear as heavy a hand upon them, as a prudent regard to their own safety, and political salvation will allow.

That a partiality is shewn, and a preference given, to the *Presbyterian* or *Congregational* CLERGY, one single fact is sufficient to demonstrate. When was an Episcopal Clergyman, or indeed a Clergyman of any other denomination, than the one above mentioned, ever selected or called upon to preach an Election Sermon? Not that I suppose the Clergy of the Church are anxious to have an opportunity to display their abilities as preachers, before the members of Assembly convened in a body, with other great personages, and a mixed multitude besides; forming altogether a large

and a learned audience. With this honor, this mark of attention and respect, they, I doubt not, can cheerfully dispense.
This is indeed in itself, a matter of very little consequence—
a mere trifle; but "feathers shew which way the wind blows."
And this single circumstance is sufficient to evince that a
marked preference is given to the presbyterian or congregational clergy.—I know the question has been gravely
asked, by men high in favour, and in office, why the Episcopal Clergy did not meet at Hartford on the day of the general
election, join the procession with the clergy, and partake
with them of the dinner provided for them at the expense of
the state? Indeed I should suppose they must be very much
in want of a dinner, before they would consent to partake of
one, which they must be conscious was never intended for
them. It is true, their people pay their proportion of the
expense of the dinner; but the presbyterian clergy, are alone
thought worthy to be the Chaplains of the day, and of
course, alone worthy of the dinner: and long, I hope, would
an Episcopal clergyman go hungry, before he would dine
under such degrading circumstances. But as I before remarked, this in itself, is a circumstance of small importance,
and I should not have dwelt so long upon it, only as it serves,
as the boy told his mother, "to shew the nature of the beast."

The rulers of this State and those who manage its
concerns, it is evident have two wills; one revealed, the
other secret—and as their clergy represent the Almighty as
governing mankind in this way, they may think it perfectly
consistent; though these two wills are no more alike, than
an apple is like an oyster. Their revealed will is, that all
should have equal privileges, and equal patronage; and in
order to make a shew of sincerity, they tell you, the call is
to all, and the door is open to all; or in other words, that all
denominations of christians are eligible to office. But their
secret will is, that all the offices of honor, and confidence,
and advantage, shall be filled by persons taken from a certain class, and of a certain complexion, whether they are
best qualified for such office or not. They have also their
decrees of election and reprobation; and these decrees are
always according to, and founded upon their secret will. Let

us see.—How many Episcopalians do we see in the Council of this State?—What—not one! is there none of that denomination in this state, capable of filling a station there? none as capable (and a little more so) as some who now fill it? Ah, but they are not predestined to sustain the office, the decree is against them!—they may now and then be allowed to fill some office where no danger can be apprehended: such as Justice of the peace, Judge of the County, and even the Superior Court, and what is more, chairman of a great caucus; and in one instance, doubtless by some error in diplomacy, a very distinguished Episcopalian, found his way into the Council: But he was too dangerous a man to be allowed to long continue there. Invention was put to the rack, to find a plausible pretence for removing him, with the least possible delay; and it was effected.—Doubtless their error or negligence in the above instance will teach them to be more vigilant in guarding against innovations. Several gentlemen of the Episcopal order are indeed allowed to stand in the nomination for Assistants; but I expect the secret will, and the decrees are against them.

There must now and then be some little shew of liberality towards the Episcopalians to keep them quiet; because they are rather a growing people in the State, and if they were to become uneasy, and jealous, and sulky, they might be troublesome, and the craft might be in danger. They must be allowed to have an Academy of their own and to call it the Episcopal Academy, of Cheshire; and as it would be utterly inconsistent and out of the question to grant them any thing from the treasury of the State, they must have the privilege of a lottery; and since they are so simple and superstitious as to suppose the office of a Bishop, necessary in their church, they must be humoured with the appointment of a board of Trustees to manage the fund for his support.—But particular care must be taken, that this Episcopal Academy does not grow into an Episcopal College, and especially that an establishment of this kind, is not made at Hartford; because such an institution in that metropolis, might in time become a rival to *Mother Yale, the great goddess of Literature, whom all Connecticut and the world worshippeth.* And with respect to a fund, for the support of a Bishop in this state, since we have passed an act of incorporation for that purpose, if they can raise a fund among themselves they must have it, but it is clear that no *Bonus* ought to be allowed to help them out; for in this case what would our *Bishops say?* They might come forward by hundreds and claim the same privilege. Such, I expect, is pretty nearly the reasoning, and such the determination of the heads of departments in this state; And one thing is clear— that no passion, or principle in them, can be operated upon to any good effect, but that of fear. As long as coaxing, and promising, and chiding will keep you quiet, their end is answered, and in a very cheap way. But if, in some situations, resistance of government authority becomes a duty, and a virtue, and several of the New-England states seem lately to have determined, I am clearly of opinion, that the Episcopalians in this state, have suffered this virtue to lie dormant quite long enough. Not that I would recommend a resistance *Vi et armis,* nor in any illegal, or unconstitutional way, but by properly exercising the invaluable right of suffrage, by withholding your votes from men, who are enemies to your prosperity and religious society, and who deny you the privileges and the patronage, which as members of the state, you have a right to claim. Of this description, it is believed, there are a number in the present Council of this State: these ought to be removed, and their places supplied by men of more enlarged, and just and liberal views and feelings. With respect to the present Governor of this state, he is certainly a very plausible man, and some think him favorable to Episcopalians, because he has been seen at Church with a prayer-book in his hand; and because he seldom issues a Proclamation, on any occasion, without incorporating in it, some detached sentences from the service of the church.— These things, however, some less charitable, or less credulous than others, view rather as a finesse, to make saving grace with Episcopalians. Be this as it may, I think a change might be made without danger to the State, and perhaps with some advantage. Among the proposed amendments to the Federal Constitution, issuing from the late Hartford

Convention, (a board in which certainly the wisdom of three states, and a little more was concentrated;) one is, that the President of the United States, should not be chosen twice in succession from the same state. The object of this, probably is, to check the arrogance of Virginia, and to give the northern, and especially the smaller states, a more equal chance. In this proposed amendment I can see no evil, nothing but what is fair and equitable. But whether southern arrogance and domination are more intolerable, and those to be complained of by the northern states, than presbyterian or congregational monopoly, is in this state, by the other religious societies in it, let the candid judge. For my part I cannot discover why an amendment to the Constitution of this State, which should prohibit the Government from being chosen two years in succession from the same religious denomination, would not be equally proper and reasonable as the above named amendment to the Constitution of the United States. Reformation, if there is room for it, ought to be the same. But is there an Episcopalian in the State, competent to the office of Governor? Ah here is the rub. I should give it as my opinion, however, that there are those, and a number of them, who would do honor to the office, equal honor; your Smith's and Treadwell's notwithstanding.

Stand fast then, in the liberty where with you are made free.—Exercise your privileges as freemen of the state, in voting for such men, and such only, as you have reason to believe will do equal justice to all classes of citizens, and to all denominations of christians. Then the genuine principles of truth, where ever found, will prevail; and so may we hope, as the Governor has expressed it in the close of his late Proclamation, "that the kingdom of Christ will come, and his will be done on earth as it is in heaven."

AN EPISCOPALIAN.[13]

As the above article lays out, the Episcopalians had many reasons to be disgruntled under Connecticut's standing order. Nevertheless, with the exception of 1811, the year the Republicans

---

13. *Republican Farmer*, Bridgeport, CT, April 5, 1815, 2.

first ran the Episcopalian Elijah Boardman as their candidate for governor, they had voted Federalist, and had returned to voting Federalist through the war. While their wealth and conservatism made them more respectable in the eyes of the standing order than the Baptists and Methodists, and they received some privileges not enjoyed by the other dissenters, they were treated far from equally. They could get into some pretty good government positions, but not the highest offices, and the legislature had repeatedly refused their requests to incorporate an Episcopalian college.

Although not having the solid support of the Episcopalians just yet, the Republicans saw big gains in the 1815 spring election. While John Cotton Smith won another term as governor, it wasn't by anything close to the margins he had won by in the previous years, with Elijah Boardman getting 4,876 votes to Smith's 8,176. The lieutenant governor's race was also closer, with Republican Isaac Spencer getting 3,129 votes to the incumbent Chauncey Goodrich's 6,399. The Republicans also gained about 20 seats in the House, increasing their strength to 57.

The Federalist papers were quick to blame the Republican gains in the spring on a low turnout of Federalist voters, and some secret plot among the Republicans, with similar articles coming from both the *Courant* and the *Connecticut Herald*.

> *Connecticut Election.*—Our annual election of state officers, and members of the legislature, took place on Monday of last week. Our present Governor, Lieutenant-Governor, Secretary and Treasurer, are re-elected by large majorities. From the general remissness of the federalists thro'-out the state, it is probable there will be a few more democratic members in the assembly this spring, than last fall. For a number of years past, the enemies of our state government have not supported any candidates of their own; in consequence of which the federalists had become extremely negligent in their duty. But at the late Freeman's Meeting, the democrats, in a secret matter, took unwearied pains to rally their broken forces, and in a great many towns have given their old candidate for Governor a considerable number of votes. It is hoped this fact will teach the friends of our excellent state government the importance of being

continually on their guard; and that a punctual attendance on the days of election will alone secure them the inestimable privileges they have hitherto enjoyed.[14]

⬿

Connecticut Election.—For the first time in some years, the democratic party in this State, have generally come forward to the polls.—But few federalists were aware that any exertion would be made by the opposite party, and of course staid at home. The consequence has been, that the democrats have gained considerable accession of strength in the House of Representatives, and their candidate for Governor has received more votes than he has for a number of years. Some of them appear quite elated at this (as they call it) *change of sentiment* in the people, and begin almost to dream that they will eventually rise into power. But unless the federalists are most shamefully negligent, the opposite party will be made to feel again, at the next election, their original nothingness, in a political point of view, in this State. The federalism of Connecticut is built upon a rock, and the gates of democracy will never be able to prevail against it.

In this town, the federalists gave only 97 votes for Governor—in New-London 84. In these two towns reside, it is fairly to be presumed, at least 700 federal freemen. In many other towns where there are large federal majorities, about the same ratio of votes has been given. If the democrats make another exertion, it will merely have a tendency to increase the federal majority. If they think otherwise, let them try again. ....[15]

The *Columbian Register* flatly dismissed both of the Federalists' claims:

The last Herald announces a democratic gain in our

14. *The Connecticut Courant,* Hartford, CT, April 19, 1815, 3.
15. *Connecticut Herald,* New Haven, CT, April 18, 1815, 3.

house of representatives and in our votes for governor, but ascribes the gain to the *secret movements* of the democrats.—Thus it stands on record that some thousands of men in Connecticut conspired to keep a secret, and that they and their wives kept it so profoundly, that it was not even suspected by federalists till after the election. How happy for federalism that it never loses without being able to assign a reason....

In this State the federalists have the command of the treasury; they can grant lotteries and incorporate banks; can receive and appropriate bonuses; can make new election laws, when the old ones will not work federally; can exorcise men for not believing that the charter of King Charles is verily a constitution of civil government; can create judges, justices, sheriffs and military officers of all grades; can make laws to disenfranchise actual freemen; can subject the qualifications of candidates for the freeman's oath to the scrutiny and sole arbitrament of their noble selves.—In fact, says the Herald, "the federalism of Connecticut is built upon a rock, and the gates of democracy will never be able to prevail against it."

This seems to be crowing, before they are out of the woods. Federalism has indeed, from the above causes prevailed hitherto. Men, seeking for offices and benefits, have voted for those, who had them in their gift; but only fourteen years of the century have elapsed: we and our descendants will keep up the contest, and if the "gates of democracy" continue to move so silently on their hinges, as not to awaken the dormant federalists, we shall finally prevail.

The federalism of Connecticut has other and more powerful aids. It can exempt from military service the rich, and has done it immeasurably beyond what has been done in any other State. It can drive the poor, who are denied the rank of freemen, to fight the battles of the rich. It can tax more heavily the poor man's cow than it does the rich man's bank share of 200 dollars. The exempts from military duty, owning 5-6ths of the property, amount to 20-48ths of all men between the ages of 18 and 45. This is the blessed offspring of Charles 2d!!!

Why do not the federal papers boast of their high prerogatives and privileges, yielding such rocky successes at elections?—Plainly because such boastings would prove, that the voters, being left to vote merely from principle, would desert them. Why do they not bring forward their 700 "federal freemen" from New-Haven and New-London? Several of them would have to come forth from their graves and some others will never come again for calling. Federalism is no longer that very fascinating thing, which has the promise "of the life that now is." Since the issue of the Hartford Convention the followers have lost confidence in their leaders. Since the peace all federal prospect of gaining the power of the general government is down. The federal war-visions are wholly at an end. Now and then a forlorn federalist, who finds himself lost in Ohio or Tennessee, writes to some northern brother, that the proceedings of the Hartford Convention are much admired in the west. The letter is published. Every body knows every word of it to be false, but it fills a space in a federal column, which might otherwise be vacant.

Ye men of Athens, when will ye be honest and place the issue of elections upon fair ground? With all the learning and talents, all the offices and wealth, all the power and nearly all the newspapers, dare you not risk one election on the votes of *all men of full age and capacity, and of fair character, who pay taxes and do military duty?* Is there any danger in trusting elections to men of this description? Is not every man of them absolutely entitled to a vote? Federalists have probably read Cobbet's opinion as to the real strength of parties in New-England. I will not quote it, as they have on hand, at present, as much affliction as they can bear, including the prospect of seeing SEVENTY-FOUR republican members in the next assembly.[16]

Seventy-four Republican members in the Assembly was overly optimistic, at least for this year, but the *Columbian Register* kept up its optimism, taunting Federalist voters a few days before the

---

16. *Columbian Register,* New Haven, CT, April 22, 1815, 3.

fall election, urging them to turn out to vote:

Connecticut Election.—The federal Freemen of this State are particularly requested to meet on Monday next for the choice of Representatives, and the nomination of Councillors.—Many friends of good order and of the ancient institutions, are much alarmed lest the democrats (whose works are works of darkness,) should undermine and finally destroy the "free" government of Connecticut. "We hope no federalist will stay at home, and say my vote will do no good; your vote may do much good."—Suppose the federal ticket should not succeed, how will you raise another Convention, &c. &c.? Federalists, be at your posts on Monday the 18th inst. or that government which Gov. Smith pronounces to be "the admiration of the world," is LOST! [17]

The Republicans' numbers in the House of Representatives held steady in the fall, and for the first time since 1810, they issued a Council Assistants list, with the highest Republican getting nearly half as many votes as the highest Federalist.

All in all, 1815 was a hopeful year for the Republicans, and things would become even more promising in 1816.

---

17. *Columbian Register,* New Haven, CT, September 16, 1815, 3.

∽ 1816 ∾

1816 was a year of transition. Now rebranded as the "Toleration Party," and with the focus on state rather than national issues, Connecticut's Republican party became broader, drawing in not only the Episcopalians but also disillusioned Federalists. Although the issue of the state's lack of a constitution was not forgotten, the biggest issue of the year was religious liberty, and with a highly unusual ticket for governor and lieutenant governor, the Republicans were able for the first time to get a non-Congregationalist into one of the top two offices in the state.

On February 21, a meeting was held by the Republicans in New Haven to nominate candidates for governor and lieutenant governor. On the same day, also in New Haven, was the consecration of the Episcopalians' new Trinity Church, drawing Episcopalians from all over the state to the town. The evidence that on this day a bargain was struck between the Republicans and the Episcopalians is undeniable. While many Federalists refused to believe that any agreement between the Episcopalians and the Republicans had taken place, there was no doubt come election day that they had indeed agreed to unite in support of an unlikely pair of candidates.

It's necessary here to back up and explain why the Episcopalians, who, with the exception of one time, had consistently voted for the standing order Congregational Federalists, in spite of the unequal treatment they received from them, were ready to break away and vote with the Republicans.

The issue that finally did it was that of the Phoenix Bank. In

313

1814, a group made up largely of Episcopalian backers petitioned the legislature to charter a new bank in Hartford. As was the customary practice, the bank's backers would pay for the privilege of being granted a charter. For the Phoenix Bank the amount of this "bonus," as it was called, was $50,000, five percent of the bank's $1 million in capital stock, to be paid into the state's treasury and appropriated by the legislature. The understanding of the bank's backers, based on what the Council agreed to, was that $20,000 would go to Yale College, $20,000 to Yale's medical school, and $10,000 to the Episcopalians' "Bishop's Fund." The Council, in 1814, voted in favor of this arrangement, but the House, although voting to give Yale's medical school its $20,000 right away, voted against the payment to the Bishop's Fund. When the Episcopalians petitioned for the funds again during the legislature's October 1815 session, the House again voted against it, and this time the Council, which had previously approved the payment, reversed itself and also voted against it. This was the last straw for the Episcopalians.

In its first issue for the new year, the *Republican Farmer* featured on its front page an article written by "A Churchman" to his fellow Episcopalians, detailing the history of the Phoenix Bank bonus:

TO CONNECTICUT EPISCOPALIANS.

It will be nothing new to inform you, that the petition of the trustees of the Bishop's Fund, for a part of the $50,000 paid into the treasury by the Phœnix Bank, received its finishing stroke at the late session of the Legislature. A force quite overwhelming, (as the yeas and nays, which have just passed the rounds of the newspapers inform us) prostrated the Petition on the floor of the house of Representatives. And, as if this were not sufficient—as if it were not enough to strangle our claim in the popular branch of the Legislature: the Honorable Council, to make assurance doubly sure, (as a writer in the last Herald triumphantly tells us,) advanced in a body, and belaboured the fallen foe, with an almost unanimous vote. ...

Yes, strange at it may seem, the same members of the same Council, who have apparently heretofore, been the sworn advocates of your claim—the same men who on former occasions voted in favour of what they were then, not afraid to term the "equity" of the petition; have in a moment, in the twinkling of an eye, bolted from their object, and at once discovered, that all their old opinions are erroneous—their former theories fallacious.—Sudden conversions we are told, generally produce the most zealous proselytes—never was the adage more faithfully fulfilled than in the case before us: the mild, the firm, the upright Council of Connecticut, we are to believe, were metamorphosed in a moment—their ideas turned quite round, and after a short struggle of conflicting feelings, have at last gone home to their constituents, filled with a new zeal, and overflowing with fresh fervour. And here the matter should in all conscience have rested. A sight of the legislative drill, should not have disturbed our nerves—the marchings and countermarchings, the windings and doublings, of the honorable phalanx, might have passed in silent review before us. But when these manœuvres are passed off in print, as cause for exultation—when you are told by way of triumphs that only "ONE" of the honorable Council was bold enough to re-assert his former opinion—and above all, when you are tauntingly told, that because the petitioners for the Bank (many of whom were Episcopalians,) respectfully proposed to give a part of the Bonus for the support of a Bishop; that therefore their petition was "*insidious*"—that it disclosed a "*cloven foot*"—when the venerable Head of the Church is thus impiously compared to the heel of Satan; our adversaries must presume much, very much, upon your forbearance—they must indeed suppose that your nerves are leaden, and your hearts cold and callous as a tomb-stone.

Think you that I am colouring this account too highly? Look for yourselves at the production of a writer in the last Herald in answer to an unvarnished statement of facts, which had previously appeared under the signature of "TOLERATION:" and when you have patiently traced through the drippings of this man's malignity, tell me, if what I have only put here as supposition, is not reality. And for what is all this? Why you have dared; yes, you Episcopalians have had the unparalleled impudence to say, that you have an equitable claim to a part of this Bonus; when, in truth, you have no claim in conscience, no equity in your favor: at least, so say the leaders of the lower house, and so at last echo the Honorable Council. ...

Turn to the records of the Council, and you find, that immediately after the Bank was incorporated, and as it were on the back of this very charter, a resolution is drawn up and passed, (as in good faith it ought to have been,) granting 20,000 Dollars to the Medical Establishment of Yale College, and 10,000 to the Bishop's Fund—Not a grant of money in the Treasury, or of "State funds"—No, they did not at that time act as if they considered the State entitled to the Bonus, except as the trustees of the institutions mentioned in the original petition: the language of the resolution was, that "out of the first monies which shall be paid into the treasury of this State, *in pursuance of the Act incorporating the Phœnix Bank,* the Treasury shall be and is hereby authorised and required to pay, &c." This resolution in part, took with the Lower House—they acquiesced in the grant of $20,000 of the money to the Medical Institution, and this sum, as I suppose, has since been paid. Not so however with the proposition which was to favor Episcopacy; the $10,000 destined for the Bishop's Fund was, (for reasons best known to the gentlemen who opposed it,) arrested in its progress by the Lower House—by the same Lower House, which had just before by a full majority granted the petition with all its provisions; here ended the business for the Spring session of 1814.

In the fall of the same year, the Trustees to your Bishop's Fund, appeared before the Legislature, and asked for a portion of the 50,000 dollars; their claim was at that time answered various ways. They were told, among other things, that the country was then at war, that the treasury was in want of the money, and that however just their claim might be, it could not at any rate be listened to at that time. After the peace, when the state was relieved from its embarrassments, the claim was again presented. The Honorable Council still remained firm in our favor; and by a majority of eleven to two, stamped this charter with another declaration that we were fairly entitled to $10,000 of the Bonus which it yielded. Indeed an influential member of the Council at that time, a Presbyterian himself, and now an honorable judge as I am told, declared, that although we could not maintain an action at law, for the recovery of the money, yet that our claim was as clear in conscience, as any that he could imagine. And unless I am much misinformed, his excellency the Governor, who presided at the board, at the time the Bank was incorporated, and who was perfectly well acquainted with all the attendant circumstances, has repeatedly expressed himself in terms nearly as strong as those above recited, in favour of our claim. The lower House, however, still refused us the money: and for the honor of our state, I wish the case ended here; but truth compels me to carry you one step further in the history.

At the last October Session of the Assembly, the Trustees once more spread their case before the consciences of the Legislature; and unaccountable as it may seem, the upper house, with only "one" exception, completely wheeled about in their opinions, and by a majority "overwhelming" indeed, fell in with the lower House, and *voted down* the claim, which they had ever before, by a majority quite as "overwhelming," been so instrumental in creating and defending.

A petition is now pending before the Legislature, from the Medical Establishment of the College, for the remaining thirty of the fifty thousand dollars; and from the reception it met with, at the last session of the Legislature, we may very safely calculate that the petitioners will receive the balance of the Bonus, at the next session. And you, Episcopalians, in the face of these facts are told, that you have been guilty of an unpardonable sin, for having suggested to a Presbyterian assembly that you have any just claim, even for a fifth part of the $50,000. You must be taught to believe that Yale College, with its professions of faith, and test creeds, is as much the institution of one sect as another; and that therefore the College, or its branches, ought to have the whole of the Bonus. ...

A CHURCHMAN.[1]

---

1. *Republican Farmer,* Bridgeport, CT, January 3, 1816, 1.

Out of the February 21 "meeting of citizens from the various parts of this State" came the Republicans' unusual nomination for governor — Oliver Wolcott, a former Federalist who had broken with that party in supporting the War of 1812 and the Madison administration. Wolcott, the son and grandson of former governors of Connecticut, had been Secretary of the Treasury under Washington and Adams, and in that position had been mercilessly abused by Connecticut's Republicans, at one point being accused of burning the treasury's books to cover up misappropriation of funds. But now he was their candidate for governor. Most importantly for the new "Toleration Ticket," Wolcott was only nominally religious and was a supporter of religious liberty.

The candidate for lieutenant governor, unanimously agreed to at the meeting, was Jonathan Ingersoll, a Federalist. A highly respected judge, and an Episcopalian, Ingersoll was also a firm advocate of religious liberty. Although only one Republican paper actually came right out and said it, these nominations were the result of a bargain between the Republicans and the Episcopalians — the Republicans would vote for the Federalist Ingersoll if the Episcopalians voted for Wolcott.

With this unconventional ticket, the Republicans hoped not only to get the votes of the Episcopalians, but of moderate and disillusioned Federalists as well. As the Federalists papers would put it, the Republican strategy was to divide and conquer.

The Republican nominations were announced in the *American Mercury* on February 27:

> At a meeting of citizens from the various parts of this State, held at New-Haven, on the 21st inst. the following Nomination for the offices of Governor and Lieutenant-Governor, was unanimously agreed on, as the one most likely to produce that concord and harmony among parties which have too long, and without any real diversity of interests, been disturbed, and which every honest man must earnestly desire to see restored:—
>
> **HON. OLIVER WOLCOTT,**
> *FOR GOVERNOR,*
> **HON. JONA. INGERSOLL,**
> *FOR LT. GOVERNOR.*

Which nomination is recommended to the citizens of all parties for their support at the approaching election.[2]

Division among Federalists over the Ingersoll nomination was seen immediately in the Federalist papers. When New Haven's Federalist *Connecticut Herald* announced Ingersoll's nomination, the announcement was quickly met with backlash from its fellow Federalist papers, the *Connecticut Journal* and the *Courant*. Neither of these papers had anything bad to say about Ingersoll, except that he was nominated by the democrats, which, as one of the papers said, was enough reason not to support him. Both the *Journal* and the *Courant* endorsed Calvin Goddard, a former Council member, U.S. representative for his district, and also a member of the Hartford Convention, for lieutenant governor. The Federalists who supported Goddard were of the opinion that he was the rightful successor of Chauncey Goodrich, who had died in office, because in the previous year's election, in which Goddard had run against Goodrich, Goddard had gotten a significant number of votes.

While Ingersoll was highly regarded by Federalists and could indeed cause a division among that party in a matchup against Goddard, Oliver Wolcott was considered an "apostate." So, while the Federalist papers were divided on who should be lieutenant governor, they were all united in endorsing the reelection of John Cotton Smith as governor.

Over the next few weeks, articles in Federalist papers expressed "regret" that the *Herald* had announced Ingersoll as the lieutenant governor nominee, and some did raise suspicions that an alliance had been formed between the Episcopalians and the democrats, as the Republicans were almost exclusively now called by the Federalists. The fact that the Republicans made their nomination in New Haven on the same day that the town was flooded with Episcopalians for the consecration of their new church, and that their candidate for lieutenant governor was not only an Episcopalian but a Federalist, was too much circumstantial evidence for some to dismiss, although others continued to disbelieve that such an alliance was possible.

The following three articles on the Republicans' nominations

2. *American Mercury*, Hartford, CT, February 27, 1816, 3.

are from three of Connecticut's most prominent Federalist papers, the *Journal,* the *Courant,* and the *Mirror.*

In the Mercury printed at Hartford, Feb. 27, is the following extraordinary nomination for Governour and Lieut. Governour:

"At a meeting of citizens from the various parts of this State, held at New-Haven, on the 21st. inst the following Nomination for the offices of Governor and Lieutenant-Governor, was unanimously agreed on, as the one most likely to produce that concord and harmony among parties which have too long, and without any real diversity of interests, been disturbed, and which every honest man must earnestly desire to see restored:—

HON. OLIVER WOLCOTT,
FOR GOVERNOR,
HON. JONATHAN INGERSOLL,
FOR LT. GOVERNOR.

Which nomination is recommended to the citizens of all parties for their support at the approaching election."

In the Connecticut Herald, published at New-Haven, by O. Steele, on the same day, is the nomination for Lieutenant Governour in a little different language, viz:

"We hear from various parts of the State that our worthy fellow citizen, the

HON. JONATHAN INGERSOLL,

will receive the votes of the Freemen, at the ensuing election, for the office of *LIEUTENANT-GOVERNOR.* His character is too well known to need any recommendation from us."

It appears from the last named paper, that at the same place and on the same day, a new church was consecrated. It is well known who the citizens were, that on this occasion, met from various parts of the State, and made the above nomination *to restore concord and harmony.* Let us ask what party set up Oliver Wolcott? And then what party set up Jonathan Ingersoll? And we shall probably learn between whom *concord* and *harmony* is to be restored.

Our worthy Chief Magistrate, JOHN COTTON SMITH, will not at the ensuing election, more universally unite the suffrages of federal freemen for Governour, than the Hon. CALVIN GODDARD will for Lieut. Governour. When the late Chauncey Goodrich was chosen Lieut. Gov. Calvin Goddard stood next to him as a candidate, and had between two and three thousand votes—Ever since the death of that exceptional man, Calvin Goddard has among federalists been considered as his successor; and, the above caucus nomination not withstanding, there is little doubt but the freemen will continue to vote for their old candidate,

JOHN COTTON SMITH,
FOR GOVERNOUR.

Hon. CALVIN GODDARD,
FOR LIEUT. GOVERNOUR.[3]

In consequence of the death of the late Lieut. Governor GOODRICH, the Freemen will soon be called upon to supply the vacancy. It was expected that they would have been left after the good example of former times, to have given their unbiased suffrages for the men of their choice—and this argument was much used (we understand) in private circles at New-Haven to prevent the General Assembly from making any appointment, and also to prevent the individual members of assembly, with other federalists, from making a nomination.

We cannot therefore refrain from expressing our regret that a newspaper calling itself federal, should have come forward and announced any individual as the candidate— we regret it because we believe it has been hitherto unprecedented—we regret it because a nomination thus made by the direction of a few or perhaps one single individual, must be either acquiesced in merely because *it is made,* or must

3. *Connecticut Journal,* New Haven, CT, March 5, 1816, 3.

be counteracted by another nomination, and thus the claims of the candidates be made a subject of newspaper discussion.

These remarks are excited by a publication in the last Connecticut Herald, that they have received assurances from several parts of the state that their worthy townsman, the Hon. Judge Ingersoll, would have the support of the freemen for Lieut. Governor of the state. ...

... Still however, we have so much regard for the gentleman who is thus named that we should probably have been silent, had we not noticed that upon the same day when this publication appeared in the Herald, at New-Haven, the Mercury at Hartford also informed us that at a meeting holden at New-Haven on the 21st February, 1816, it was unanimously voted to support the Hon. Oliver Wolcott, for Governor, and the Hon. Jonathan Ingersoll, for Lieut. Governor.

The circumstance that the nomination of Mr. I. was made in a paper which has all the winter been scandalously attacking the legislature of this state, especially the Council, because they would not grant 10,000 or 15,000 dollars to the Bishop's fund, and made directly after a great number of Episcopalians had been convened to consecrate their church and ordain its pastor—and the same day announced in the American Mercury, a paper which for years has been filled with the grossest abuse of the officers and institutions of this state—tend so strongly to excite a belief that there has been a combination to effect a certain object by these means, that we deem it our duty no longer to remain silent—or to acquiesce in a nomination thus made.—When we say this, however, we do not mean to be understood to charge Judge Ingersoll with being privy to this—we do not believe that he is, and we trust that many of the most respectable Episcopalians are not. ...

We look upon a secret combination with democracy as more dangerous to the cause of federalism than any open attacks—we cannot trust the men who are daily talking to us about allaying party spirit, and at the same moment are exciting their partizans to take up their former weapons. In Connecticut we must set our faces like a flint against any compromises with those whose business it has been for years to rail at our most valuable institutions and our most valuable men—who preach peace when war is in their heart— such combinations have been the bane of federalism in other states, and must prove its destruction here. If Mr. Ingersoll is chosen Lieut. Governor by such means, the Council will next be attacked—individual members will be marked and abandoned, and in two years the democrats will impose a Governor upon the state.

For these reasons we cannot lend our aid to the nomination which has been made—For these reasons we feel it our duty to say, that we do not consider Mr. I. as the federal candidate—and although we claim no authority to dictate upon this subject, yet we think it would not be right to suffer the democrats, or even a minority of federalists, to direct who should occupy the second office in the state—and to prevent a minority from ruling a majority, to cut off the expectations of democracy, to shew that the combination between federalism and democracy is not extensive, and to give its proper weight to the suffrages of the freemen on former occasions, we feel compelled to adopt the example that has been set us, and say, that from the remarks we have heard from various gentlemen from different parts of the state, and more particularly from the votes of the freemen upon former occasions, that the federal candidates will be His Excellency JOHN COTTON SMITH, for Governor, & the Hon. CALVIN GODDARD, for Lieutenant Governor.[4]

◠

The American Mercury of the 27th ult. contains the following Nomination:

"At a meeting of citizens from the various parts of this State, held at New-Haven, on the 21st. inst the following Nomination for the offices of Governor and Lieutenant-Governor, was unanimously agreed on, as the one most likely

4. *The Connecticut Courant*, Hartford, CT, March 5, 1816, 3.

to produce that concord and harmony among parties which have too long, and without any real diversity of interests, been disturbed, and which every honest man must earnestly desire to see restored:—

HON. OLIVER WOLCOTT,
For Governor,
HON. JONATHAN INGERSOLL,
For Lieutenant Governor.

Which nomination is recommended to the citizens of all parties for their support at the approaching election."

Thus we learn that our Democrats are willing to uphold for Governour the man who a few years since they pronounced as incendiary. Who they accused of burning the treasury books to hide his infamy. And if they really believe this charge we ought not to be surprized.

But what is there in the character of Judge Ingersoll for them to admire: He has always been reputed an honest man, and a federalist—why then should he be their candidate?—

Have they been induced to make this mongrel nomination from any concert with federalists: Federalism never gained any thing from an union with democracy.—We never attempted such an union without being in some measure degraded, and always deceived.

But this nomination was made at New-Haven on the same day the new Episcopal church was consecrated. From which circumstance, and because Episcopalians have failed to obtain money from the State for support of a Bishop, it has been reported that they are consenting to this arrangement.

That many federal churchmen do wish Judge Ingersoll be elected Lieut. Governour is probable. But that they can be persuaded, under existing circumstances, to support Mr. Wolcott as Governour cannot be true—and if any person suspects them of such a design, in my opinion he wrongs this worthy class of citizens.

If there are federalists among us, who for the sake of effecting an inferior object will unite with the enemies of the State in their destructive views; we need only to know and we will despise them. But surely there is nothing in the principles of government of the church of England congenial with democracy.—Nor have the members of this church ever been supposed to lean that way; if we except those who have joined it within a few years from unworthy motives, and these were mostly democrats before.

Notwithstanding the Hon. Mr. Goddard on a former occasion received a large number of votes for Lieut. Governour, the General Assembly omitted at their last session to appoint any person to that office; because it was thought more proper that the Freemen of the State should make the selection. An opportunity for expressing their minds will soon occur.

If a majority of votes are not bestowed upon some one man it will then become the duty of the Gen. Assembly to fill this vacancy, and it will be equally our duty to acquiesce in their doings.[5]

The *Mirror's* confident assertion that while many Federalist Episcopalians might want to see Ingersoll elected lieutenant governor, they could never be persuaded to vote for Wolcott for governor, was wrong. According to the *Columbian Register,* a bargain had indeed been made between the Episcopalians and Republicans. The Republicans would vote for the Episcopalians' man Ingersoll if and only if the Episcopalians voted for the Republicans' man Wolcott.

... We stand on high ground, being on the side of an overwhelming majority in the United States. To us the local government of the State is of comparatively small account, yet as we constitute a political minority, and as the episcopalians constitute a religious minority, both of which are oppressed by the congregational order, we have offered a ticket, which the two minorities, if united, can carry. We have placed the issue of this ticket on the ground of *Toleration.*

But it is said by some, that episcopalian federalists cannot consistently unite with republicans in support of a ticket. Of this episcopalians will judge for themselves. They may

5. *Connecticut Mirror,* Hartford, CT, March 11, 1816, 3.

be assured that we have no more attachment to federalism than they have to republicanism, and that it is impossible for them to respect their political opinions more than we respect ours. It is not believed that they will, universally, vote for Mr. Wolcott, or that we shall all vote for Mr. Ingersoll; but if they do not generally, openly and without reserve vote for our candidate, we shall not, in like manner, vote for theirs. Our votes will amount to two or three thousand over the number of episcopal votes; ours will be given to Mr. Wolcott at any rate, and also to Mr. Ingersoll, if his friends vote for Mr. Wolcott, not otherwise. ....[6]

The *Courant* responded to the *Register's* ultimatum to the Episcopalians with this paragraph:

A *Challenge.*—One of the democratic papers has come out and avowed that unless the Episcopalians openly and without reserve support Mr. Wolcott, they shall not support Mr. Ingersoll. We hope the Episcopalians in some of our large towns will immediately have a meeting and authorise us to inform the public they do not agree to the terms.[7]

And the *Herald* responded to the backlash it was getting from the *Journal*:

In yesterday's Journal appeared no less than four long, stupid pieces, all laboring to prove that JONATHAN INGERSOLL ought not to be Lieutenant-Governor, because he has been nominated for the same office in the Herald and Mercury. The author of one of the pieces *dares* us to come out and tell who had the impudence and assurance to recommend him. We will inform him, that, if he will have a little patience, the names of those gentlemen will be given to the public very shortly.[8]

Although breaking with the other Federalist papers with its

6. *Columbian Register,* New Haven, CT, March 16, 1816, 2.
7. *The Connecticut Courant,* Hartford, CT, March 26, 1816, 3.
8. *Connecticut Herald,* New Haven, CT, March 19, 1816, 3.

endorsement of Ingersoll, the *Herald* was still a Federalist paper, and as such was right in line with other Federalist papers in vilifying the democrats and their nomination of Wolcott, and also in its disbelief that there was any arrangement between the democrats and the Episcopalians.

Governor and Lieutenant-Governor.

In the Mercury, we have seen a paragraph, in which we are told, that at a late meeting of certain persons in the city of New-Haven, OLIVER WOLCOTT, Esq. and the Hon. JONATHAN INGERSOLL, were nominated to the two highest offices in the gift of the people of this State. We have long had occasion to remark the insidious machinations and dark intrigues, which have distinguished the efforts of the leaders of Democracy, to revolutionize Connecticut. The zeal and perseverance which they discover in a cause so hopeless, would appear somewhat surprising, were we not aware of the bitter animosity which they feel towards those men, whose talents and virtues have so long merited and received the confidence of the people. In all their measures, they have shown themselves to be actuated only by a strong desire to enjoy the honours and emoluments of office. They have proved how much their unworthy passions would be gratified, by having occasion to proclaim to the world, that Connecticut has changed her political creed—forsaken those maxims and principles which have hitherto governed her councils, and was ready to support those wild theories, and pernicious systems, which are the *ne plus ultra* of democratic legislation. To effect this object, they have brought forward every measure which ingenuity could devise. They have resorted to every form of exaggerated misrepresentation, and have searched every vocabulary, for terms of reproach, invective, and defiance. But they have failed. The intelligence and good sense of the people of Connecticut, have risen superior to all their arts ...

... Indeed, the leaders of Democracy despair of success in the ordinary way. They no longer rest their cause upon principle, but resort to management and intrigue. They seize hold of the broils of neighbourhoods, the quarrels of towns, and the dissensions of religious sects, and endeavour to turn them in the advantage of their party. In pursuance of this principle, they have lately made uncommon efforts to connect their own sinking fortunes with the higher destinies of the Episcopal order.

The nomination to which we have alluded, is a master stroke of policy of this kind. The manner in which it has been communicated to the public, is deceptive in the highest degree. The object appears to be, to convey the idea, that there has been a coalition between Episcopalians and the democratic party. Accordingly we are told, that the nomination was made at New-Haven; and not only so, but at the precise time when the city was crowded with Episcopalians from every part of the State, for the purpose of witnessing the consecration of Trinity Church. But, upon inquiry, we are satisfied that this meeting was not countenanced by a single federal Episcopalian. On the contrary, this information was received with surprise by the people of New-Haven; and the general inquiries were, Where was this mighty convocation held? and of whom did it consist?

The connexion of Judge Ingersoll's name with that of Oliver Wolcott, stands solely upon democratic authority.— A coalition between Democracy and Episcopacy!!! This would be a new thing under the sun. Such a union would be, to join principles repugnant in their nature—to combine the mephitic damp with the healthful air. What! can it be supposed that federal Episcopalians, impelled by a sense of injury and feelings of resentment, would give up those principles which are founded on the immutable distinction between right and wrong? Are there any who can entertain the derogatory opinion, that they are about to desert those institutions which they have concurred to defend with so much ability and zeal? Is it not perceived, that they must reject with indignation the hand of friendship from the democratic party, which is proffered with a hollow heart, and with selfish views?

But we have something more substantial than *a priori* reasoning, on which to found an opinion. We know, from actual information, that no such union has taken place; and we wish to have it generally understood, that there is no occasion to entertain a single apprehension on this subject. ...[9]

The Republicans' unusual choice of candidates naturally required an explanation to the state's rank and file Republicans, who would certainly have been curious as to why their party had nominated the former Federalist Wolcott and Federalist Ingersoll. So, in an article addressed to the Republicans of Connecticut, the *Register* explained that with the national government secure in Republican hands, and the divisive national issues of embargoes and the war behind them, it no longer mattered what party the state's rulers belonged to, as long as they were firm friends of civil and religious liberty.

To the Republicans of Connecticut.

We invite you to the support of this ticket by your votes at the approaching proxies on the 8th day of April next; but we do not seek your votes, unless they can be given consistently with the principles, which have guided you on former elections.

There was a season, when it appeared important for us to support men, devoted to the republican administration of the United States; but the administration is so well established, that it is wholly unimportant to its success whether Connecticut support it or withhold her support. We are imperiously called to look to our altars and fire-sides, and to establish in our towns and neighborhoods a government favorable to our civil and religious privileges.

Such a government is not now administered in Connecticut. The Congregational order is dominant; it has the control of our colleges, commencements and general elections. It gives abundantly of our substance to those who have, and withholds most manfully from those, who have not. The address of the Rev. Lyman Beecher exhibits in its

9. *Connecticut Herald,* New Haven, CT, March 12, 1816, 3.

spirituality and purity the present views of the Congregational order.[10] Not content with an unprecedented degree of
power, it claims to spread its wings over all the religious
denominations, to drive out of their desks all the uneducated
clergy and to supply their places with the sons of Yale
and Andover. This is the English translation of it; and this
address, being got up under the patronage of Judge Reeve
of the Charitable Society, of Gov. Smith of the Bible Society,
of Gov. Treadwell of the Moral Society, and of several of our
state Counsellors, as promoters of Congregational schemes,
is to be considered as the great battering ram, by which our
walls are to be destroyed.

If the present men and measures in Connecticut are to
go on, we are to have no freedom of conscience and of
worship. The bonus to the church is of little present consideration, a mere 20 per cent. of what cost nothing to the
State; but it shews by a little what a great deal means. The
episcopal, methodist and baptist churches are to be kept
down at any cost and all hazards, and we are challenged to
come out, one and all, and to assert our rights of conscience
and of worship, if we dare.

You, republicans, will accept this challenge, and since
political considerations are mostly out of the way, the
candidates named are probably the best for the exhibition
of our electoral opinions.

The grandfather and father of Mr. Wolcott were highly
respected governors of this State. He has been secretary of
the treasury of the United States, which office he executed
with acknowledged ability and integrity. In New-York, where
he was president of the Merchant's bank and subsequently
of the bank of America, he has long been respected as a
supporter of sound moral and political principles, has had
several appointments of trust under the republican presidents,
and he has now resumed his abode here, and can doubtless
say with Mr. Dexter, the republican candidate for the office

---

10. The reference to Lyman Beecher is sarcastic. In the address referred to, Beecher asserted
that only college educated ministers, preferably of the Congregationalist order, were qualified
to preach, and that ministers of dissenting denominations, who largely lacked such formal
education, should be disqualified from preaching.

of governor in Massachusetts: "It is a leading principle with me that the duty, which every citizen owes his country, requires that he should support that administration of civil government, which they choose to appoint, in all measures, which his unprejudiced understanding does not shew him to be wrong, and consequently that every combination for general opposition is an offence against the community."

Our late worthy candidate for the office of governor, Elijah Boardman, esq. has requested to be excused and has expressed his disposition to vote for Mr. Wolcott.

As to Mr. Ingersoll, no man can be more respectable on such a ticket. He is eminently a friend of toleration, of high standing as an episcopalian. His present office of judge, and the offices, which he has held in life, attest the universal estimation, it may be truly said, that they are always the result of principles well digested and aiming at honest and useful ends, and whether he may agree with or differ from us, he will always be as rational, intelligent and useful as the best of us.—Civil and religious rights can never be in hazard, while such men have dominion.

Fortunately at the approaching proxies there will be no question as to the merits or demerits of the general government, the claims or pretensions of opposing candidates for the presidency, or even the correct administration of the State government. The great question to be decided, is, whether we shall continue for another year under ecclesiastical domination, the congregational order holding all power and control.

The man, who believes that other orders have been equally patronized, must have had his eyes closed during the long night of congregational dominion in this State. To such we can address nothing, which would rouse them to the exertion of a vote; but of republicans we believe that all will feel the importance of this crisis, and as our candidates are of character established, that their opponents will not venture to assail them, we expect a strong, harmonious and universal republican support of the ticket.[11]

---

11. *Columbian Register,* New Haven, CT, March 12, 1816, 2.

One writer in the *Journal* urged the Episcopalians to "extricate themselves" from the "dilemma" of their reported pact with the democrats:

A DILEMMA!

In private life he who pursues a straight forward path, generally gains friends and meets with success. So it is also in Politicks. Insincerity always breeds suspicion; and suspicion soon destroys all *Confidence.*

A union is said to exist between Episcopacy and Democracy for the purpose of the approaching Election. Though a single word from the Episcopal Candidate would dissipate all suspicion, he and his friends preserve the most ominous silence.

Were they to disavow the Union, the alarms of the Federalists would be quieted; but then they would lose the unprincipled aid of Democracy. If they persist in their obstinate and ominous silence, they will probably lose the support of all honourable and intelligent Federalists.

This is indeed a dilemma! but they may easily extricate themselves from it, by immediately abandoning what appears to me a disingenuous and dishonourable course. If by so doing their Candidate should lose his election, they would have nothing to accuse themselves of; they would still preserve entire their Political Integrity.

FAIR PLAY.[12]

In a letter to the editor of the *Mirror,* allegedly written by "Several Episcopalians," these supposed Episcopalians didn't believe their fellow Episcopalians would sacrifice the interests of the state for their "sectarian wishes," and opposed an Episcopalian college and the Bishop's Fund as "the political baseness of Churchmen."

SIR—

We have heard it asserted that a secret bargain has been made between the Democrats and Episcopalians of

12. *Connecticut Journal,* New Haven, CT, April 2, 1816, 3.

Connecticut, by which the latter at the ensuing election are to vote for Oliver Wolcott as Governour, and the former for Jonathan Ingersoll as Lieut. Governour. By this arrangement it is said the democrats expect to produce collisions on the federal party—to unsettle the steady habits and good order of society—to destroy the present system of government—and ultimately to raise themselves to office and power on the ruins of religion and social happiness. The expectations of the Episcopalians are thought to be less elevated. They only hope to get one of their men into office—and by some manœuvre or other to force from the state certain endowments upon their sect, which three fourths of the freemen of Connecticut have hitherto thought they had no reasonable claim to.

Mr. Editor, we do not believe in such a bargain—we do not believe that federal Episcopalians will sacrifice the paramount interests of the State to their sectarian wishes. We cannot yet believe that a society of Christians, hitherto respectable, will throw aside their honour, their honesty and their political integrity and stoop to chaffer with democracy!—At least while Episcopalians retain the spirit of their religion we know they will not be guilty of a conduct so flagitious in principle, and so poisonous in tendency.

With regard to the coming election, we shall take the direction of reason and religion, and vote for such men as in our consciences we think best fitted for office. Our present Governour has demonstrated his ability and his claim to our confidence—and we shall most cordially continue to him our support.

For the office of Lieut. Governour, Mr. Goddard and Mr. Ingersoll have been nominated. The latter has been reputed an able lawyer—but as his life has been almost exclusively devoted to his profession, he has never till lately been thought of for high political office. Mr. Goddard is better known—In the Congress of the United States he has held a distinguished reputation, and the freemen of Connecticut have long been accustomed to give him eminent consideration for all the requisites of the first offices in their gift.— And in addition to this it is no small recommendation to us that he was the friend and respected counsellor of both the late Governour Griswold and Lieut. Governour Goodrich, and that the first men who have been associated with him in office have always acknowledged his ability, his wisdom, and his integrity. Under these circumstances we shall think it a duty enforced by every patriotic and religious principle, to give him our votes at the next election for Lieutenant Governour.

We cannot here refrain from addressing a few remarks to our religious federal brethren, on the subject of Mr. Ingersoll's democratic nomination.

The democrats have nominated Mr. Ingersoll because he is an Episcopalian—not that they respect our Church, for they are the broad-mouthed ridiculers of all religion—but they hope by this to induce you to take hold of their hands and walk with them—to soften your aversion to their party—to flatter away your honesty—to unloose your attachment to federalism—and ere long to manœuvre you into democracy. These are their hopes, and we are to see whether you will disappoint or realize them. Whatever may have been your opinions of Mr. Ingersoll, you must now view him as a man that democrats are willing to vote for.—This should determine every federalist against his election, for the designs of democrats are "only evil and that continually" and whoever votes for their candidate accelerates their iniquity. These are considerations which will operate on every honest mind, and let those who are too foolish to be honest remember, that he that walks in the same paths with democrats must not expect to come off untainted with pollution, or unspotted with disgrace.

For ourselves, though we adore our Church, and most heartily desire its prosperity, yet we sincerely hope we may never see a "Seabury College" or a "Bishop's Fund" established by the political baseness of Churchmen, and we pray Heaven we may never behold Episcopacy cajoled into wedlock with democracy.

SEVERAL EPISCOPALIANS.[13]

13. *Connecticut Mirror,* Hartford, CT, March 25, 1816, 3.

The Republican papers didn't buy for a minute that this "Several Episcopalians" *Mirror* letter was really written by any Episcopalians, and promptly responded:

"BROAD-MOUTHED RIDICULERS OF ALL RELIGION."

This charitable expression is extracted from the last Mirror; and was no doubt written by one of those pious gentlemen who consider religion as *peculiar* to their sect. ...

The most candid must believe this writer at least a hypocrite. Under this cloak the supporters of church and state have long succeeded in making the people believe that the government of Connecticut is founded on the principles of truth, equity and justice. There are ten chances to one, in my opinion, that most of the writers who support the present system of our state government, could they be brought forth to public view, would prove a similar character with that of the writer in the Mirror.

Because republicans, (consisting of nearly all the Baptists, Methodists and many congregationalists,) have united with the Episcopalians in nominating for the two first offices in the State, men who are friends of toleration—men who believe that Christ's 'kingdom is not of this world,' and who believe that Christ will take care of his church without the aid of Connecticut, the whole are denounced as infidels and *"ridiculers of all religion."*

Yes—when the Baptists, Episcopalians, Methodists, &c. assert their right to an equal degree of privileges with the denomination which now obliges them to 'bow to their political Baal,' they are represented as wishing to "rise in power on the ruins of religion." ...

Episcopalians, Methodists, Baptists, &c.! You verily believe that you do not enjoy equal religious rights with the Standing order. You have remonstrated against this—and remonstrated in vain. *If you do not improve this opportunity in giving your opinions of the conduct of your rulers, can you ever again, with the least propriety, complain of congregational treatment?* Answer this question, by unanimously coming forth and exercising the privilege of freemen; and the spell which has long cemented Church and State will be dissolved forever.[14]

The *Mercury* got creative in treating the Federalists' candidate as disrespectfully as the Federalist papers had been treating the Republicans' candidates.

> We wish to enquire of some of the sagacious *"broad-mouthed"* bellowers of religion and morality, the origin of the Hon. CALVIN GODDARD—in what part of the world he first inhaled the vital air. Perhaps, like Æneas of old, he may be a descendant of the Cyprian Goddess, or even of Jove himself. We are the more inclined to this opinion from a case reported in Judge Root's Reports, page 472, vol. 1 —
>
> "MOTT *versus* GODDARD"
> "Action for breaking and entering his house, AND GETTING HIS DAUGHTER WITH CHILD. Plea—Not guilty. Issue for the jury.
> "The daughter was offered as a witness, and objected to; that she had a suit depending for the maintenance of said child; also an action *FOR A BREACH OF PROMISE TO MARRY HER.*
> "By the court—She is admissible from the necessity of the case, and upon the ground of former precedents from books, and in this state. The action was withdrawn."
>
> This Goddard may not be the honorable *Calvin*—If he is the same, this accounts for his having "been thought of for high public office," instead of Mr. Ingersoll, who has never performed any feats of the like nature.[15]

And the *Register* followed with a clear message to the Federalist papers that the gloves were now off.

TO CONGREGATIONAL FEDERALISTS.

You understand perfectly our course at the approaching

---

14. *Columbian Register,* New Haven, CT, March 30, 1816, 2.
15. *American Mercury,* Hartford, CT, April 2, 1816, 3.

proxies and that to you we owe no apologies or explanations respecting our ticket; but one thing you appear not to understand, and we shall improve the present occasion to enforce it on your minds.

It is not believed, that the most respectable of your number approve the abusive manner, in which your writers in the Courant, Journal and Mirror manage your election concerns: but you have not used your influence to bear down such writers; you have been even willing to profit by their impressions, which they could make on weak and base minds.

We commenced the present contest in mild language and avowed our candidates and motives without any reflection on your candidates and motives. By degrees your papers after some odious vaunting about religion and jacobinism, rose to their former style of insolence & abuse, & the American Mercury was driven to the necessity of retaliation by publishing from Root's reports the case of

MOTT *versus* GODDARD.

If our candidate for governor is to be called a renegado, a traitor, a deserter, mark you the consequence. You have already marked it and what you have seen is only a text to a volume, which no friend to humanity will ever wish to see in print. You feel keenly when any of your number is assailed, but have democrats no wives, no children, no souls, no reflections on time or eternity? If you have a high opinion of your own holiness or of your party societies or of Mr. Beecher's scheme about educated ministers, keep these things to yourselves, especially while elections are pending; for assuredly, if you bring them forward at such times for your benefit and our injury, you will hear from us in reply.

For more than 15 years the republicans of this State have been treated like slaves, for no other crime than their adherence to the principles of the revolution and to the avowed policy of the general government. Driven from participation in the civil and military administration of the State government, punished for declaring that there was no written constitution, deprived of the benefit of the old election law, harassed in courts, officered by men, hostile to us, stigmatized in the papers by every opprobrious name, written down, preached down and pressed down, till further endurance becomes criminal!

You have foreseen this day and have prepared yourselves in every form to meet it, and you have calculated minutely how much men might be made to bear and you have puffed them, unintentionally, a little beyond the point of endurance. Not content with a fulness of civil power, you have claimed uncontrouled ecclesiastical dominion.

Did you believe that all orders of christians would submit and bow before your order? or did you expect that resistance to you could always be born down by the cry of *Religion is in danger?*

Every friend to real religion will lament that the cant of sanctity is brought forward at our proxies, and that your market religion is constantly at vendue or private sale. You have now the power of the State: your numerous appointments to office constitute a regular organization for your support at elections. Yale College, with all its patronage and funds, and the Medical College and the privileged corporations are at your service. Many of the newspapers are in your pay and employ. For the approaching election these advantages have not sufficed you. No! We must again be passed through your fires: but you will please to remember, that if in any future paper the late language of your Courant, Journal and Mirror are repeated, we will not content ourselves with the profit, which our cause will reap from the impudence of your writers.—The state of society requires a radical operation, which however painful it may be to you for the present, will teach you a lesson, long to be remembered.[16]

On April 8, for the first time, a non-Congregationalist was elected to one of the state's two highest offices. The Episcopalian Jonathan Ingersoll won the lieutenant governor's race with 10,494 votes to Calvin Goddard's 8,635. John Cotton Smith was reelected

---

16. *Columbian Register,* New Haven, CT, April 6, 1816, 2.

governor, but the race was very close, with Smith getting only 11,386 votes to Oliver Wolcott's 10,170.

The Republicans also made significant gains in the legislature, with the *Register* reporting:

> In the House of Representatives of this state at its next session, there will be about *ninety* firm republicans, at least ten more than at any former period; these with the toleration federalists will make the parties nearly equal. This will be a novel case in Connecticut.[17]

The Federalist papers quickly blamed the outcome of the election on some sort of extraordinary exertions on the part of the Republicans to get more of their voters out, and complacency and low voter turnout among the Federalists, with the *Courant* saying of the Republicans:

> ...They have now been organized and marshaled, and all called into service and put under the most severe discipline.[18]

And of the Federalists:

> ...The federalists on the other hand, secure in their own strength, and despising the enemy they had so often conquered, in most of our towns made no exertions. They did not believe that men who were groaning under the burden of the late unjust war, could have been brought up to vote for the supporters of that war. Experience however has falsified all such calculations. We now know what to expect and must be ready to meet it. We have cause for exertion, but none for despondency. The federalists can again it is believed bring into the field 15,000 voters, and now it is generally understood what exertions the democrats have made and are making, it is believed that this will be done.[19]

And of the Republicans' success in the *Courant's* own city of

17. *Columbian Register,* New Haven, CT, April 20, 1816, 3.
18. *The Connecticut Courant,* Hartford, CT, April 16, 1816, 3.
19. Ibid.

Hartford, which had gone for Wolcott and Ingersoll, and also for the first time elected Republican representatives:

> The success of democracy in this town was as unexpected to our enemies as to ourselves. We began balloting with a federal majority of 70 votes and ended after sun-set with a democratic election; our friends abroad however need not be alarmed for us, though we know they will be surprised. We have been too confident in our own strength. The potion though bitter may be salutary, and we trust that our united exertions will yet do honor to the federal cause.[20]

The *Journal's* city of New Haven had also gone for Wolcott and Ingersoll, and for a Republican representative in the one of its two seats for which there was a contest. The city's other representative, although a Federalist, was an Episcopalian, and had the votes of both the Federalists and the Republican-Episcopalian alliance. The *Journal,* like the *Courant,* made excuses for the Republicans' success, attributing the victory of its new Republican representative by a vote of 236 to 157 to the Federalists not believing that the Episcopalians were really going to vote with the Republicans.

NEW-HAVEN ELECTION.

> The Federalists of Connecticut are astonished at the result of the late Election in this city. They have a right to know how it was brought about. ...
>
> The uncommon number of democratic votes was owing to the following facts:
>
> 1. Every democrat, who could be found, was brought to meeting. One of their number stationed at the polls counted them. Their number was 150.
>
> 2. The remaining 86 were Episcopalians, who heretofore have been federalists; and who, on that day, voted in a body for the demo. candidate. ...
>
> The smallness of the federal vote may be thus explained:
>
> 1. The federal ticket lost 86 Episcopalian votes gone

---

20. *The Connecticut Courant,* Hartford, CT, April 16, 1816, 3.

over, and 20 scattering, or 106 in all.

2. Express assurances were given to several of the principal federalists that no union had taken place between the Democrats and Episcopalians. These assurances were believed; and the impression, which they made, extensively circulated among the Federalists. Supposing that they were intended not to lull the watchfulness of the Federalists, but to produce harmony; yet their only effect was to inspire a false security; and thus to paralyze exertion. No attempt was made to get the Federalists out to the polls.

The federalists of Connecticut ought also to know that no men in the community are as much mortified at this result, as those Episcopalian gentlemen who maintained their integrity. Several of them finding what course the great body of Episcopal Federalists were about to take would not go to the meeting. The others would not believe the coalition possible, until they heard the votes declared.[21]

The *Register* promptly responded to the *Courant* and the *Journal,* giving them ample advance warning that the Republicans would also be out in force at the September election, so as not to take the Federalists by surprise again:

NOTA BENE.

Know all Congregationalists by these presents, that on the 18th of September next the friends of toleration will be out at proxies with their ticket, which notice is given on this 29th day of April, to save the Journal and other federal papers from complaining that they were taken by surprise.

———

The Hartford federal papers state that the success of democracy in that town will be a *'bitter potion,* though it may be *salutary;'* and we will add our wish that it may also work an effectual cure—for surely federalism is much disordered.

21. *Connecticut Journal,* New Haven, CT, April 16, 1816, 3.

The Courant and Mirror in face of the election of Mr. Ingersoll to the office of Lt. Governor, state that *"fifteen thousand voters* can be brought into the field" to put down the Friends of Equal Rights and Toleration at another election. How consistent! ...[22]

The *Register* also responded to another post-election piece from the *Journal,* which declared "apostacy and fanaticism ... triumphant" in New Haven's election:

> The following specimen of fine writing, and philanthropy, we extract for the benefit of our Episcopalian fellow citizens, from the Connecticut Journal of last Tuesday.
>
> "O, SHAME!
> "Triumph of Apostacy and Delusion!!!
>
> "In this federal town of New-Haven, where four fifths of the FREE-men are the friends of order and "steady habits," prejudice, apostacy and fanaticism are triumphant! The result of the election this day furnishes the fullest evidence that moral depravity and personal debasement form no barrier to political delusion and sectarian prejudice.—O, SHAME!—"Judgment hath fled to brutish beasts, and men have lost their reason."
>
> Such an eruption of spleen, and ill nature, we were hardly prepared to find, even in the prostituted columns of the Journal. We had hoped, after all the puerile calculations, the boastings, and challenging, which have for nearly two months past, been teeming from the Journal, that its half-fledged scribblers would content themselves now the election agony is over, to writhe in silence under the effects of their ridiculous efforts. But this will not answer—the overwhelming majority of our fellow-citizens must be branded, as a pack of Apostates and deluded Fanatics! And for what? Why because they have not, (after their better experience,) entrusted the legislative concerns of the town to a political

---

22. *Columbian Register,* New Haven, CT, April 20, 1816, 3.

madman; and secondly, they have resisted with the indignation of men, the unceasing efforts, which have been made to vilify their favorite candidates.

Well might the writer of the above article exclaim, "Judgment hath fled to brutish beasts;" and if he will only look at the returns which we this day publish from the different towns in the State, he will find that the "brutish beasts," have been visited with a much heavier "Judgment," than the votes of this town afford. [23]

With the victory of Ingersoll, the closeness of the governor's race, and their gains in the House of Representatives, the Republicans next set their sights on the Council. In the fall, both parties issued assistants lists. On both lists were two Episcopalians, Asa Chapman and Samuel Johnson. These two Episcopalians, supported by both the Republican-Episcopalian alliance and a few thousand Federalists, topped the list of the twenty nominees. One Republican, David Tomlinson, also received enough votes to make the list, although coming in at number twenty.

Although the Federalists made great efforts to get out as many of their voters as possible, and flipped a few seats back to Federalists, the number of Republicans in the House remained steady.

The Republicans also pulled an interesting trick to break the Congregational-Federalist stranglehold on Connecticut's representatives in the U.S. House of Representatives, voting for the lowest men on the Federalists' list, one of whom was Charles Denison, the Episcopalian state representative from New Haven. By doing this, only two of Connecticut's seven existing U.S. representatives were reelected, and five new men, only nominal Federalists, and one of them a non-Congregationalist, were elected.

Referring to Connecticut's election, Boston's Federalist *New-England Palladium* labeled Connecticut's Republicans "political persecutors," a charge that the *Register* begged to differ with:

THE PERSECUTORS!

The Boston Palladium of the 13th ult. says "In Connecticut

23. *Columbian Register*, New Haven, CT, April 16, 1816, 3.

the *political persecutors* have come forward with a *toleration* ticket."

This Palladium was set up as the great religious trading paper of New-England: of course the platform has a share of its sympathies. Several classes of men in this State, who have long been deprived of their rights, civil and religious, are denominated persecutors, because having borne, so long as evils were tolerable, they are driven to the necessity of declaring that they can bear no longer.

What has been the condition of the minor religious orders and of the republicans in Connecticut for the last 16 years? They have been borne down, proscribed, kept from all share of the common power, except a few crumbs, habitually slandered by those, whom the Palladium would naturally call *the persecuted!* [24]

The Federalists were understandably worried. Knowing that this might very well be their last year in power if they didn't find a way to get the Episcopalians back and somehow unbrand themselves as the party of intolerance, they passed at the October session of the legislature *An Act for the support of Literature and Religion,* an act that would give significant amounts of money to all the religious denominations — Baptists, Methodists, and Episcopalians as well as the state-supported Congregationalists.

At the end of the War of 1812, the federal government owed the state governments money for their military expenditures during the war. Connecticut calculated that the amount it was owed was $145,000. By the *Act for the support of Literature and Religion,* this money, whenever it was received, would be divided among the different religious denominations and Yale College, with a third distributed among the Congregationalist societies, a seventh going to the Episcopalians' Bishop's Fund, an eighth to the Baptists, a twelfth to the Methodists, a seventh going to Yale, and the remainder to be put in the treasury. Because the Baptists and the Methodists had no corporate body to receive the money, the act appointed trustees for them, chosen by the legislature and named in the act.

None of the denominations was pleased with this act. The

24. *Columbian Register,* New Haven, CT, October 19, 1816, 1.

Congregationalist were happy to receive money from the state, but thought they should get more than a third of it. The Episcopalians saw it as a bribe for their votes. And the Baptists and Methodists not only didn't want public money, but were outraged that the legislature would appoint boards of trustees for them without their knowledge or consent.

As the *Mercury* put it, the act was seen by the dissenting religious denominations as nothing but an attempt by the Federalists to "extricate themselves from the abyss of contempt."

A HINT IN SEASON.

... The faction of federalism now struggling as we fondly trust with its last paroxism, seems still to indulge a faint hope, which like that of the hypocrite appears to be one of its own manufacturing, and well calculated to afford in the end a horrible death.

The tune of "one hundred and forty-five thousand dollars" played in the legislature on the "harps" of Gen. Sterling and other federal performers, has swelled the anticipation of that party with some cheering ideas, which added to those excited by pulpit "melody," almost makes them dare to hope that they shall extricate themselves from the abyss of contempt, into which their rebellion against the government of their country, and their thirst after aristocratical glory have plunged them.

But thank God this music makes a doleful discord with the feelings of every true republican and honest statesman. Not because republicans are opposed to the support of "literature and religion," as has been asserted by some of the federal scribblers, but because they well know the designs of the federal party. Like the serpent that charms his prey they sing only to allure. Can it possibly be supposed that if the three denominations of christians, viz. Baptists, Methodists and Episcopalians, had applied three years ago to the legislature for sums of money for the support of their institutions they would have received any? No! a grant has actually been refused to the Episcopalians, which denomination has now received a *promise* of the largest donation of the three. But our readers are well informed of this and other circumstances which incontestibly prove that the federal party did not think it best to *hire* any help until they actually found themselves in need of it. Let it suffice to say that circumstances previous, as well as those that attended the passage of this bill, and even the very words of those who agreed in its favor in the house of representatives proves it to be *intentionally* a base attempt to prolong the life of the federal aristocracy. But *eventually* it turns out a fine stimulus to the rising vigor of republicanism, and proves our federal statesmen to be all Quack Doctors, unskilled in the theory of political diseases.—Republicans of Connecticut! the busy wheel of time will soon roll on the day when you will again have a chance to try your increased strength against the broken and deserted ranks of federalism. You have long been under the weight of its tyrannical oppressions, and long witnessed the corruption, intolerance and rebellion, that has distinguished its reign. You have witnessed the undue superiority the federal Clergy have held over those of other denominations; you have seen them sporting in "gay apparel" surrounded by wealth and luxury, while some of their brother Baptists and Methodists have travelled the country on foot, spreading the sound of peace, without at sometimes, even a whole coat to cover their backs; still we hear no complaint from the persecuted servants of Christ, and find them engaged in nothing else of a public nature, but the duties of their honorable calling.

You have witnessed, republicans, an "organized rebellion" against the general government even in this land of piety and "steady habits." A council of influential men assembled at the seat of our state government secretly meditating an attack upon the Congress of the United States which might eventually have ended with the loss of our liberty and independence, and subjected us to all the horrors of civil war! Yes, it is a truth however painful it must be for every true American to hear it, that while our country was engaged in a war with a foreign enemy, for the protection of our commercial rights, while our coasts were invaded by the fleets of a powerful nation, and the infant settlements on our frontiers exposed to the depredations of a merciless savage foe, at a time when the internal affairs of our republic seemed to wear a gloomy cast, and needed the combined efforts of all its supporters: it is a truth, that the government of this State refused to assist our country. The standing Clergy even from the pulpit loaded our Administration with bitter reproaches, and shamefully abused with their lawless tongues all those that dared even to declare themselves to be Republicans, while they were heard to pray fervently for the success of a parcel of rebels assembled at the city of Hartford meditating a division of our Union!!! Justice seemed to be trampled upon—and patriotism to have forsaken the state—moral obligation was despised—the federal party had become like Bedlamites, and confusion was the only order of the day.

Not to notice other conduct of the federal party which has marked their reign with disgrace, and proved them to be unworthy to hold the reins of government, I trust I shall be pardoned for cautioning the republicans, and all others who feel willing the people should enjoy their dearest rights and liberties, free from the tyrannical restrictions of a political party, not to be deceived by their present flattering policy. You have all heard the fable of the fox commending the singing of the crow when she had some what in her mouth that the fox lied. Their "harping" is totally unworthy your notice, unless you honor it now and then with a little contempt. Only stand firm and undaunted in the cause of virtue and your now deluded opponents if they find they can make no impression on you with their music, will either retreat from the political contest, or join the ranks of Toleration. Come then "let us go on our way of rejoicing" and when we have fairly gained the victory and have taken our rights and privileges from the grasp of a party and placed them in the hands of the sovereign people; we will all devoutly say with good old Simeon of old "now let thy servants depart this *political life* in peace, for our eyes have seen the *salvation of our country."* [25]

25. *American Mercury,* Hartford, CT, December 10, 1816, 3.

The *Register* described the act's giving away of money that the state didn't actually have yet and couldn't even be sure that it was going to get as a rough draft of the Federalists' will:

> Federalists being about to depart this political life, have made a rough draft of their will, giving their first-born something more than a double portion, viz—68,000 dollars, and to the favored members of the family, smaller but very handsome legacies.
>
> This is like a father, who having squandered what otherwise would have gone to his children, made a will giving each of them a large portion. On being enquired of where they were to find their portions after his death, he said they might go and earn them, for he had shewn his good disposition.[26]

Even outside of Connecticut, the act was seen for what it was — a political maneuver by the Federalists — as Rhode Island's *Providence Patriot* reported:

> *Curious Legislation.*—The federal legislature of Connecticut have trumped up a demand against the U. States, for monies expended by them during the war, amounting to $145,000, and have very seriously gone to work, and appropriated portions of it to the several religious denominations in the State, (to prevent any more squabbling about *toleration,* we presume) as if the money was already in the Treasury, or likely to get there! This is one of the most curious manœuvres of the steady habits folks. ....[27]

The *Mercury* summed up the year of 1816 "the birth of liberty" in Connecticut, and rightly predicted that "nothing less than complete victory" was coming:

MORE RAYS OF LIBERTY.

"Take an harp, go about the City thou Harlot, make sweet

26. *Columbian Register,* New Haven, CT, November 2, 1816, 3.
27. *Providence Patriot & Columbian Phenix,* Providence, RI, November 9, 1816, 2.

melody sing many songs that thou mayest be remembered."
Isa. 23 chap. 16 ver.

When federalism was at the zenith of its glory in Connecticut, and the "bulwark" of "steady habits" was proclaimed invulnerable even to the "lapse of time," our standing Clergy, under the influence of a political phrenzy, united themselves with a political party, and by that union, rendered their influence as transient, as the existence of the faction it supported.

Confident of a support from their deluded followers, each took his station, not as one dependent upon the people for subsistence, but as one on whom the *people* were dependent not only for the light of divine revelation, but for the salvation of their souls! All other denominations of christians were driven from their communion table with contempt, and those of their constituents who had not subscribed to their articles of faith, were placed under sentence of Hell until they would embrace their creed. Their language to all but those of their flock was, "stand by, for I am more holy than thou." Instead of the soft inviting airs of the gospel of peace, they sounded the harsh trumpet of eternal warfare, and "out of their mouths went forth perpetual streams of fire and brimstone."

In the midst of this splendid career a sound was heard which made even these "mighty ones" tremble, while it filled with gladness the heart of every genuine christian who looks forward with anxious expectation for the dawnings of Millennial glory. It was the blessed sound of TOLERATION! It reiterated like the twilight song of Virgins upon the margin of some "silver lake," while every sacred temple of truth and virtue proved vocal to the sound. The face of politics and religion at once seemed to be changed. The boasted structure of "steady habits" began to totter upon its sandy foundation, and the storms of public odium threatened final destruction to the Altar of superstition and ignorance. Justice awoke from her stupor and waved her long forsaken standard amid the shouts and joyful acclamations of one party, and the fears and distorted grimaces of the other.

From this period we may date the birth of liberty, and the downfall of priestcraft and religious tyranny in old Connecticut. Though the triumph of Republicanism at present is not complete, yet as she has marshalled her forces beneath the standards of justice, truth and virtue, with the motto of TOLERATION enstamped upon her ensigns, we think that nothing less than complete victory can be the glorious fruits of her political warfare. And our expectations are still strengthened when we view our "standing clergy" at the present day, who think we may with propriety be styled the "great political bulwarks" of the state, striving by all the power of their eloquence and *political religion* to procure for themselves an "honorable retreat." They have spiked their engines of fire and brimstone—thrown down the barrier of separate communion—proffered their fellowship to the Baptists, Methodists and Episcopalians—proclaimed many of their articles of faith to be unnecessary for the salvation of the soul—and have thrown down their harsh trumpets of war, and "taken their harps" to "go about the city" and "make sweet melody" and "sing many songs" that they may "be remembered." Some persons, we are credibly informed, have been taken into the church without receiving their ordinance of sprinkling; and even an orthodox preacher has been heard to say that "he believed there were many good christians among his people, that did not belong to the church."

The policy of the established priesthood at present, is framed with much cunning and deceit, and much better calculated to secure to them a continuance of the "loaves and fishes" than it was three years ago; yet I shall take the liberty to remind them by way of a "modest hint" that it is "too late to secure the stable after the Steed is stolen." It is well for them that they are preparing to take their exit with as good a grace as possible, for be assured that the political stage of Connecticut will soon exhibit a scene in which they will not be allowed to act so conspicuous a part. Therefore we say again it is a good thing for them that they have taken their "HARPS." As to their federal constituents we can say no "comforting thing" to them, but must salute their ears with these harsh words from the prophet Isaiah: "HOWL YE SHIPS OF TARSHISH FOR YOUR STRENGTH IS LAID WASTE." [28]

1816 was also, of course, a presidential election year, and as the Federalists were taking their last gasps in Connecticut, so too was the party nationally. This would be the last time that the party would run a presidential candidate, with Federalist Rufus King getting only 34 electoral votes to Republican James Monroe's 183. The Federalist party became a thing of the past nationally, and was soon to be put out of power in Connecticut.

28. *American Mercury,* Hartford, CT, November 12, 1816, 3.

∽ **1817** ∾

The contest between the Tolerationists and the "Platform" men, as the Republicans had begun calling the Federalists for their attachment to the Saybrook Platform, was on. With such a crucial part of the contest being for the votes of the religious dissenters, the Federalists were none too happy with this new designation of the "Platform" party, as the *Register* reported:

WHINING.

A piece in the last Journal headed Saybrook Platform whines about our use of the word Platform as designating the dominant religions and political sect in this State.

The writer seems to regret, that the good old days are past, when the platform was established by law, when the Common Prayer book was treated with ridicule, when all dissenters were driven by law from the state, when Churchmen were openly reviled and persecuted, when a sacredness and authority were attached to the Platform, superior to the Bible.

These days are passed away;—The people are shewing a disposition not longer to bend their neck to the Clergy of the standing order; to think in religious and political matters for themselves; to determine and act without fear, without arbitrary force. Does not the term platform more accurately designate the intolerant party or faction which now misgoverns our state, than any other name? The names Republican, Democrat, and Federalist do not distinguish parties, as they now exist. They are justly becoming obsolete—they ought not to be used: *Toleration* and *Platform* are the significant terms which truly describe the division of parties. Are the friends of Toleration bound in honor not to use a name which may be disagreeable to the persecuting faction?

The Editor of the Journal may whine about the destruction of religion and morals and learning because the minor sects apply the epithet Platform to the governing religious party; but this is not the only *truth* about which he *whines*. We assert, then, that the term Platform is well applied to one party, and the name Toleration, including the minor sects, properly designates the oppressed party. ....[1]

Passed by the Fedetralists in an attempt to get votes from the dissenters, and particularly to get the Episcopalian vote back, the 1816 *Act for the support of Literature and Religion,* commonly known as the "Appropriation Act," was backfiring tremendously. Beginning at the end of 1816, and continuing right up to the 1817 spring election in April, meetings were held in towns across the state by the dissenting denominations, sometimes alone and sometimes with the different denominations coming together, passing resolutions against the appropriation.[2] The Republican papers were filled with the resolutions passed at these meetings, sending a clear and unified message — their votes could not be bought.

At a meeting of the Methodists and Baptists in New-Canaan, assembled for the purpose of taking into consideration, and expressing their opinion of the late extraordinary act of the Legislature of this State, making appropriations to several religious denominations of a certain sum of money which is claimed to be due from the General govern-

---

1. *Columbian Register,* New Haven, CT, April 5, 1817, 2.

2. While opposed to the appropriation, the Episcopalians' Bishop's Fund did accept the money, as eventually did the trustees appointed by the legislature for the Methodists and the Baptists, but this did not change their indignation at the act or the Federalists' attempt to buy their votes. The Baptists didn't accept their share until 1820, and while the Methodists' trustees accepted that denomination's share in 1818, some of the Methodist societies returned their portions.

ment to this State, for services rendered for public defence during the late war with Great Britain. The said meeting ... unanimously adopted the following resolutions:—

Resolved, That although we differ in opinion as respects our religious sentiments, yet we will unitedly protest any measure which is calculated to wrong the public, or do injustice to individuals.

Resolved, That we view the late appropriation act of the General Assembly unjust, and dangerous in principle, for on the ground that one hundred and forty-five thousand dollars has been collected and distributed, the Legislature can tax the good people of this State, to ten times that amount, and to appropriate the money to any use or purpose whatever. ...

Resolved, That we unitedly protest against the usurped power of the General Assembly in making legal corporate bodies for us, without our knowledge, approbation or consent.

Resolved, That we view the said act, not sincerely expressive of any real good will to us, but an act of mere political intrigue; for we have ever been in a greater or less degree, the subjects of ridicule, slander and persecution, by the ruling party of this State; and we believe it to be the duty of the several corporate bodies (if ever received) on any conditions, but to refund it to the people from whom it was obtained.

Resolved, That we believe this novel and ridiculous act of giving away money that has no existence, only in the imaginary ideas of men, to be a legislative farce, designed to set each of our sects against the general government in case it should refuse to refund the money, agreeable to the requisition; and in this way to increase the popularity of the present rulers in the state, and secure their future election.

Resolved, That we will never be duped or bribed by our Legislature, to become supporters of that tyranny which exists in a union of Church and State, which has drenched the earth with blood, and been the curse of Christendom almost ever since the reign of Constantine; but will ever protest against it as being derogatory to the spiritual nature of

Christ's kingdom; the subjects of which will yield voluntary obedience to their master's requirements, without the agency of human laws or legal appropriations. ....[3]

At an united meeting of Baptists, Episcopalians, and Methodists, convened in the society of Andover, on the 12th of February, and by an adjournment on the 18th day of March 1817, for the purpose of taking into consideration, and expressing their opinion, on the late extraordinary act of the legislature of this state making appropriations to several denominations of a certain sum of money, &c. entitled "An act for the support of Literature and Religion" ...

Resolved, That we disapprove of the act of our legislature, in appropriating certain sums of money to Yale College, and several religious denominations in this state, because we view it as designed to give a bias to the freedom of religious opinion, by holding up to view a determination to advance the temporal interest of one favorite sect at the expence of every other; as designed to influence the freedom of elections, by uniting Church and State under the same banner, to fight not the battles of the Lord, but the political and hypocritical battles of Pharisaical priests and aristocratical demagogues, and thereby corrupt the simplicity of the Christian character, and subvert the liberties of the state. ...

Resolved, That in our opinion the aforesaid act is a counterpart to the certificate law, and a like intolerant attempt to coerce and enslave our conscience, to prejudice the understanding of the weak and uninformed; a political bounty to fill federal skeleton regiments; an imbecile and unavailing attempt to paralize the feelings of the injured, and thereby maintain party predominance at the expence of public treasure and private sensibility. ...

Resolved, That we view in the said act a renewed source of grief and mourning for every pious mind over the unhappy state of Connecticut, which, having so great advan-

---

3. *Columbian Register,* New Haven, CT, January 11, 1817, 2.

tages for religion and literature, has demonstrated so great weakness in the choice and conduct of its rulers for years past; we expected that such men would have manifested a due regard to justice and equal rights in their legislative dispositions of money, but this appropriation is unjust in principle and distribution. Where is the Quaker, the Universalist? &c. Their certificates are lawful, and they paid their share of this money. Their share is taken by legislative authority, and given to others.

Resolved, That we doubt whether said appropriation was made from the motives thereto specified. We view the appropriation made to the Baptists, Episcopalians, and Methodists, a matter of intrigue, designed to make a tool of these religious denominations, to aid the elections of this state to secure the seats of those now in power. ...[4]

Meanwhile, the *Mirror,* along with the other Federalist papers, extolled the "benevolent minds of the legislature" for making the appropriation:

TRAITS OF DEMOCRACY.
No. IX.

The very liberal appropriation made by the Legislature at their last session, of the balance due from the United States to this State, for expences incurred in support of Mr. Madison's War, has opened a wide field, for the display of democratic intolerance, illiberality, and vulgar abuse. It is evident from their conduct on this occasion, that they are determined on keeping the State in a ferment, and that nothing will satisfy the leaders of democracy, short of a complete surrender of the government into their hands. ...

To those who are best acquainted, with the true character of Connecticut democracy, and understand the dark designs, and vile intrigues of the leaders of this party, can easily account for the violent opposition, which the benevolent minds of the Legislature, in making this appropriation,

4. *American Mercury,* Hartford, CT, April 1, 1817, 2-3.

has met with from this class of men. It is a well known fact, that the leaders of democracy, have exerted themselves, and are still using their utmost endeavours, to prevent the claims of this State, ever being allowed and paid by the United States; and if this State should fail of receiving this balance, which is so justly its due, it will be owing to the hostile endeavours, which this party are making use of to prevent it. To this deep rooted prejudice against the claim of this State, may be attributed, more than to scruples of conscience, or any thing else, the virulent opposition of this party to this appropriation. Another, and perhaps a primary cause of this opposition is—that this measure of the Legislature, has shut a door in some degree, against their wicked attempts, to seduce certain religious denominations, to join their ranks and aid in their designs, to revolutionize the State. ....[5]

At the end of March, less than two weeks before the election, the news broke that Connecticut had received a portion of its claim, a payment of $50,000.[6] The Federalist papers jumped on this news, using it to make another effort to entice the dissenting denominations away from the Republicans.

☞ $50,000 ! !

A part of the 145,000 Dollars due this State from the United States, for expences incurred during the late war, and appropriated last Session of the Legislature to the support of Religion and Literature has already been paid on account to the Agent of this State, and deposited to the credit of this State, in the bank of the United States.

This is a pretty good BEGINNING!—a little more than one third of the sum due is realized by the first payment. Let it

5. *Connecticut Mirror*, Hartford, CT, March 17, 1817, 3.
6. Of the $145,000 Connecticut made a claim for, the federal government only allowed $115,000 as reimbursable expenditures. After the payment of $50,000 in 1817, it would be over two decades before Connecticut would receive another payment, getting $65,000 in 1838, which wasn't even enough to cover the interest. Connecticut was still trying to get the balance of this War of 1812 debt in 1936, which by that time, with interest, amounted to nearly $600,000.

be remembered that if any small number of the Minor Sects have by designing men been influenced to refuse to accept their share of the money there will be more for those who are wiser and better disposed.

FREEMEN OF CONNECTICUT of all religious denominations, pause for a moment and reflect upon the course pursued by those who aim at the destruction of the INSTITUTIONS of this STATE.

Until within a few years, the Democrats have laboured with all their arts to induce you to change your *political* institutions. They have informed you that your Laws regarding Elections are oppressive; that you had no Constitution of civil government, and have kindly offered to assist you in forming one. These kind offers you steadily rejected, and uniformly said Nay, we will abide in our good old Steady Habits where we have found prosperity and happiness. ...

Let every serious man, of whatever religious denomination he may be, pause and reflect, and ask himself in the presence of God, what he expects from such a party, and whether he is prepared to deliver into the hands of Democracy the Religious Institutions of Connecticut!! [7]

The Republican papers also, of course, reported on the Federalists' pre-election windfall:

$50,000!

What a world of money!—all safe arrived in the best market that ever was known. "After such a flood of specie the banks must certainly discount; and I'll bet a beaver hat his Excellency will be re-elected by a majority of 5000 votes." A man can scarcely turn a corner in New-Haven without having his ears assailed with this clamor. But is it to be wondered at? What was the appropriation made for, but to buy votes on the 7th of April? It will be surprising indeed if the whole amount of our constitutional claim does not arrive before another week goes out. The person who

7. *Connecticut Journal,* New Haven, CT, March 25, 1817, 3.

does not yet perceive the vast improvement made in the literature of Connecticut, by the strength of this money, must be too blind to read the Journal.[8]

The platform gentry are making a wonderful deal of fuss of their having received—yes, and actually paid into the Treasury too, $50,000 of the claim upon the U. States. Before freemen's meeting they will have sent runners into every town to proclaim the joyful news. It is well for their poor brains that the whole sum was not paid, else, judging from the effect which this part has upon their senses, they would go stark mad for joy. No one ever doubted that a part of the claim would be paid—yet as they must have some great news on the eve of an election, this subject is presented to the people in glaring capitals. But, taking it as they wish to have the subject viewed, it only proves that instead of $145,000, *the note has lost by their mismanagement only about two thirds of that sum,* viz. 95,000.

Or, if it will better suit them, they may take for granted that the whole sum will be reimbursed, and how then stands the account? *They have gratuitously given, without their being applied to therefor, $145,000 of the people's hard earnings for the very charitable purpose of securing an election.* A very benign act indeed—and this too at a time when the treasury was exhausted, and the state largely in debt! The whole of this sum had been collected of the people by taxes of three and four cents on the dollar. Now when these benevolent souls shall have convinced the freemen that the act of appropriation, under the above circumstances, was expedient, just or politic, we will then acknowledge that they ought to be rewarded for their benevolence by being retained in office.[9]

8. *Columbian Register,* New Haven, CT, April 1, 1817, 3.
9. *American Mercury,* Hartford, CT, April 1, 1817, 3.

To His Excellency
JOHN COTTON SMITH.

SIR—The period has arrived, when your excellency must be addressed in stronger language than that to which you have heretofore been accustomed. Nearly fourteen thousand of your fellow-citizens will declare by their votes that the law granting 145,000 dollars to the different denominations of christians and Yale-College, and to which you placed your signature as governor, was intended as a bribe to secure their support. In this act of your political friends and yourself, the cloven foot is distinctly discovered.

An injured citizen will close his communication by asking your excellency a few serious questions—and he hopes they will sink deep into your heart.

Have you in your administration the honor of your country—the constitution of this republic—and the farewell injunctions of the departed Washington? Did you not believe, while you approved of the conduct of the Hartford Convention, that association of infamy, would eventuate in producing the horrors of civil war, and the disunion of the States? Have you not, while attempting to cajole episcopalians by Fasts,[10] done all in your power to hinder their growth and prosperity by denying them a college and the power of conferring degrees at their academy in Cheshire? Have you not done your utmost to keep down the minor sects? Did you not in your own soul believe that the money which you gave your consent to be squandered for votes would purchase your re-election? In fine, sir, are you not sensible that MENE TEKEL[11] is written upon your conduct by your indignant constituents?

Answer these questions at the bar of your conscience.

Your injured Constituent.

---

10. One of the crumbs given to the Episcopalians in the Smith administration to conciliate them was to make the state's annual fast day coincide with the Episcopalian observance of Good Friday.

11. In the Bible's Book of Daniel, the words "MENE, MENE, TEKEL, UPHARSIN" were the miraculous writing on the wall interpreted by Daniel as foretelling that Belshazzar's days were numbered and his kingdom would fall.

"The several printers in this State are requested to copy the following notice for the information of all concerned"—says our honorable State Treasurer; and we cheerfully comply with his request, remarking however that we consider it a high-handed attempt to influence the votes of the freemen.

"Fifty Thousand Dollars

"Of the MONEY appropriated by the act for the encouragement of literature and religion, has been received into the Treasury of this State, from the Treasury of the United States, and is ready to be distributed agreeable to the provisions of said act.—Previous to the distribution to the Presbyterian or Congregational denomination of Christians, it will be necessary that they should make return of their respective lists, conformably to the provisions of said act.

"A. KINGSBURY, Treasurer.

"Treasury-Office, Hartford,
March 27th, 1817." [12]

To the Freemen of Connecticut.

It is now about a twelve-month since men of opposite political and religious tenets, threw aside their prejudices and became united in the common object of obtaining a REFORM, in the political intolerance which has too long tinctured the councils of Connecticut. Such were the feelings which animated all classes on this interesting subject, that the "TOLERATION TICKET," was no sooner announced, than it acquired the confidence and support of a large and powerful body of Freemen. The struggle that ensued, is familiar to us all. It was a struggle peculiar in the annals of Connecticut elections;—peculiar, because the People, unaided by the annual Legislative caucus at Hartford, came forward in their

12. *Columbian Register,* New Haven, CT, April 5, 1817, 2.

strength, to win an independence which panic-struck the ruling party, dared to vote for such men as they deemed most worthy of public confidence. The semi-annual proxies in September, ended in the election of an increased number of men of liberal principles to the Assembly, and in the elevation of one of our ticket, in spite of the returning officers, to the Nomination list for Council. And there can remain no doubt but that at the ensuing election in April, the cause which now mingles with the feelings and has become interwoven with the hearts of so many of your number, will be crowned with complete success. ...

What is there in the history of the year past which looks as if the ruling party would breathe a more tolerant spirit hereafter, than has hitherto marked their career? True—at a moment when the gloom of political death was gathering around them—as if to lessen the account which was soon to be rendered at the bar of public opinion, the fruits of their mismanagement during the war, were by every legal solemnity, bequeathed to the *pious uses of Religion!* But fellow-citizens, this death-bed repentance cannot—it ought not to save them. Nay, the very persons from whom it proceeds would be the first to ridicule it, could their sense of immediate danger only be removed. What,—after the strange management with the Phœnix Bonus, which we have witnessed at the hands of the ruling party when in the hey day of their power, can any man be so moon-struck as to believe the "Appropriation Act," proceeded from a real regard to the interests of the minor sects? ...[13]

Voter turnout on April 7 was the highest it had ever been, with virtually every freeman in the state coming out to vote. The Toleration ticket was once again Oliver Wolcott and Jonathan Ingersoll. The Federalists, as expected, renominated John Cotton Smith for governor, and, in yet another effort to lure some of the formerly-Federalist Episcopalians back to their side, also nominated the incumbent Ingersoll for lieutenant governor.

This time, Wolcott won, with 13,655 votes to Smith's 13,119.

13. *Columbian Register,* New Haven, CT, March 15, 1817, 2.

The Republicans also, for the first time, had a majority in the House of Representatives. Because the Council nominees had been chosen the previous September, the Council remained Federalist for now, but this would be the last time.

The Federalists responded to the Republican victory with their usual excuses and blame — that they were taken by surprise by the "unparalleled zeal" and "unexampled means" of the Republicans; there was "listless apathy" among their own party. But, the *Mirror* wrongly predicted, the Federalists would again "rise in their strength" when the true designs of the Republicans were found out:

> ... We shall not pretend that the result of this election has not disappointed and chagrined us.—We find that we did not attribute sufficient consequence to the unparalleled zeal, and unexampled means of our opponents; to the listless apathy of some, and the treacherous neutrality of other among our own party. Many true federalists, have viewed the exertions of democracy, as contemplating at present nothing more than the election of Oliver Wolcott, and believing him heartily attached to the good of his native State, have seen no reasons why particular exertions should be made to prevent his election. If these views were correct we should scarcely blame their conduct; but it should have been understood that Mr. Wolcott is only the democratic stepping-stone to power; that he is the instrument not the object of their purposes. When this is thoroughly known— and this election will go far to make it so—the federalists of Connecticut will rise in their strength and rebuild the breach which has been effected in the citadel of our social blessings and political happiness.[14]

The reporting by Connecticut's Republican papers was rather subdued for an event so momentous. From the *Mercury*:

The Election.

Monday of last week was a proud day for Connecticut.

14. *Connecticut Mirror,* Hartford, CT, April 14, 1817, 2.

A majority of her citizens burst the chains which for years had bound them to an ignominious servitude, and proclaimed their freedom. Connecticut, so long estranged from her sister states, has at length enrolled herself under the banners of the republic. *For the first time* the republicans have succeeded in placing in the Gubernatorial chair their candidate, and for the first time also, they have a *majority* of members in the house of representatives. On this subject we would not affect an indifference—for we frankly confess we sincerely rejoice at the arrival of that epoch which we have labored for so long a time to bring about: but on the other hand, we are far—very far we think from exulting over a prostrate enemy. We believed that the persons who governed this state, independent of their hostility to the general government, had been in power long enough—that they were tied up to a system which is poorly adapted to the present exigencies of the state, but which they could not without the loss of power abandon—we therefore were willing to see them displaced by men, who we hope, will adopt a system of liberality and toleration—a system of equality in religious and political rights. We trust the time has arrived when a democrat can be named without having attached to his character a term of *reproach,* and when the offices in the gift of the legislature will not be confined to a religious sect, or political party. ...[15]

In contrast, the reporting by Republican papers outside of Connecticut took a much more jubilant tone, especially in the papers of Boston:

☞ *All hail, Sister Connecticut!*

We have the satisfaction of announcing that in the long-benighted State of Connecticut, Republicanism has at length most gloriously triumphed. There can be no doubt of the election of the Hon. OLIVER WOLCOTT as Governor of that State. ... "On the decisive evidence furnished of the

---

15. *American Mercury,* Hartford, CT, April 15, 1817, 2.

election of Mr. WOLCOTT, (remarks the Hartford Times) we congratulate most sincerely all our friends, and indeed the whole community, which has the deepest and happiest interest in the result of this election." It is, indeed, a most glorious event; and the more so, as Connecticut has *never before had a Republican Governor.* The atrocious and disorganizing principles which gave birth to the *Hartford Convention,* become every day more and more unpopular, and will finally be scouted even from Connecticut.[16]

⤷

"Roll on, loved Connecticut."

The election of a Republican Governor in Connecticut is a great event. Connecticut was federalism's *last hope.* It was the rock of their salvation. It was their sheet-anchor— their last remaining stay—the *nucleus,* around which all the discordant fragments of which their party was composed were accustomed to form and conglobate. In losing Connecticut, they lose all; and may now be looked upon as shipwrecked mariners, tossing upon the seas in a crazy weather-beaten bark without rudder or compass. The republicans, as magnanimous as they are successful, disdain to exalt over a fallen foe, and stretch forth a friendly hand to their drowning opponents. All they ask in return, after assisting them to get on board the good old live oak timbered ship UNCLE SAM, is, that they will not mutiny a second time, and again endeavor to run the ship into Regent's cove, or to strand her on the flats between Capes *Henry* and *Convention.* Should they offend a second time in this way, they will inevitably be hanged at the yard arm, without benefit even of Connecticut clergy.[17]

⤷

Toleration and Consistency predominant over the "Blue

16. *Boston Patriot,* Boston, MA, April 12, 1817, 2.
17. Ibid., April 16, 1817, 2.

Lights" of Connecticut.—The late election in the State of Connecticut, (says the N.Y. Republican Chronicle) has terminated in the probable success of the candidates held up by the Republicans and friends of tolerant principles, for Governor and Lieut. Governor. From several letters from Gentlemen in different parts of that State, we are pleased in being able to announce this agreeable information, and likewise to anticipate that there will be a Republican Majority in the Assembly; a circumstance which never occurred in that State—and which the friends to *lights* that are *blue,* and *Conventions* that are *infamous,* have often said never, never should take place.

Feeling an interest in a success so unexpected, a correspondent observes, that in all probability, if union and harmony continues among the Republicans another year, nothing but the acts of the late predominant party in that State will be left to keep in remembrance, the power of an execrable junto, and it is hoped that the first proceedings of a new administration, will be to call a convention for forming of a Constitution, with which the State never yet has been blessed, unless King Charles' Charter, and volumes of *Blue Laws* can be considered as such.[18]

It was upon hearing the results of this spring election that Thomas Jefferson, over fifteen years after writing his famous "wall of separation" letter to Connecticut's Danbury Baptists, wrote to John Adams:

... for what need we despair of after the resurrection of Connecticut to light and liberality. I had believed that, the last retreat of Monkish darkness, bigotry, and abhorrence of those advances of the mind which had carried the other states a century ahead of them. they seemed still to be exactly where their forefathers were when they schismatised from the Covenant of works, and to consider, as dangerous heresies, all innovations good or bad. I join you therefore in sincere congratulations that this den of the priesthood is at

18. *Independent Chronicle,* Boston, MA, April 17, 1817, 2.

length broken up, and that a protestant popedom is no
longer to disgrace the American history and character.[19]

Leading up to the fall election, with its all-important contest for
Council nominees, the Federalists revived their old scare tactics
from years past. The Republicans were once again called Jacobins,
tools of Bonaparte, and religion was of course in danger.

> ... Since the Jacobins of Connecticut commenced a series
> of desperate exertions for the ascendancy in State Govern
> ment, their great object has been to convince the people,
> that the federalists have not only differed from *them* in point
> of principle, but from all wise and good men; not content
> with attacking their political tenets, which in practice, have
> so long rendered the government of Connecticut the happi-
> est on earth—they have professed to espy a monster in the
> religion of their opponents, and endeavored to cloth the
> pretended Bugbear in the dress of Inquisitorial Persecution.
> ... Bonaparte probably owed more of his success, to his
> Emissaries, (whose business was to corrupt the people and
> divide the government marked for his prey) than to his
> arms.—Mankind are influenced only by motives, and when
> the motives to be held out, are manifestly *bad,* they can of
> course effect nothing, until those whom they are intended
> to influence are rendered regardless of their moral nature.—
> The Jacobins of Connecticut have for a long time reasoned
> in this manner, and for the purpose of preparing the people
> to relinquish all claims to whatever is in reality *dear* to
> them, they have begun (in conformity with the precepts and
> example of their Gallic Master,) at the foundation. The corner
> stone of those pillars which support the Temple of Liberty,
> must be removed—THE RELIGION OF THE GOSPEL must be
> brought into disrepute—The strict observance of the Sabbath
> must be rendered unpopular, and those foolish notions
> about morality and good order, so long cherished by the peo-
> ple of Connecticut must be given up. This is no dream, it is

19. Thomas Jefferson to John Adams, May 5, 1817. Albert Ellery Bergh, ed., *The Writings of Thomas Jefferson*, vol. 15, (Washington D.C.: Thomas Jefferson Memorial Association, 1907), 109.

no fiction, but plain matter of fact. There are many Jacobins in the State who wish for this state of things, and who are making all possible exertion to bring it about—most of the writers for the Democratic Newspapers, if we may judge from their productions are of this stamp. They have commenced their operations to be sure with some degree of caution, their first attack is not an open one, made upon religion in general, the people are not yet ripe for such an event, but it is an attack made upon what they are pleased to term "one of the Religious Sects."...

Those people who come out against Congregationalists, in the style which every one may witness who will look into a Democratic Newspaper, and attempt to prove that *"Platformist"* is synonymous with hypocrite and persecutor, are not aiming at *Congregationalists*—this is only a pretence, to conceal the real design.—To Baptists let an appeal be made for a decision—These disciples of Bonaparte profess to hold the Baptists and their religion in high estimation. The Congregationalists and Baptists agree in every thing of any importance, relating to their religious tenets, except in the ordinance of Baptism, and even in this the difference is considered so unimportant, as to render it perfectly proper for the two sects to commune together at the same table.

Now let reason and candor decide, whether an enemy to the religion of a Congregationalist, can be a friend to that of a Baptist, seeing both are acknowledged to be the religion of the Gospel. The same reasoning will hold, in relation to Episcopalians and Methodists.—The truth is, *religion* itself is the thing aimed at, and must be rendered *odious*. ...[20]

The *Courant* argued that Connecticut's laws were perfectly fair to all religious denominations and that the offices of the state were equally obtainable by all. As one example of this claimed equality of all denominations to ascend in office they reached back in history to the ninety-year-old William Samuel Johnson, an Episcopalian who thirty years earlier had represented Connecticut at the Constitutional Convention, and had been one of the state's U.S.

20. *Connecticut Journal*, New Haven, CT, August 12, 1817, 3.

senators in the first Congress in 1789. As another example they used the present lieutenant governor Jonathan Ingersoll, ignoring the obvious fact that the reason Ingersoll was in office was because the Episcopalians had left the Federalist party to put him there.

> ... But a different cause of complaint, and of revolution, has been discovered within a couple of years, which seems to have been urged with an unexpected degree of force and success, in this extraordinary attempt to destroy the state— I allude to the magic word *"TOLERATION."* Yes, without one single obstacle in the way of any class or denomination of christians, either in the acquisition of wealth, the attainment of office, or the gratification of ambition—without one shackle upon the mind, or one ligature on the conscience, it has been discovered, by some profound searcher after political mischief, that somewhere in our system there exists a rigid and unfeeling intolerance. Let the enquiry be put to any one of these reformers of government. Pray, Mr. Alexander Wolcott, or Mr. Abraham Bishop, are you not at liberty to worship God in the way which your judgment dictates, or your conscience approves? If either of you should prefer the episcopal, the baptist, the methodist, or the universal mode of worship & confession of faith, to the congregational, do not the laws make abundant provision for you to pursue your wishes, and obtain the object of your choice? Is there any legal disqualification to your holding any office in the state government, to which the freemen might, if they were disposed, elect you, except, indeed, that you hold offices under the United States, and even that might be removed by resignation? If either of you should be desirous of changing from the denomination of christians to which you now nominally belong, & to join another more consonant to your wishes, are you not at perfect liberty to do it? Where then is there to be found either civil or religious intolerance? Surely it will be difficult to say, as long as the laws equally protect all classes, while the avenues to office are equally open to all, and every man may worship in the mode most agreeable to his conscience, or even his whims.
> But it seems to be supposed, that one particular class of

christians, and that a very respectable one, labour under some hardships of this sort, and on that supposition a perfect phenomenon exists, viz. that of professed presbyterians, baptists, and methodists, and above all, democrats, are full of anxiety, and full of sympathy, for the hardship of the episcopalians. Let the eldest, most intelligent, and pious episcopalians be enquired of on this subject, and see if they will complain of intolerance? Let the aged and venerable JOHNSON, over whose sacred head the last half score years of a century are now fleeting, whose eyes almost see within the veil which separates him from, and whose ears almost hear the songs which are chaunted in, the celestial regions, whether through his long life he has endured the pangs of intolerance from the government of his native state? Ask the present Lieut. Governour, the Speaker of the House of Representatives, two or three members of the Council, and others to whom offices have been recently offered, and rejected, whether they are conscious of any intolerance? And if they, one and all, answer as they must, and as they will cheerfully, in the negative, let the enigma of the extreme solicitude of the various descriptions of persons above-mentioned be solved by whom it may. It is an insult to common sense to pretend that there is any want of toleration in this state, unless it may be the *toleration of vice and immorality.* Yet, strange as it may seem, *"Toleration"* has had seemingly more agency in throwing the state into confusion, and endangering its government, than all other causes put together. Yet, Abraham Bishop, and Alexander Wolcott, and men like these, have discovered that, which has escaped the searching eye of the great Johnson for almost a hundred years. And can it be thought the firm, enlightened, and high minded freemen of this state will yield up all that is valuable and venerable in their government, at such an undefined, unfounded, and ridiculous pretence, as this? Will they leave the rich inheritance derived from their ancestors, for such a jack-a-lantorn as these restless, designing, and vindictive men have set up? ... [21]

---

21. *The Connecticut Courant,* Hartford, CT, September 2, 1817, 1.

In its last issue before the election, which carried on its front page a large advertisement for the Toleration ticket for Council nominations, the *Connecticut Herald,* which had changed hands and was now a Republican paper, urged the Episcopalians and other dissenters to vote the "Platform Aristocracy" out, relying on the issue that had brought the Republicans such success in the spring — the Appropriation Act:

To Episcopalians and the Minor Sects.

The Aristocrats request you to vote on the 15th inst. for their Nomination of Councillors, most of whom were bitterly inimical to granting you that proportion of the Phœnix Bonus which was equitably your due. They desire you to support those men, who, one year since, by their famous Appropriation of one hundred and forty-five thousand dollars, attempted to purchase your consciences with a sum of money, the greater part of which they have not obtained, and probably never will.

Indeed, they did not expect to obtain it when they passed the bill for the appropriation. Suppose, however, that contrary to all probability, the whole amount of the $145,000 should be allowed by the General Government— This allowance would not put the case of our appropriators upon better footing. ...

... Because, the Episcopalians, (to quiet whom, as well as to coax over the other minor denominations, the appropriation was made,) it is well known, never asked, expected or wished to receive their just proportion of the Phœnix Bonus from *this* sum of 145,000 dollars, or from any other fund than that which was intended by the petitioners for the Phœnix Bank to be applied to their benefit. The Episcopalians, together with all the minor sects, *contributed by taxes equally in proportion to their numbers, with the prevailing religious denomination,* to the one hundred and forty-five thousand dollars; and the Episcopalians and minor sects have no greater proportionate share of the sum than the Congregationalists—that is to say, they all share in exact proportion as they paid; or in other words, according to their numbers. Yet in the face of this undeniable truth, the champions of this Platform Aristocracy took great credit in themselves for their generosity to the Episcopalians, Methodists and Baptists. Singular generosity, indeed! and what renders it still more striking is, that Yale College also comes in for a large share, independent of the great sum which is specifically given to the Congregational denomination! The share of Yale College is equal to that of the whole body of Episcopalians. If the principle of the appropriation be sanctioned, the precedent will authorize some future Legislature to levy a direct tax upon the people, either to support any of the minor denominations, or perhaps to prop up the dominant one which has hitherto been effectively the established religion in Connecticut. ...

Episcopalians, Baptists and Methodists!—You are requested to examine attentively the features of the celebrated Appropriation Act, and to form your unbiased opinion whether it was passed to promote its declared, ostensible object, "literature and religion," or whether it was passed for the purpose of buying the votes of the minor religious denominations. It has been frequently said that the last mentioned purpose was hinted at even in the House during the passage of the bill, and was directly mentioned out of doors by some of the advocates of the Appropriation, in order to obtain the consent of those religious dissenters who were federalists. It is notorious, that immediately after its passage, the Platform Aristocrats publicly boasted that the Appropriation had given the death-blow to Republicanism. ...[22]

In the same issue, the *Herald* exhorted its readers to "Stand Up" in the face of the Stand Up Law that had intimidated voters for so many years:

☞ STAND UP! STAND UP!
"United, let us STAND"

FELLOW-FREEMEN—On your votes next Monday, for

22. *Connecticut Herald*, New Haven, CT, September 9, 1817, 1-2.

Assistants, depend perhaps the future good or evil destinies of the State.

If you are opposed to a "host" of Lawyers for Councillors, and are friendly to the Ticket which is proportionally composed of Farmers, Merchants, Mechanics, and Lawyers, be in season at the polls on Monday, STAND UP for the TOLERATION Ticket, and remain until the whole list is voted for.

If you disapprove the secret sittings of our past and present Councils—if you believe the "Stand-up Law" to be oppressive in its operation, and the Upper House reprehensible for their stubbornness in refusing to concur with the Lower House in its repeal—manifest your displeasure by a general STANDING UP.

If you are adverse to a Union of Church and State, fearlessly discountenance the adulterous connexion, by STANDING UP.

If you condemn the late appropriation of $145,000, say so by STANDING UP. ...

If you would have a written Constitution, defining the powers and duties of our State Rulers, STAND UP and vote for the friends of such a Constitution.

If you think it equitable that the public offices should be distributed among honest and capable men of every religious and political denomination throughout the State, declare it by STANDING UP.

If you are anxious that the State government should harmonize with that of the Union, you will STAND UP for the Friends of the Union.

In a word, if you would for ever prevent another Convention in the State to plot treason—if you would at once get rid of the frowns, the gibes and jeers of a set of supercillious patricians—if you would put down Aristocracy in Connecticut at a single blow—*NOW* is your most favourable opportunity—STAND UP as one, on Monday next, and the victory is yours.—A determined boldness and an Union of Effort will insure a permanent triumph to the friends on Toleration.[23]

---

23. *Connecticut Herald,* New Haven, CT, September 9, 1817, 3.

And stand up they did. Every single one of the Toleration Ticket's twenty nominees was chosen, guaranteeing that as of the following May the entire Council would be Republican. And, as both the *Mercury* and the *Register* reported, the Republican majority in the House of Representatives would be at least 50.

Republicanism Triumphant.

We have the high satisfaction of informing our readers, who have anxiously waited for the result of the recent election, that the republican ticket for councillors has entirely succeeded, by a large majority. The odious *stand-up law,* under which the present council compelled us to vote, had lost its terrors, and that aristocratic influence, which had so long awed the freemen, vanished before the firmness of their united exertions. The 15th of September 1817 will ever be remembered with undissembled pleasure, by the long oppressed republicans of the State of Connecticut.

No longer shall we be pointed out as a dim star in the national constellation, but united and reformed, we shall co-operate with the general government, both in the defence of our rights and in the establishment of a national character.

We indulge the grateful prospect, of a reign of peace and of principle, when the weapons of party scurrility will be blunted and the bonds of oppression will be broken asunder. Our political opponents have long claimed all the religion, wealth and talents in the State, but their pretensions, like their ungentlemanly abuse and scurrility, have lost their weight. The cloak of pretended sanctity may protect for a while, but the spirit of truth will at length expose the false covering of the impostor.

Republicanism now stands forth *"bearing her own proper name and character;"* and as earnestly invites the scrutiny and liberal comment of the upright politician, as she compassionately despises the low slander and malice of the modern scribblers for the aristocratic papers. Republicans make no pretensions to perfection, but they have so much respect for themselves as to demand their rights.

Our majority in the house of Representatives will be between fifty and sixty, enough to protect us from the dying malice of exasperated Aristocracy, which so much annoyed us at the Spring Session.

We feel ourselves simply rewarded for the years of toil, and the torrents of abuse, which we have suffered, and hope to enjoy under an equitable administration the peace of neighbours and the rights of freemen.[24]

⌒

Final Result.

In our last we stated that the republican majority in the popular branch of the next legislature, could not vary much from 45.—It seems now to be generally admitted that it will exceed 50. Litchfield county sends 16 republicans, instead of 11, as we supposed. The majority on the Council Ticket, it is believed, will exceed 2500.

On this auspicious result, we cannot forebear making further remarks. It is well known that the aristocratic faction expected much assistance from the "stand up law"—that on this law they placed their chief dependence—coolly calculating that the independent freemen of Connecticut were to be intimidated in their attempts to effect a reform and obtain equal rights; but the event is highly honorable to them; and we believe it will prove a lasting blessing to the State,—inasmuch as it has shown the citizens that the sovereign power is in their hands—that their rulers are their servants, and accountable to them for their conduct; and we trust our citizens will hereafter view the measures of their rulers with the eyes of freemen, jealous of their rights.

There is a class of men particularly, whom we congratulate with the most heartfelt satisfaction on this triumph: we mean those republicans who have for seventeen years borne the brunt and heat of action. Republicans! you have at last beheld in Connecticut the victory of principle over superstition, bigotry, intolerance and hypocrisy: You have

---

24. *American Mercury*, Hartford, CT, September 23, 1817, 3.

seen your fellow-citizens adopt the very sentiments and measures you advocated, and for which you have been persecuted and stigmatized with every epithet which a depraved heart could invent—and your principles have not only been adopted, but they have been adopted with a pleasure and satisfaction surpassing the most sanguine anticipation.

Nor indeed is the result much less uninteresting to the republican youth of Connecticut: treading in the steps of their worthy sires, and directed by their own convictions of truth, rather than the mandates of aristocratic partizans, they were becoming the objects of hatred and persecution to the ruling party.—We hope they will no longer be obliged to seek the wilderness for a home and society [25] —but that they may enjoy the comforts of civilized life in the land of their fathers.

To the friends of civil and religious liberty, not only in our own state, but throughout the union, the triumph of toleration will be a subject of rejoicing.

But we would warn our fellow-citizens, that although our enemies have been conquered, they are not annihilated— although they have been driven from the field, they yet lie in the marshes and fens of some appropriation law or freemen grinder; and it becomes us still to be on the alert— still to consider that we are in the neighborhood of an enemy who want nothing but power to place us in the situation from which we have just extricated ourselves. [26]

The *Courant*, the *Mirror*, and the *Journal* reported the story that no Federalist would have dreamed they'd ever be reporting seventeen years earlier when they predicted with much certainty that Connecticut's Republican party would last but a few years.

THE ELECTION.

It is now ascertained that the democratic, *alias* the

25. A problem that had plagued Connecticut for years was its loss of significant portion of its younger population who were emigrating to the Republican western states in droves.
26. *Columbian Register,* New Haven, CT, September 27, 1817, 3.

toleration, *alias* the republicans, *alias* the union and reform ticket for nomination has prevailed by a large majority; and that the house of representatives will contain only about 80 federalists of 201 members. Such a revolution in a state so signal for its steady habits, may excite surprise among our friends through the Union. To those who have witnessed, for the last eighteen months, the course pursued by those who wished to revolutionize the state, and by those who wished, in *any event,* to be secure with the strongest party, the event creates much less surprise than mortification, and much less indignation than contempt. ...

We rejoice in the reflection of seventeen years so many freemen have remained firm and incapable of seduction— that neither the flattery of courtiers, nor the falsehoods of unprincipled jacobins, nor the treachery of traitors, could shake the most upright, the most intelligent, and most valuable part of this community. To those of our political friends who have come from this fiery trial, glorying in the principles of Washington, and rejoicing that they are federalists, we look with no common feelings of respect and attachment. To those few who have sustained an elevated course till they saw a Lion in the way, we wish a more desirable retreat than they will probably find; and to those small lawyers in various parts of the state, somewhat large in numbers but small in every other view, who have meanly deserted the federal standard, to obtain the loaves and fishes of office, we wish the crumbs which fall from the tables of full grown democrats.

We will only add that the most foul falsehoods respecting men and measures have been propagated to deceive the people; and that news-papers teeming with such malignant slanders have been carried to the doors of thousands who have had no opportunity to be undeceived. It would have been strange if such engines of evil had been harmless— they have done the mischief intended by their authors, who look with peculiar delight upon their baneful effects. To such we may speak at a more leisure moment.[27]

27. *The Connecticut Courant,* Hartford, CT, September 23, 1817, 3.

It falls to our lot, this day to record the complete success of the democratic party in this State. A majority of between 40 and 50 in the house, and between 1000 and 2000 votes for their council ticket, attest their triumph. To our friends abroad it may be unexpected; but those who have watched the course of things in this State, for some time past, cannot be surprised. As the constant dropping of water will wear even upon stone, so the constant abuse of men and measures, may leave an impression upon the hearer—and a falsehood often repeated may be made to pass for truth. Those who have seen our democratic papers for some time past, will be at no loss for an application of these remarks. Torrents of scurrility have been constantly issuing from these fountains, upon men the most respectable, and upon institutions the most venerable. Every artifice has been used which ingenuity could devise, and every misrepresentation made which could be tortured into plausibility. Every passion has been enlisted, and every prejudice has been excited. A religious warfare has been attempted to be enkindled in the 19th century, and these modern Crusaders with the talisman "toleration" for their banner, have, like Peter the Hermit, filled their ranks with men, panting for the success of what they would consider, a holy war.

In addition to this, our opponents have attempted to make the people believe they were about to reform abuses, and unite parties, and with the magic words, "toleration," "reform" and "union," democracy has accomplished in a few months what she attempted in vain, for years, when she stood forth bearing her own proper name and character.

That many have been deceived by the new names which have been assumed, and the professions which have been made, there can be no doubt—we hope however they will not be of the number of those "who love to have it so,"

It now remains to be seen whether democracy will perform the promises she has made, whether the golden dreams she has excited will be realized—whether her toleration permits any difference of opinion upon political subjects—whether her pretended union is any thing more than a permission to unite in thinking and acting with her,

whether the new public officers will really be better friends
to the people, more disinterested, more patriotic than their
predecessors—or whether these pretences have been held
forth as passports to office.

And if it should appear that these men, while pretending
to seek the people's good, have merely meant their own—
we trust there is still a redeeming spirit in this State, which
will teach demagogues that altho' for a while our Freemen may
be deceived, yet that in the end, imposture cannot triumph.[28]

The election has terminated in a result unfavourable to
Federalism, and of consequence, as we in our souls believe,
unfavourable to the highest and dearest interests of Connecticut. What Federalists might have done to avert this
calamity from the land of steady habits, of correct morals,
and of true civil and religious liberty, it is not our purpose
at present to enquire. The calamity is upon us, the report
of it has gone abroad, and we must stand in the view of our
sister states, disrobed of that high character for political
firmness, and for hatred of rash innovation, and unshaken
attachment to the free and venerable institutions of our
ancestors, which have always been the glory of Connecticut,
and made her sons in every clime proud of the land of their
nativity. A restless party, which has long been organized
against our government, and which for two years past has
been industriously stirring up every thing that is odious in
bigotry, and every thing that is contemptible in faction, in
pursuit of that power which they had neither the virtue
nor the talents to attain by other means, have at length
accomplished their object. For a season at least we must
suffer the disgrace, and if we escape with disgrace only, if
in the madness of revolution our institutions are not pros-
trated, and our morals not lost, we may think ourselves
happy indeed.

The period has at length arrived in Connecticut, when

28. *Connecticut Mirror*, Hartford, CT, September 22, 1817, 3.

Rulers of great experience, of acknowledged talents, of tried and spotless character, and of at least as much public or private virtues as their opponents, are unceremoniously driven from office,—and for what? What evil have they done? What sober man, accustomed to observe public affairs, can review their long and peaceful administration, without astonishment at the folly of those, who could wish to dismiss experienced and faithful public servants merely for the sake of a *change*. The men who have come into power, have performed no public services which would entitle them to claim office as the reward of their merit; nor have they heretofore furnished us any very high evidence of their superior ability to their predecessors. The great principles which have always kept them together as a party, have not recommended them to the confidence of the people, for their principles ever have been odious, and we believe they were never more odious than at the present moment to the great majority of the Freemen of the State.—Something beside their own merits or the principles upon which their party was formed, the leading democrats well know, has had a powerful agency in bringing them into office.

What is to be the effect of this Revolution? If we have not got wiser or purer men than before, shall we have wiser or better laws? Can it be supposed that our burthens will be lighter, or that we shall enjoy more tranquility and genuine liberty than we have done? Shall we be more respectable abroad when our present Councillors retire into private life, and leave their places to be filled by men of the Democratic Ticket? We know how these questions will strike every Freeman in the State, and we only wish they had been more seriously weighed and reflected upon before the late election.[29]

With Republican control of both houses of the legislature guaranteed in the spring, the year of 1817 ended with the first of many town meetings that would be held across the state in the coming months, passing resolutions to instruct their representatives

29. *Connecticut Journal*, New Haven, CT, September 23, 1817, 3.

in the next General Assembly to make the push for a convention to form a real state constitution.

STATE CONSTITUTION.

At a meeting of the friends of Toleration and Reform, holden at Cheshire, on the 10th November, 1817, the following preamble and resolves were approved and adopted:
Whereas, we firmly believe that "all men are created equal, and endowed with certain unalienable rights." That the power and right of self government are inherent in the people. That rulers possess no power, but by express delegation. That in the formation of Society for the mutual safety and benefit, each citizen by compact, resigns a portion of his natural rights to the body corporate. That this body politic, thus formed, and vested with authority by the individuals who compose it, must delegate certain powers and privileges to those who are elected to manage the public concerns. That the perfection of every government depends upon its written Constitution, and a faithful administration; and that rights and power not expressly delegated, are reserved to the people.

Resolved, as the sense of this meeting, that a written Constitution, defining precisely the powers of the rulers, and securing the invaluable rights of the citizens, is indispensably necessary in every well regulated State—and we hereby recommend that our representatives be instructed to use their influence in the next General Assembly, to induce that honorable body to recommend to the people of this State to choose delegates, for the purpose of forming a Constitution of civil government, to be submitted to the people for their consideration and adoption.

Resolved, That the inhabitants of the several towns in this State be, and they are hereby requested to adopt such measures as they shall judge best calculated to effect this desirable object. ...[30]

---

30. *American Mercury,* Hartford, CT, November 25, 1817, 3.

STATE CONSTITUTION.

At a Town Meeting legally warned and held in Stamford, on the 15th day of December, 1817, the following resolutions were passed, viz:

Resolved, 1st, That we deem the civil liberties of the inhabitants of this State as insecure without a written Constitution, bounding and defining the Legislative and Executive powers of the government.

Resolved, 2d, That we do not find in the Charter of Charles 2d. of England, declared as the Constitution of this State by an authority wholly incompetent to such a purpose, any of the essential requisites of a Constitution of civil government in a Republican country. Therefore,

Resolved, 3dly., That the Representatives of this town, in the next ensuing Legislature, be instructed to use their utmost influence in procuring a convention of delegates for the purpose of framing a Constitution of civil government for this State. ....[31]

From the *Mercury* — an allegorical recap of Connecticut's long struggle between her Federalists and her ultimately victorious Republicans:

MARRIED.

On the 15th of September last. MISS STEADYHABIT CONNECTICUT, to the AMERICAN REPUBLIC.

This young lady was married many years since to her present spouse, with whom she had a violent quarrel, living at open variance with him for a long time, and about three years ago threatened TO SEPARATE FOREVER. She was instigated to this outrageous conduct by her elder sister Massachusetts, who, being a jealous shrew, was never contented unless she could rule every thing herself, and therefore took desperate dudgeon because her sister Virginia was preferred by most of the family. The unfortunate dis-

---

31. *Connecticut Herald,* New Haven, CT, December 23, 1817, 3.

agreement between Miss Steadyhabit and her spouse was in a train of reconciliation last spring, and, maugre the insidious efforts of certain cunning councillors of wrath, was happily adjusted to entire satisfaction on the 15th of September past. The grand nuptial festivities will not, however, take place before next May, as some of the aforesaid strife-seeking Councillors claim, by virtue of a lease, to hold possession of the Hall of Ceremonies, called the Council Chamber, until that time. The former marriage was considered so nearly dissolved in every thing but name, that it was thought proper to have the parties concerned, go over the ceremony of Marriage again.—This even forms a new æra in the annals of *New* England, which will shortly, we trust, have no more relationship with *Old* England than is to be found in the partial resemblance of their names. Now that Miss Steadyhabit has escaped from the leading-strings of her sister Massachusetts, and declined the further guardianship of Old England whose views she begins to understand, it is supposed that little Rhoda will free herself entirely from the control of the Essex Junto, and even that many "good men and true" who belong to the household of Massachusetts will open her eyes also, to the error of her ways and to a just perception of the characters of those who, by their wicked delusions, have degraded her in the estimation of the world, and by their artful and patricidal conduct "kicked into a war" the whole American family of the Union, and then attempted to render it disastrous and disgraceful. ...

... The "famous Doctor"—JOHN HENRY—said, some years ago, that Miss Connecticut needed no change—but many physicians of sagacity had ascertained that the Constitution, *if worthy of being so called,* was almost good for nothing, decided that a change was indispensably necessary. They knew that she had been a great time troubled with hysterics, with wind in the stomach and intestinal passages, the most rigid constipations, and tenesmus, with flatulent cholics, nausea, extreme chills, heart burning, eructations, depression of spirits, superstitious vapours, and with all the childish bugbears of a disordered fancy. She would sometimes conceit that all the meeting houses were going to be pulled down about her ears—then take it into her head that all the bibles belonging to her family were going to be burnt up, and actually once went so far as to prepare for burying them in order to ensure their safety. Some of her servants who were right-cunning craftsmen, fellows of marvelous acuteness and of most prolific invention in the trade and mystery of story telling, used to delight in worrying the poor lady almost out of her senses. They likewise, frequently practised optical tricks upon her by saddling her nose with a pair of *Magical Spectacles* so contrived as to turn objects up side down—in consequence whereof her vision, by long habit, became perverse to that degree that, even without her glasses, it converted, like a *camera obscura*, every thing she beheld. Nay more, the *Magical Spectacles* had so completely disordered her visual faculties that when by chance she happened not to wear them, the most extraordinary deceptions of sight perpetually tormented her. She supposed both men and women were walking upon their heads. She would take the most harmless domestic animals for beasts of prey, and one night she disturbed the whole family, and not a soul could get a wink of sleep, as she clamorously persisted that a little bob-tailed cur which had slipped into her room, was a huge mammoth pursuing her through the woods. At another time she went half crazy from mistaking some kittens newly littered, for furious tigers come to devour her alive and whole, and had like to have burnt down her house by throwing blazing fire-brands at them to frighten them away. In process of time her other senses became affected—the nerves of her ears were so tremblingly susceptible that the slightest motion of air sounded to her like a tornado, and she once went into a swoon from her alarm at the chirping of a nest of young chimney-swallows just hatched, which she insisted was the screaming of Vultures in the act of destroying the tenants of her poultry-yard.

Some laborers who cultivated her farm and who were attached to her former spouse, were forced to sleep in the barn both summer and winter. Whenever they endeavored to come inside of the house for shelter or protection, the facetious knaves within set up a dismal hue and cry, in which the good lady joined to the very top of her lungs, exclaiming that all the maids would certainly be ruined. At such times she would invariably be overtaken with extremely sanctimonious fits, in consequence of some sly doses given her by her roguish servants, under the name of reviving drops. She would then sit down, cross the bridge of her nose with the Magical Spectacles and sing some staves of a hymn so loudly through her nasal organ, that she might be heard half a mile off, to the great annoyance of the neighborhood, who were a religious, good sort of people, but who, nevertheless, thought there was a proper time for all things, and who, from constantly observing that her devotional fits always came on much stronger just as she was in the greatest heat of the quarrel with her spouse or with the laborers attached to his cause, shrewdly suspected her of a little sanctimonious affectation and pharisaical ostentation.—It was amusing to see the conduct of the arch jugglers of house servants upon these occasions. They would form a complete circle round their mistress, carry up the stave in a truly edifying manner, sometimes shut their eyes as if in a trance of ecstasy, at other times open them and roll them back so far that nothing but the whites could be discerned. Now and then, when they thought they were unobserved, they would interchange jokes in whispers accompanied by winks, shrugs and ill-suppressed tittering, at the success of their artifices. But the moment they knew they were looked at by others, their faces were as long and as demure as ever. Some of them would seize the opportunity of the good lady's fits of devotion to creep secretly into the pantry or cellar, to make sure of a dainty tid-bit or some refreshing cordial that might comfort the inward man of the stomach—while others who were always promoting law suits and spouting in court, got suitably rewarded for their zeal by appointments from chief butler, steward, &c. down to bottle corker, dog whipper & overseer of the henroost. It was remarked that the last mentioned spouting, wind selling set, after joining in the devotional conferences of the house with solemn visages, at least half a yard in longitude, were frequently, when in private among themselves, a little humorous and sarcastic upon the scenes they had just left—but of this the good lady knew nothing, for they wore a most rigid, screwed-up aspect in her presence, especially at the period- ical seasons when they went to quarreling with her spouse and his trusty servants. Then was there a most doleful spirit—a most soul stirring and ear confounding noise— then, indeed, were the ram's horns blown before the wall of Jericho. Such a hurly-burly was raised that a quiet drowsy headed, way-faring man could scarcely sleep in his bed for the clatter. Then a trained troop of as valiant and trusty squires errant as the renowned Sancho Panza, being for the most part litigant spouters, some manfully mounted on their Dapples, others on their Rozinantes, each one armed with an enormous bag of wind, rode constantly, by night and by day round the neighborhood at full gallop, with huge speak- ing-trumpets in their gaping mouths and blowing out from their air swollen, bursting cheeks the horrid sounds of "Infidels, Jacobins, Vandals, Anthropophage, Heathens, Ruffians, Scoundrels, Democrats, Villains, and Devils incar- nate!!!! Down with them, destroy them, or else we shall be all murdered and ravished. We are going to be attacked by ragamuffin cannibals who will first eat *us* without cooking and then swallow up *themselves!!*"—Handbills too, as large as the side of a house, and in types as big as little boys, were scattered upon the four great winds. To catch these awful tidings every eye, every ear and every mouth was a jar for some eight or ten days and nights. The simple folk looked sillier, and the wise men of Gotham looked wiser than ever. The wise conjurers of the East, wore such ambiguous, knowing physiognomies that if their constant activity had permitted them to be caught by a portrait painter, they would have furnished him with so many legitimate like- nesses of Solomon. In the mean time the litigant troopers were not idle, though often sore galled, they deserved well of their country by riding and laboring hard for their poste- riors—that is, for the posterior part of the human race which follow them in the capacity of lineal descendants. Ever and anon, these redoubtable cavaliers obstreperously let off their bags of wind with marvelous dexterity. Incontinently thereupon all the old women fainted, the young ones shrieked, while the little boys set up their shrill pipes and cried as if their hearts would break.—The whole family were nearly terrified to death at hearing the hideous stories of gumbolumbo, of raw-head and bloody bones, and other nursery tales of terror which had long been told to scare children, and some old women in breeches and others in petticoats.—"Keep them out—kill them," was the universal cry of the house servants, and whenever two or three of the honest ploughmen who cultivated the farm, and who were harmless as the man in the Moon were seen together, they were immediately denounced as philosophers, illuminati, assassins, incendiaries, and outlaws, utterly unfit to live. Then those within doors prayed and preached most efficaciously against them, and made such wailings, such woe begone vinegar countenances, and such puritanical exhortations, that a stranger would have thought himself suddenly carried back to the days of Oliver Cromwell and his celebrated Rump Parliament.—Prodigies & wonderful things happened to the great consternation of Miss Steadyhabit and divers others of her family. Strange sights and apparitions were seen which set the dogs a-barking, made horses break their bridles, and once, as it is credibly reported, caused a brindled cow to be taken in labor before her time. Windmills built of paper and pasteboard were raised, then attacked and destroyed by swords, muskets and artillery. Terrible giants were killed who were made up of rags and straw, expressly to be hacked to pieces. Shouts of applause followed these noble feats of arms—the speaking-trumpets sounded a salute of thanks, and the wind troopers wriggled almost lustily.

Things went on thus for some time—at length, all liberty of opinion on religious points was interdicted—a certain creed was promulgated, from which none must dare to deviate on penalty of excommunication.—Peradventure, it may have been fortunate for the Hebrew Jews that none of them were to be found in the household. Nor were there any Mahometans, Geentoos, Tunkers or Swedenborgians—nor any Roman Catholics, albeit there was much discussion as touching manifold hidden mysteries. Neither were there, according to report, any open and acknowledged Socinians, a sect held in particular abhorrence, and perchance, one of these unlucky gentry, if fairly caught in a brimstone rat trap, would have owed his security from being boiled, barbecued or roasted, at least as much to the want of power to do it as to any other three united reasons in the whole chapter of Steady habit liberality, as then explained and understood.—Indeed, opinions of all kinds were to be exactly squared according to a regular pattern publicly established and elevated upon a lofty and terrific Platform. Some old and faithful servants were turned, neck and heels, out of the house, for the heresy of not implicitly believing that their valetudinarian mistress possessed the best possible Constitution in the whole universe. Whoever dared to doubt this dogma, which for a long period was a principal test of orthodoxy, was unceremoniously branded with the stigmatizing appellations of "Jacobin, infidel, heretic and whig," & all who were supposed to harbor any lurking feelings of common christian charity to Miss Steadyhabit's spouse, were called "pests of society," shunned like nefarious malefactors, and delivered over to the most slanderous calumnies, until they recanted their odious sentiments, when they were again declared to be virtuous and honest. But so long as they persisted in their charitable opinions, it was a common custom with the troopers aforementioned and the training bands of the household whenever they met the poor heretics to salute them with cards of compliment to their unfortunate wives and children, who were almost equally excluded from the pale of social communion. This plan was of an admirable contrivance and effect; for by keeping their mistress at variance with her lawful spouse, the confidential servants controlled her, and managed all her concerns according to their own good pleasure with high hand and much profit to themselves and no one dared to say "why do ye thus?"

Their undisputed authority made them exceedingly bold, and they prohibited many things not before looked upon as sinful. Sunday divertisements, not deemed improper in most parts, were severely handled. The game of football was beheld with eyes of reprobation, because it threw the persons of men into unseemly postures, and caused them to leave that line of perpendicular uprightness which they should constantly preserve in all their actions.—Three old women were sorely admonished in public meeting, for having got together on Saturday evening on private business, and drank Souchong & mumbled a little buttered biscuit.— A journeyman leather-breeches maker was hotly reprimanded for dancing cut out jiggs with a traveling bellows mender and two barber's apprentices, every Tuesday and Friday evening for a whole fortnight together—a sport to which they were much addicted, and which was unanimously declared to be not only unprofitable, but a profane and unlawful amusement. It was also taken into grave and serious consideration whether the ancient Blue Laws should not be enforced so far as to cause the hair of the whole household to be cut in one sober, uniform manner, by clapping the half of a pumpkin shell upon their heads; and moreover, certain of the more zealous did propose to renew the good old practice of whipping a barrel of beer for working upon the Sabbath.

While matters proceeded in this wise, the house-jugglers chuckled mightily and laughed in their sleeves to see how swimmingly their schemes were going on. But it fell out at last that sundry difficulties arose in the household. The jugglers were suspected of conniving with a certain violent man named Bullcalf, sometimes called Bulwark, who strove hard to get away the extensive family lands, an estate of great value; and they were likewise accused of divers other evil practices. They now began to be sore afraid lest they should be dismissed from their places of honor and profit which they had held exclusively for so many years, as it were by chartered right, and which they hoped to render *offices in fee simple* to themselves and their heirs forever. Whereupon, being in grievous tribulation, they bethought themselves of a crafty device. They went forthwith to the treasury that held the money in which each man of the household, and of the farm, had thrown in a purse containing his equal part, and they took up each man's purse, and, with a deceitful ceremony nicknamed "Appropriation," they carried it to him, saying, "Dearly beloved! surely thou needest help to pay for thine education and for the preaching of the Gospel. Lo! here is money therefor, which we give unto thee. Come now, let us be good friends together, and do thou be grateful to us for the gift, and do thy uttermost to persuade our mistress to continue us in our offices."—Thereat many waxed wroth and said, "Verily, this money is our own and not yours—ye have no right to give it away. Ye would purchase our consciences with a bribe, and moreover would buy us with our own money. Depart from us and avoid our hot indignation, oh! ye generation of vipers!"—This and other high handed offences, came at last to the knowledge of their mistress, who now began to think that much wrong had been worked by the confidential servants of her household. The physicians who understood her disorder, her secret infirmities, and the impositions practised upon her by the jugglers, were admitted to her presence. They immediately prescribed a Reform of regimen. They administered salutary Alternatives which were completely successful in renovating her system. With returning health of body the sanity of intellect was restored. She no longer implicitly believed the scare-crow tales fabricated by her principal domestics. She undertook to think and to examine for herself—found good grounds for her suspicion of their malpractices—indignantly dashed the Magical Spectacles to atoms—dismissed the servants who by their deceptions, had alienated her from her spouse, and cordially re-united herself with him in the bonds of harmony and affection.

FLOREAT REPUBLICA.[32]

---

32. *American Mercury,* Hartford, CT, October 14, 1817, 2.

⌁ 1818 ⌁

Oliver Wolcott and Jonathan Ingersoll were unopposed in the 1818 election. The Republican majority in the House of Representatives remained as large as it had been in the fall, and, as was guaranteed by the nominations in the fall, the Council became entirely Republican. Nothing now stood in the way of altering or repealing the old election, religious, and other laws that the Republicans and religious dissenters found so repugnant, and, of course, nothing stood in the way of calling for a convention to form a state constitution.

At its May session, the legislature passed a resolution calling for a constitutional convention, choosing the 4th of July as the day for the towns to hold an election to select their delegates to the convention. And, because the legislature also passed at its May session a suffrage act extending the right to vote to all white males of twenty-one years who paid taxes or served in the militia and were of good moral character, the election of delegates to the constitutional convention was to be the first election in which many new voters who previously didn't qualify to be freemen were able to vote.

Although the Republicans had a majority of 65 in the House of Representatives, their majority in the convention was much smaller, with nearly as many Federalists as Republicans being chosen to represent their towns in the framing of the constitution.

The convention convened at Hartford on August 26. Governor Wolcott presided, and Pierpont Edwards, the man who had hosted the very first formal meeting of Connecticut's Republican party eighteen years earlier, was elected chairman of the committee to draft the constitution.

Just two days later, on August 28, the committee reported a draft of the preamble and bill of rights to the convention. As journalists were allowed to attend and report on the convention's proceedings, the committee's first report appeared in the newspapers a few days later.

The sections of the bill of rights regarding religious liberty, as reported by the committee, were:

> *Sec.* 3. The exercise and enjoyment of religious profession and worship, without discrimination, shall forever be free to all persons in this State, provided that the right hereby declared and established, shall not be so construed, so as to excuse acts of licentiousness, or to justify practices inconsistent with the peace, and safety, of the State.
>
> *Sec.* 4. No preference shall be given by law, to any religious sect or mode of worship.[1]

On September 1, a debate took place over section 4, when John Treadwell, the Congregationalist former lieutenant governor, one term governor, and delegate to the Hartford Convention, objected to its use of the word "religious" instead of "Christian." Most of this debate was reported in the *Mirror*.

> Mr. Treadwell, wished to move one amendment to the 4th section, which would render it unexceptionable to all parties; he was not ashamed of our religion, or mode of worship; our religion came from God, it was the *Christian* religion: and he knew it to be the power of God unto salvation; he would not change the object of worship; he had no idea of setting up Jupiter, Ammon, of Mahomed, of Confucius, or any other heathen God, as a proper object of worship; nor would he substitute any other worship for that of Jesus Christ, the present mode should not be changed; and here he hoped it would be understood that he had nothing personal in view—that he was expecting no office

---

1. *American Mercury*, Hartford, CT, September 1, 1818, 2.

and no emolument, but being called upon to act as a member of this Convention, he had a duty to discharge, that duty should be conscientiously discharged, and he should not be accountable for any consequences which might result from the Constitution. He was not prepared to place Jesus Christ on par with false Gods, and would therefore move, that the word *"religious"* be erased, and the word "Christian" substituted—so that the section would read, "no preference should be given, by law to any Christian sect, &c." He was willing that all should enjoy equal privileges—that no preference should be given by law to any *Christian* sect—but that in point of law all should be equal—substituting the word Christian for Religious he thought removed the ambiguity and would render the section acceptable to all—as it stood the section might be construed to mean, that no preference should be given to the Christian religion above any other, but he was not prepared to say, that the Christian religion should not be ranked above any other.[2]

Alexander Wolcott, the Republican party leader from years past, and now the leader of the Republican delegates to the convention, questioned Treadwell's intent:

Mr. A. Wolcott, said that he could not find that he had any idea of his own on the subject, but he found some difficulty in settling what the gentleman would mean, or what was intended by the amendment; was it intended to exclude Jews or Mahomedans, or any other religious sect? If the section was designed to place them all on a footing, *well*—but unless that were the case, he was prepared to say that Religion was not an affair of the State. The Convention or the Legislature had nothing to do with the subject; it become necessary to alter the phraseology of the laws, he could not see that they had power to frame such laws, there should be no distinction between Jew and Gentile.[3]

Pierpont Edwards reasoned that not giving a preference to any

2. *Connecticut Mirror*, Hartford, CT, September 7, 1818, 2.
3. Ibid.

Christian sect couldn't infringe the rights of non-Christians, saying: "the Legislature should tolerate Jews and Mahommedans, at the same time, there had never been any in the state, and probably never would be; but if there should, the amendment would not infringe their privileges," and was therefore not opposed to Treadwell's amendment.[4]

After a bit more debate, Treadwell got his way, and "religious" was changed to "Christian."

This change was inconsequential. The debate was yet to come on the infinitely more important section on religious liberty, the article which would abolish the odious certificate law — the "degrading acknowledgements" as the certificates were called by the Danbury Baptists in their 1801 letter to Thomas Jefferson — and put an end to the requirement that everyone belong to some Christian society or congregation. On this section, the Republicans were not going to concede.

This was Article 7, as initially reported by the committee on September 4:

ARTICLE SEVENTH.—RELIGION.

§ 1. It being the right and duty of all men to worship the Supreme Being, the great Creator and Preserver of the universe, in the mode most consistent with the dictates of their consciences; no person shall by law be compelled to join or support, nor be classed with, or associated to any congregation, church or religious association.—And each and every society or denomination of Christians in this state, shall have and enjoy the same and equal powers, rights and privileges; and shall have power and authority to support and maintain the ministers or teachers of their respective denominations, and to build and repair houses for public worship, by a tax on the members of the respective societies only, or in any other manner.

§ 2. If any person shall choose to separate himself from the society or denomination of Christians to which he may belong, and shall leave a written notice thereof with the

4. *Connecticut Mirror*, Hartford, CT, September 7, 1818, 2.

Clerk of such society, he shall thereupon be no longer liable for any future expences which may be incurred by said society.[5]

Not surprisingly, strong objections were raised against this article in the Federalist papers, as in this item from the *Journal:*

… The committee of the Convention have declared in their report that it is "the right and duty of all men to worship the Supreme being," and that the citizens of Connecticut might support religion if they pleased, and not without— that is, in the language of the report, if a person belongs to a particular religious society, "by leaving a written notice with the clerk of such society, he shall thereupon be no longer liable for any future expenses which may be incurred by said society." Here the committee have provided the means by which men may absolve themselves from all civil obligations to support the gospel; they have only to leave their certificate with the clerk of the society to which they belong, and they may support the gospel or not, as they please. A *right* is declared which no one need to exercise— a *duty* is established which no one need perform. This is their boasted Toleration: a toleration to be without religion: a toleration suited to the ideas of a few ambitious leaders, whose whole lives have been at open warfare with all religion; who, for many years, have hung like dark clouds upon our political horizon, portending destruction to the morals of Connecticut. "O my soul, come not thou into their secret: unto their assembly, mine honour, be not thou united."[6]

Article 7 was hotly debated by the convention on September 11, with Treadwell being the first to object to it.

Mr. Treadwell agreed that it was a very important section, and moved to divide the question: the first to be taken on that part of the section ending with the words "or religious association,"—which was agreed to, and he then made the

5. *Norwich Courier,* Norwich, CT, September 9, 1818, 3.
6. *Connecticut Journal,* New Haven, CT, September 15, 1818, 3.

following remarks:—I rise, Sir, for inquiry on this part of the article. As it regards conscience, I know it is the duty of every person to worship the Supreme Being, in spirit and in truth—but conscience may be perverted, and man may think it his duty to worship his creator by images, or as the Romans and Grecians did. My objection, sir, is the word duty. I would tolerate all modes of worship, but would not recognize it in the Constitution, as the duty of a person to worship as the heathens do. Again Sir—"No person shall be compelled to join or support, or by law be classed with, or associated to any congregation, church or religious association." I wish to know the extent of meaning in this expression. If I understand, it goes to dissolve all ecclesiastical societies in the State. Ecclesiastical societies are now associated by law, and have certain privileges by law. This Sir, takes away their rights and privileges, it recognizes no ecclesiastical association, but leaves all, as it were, in a state of nature. Sir, I have no idea of making *distinctions* between different religious denominations; whether congregationalists, episcopalians, baptists or methodists, all should be placed on equal footing. When a particular denomination prevails, I would make it the standing denomination of the place, and others should enjoy the privilege of separating from it. If the episcopalians or baptists prevail, the other denominations should certificate. Sir, there can be no objection to this principle; I know that in most societies, congregationalists prevail, but what then—this makes no distinction, the principle associates no particular denomination by law. But the article dissolves *all* associations: "no person shall be classed with"—now, all persons are classed with and associated together; this is to dissolve the whole union. Sir, I am unwilling that these associations should be thus dissolved; they have rights and privileges, as corporate bodies, and unless they have forfeited those rights, they cannot be justly taken from them. Justice would demand a trial in this case, and unless my views should be very much corrected on this subject, I am altogether opposed to the article.

Mr. A. Wolcott said, in order to conciliate the feelings of gentlemen, he would move to erase the words "and duty," which was not done.

Mr. Stow—We are called upon, Mr. President, for the meaning of this section. I will give what was my opinion of its meaning, when it passed the committee. It had always been my opinion, that Connecticut had been parceled out; that religion had been established by law, and that congregationalists had been the order established. I believe, Sir, if it had never been the case, the people would not do it now; but it has been done, at a time when men were not as liberally disposed as they now are, or at least when there were not as many denominations as there now are. I acknowledge, Sir, that certain societies have corporate rights; some societies have funds, and if we do away with these rights, we infringe on *private* rights. To steer clear of that, I would say in *future,* that is, I would not say hereafter that a person shall contribute to support, but with voluntary consent. If an individual enters a town now, he must enter his name as belonging to some denomination of Christians. This law was made so broad as to compel no such thing; but it designs that all who have been caught in these bands may be let out. If any man says he has been imprisoned unlawfully, this will let him out, and he may go free; hereafter we will have no such restraint. As to the present section, if it is altered in any way, it will curtail the great principles for which we contend, and society will be disturbed as heretofore; and Sir, to come to the established order, for whatever you may call them, although they were established by the Saybrook Platform, they do not all agree among themselves. Some say, that if their preachers continue to preach certain doctrine, they shall be dissatisfied; they will not pay for preaching which they don't believe—and Sir, on this principle of liberality they will not need to. Some societies will tax themselves, and some will not—they will find it inconvenient, they will find themselves losing members by it, for those who are dissatisfied will go away, and finally adopt principles, which otherwise they would not own. Some societies will sell their pews, and others will rent them for the support of their minister, according to circumstances. Sir, this provision is necessary, to secure the rights of those who are incorporated, and those who are not. The gentleman from Farmington would make the congregationalists the predominant order; but Sir, this is not agreeable to the spirit of the times. It is well known that certain orders don't want this privilege, and it would be idle to grant them what they don't want. I hope the section may pass, that the thing may be set at rest, and the State settle down quietly.

Mr. Treadwell said the gentleman certainly misunderstood him. He *expressly* declared, that all denominations should be placed on equal footing.

Mr. A. Wolcott would not have a man compelled to join, or pay, to any political group.

Mr. G. Tomlinson expressed himself in favour of the section, as it stood, and declared that it placed the subject exactly on the footing of the present law.

Mr. N. Terry—Sir, I cannot agree with the gentleman last up; if I could I should be very glad. Nay, Sir, my ideas on this subject are exactly *contrary to his.* The principle contained in this section, is entirely different from our present law on the subject. The principle on which our law is founded, is here cut up by the roots; our law does compel a person to belong somewhere, though he has the liberty to belong where he pleases; but here it is declared, that it shall be at the option of the person, whether he belongs to any denomination: "No person shall by law be compelled to join or *support,* nor be *classed with,* or associated to, any congregation, church or religious association"—if gentlemen would stop here, the Article goes to withdraw all support from present corporations—turn Sir if you please to the 2d Section: "If any person shall choose to separate himself from the society or denomination of Christians to which he may belong, and shall leave a written notice thereof with the Clerk of such society, he shall thereupon be no longer liable for any future expences which may be incurred by said society"— now Sir, put these two passages together, and I submit, whether it does not dissolve all obligation; *this* is to be the operation of it: I am not opposed to the free enjoyment of the rights of *conscience,* I should be the last man to oppose a principle of that nature; Sir, no man should infringe *my* rights of conscience, and I am willing that all others should enjoy the same—but the question is, whether religion shall be supported *somewhere;* does this interfere with the rights of conscience? this law is to be established for the health of the *community*—we are taxed to support many things which we don't like; suppose I do not like a particular religious denomination, and am taxed to support it, unless I unite myself to some other; does this interfere with my rights of conscience? no more Sir, I beg leave to say, than it does to be taxed for the support of a war, which I don't approve of. I suppose I should not think it necessary for my children to be *schooled;* if laws are made for the support of schools, shall I be absolved from taxes? no Sir. Schools are a benefit to the community, and all men should be made to support them; although some may be of a different opinion. On the same principle, would I make all men support public worship *somewhere;* but on the question *where,* every man should be left to act at pleasure; this is the object of all our laws, the public good. I do not understand that any one denomination is placed over another—Sir, what is our *law?* why, that if a person wishes to leave a society of one denomination for that of another, he has only to signify his desire in writing, and lodge it with the Town Clerk; and can you get along without this? will you go counter to the very principle which has produced so much happiness to the people? but gentlemen say, you must "certificate to the standing order"—can it be otherwise? Sir, I defy the gentleman to make a practicable alteration in this respect: the attempt has already been made by a party on coming into power, and what was done? the same law continued with a very slight alteration. On this principle, if a man moves into the society of West-Hartford, he is presumed to belong to the congregationalists—and if he comes into Hartford, would you certificate if he don't belong to the Episcopal Church? *No Sir,* there is no propriety in this: in carrying this law into effect, you must have a place, a *quo* to start from; it is impossible that a law should be more equitable, or more just—but this Article goes to destroy the law, and puts it in the power of every man to contribute or not, as he pleases.

But gentlemen would permit those to be taxed who are willing—what sort of regulation is this? here is a meeting house to be built, and the society votes to build it—certain persons choose not to pay their part, and withdraw from the society; but as soon as the house is built, and the minister settled, these same persons come directly back and enjoy the privileges. But Sir, I have been up long enough, I cannot vote for the Section, and am obliged to say, for the Constitution with such a provision in it—*for Sir,* it strikes at the root of good order in society.

Mr. Burrows and Mr. Treadwell both spoke here, but we must omit their remarks.

Mr. Stow—In answer to the gentleman from Hartford, Sir, I deny that the Legislature have a right to compel a man to support public worship: if they have that right, they have a right to say what is public worship, and where, and in what manner he shall support it: this is impolitic—it has been the cause of all the martyrdoms down to the present day; they have a right to legislate on all subjects relative to civil liberties, and in such cases the majority shall rule; but if a society can say that individuals shall worship, it can say *how* they shall worship: to direct worship on this mountain or on that mountain. And if they vary from this, the right is infringed. It is the *duty* of all to worship in sincerity and in truth; but I deny the right of any power to make a man worship—all should be left free, and if men differ, it amounts to only this; if my neighbor don't think as I do, he is accountable to his God for it. If a power has a right to say what is public worship, it may go to support idolatry. The Bill of Rights says that it shall be free for all men to worship God according to the dictates of their own consciences: now if you make a law that a man shall worship somewhere, and that man should think it his duty to worship the *devil,* you would compel him to worship the *devil;* and is the gentleman prepared to say, a man shall do that? Let every man have a *right* to render voluntary worship, and not *compel* him to render it. …

Mr. Tomlinson moved to amend the first part of the section, so as to read thus—"It being the duty of all men to worship the Supreme Being, the great Creator and Preserver of the Universe, and their right to render that worship, in the mode, &c."—which was done. The question was then taken on the section and approved.—103 yeas to 86 nays.[7]

The article's second section, which did away with the requirement that everyone belong to some Christian society or congregation, was then read. Treadwell's fellow Farmington delegate Timothy Pitkin moved to strike the whole section, but this was voted against, with only 84 voting in favor of Pitkin's motion and 105 against it.

Treadwell again kicked off the debate.

> Mr. Treadwell then moved the following amendment, to the 2d section—by inserting after the words—"clerk of such Society"—this clause—and shall join himself to a society of christians of a different denomination, so as to become subject to their lawful orders and regulations, with respect to its common expences" he shall, &c. This amendment, said Mr. T. will compel those who belong to a particular society, to continue their support or contribute to some other society. His connection with one, can't be dissolved, till he has prepared to become subject to the regulations of another. It therefore places the subject on this solid principle that every individual shall support public worship, somewhere—and the proportion will be properly distributed. Expences incurred for the common good should not be defrayed by a few individuals. I do not like the idea of taxing one part of the community, and excusing another. The support of public worship is *necessary* to the good of the State. On what principle, therefore, can any man be excused from the burthen?
>
> Mr. Waldo—In old times, we are told that Pharaoh, would not let the people go—and when the disciples deserted our Saviour, and walked no more with him, we don't hear of any force being used to make them return. Much is said, Mr. President, about religion. In what does it consist? "Love thy Lord thy God, &c." Those who do not do this, must take the

---

7. *Connecticut Mirror,* Hartford, CT, September 21, 1818, 1-2.

consequences, I would not compel them to do it. The worst thing that ever was, is an established religion. This has been the case with the Mahomedan and Roman Catholic. When I was a little boy, it caused more bloody noses, than anything else; ah *you separate, you separate,* the other boys would cry; I'm sorry I ever took so much notice of them, but, now I thank God for the privilege of expressing my opinion, and giving my vote against it.

Mr. Hart said, there has been an established religion here, and can it be the true religion? There is but one true religion—and what shall we do with Catholics and other denominations? (Tolerate them all said Mr. Treadwell.) Mr. Speaker, this looks a little like this—one man says to another, you help me support my truth, and I will help you support your falsehood. I have no idea of supporting error. I don't like it,—and I shall make use of all my weapons to destroy it. There are two kinds of religion brought in here, one of the heart, and the other of the head. It seems we can do nothing about supporting the religion of the heart—but you can compel a man to pay money—and will this promote the good morals, happiness, and peace of society? Many people think that religion may be supported without money—and for my part, I have no mind to make a monied institution of it. According to reasoning of the gentleman, the more money you spend, the more religion you have—and what right has a man to make another support a monied religion? I know of but one man who undertook to purchase the gift of God with money, and he didn't succeed very well. Let us refute each other's errors, and support *truth.* Mists and darkness are now cast around it. We had much better support truth, than compel the people to pay money.

Mr. D. Burrows said, if a man went off from society, as it was represented he might do, by the gentleman from Hartford, he was a mean fellow, let him go: but we ought not to make a man pay so much money for going to Heaven. ...[8]

After some further debate, which continued into the evening,

8. *Connecticut Mirror,* Hartford, CT, September 21, 1818, 2.

the section was ultimately passed, by a vote of 97 to 69.

On the last day of the convention's proceedings, the Federalists made one more attempt to keep their certificate law, with Timothy Pitkin moving to strike the entire seventh article. The attempt was unsuccessful, and the article, with only minor wording changes from what was originally reported by the committee, appeared as follows in the final constitution:

ARTICLE SEVENTH.

OF RELIGION.

§ 1. It being the duty of all men to worship the Supreme Being, the great Creator and Preserver of the Universe, and their right to render that worship, in the mode most consistent with the dictates of their consciences; no person shall by law be compelled to join or support, nor be classed with, or associated to, any congregation, church or religious association. But every person now belonging to such congregation, church, or religious association, shall remain a member thereof, until he shall have separated himself therefrom, in the manner hereinafter provided. And each and every society or denomination of christians in this state, shall have and enjoy the same and equal powers, rights and privileges; and shall have power and authority to support and maintain the ministers or teachers of their respective denominations, and to build and repair houses for public worship, by a tax on the members of any such society only, to be laid by a major vote of the legal voters assembled at any society meeting, warned and held according to law, or in any other manner.

§ 2. If any person shall choose to separate himself from the society or denomination of christians to which he may belong, and shall leave a written notice thereof with the clerk of such society, he shall thereupon be no longer liable for any future expences which may be incurred by said society.[9]

---

9. *Republican Farmer,* Bridgeport, CT, September 23, 1818, 2-3.

On September 15, by a vote of 134 to 61, the constitution was adopted by the convention. All that remained was for the people to vote on it.

The Federalist papers, as expected, urged their readers to vote *no,* with the *Mirror* making its final pitch on the day of the vote:

On the first Monday in October, the freemen of this State are to exercise a duty of the highest importance, that will ever fall to their lot. I allude to the vote they are to give on the great question of adopting the Constitution, formed by the Convention, which lately met in this town. Let no man who loves his country, or regards the well-being of the State in which he lives, or the comfort, security, and happiness of himself, or his posterity, view the present occasion as one of ordinary importance. No generation of men in Connecticut, since the little band led by Hooker first planted their tents on the banks of our river, were ever called upon to perform so solemn a duty, as that which we are to engage in, on that day. With feelings like these—with impressions too deep to be effaced, and motives too interesting to be trifled with or disregarded, I venture to call the attention of such as may chance to light on this address, to the subject which lies before you.

At this freemen's meeting WE, who have hitherto passed our lives in peace, comfort, prosperity, and happiness, under the shadow of that VINE which our fathers planted, and which the GOD of our fathers caused to grow and flourish, must by our own free & voluntary act, annul & destroy our good old government, and forever hereafter strike it out of existence, and at the same moment, adopt one made up of modern theory, new to us, and unsanctioned by the test of experiment—or, we shall prove by our acts, that we will maintain the ground on which we have hitherto stood, adhere to the institutions which our ancestors planned and established, and on which the blessing of God has rested for nearly two centuries past. On this subject, no man who reveres the character of his ancestors, the government that they formed and transmitted to us, the laws they enacted, the Institutions they established—no man who loves freedom, and the highest state of social happiness to be found beneath the sun, who cherishes good order and good morals, or reverences the religion of the Holy Scriptures, can feel indifferent, or act with a cold and sluggish spirit.

It is the indispensable duty of every such man as I have described, to lay aside all minor considerations—attend the meeting, and give to this instrument, now about to be fastened upon us, his most determined negative. The man who hesitates, hesitates over ruin:—the man who votes for this Constitution is either blind to, or regardless of, the best interests of the State. The question is to be decided by a bare majority of votes—not a majority of towns. Every vote, therefore, let the majority in any individual town be as it may, is of great importance, because they all must be brought together and counted, and the balance be struck upon the votes of the whole State.

Need any thing further be urged? My fellow freemen, *the existence of your Ecclesiastical Societies, the character of your courts, the safety of the militia, the long established habits of elections and of the legislative sessions, with many other things of more or less importance, are all at stake. This single day settles the question forever—of course, let no man put off his exertions till to-morrow—for to-morrow it will be too late.*[10]

And the Republican papers, of course, urged their readers to vote *yes,* with the *Register* publishing two days before the vote:

ALL DEPENDS.

On the first Monday of October, all the enemies of the Constitution, if not prevented by sickness, will turn out to vote. Let its friends be equally diligent and there will be a majority of thousands in favor of its adoption.

The Constitution has provided well for life, liberty, property and reputation; has established the rights of suffrage and of conscience. Adopt it and your lands will rise in value,

10. *Connecticut Mirror,* Hartford, CT, October 5, 1818, 3.

your agriculture and your arts will be protected, navigation will flourish, religion will be safe, and you will be freemen in deed and in truth. If you reject it and become again the subjects of Charles 2d, the victims of stand up laws, unequal taxation and dependent Judiciaries, you will be poor and helpless, your sons will emigrate to the west and your state will lose its name in the nation.

The majority of votes throughout the state is to decide the question. In every town, federal or republican, every vote in favor of the Constitution must be obtained. On the day of decision new freemen will be admitted. After this the ballot-boxes will be opened: you will put on the box your ballot with the word YES fairly written on it; you may then retire in peace, with the reflection that you have done your best for yourselves and your children.

No one will go to meeting undecided how to act. Long harangues on a subject, which occupied the Convention three weeks, will not be offered, unless it be for the wicked purpose of fatiguing the freemen.

If the Constitution be now rejected, it is rejected for time and eternity. It is, take it all in all, the best instrument of the kind ever offered to a free people. Be punctual in your attendance and make the First Monday of October the anniversary of the birth-day of the State.[11]

On October 5, 1818, the people of Connecticut ratified their constitution by a vote of 13,918 to 12,364.

The "Constitution State" at long last had a constitution.

---

11. *Columbian Register,* New Haven, CT, October 3, 1818, 3.

∾ Index ∾

Printed in Great Britain
by Amazon

54671418R00244